CONTENTS

Introduction

The idea of eating healthy foods, maintaining a fit physique, or losing excess weight, is often perceived as a myth by many. True, there are many advice and dietary regimens out there, many of which you have sampled and disappointedly discovered is not suited for you. Quite frankly, the amount of dietary information we're bombarded with today can be misleading, especially for a novice who wants nothing but a healthy eating lifestyle. But, what if you discover that shedding that weight and achieving better health isn't nearly a rocket science as you thought it was? What if starting a healthy eating habit is much easier than you thought it was? The good news is that it very much is - you can achieve better health, without going to the moon or even seeing a dietician.

The content of this book is rich with unique, easy-to-make recipes that can be made at home. All that is required of you is the discipline and simple commitment it takes to implement these recipes. This book elaborates on crockpot dieting, listing out different recipes and methods of preparing them. A crock pot, also known as a slow cooker, is a countertop electrical cooking appliance that is used to simmer foods at much lower temperatures and for several hours than regular cooking methods such as baking, steaming, boiling, and frying. What this means is that crock pot cooking extends for many hours, even for dishes that could be made quicker and in less time. Interestingly, as illustrated in the recipes included in this book, crockpot or slow cooking can be used for a wide variety of dishes, including pot roast, soups, and stews.

If you're planning or thinking about starting out on healthy eating or just in need of healthy meal cooking ideas to add to your fitness program, you probably would want to consider crock pot meals. Crock pots were initially designed to save time and have your meal ready after long hours at work, without necessarily spending long hours in the kitchen cooking. They became popular in the US in the 1940s when many women began to work outside the home. A typical benefit here is that you could start dinner in the morning and finish preparing it in the evening when you return from work.

While saving time spent on making meals is obviously one of the benefits of using slow cooking, there are many other excellent benefits, which will be highlighted in the following paragraphs. You most likely have enjoyed the benefits of instant cooking and several other healthy cooking methods, but hey, who wants to spend so much time prepping meals when I could actually prep up the meal, set it on, and face other important business I have for the day. If you work a regular day job and have kids at home, you obviously do not have too much time to go around for all your activities. Some of the recipes discussed here do require some preparation before going in, but they are still a great way to get your dinner on the table, especially on days when squeezing out time to make a meal is such a hard job.

What`s The Fuss About Crock Pot Meals

Have you thought about leaving the house while your food cooks? Well, now you have it, and there's more. How exactly? You may ask. That's why we have prepared these recipes. But beyond having your meals cooked in your absence, here are some other ways slow cooking can simplify your life. I bet this part will stimulate your interest further.

1. Having a meal in the crock pot eliminates the never-ending temptation to go for take-out orders. And as we all know, we simply spend more when we eat out. Worse still, the meals aren't always excellent compared to when you make your meals at home.
2. Crock pot recipes can turn out super delicious dinners. Often, they offer great-tasting meals that you can stash away in the fridge and quickly reheat when needed. Chilled lasagna, for instance, can be gently reheated to a warm temperature and neatly sliced into little squares. Chilled stews and soups are known to have improved tastes when reheated, which is the case here.
3. Crock pot recipes are great for any weather situation - cold or hot. The aroma of hot soup would most likely be dearly inviting when you come in from a cold winter day. On the other hand, they work just as fine during the summer. Besides, they do not heat the kitchen as would be expected of an oven.
4. Are you worried about electricity? Well, unlike an oven, a crock pot consumes less electricity. Hence, they are generally economical.
5. Crock pot meals generally involve a one-step meal preparation, which can be done and placed in the pot all at once. This is another way you can cut back on time spent in the kitchen.
6. Crock pots are just great for getting tender fall-off-the-bone meat. A lot of the foods that are ideal for crock pot meals seem a bit more expensive too. To get the best out of these meals, slow cooking is almost inevitable. Beef chunks, rump roast, and pork butt are all budget-friendly, but they come out better-tasting when cooked in crock pots. The prolonged cooking softens the connective tissues of the meat without toughening the muscle, thereby making them tender meat.
7. Are you worried about doing dishes all the time? Yes, we all do. Crock pot, however, uses fewer dishes. It's an effective way to do away with dishes.
8. Cooking your meal is an effective way to cut back on water usage -for cooking and for cleaning after cooking. The low cooking temperature contributes to the ease of cleaning. If my guess is right, I'm sure

you`re wondering about seeing your precious pot get burnt when you get back. Worry not. The inside of the pot is designed to withstand heating for a long time. Besides, the low temperature of crock pot cooking makes it almost impossible to burn. However, you want to tone down on the length of cooking time for vegetables and some kinds of meat.

9. Other health benefits of crock pot meals include: getting more nutritious foods, making home-made healthier meals, controlling what you eat, and keeps you on track with your fitness program.

Slow Cooking On High Heat And Low Heat

For the best results, it is advisable to cook your meals at the best temperature. To someone who's new to slow cooking, the concept may seem pretty much the same, but there is quite some difference between cooking at low temperature and high temperature. The truth is that even though it is called slow cooking, simmering your recipes over long periods tends to drain the ingredients of all the nutrients and flavor, leaving your meal bland and tasteless.

A common consideration when it comes to slow cooking is about saving time. However, before you think of turning up the dial on your crock pot, you should also consider the simmer point. The simmer point is the typical time it takes to bring all the content of the pot below the boiling point. The temperature is around 209 degrees celsius. Normally, it takes about 7-8 hours to arrive at this point on low setting, while it takes up to 3 or 4 hours to achieve the simmer point on high setting. Getting the best out of your crock pot meals also depends on knowing how to use the pot and not just the recipes.

Using the default temperature settings is advised; you can also adjust it to suit the meal you`re preparing. This depends on the amount of time you`re willing to allow the food to cook, the suggested temperature setting for the recipe, and the flavor you want to get out of the meal. What this means is that a recipe that calls for an eight-hour simmering can be converted to 4 hours on high setting. Recipes that suggest a high location for about 4 hours can be converted to low and left to cook for long hours. However, it's important to note that extending the time for cooking the meal will alter the flavor of the food.

What Kind Of Recipes Should You Expect To Find?

Generally, getting the best out of your crock pot cooking requires slight to a significant adjustment in the recipes. Reason being that recipes intended for other cooking methods may not be well-suited for slow cooking. For instance, the amount of water required to cook rice or boil meat in a crock pot will be lesser than the required quantity of water needed for other cooking methods. Typically, there is a little evaporation since the food simmers for longer hours, but there should be enough water to cover the food.

In the addition to the above, keep in mind that several of the recipes recommended for crock pot cooking usually use prepared seasonings, sauces, and ingredients. This is consistent with the idea of saving time. The following are some example of recipes that can be made using a crock pot:

1. 1 Slow Cooked Brown Rice (Never Dry)
2. Crock-Pot Chicken Fajitas
3. Slow-Cooker Chicken Cacciatore
4. Slow-Cooker Turkey Chili
5. Steel-Cut Oats
6. Slow-Cooker Split Pea Soup

There are several other recipes included in the book, ranging from quick meals for breakfast or brunch to meals that are ideal for dinner and desserts. By and large, they are easy to make. Using the included guidelines makes the process even more fun. With practice, you quickly get them under your fingers. You could start by trying your hands on the recipes with shorter lists of ingredients and then later move on to more interesting recipes. The recipes come with steps and tips to get the best rates out of each meal. Meanwhile, you could tweak the recipes by adding your flavors to the mix to achieve your desired taste.

Tips For Achieving Great-tasting Crock Pot Meals

To get the best tastes from your crock pot meals, you can use the following easy-apply tips:

#1 Crock pot meals often need a little oomph at the end of the cooking. You may add some freshness by slicing up the meal with some neatly chopped fresh herbs or green onions to brighten up the flavors. A slight splash of acidic flavor is also a great addition. But this depends on the recipe you're making. A squeeze of lemon juice will often suffice to do the trick.

#2 It's essential to know how to use your crockpot, very well. If you're new to crock pot recipes, you might want to first check out some safety tips before using the pot. Watching some videos online will also give you some practical experience. Also, stick to the suggested regulations for each recipe. For example, if five hours of low summering is indicated for a particular recipe, it's best to stick to the recommendation. If, however, you wish to adjust the temperature, also be sure that the time for the cooking is in line with the provided advice. Also, keep in mind that all crock pots cook differently. So, if you have more than one of them, bear in mind that they all cook differently, depending on the design and size of the pot. Typically, the larger the crock pot, the longer it will take to heat and cook.

Crock pots have high and low settings. Some have up to three settings. With the low setting, your food will cook between 6-10 hours. The high setting, on the other hand, allows the food to cook in 4-6 hours, at a higher temperature. As I mentioned earlier, once you get the hang of it, you can use the setting that fits your needs. One hour on high is approximately equal to two hours on the low setting. The high and low location is perfect, depending on the food you want to cook. Slow cookers or crock pots vary in size from 1 to 7 quarts. Smaller slow cookers are good for dips or sauces, while the larger ones are great for massive cuts of meats and soups. If you intend to cook for up to four people or less, a 3.5-4 quart size slow cooker would be perfect. A 5-7 quart size or larger slower cooker is best if you're cooking for 5 or more people.

#3 Prep what you can the day before, or at least hours before you start. If you belong to a busy world like mine, you would need to prepare your ingredients long enough before slow cooking, at least a day before. Vegetables, onions, meat, and others are to be washed and ready to go into the pot.   be shopped or meat to be cooked. You can either proceed with the cooking at night when you arrive from work or neatly place the ingredients in a fridge and start cooking in the morning.

If you're hesitant about cooking your meals while you're away at work or on some other task outside the house, you can set the cooker on while you're in the house, but not necessarily spending in the kitchen. You may then allow the meal to cool down and add them to your refrigerator for eating later.

#4 Let's not forget about cleaning up. Although, we've said earlier that you don't have to do much dishwashing as compared to other cooking methods, at least you still have to care for the pot. Properly caring for your pot ensures you enjoy it for a longer time. For easy cleanup and care of your crock pot, you may rub the inside of the stoneware with oil or spray it with a nonstick cooking spray before using it. You may also get slow cooker liners to ease up the cleanup.

#5 It is best to always thaw frozen meat and poultry in the refrigerator before cooking it in the crock pot. Instead of directly putting frozen meat in the pot, allow it to defroze for some minutes before cooking. This ensures that the food cooks completely.

#6 Fill the pot appropriately. To get the best results from your crock pot recipes, it's important that you fill the pot appropriately. Too much food or too little food can affect the taste, quality, and durability of the pot. So, when filling the pool with food content, always ensure that it is not less than half full and no more than two-thirds full to get the best quality.

#7 Appropriate layering of food in the pot. Since vegetables usually cook slower than meat and poultry, it's best to place the vegetables in the crock pot first, then place the meat on top of the vegetables and top it up with liquid, such as broth, water, or an already prepared sauce.

#8 Use the appropriate liquid for cooking your meals. Each recipe discussed in this book has a recommended liquid to go along with it. To get the best taste, you can use the included liquid. The fluid may be broth, water, or barbecue sauce, suggested in the recipe.

#9 Use an adequate amount of liquid for cooking. Liquids do not boil away from the pot, so you want to be mindful of the amount of liquid you're adding to the mixture. You may reduce the liquids by one-third to one-half when you need to use slow cooking to prepare a non-crock pot recipe.

#10 Always keep the lid in place during cooking. Whether you're leaving the food to cook in your absence or doing the cooking when you're around in the house, always remember to leave the lid on—removing the lid of the pot further slows down the cooking time. About 15-20 minutes of cooking time is lost every time the lid of the pot is lifted.

#11 Exercise caution when cooking pasta. To avoid ending up with mushy or marshy food, always add grains such as pasta at the end of the cooking process. It is best to cook your pasta and rice, including other grains, separately, and add it to the pot just before serving.

Adopting a healthy eating lifestyle has never been easier. As you'll discover in the subsequent pages, the recipes included here are pretty easy and offer many benefits to your body. They are safe and can fit just fine into your fitness program if you're currently on one. All that you need to implement the recommended cooking tips, follow the recipes, and use the suggested care tips for your crock pot. The journey towards a fitter and healthier body is just as possible as you can imagine it.

Breakfast Recipes

Cauliflower And Eggs Bowls

Servings: 2   Cooking Time: 7 Hours
Ingredients:

Cooking spray
4 eggs, whisked
A pinch of salt and
black pepper
¼ teaspoon thyme,
dried
½ teaspoon turmeric
powder

1 cup cauliflower
florets
½ small yellow
onion, chopped
3 ounces breakfast
sausages, sliced
½ cup cheddar
cheese, shredded

Directions:
Grease your Crock Pot with cooking spray and
spread the cauliflower florets on the bottom of the
pot.   Add the eggs mixed with salt, pepper and
the other ingredients and toss.   Put the lid on,
cook on Low for 7 hours, divide between plates and
serve for breakfast.
Nutrition Info:calories 261, fat 6, fiber 7, carbs
22, protein 6

Milk Oatmeal

Servings: 4   Cooking Time: 2 Hours
Ingredients:

2 cups oatmeal
1 cup of water
1 tablespoon liquid
honey
1 teaspoon vanilla
extract

1 cup milk
1 tablespoon coconut
oil
¼ teaspoon ground
cinnamon

Directions:
Put all ingredients except liquid honey in the Crock
Pot and mix.   Close the lid and cook the meal on
High for hours.   Then stir the cooked oatmeal
and transfer in the serving bowls.   Top the meal
with a small amount of liquid honey.
Nutrition Info: Per Serving: 234 calories, 7.4g
protein, 35.3g carbohydrates, 7.3g fat, 4.2g fiber,
5mg cholesterol, 33mg sodium, 189mg potassium.

Asparagus Egg Casserole

Servings: 4   Cooking Time: 2.5 Hours
Ingredients:

7 eggs, beaten
4 oz asparagus,
chopped, boiled

1 oz Parmesan, grated
1 teaspoon sesame oil
1 teaspoon dried dill

Directions:
Pour the sesame oil in the Crock Pot.   Then mix
dried dill with parmesan, asparagus, and eggs.
Pour the egg mixture in the Crock Pot and close the
lid.   Cook the casserole on high for 2.5 hours.
Nutrition Info: Per Serving: 149 calories, 12.6g
protein, 2.1g carbohydrates, 10.3g fat, 0.6g fiber,
292mg cholesterol, 175mg sodium, 169mg
potassium

Vanilla Maple Oats

Servings: 4   Cooking Time: 8 Hrs
Ingredients:

1 cup steel-cut oats
2 tsp vanilla extract
2 cups vanilla almond
milk
2 tbsp maple syrup

2 tsp cinnamon
powder
2 cups of water
2 tsp flaxseed
Cooking spray
2 tbsp blackberries

Directions:
Coat the base of your Crock Pot with cooking spray.
Stir in oats, almond milk, vanilla extract,
cinnamon, maple syrup, flaxseeds, and water.
Put the cooker's lid on and set the cooking time to 8
hours on Low settings.   Stir well and serve with
blackberries on top.   Devour.
Nutrition Info: Per Serving: Calories 200, Total
Fat 3g, Fiber 6g, Total Carbs 9g, Protein 3g

Eggplant Pate

Servings: 15   Cooking Time: 6 Hrs
Ingredients:

5 medium eggplants,
peeled and chopped
2 sweet green pepper,
chopped
1 cup bread crumbs
1 tsp salt
1 tbsp sugar
½ cup tomato paste

2 yellow onion,
chopped
1 tbsp minced garlic
¼ chili pepper,
chopped
1 tsp olive oil
1 tsp kosher salt
1 tbsp mayonnaise

Directions:
Place the eggplants in a colander and drizzle salt on
top.   Leave them for 10 minutes at room
temperature.   Whisk tomatoes paste with sugar,
salt, mayonnaise, and garlic in a bowl.   Grease
the base of your Crock Pot with olive oil.   Spread
chopped onion and eggplant in the cooker.   Pour
the tomato sauce over the veggies.   Top the sauce
with green peppers and chili pepper.   Put the
cooker's lid on and set the cooking time to 6 hours
on Low settings.   Blend the cooked eggplant
mixture with an immersion blender until smooth.
Top the eggplant pate with breadcrumbs.   Serve.
Nutrition Info: Per Serving: Calories 83, Total Fat
0.8g, Fiber 7g, Total Carbs 18.15g, Protein 3g

Raspberry Oatmeal

Servings: 4   Cooking Time: 8 Hours
Ingredients:

- 2 cups water
- 1 tablespoon coconut oil
- 1 cup steel cut oats
- 1 tablespoon sugar
- 1 cup milk
- ½ teaspoon vanilla extract
- 1 cup raspberries
- 4 tablespoons walnuts, chopped

Directions:
In your Crock Pot, mix oil with water, oats, sugar, milk, vanilla and raspberries, cover and cook on Low for 8 hours.   Stir oatmeal, divide into bowls, sprinkle walnuts on top and serve for breakfast.
Nutrition Info:calories 200, fat 10, fiber 4, carbs 20, protein 4

Pork And Eggplant Casserole

Servings: 2   Cooking Time: 6 Hours
Ingredients:

- 1 red onion, chopped
- 1 eggplant, cubed
- ½ pound pork stew meat, ground
- ½ teaspoon chili powder
- 3 eggs, whisked
- ½ teaspoon garam masala
- 1 tablespoon sweet paprika
- 1 teaspoon olive oil

Directions:
In a bowl, mix the eggs with the meat, onion, eggplant and the other ingredients except the oil and stir well.   Grease your Crock Pot with oil, add the pork and eggplant mix, spread into the pot, put the lid on and cook on Low for 6 hours.   Divide the mix between plates and serve for breakfast.
Nutrition Info:calories 261, fat 7, fiber 6, carbs 16, protein 7

Baby Spinach Rice Mix

Servings: 4   Cooking Time: 6 Hours
Ingredients:

- ¼ cup mozzarella, shredded
- ½ cup baby spinach
- ½ cup wild rice
- 1 and ½ cups chicken stock
- ½ teaspoon turmeric powder
- ½ teaspoon oregano, dried
- A pinch of salt and black pepper
- 3 scallions, minced
- ¾ cup goat cheese, crumbled

Directions:
In your Crock Pot, mix the rice with the stock, turmeric and the other ingredients, toss, put the lid on and cook on Low for 6 hours.   Divide the mix into bowls and serve for breakfast.
Nutrition Info:calories 165, fat 1.2, fiber 3.5, carbs 32.6, protein 7.6

Baby Carrots In Syrup

Servings: 5   Cooking Time: 7 Hours
Ingredients:

- 3 cups baby carrots
- 2 tablespoons brown sugar
- 1 cup apple juice
- 1 teaspoon vanilla extract

Directions:
Mix apple juice, brown sugar, and vanilla extract. Pour the liquid in the Crock Pot.   Add baby carrots and close the lid.   Cook the meal on Low for 7 hours.
Nutrition Info: Per Serving: 81 calories, 0g protein, 18.8g carbohydrates, 0.1g fat, 3.7g fiber, 0mg cholesterol, 363mg sodium, 56mg potassium.

Green Muffins

Servings: 8   Cooking Time: 2 ½ hrs
Ingredients:

- 1 cup spinach, washed
- 5 tbsp butter
- 1 cup flour
- 1 tsp salt
- ½ tsp baking soda
- 1 tbsp lemon juice
- 1 tbsp sugar
- 3 eggs

Directions:
Add the spinach leaves to a blender jug and blend until smooth.   Whisk the eggs in a bowl and add the spinach mixture.   Stir in baking soda, salt, sugar, flour, and lemon juice.   Mix well to form a smooth spinach batter.   Divide the dough into a muffin tray lined with muffin cups.   Place this muffin tray in the Crock Pot.   Put the cooker's lid on and set the cooking time to 2 hours 30 minutes on High settings.   Serve.
Nutrition Info: Per Serving: Calories 172, Total Fat 6.1g, Fiber 1g, Total Carbs 9.23g, Protein 20g

Scallions And Bacon Omelet

Servings: 4   Cooking Time: 2 Hours
Ingredients:

- 5 eggs, beaten
- 2 oz bacon, chopped, cooked
- 1 oz scallions, chopped
- 1 teaspoon olive oil
- ½ teaspoon ground black pepper
- ¼ teaspoon cayenne pepper

Directions:
Brush the Crock Pot bowl bottom with olive oil. After this, in the bowl mix eggs with bacon, scallions, ground black pepper, and cayenne pepper.   Pour the liquid in the Crock Pot and close the lid.   Cook the meal on high for 2 hours.
Nutrition Info: Per Serving: 169 calories, 12.3g protein, 1.4g carbohydrates, 12.6g fat, 0.3g fiber, 220mg cholesterol, 406mg sodium, 179mg potassium

Breakfast Meat Rolls

Servings: 12   Cooking Time: 4.5 Hours
Ingredients:
- 1-pound puff pastry
- 1 cup ground pork
- 1 tablespoon garlic, diced
- 1 egg, beaten
- 1 tablespoon sesame oil

Directions:
Roll up the puff pastry.   Then mix ground pork with garlic and egg.   Then spread the puff pastry with ground meat mixture and roll.   Cut the puff pastry rolls on small rolls.   Then sprinkle the rolls with sesame oil.   Arrange the meat rolls in the Crock Pot and close the lid.   Cook breakfast on High for 4.5 hours.
Nutrition Info: Per Serving: 244 calories, 4.9g protein, 17.3g carbohydrates, 17.2g fat, 0.6g fiber, 20mg cholesterol, 106mg sodium, 31mg potassium.

Cowboy Breakfast Casserole

Servings: 6   Cooking Time: 3 Hours
Ingredients:
- 1-pound ground beef
- 1 cup grass-fed Monterey Jack cheese, shredded
- Salt and pepper to taste
- 5 eggs, beaten
- 1 avocado, peeled and diced
- A handful of cilantro, chopped
- A dash of hot sauce

Directions:
In a skillet over medium flame, sauté the beef for three minutes until slightly golden.   Pour into the CrockPot and pour in eggs.   Sprinkle with cheese on top and season with salt and pepper to taste.   Close the lid and cook on high for hours or on low for 6 hours.   Serve with avocado, cilantro and hot sauce.
Nutrition Info: Calories per serving: 439; Carbohydrates: 4.5g; Protein: 32.7g; Fat: 31.9g; Sugar: 0g; Sodium: 619mg; Fiber: 1.8g

Maple Banana Oatmeal

Servings: 2   Cooking Time: 6 Hours
Ingredients:
- 1/2 cup old fashioned oats
- 1 banana, mashed
- ½ teaspoon cinnamon powder
- 2 tablespoons maple syrup
- 2 cups almond milk
- Cooking spray

Directions:
Grease your Crock Pot with the cooking spray, add the oats, banana and the other ingredients, stir, put the lid on and cook on Low for 6 hours.   Divide into bowls and serve for breakfast.
Nutrition Info:calories 815, fat 60.3, fiber 10.7, carbs 67, protein 11.1

Potato Muffins

Servings: 4   Cooking Time: 2 Hours
Ingredients:
- 4 teaspoons flax meal
- 1 bell pepper, diced
- 1 cup potato, cooked, mashed
- 1 teaspoon ground paprika
- 2 oz Mozzarella, shredded
- 2 eggs, beaten

Directions:
Mix flax meal with potato and eggs.   Then add ground paprika and bell pepper. Stir the mixture with the help of the spoon until homogenous. After this, transfer the potato mixture in the muffin molds. Top the muffins with Mozzarella and transfer in the Crock Pot.   Close the lid and cook the muffins on High for 2 hours.
Nutrition Info: Per Serving: 107 calories, 8g protein, 7.2g carbohydrates, 5.7g fat, 1.7g fiber, 89mg cholesterol, 118mg sodium, 196mg potassium

Eggs And Sweet Potato Mix

Servings: 2   Cooking Time: 6 Hours
Ingredients:
- ½ red onion, chopped
- ½ green bell pepper, chopped
- 2 sweet potatoes, peeled and grated
- ½ red bell pepper, chopped
- 1 garlic clove, minced
- ½ teaspoon olive oil
- 4 eggs, whisked
- 1 tablespoon chives, chopped
- A pinch of red pepper, crushed
- A pinch of salt and black pepper

Directions:
In a bowl, mix the eggs with the onion, bell peppers and the other ingredients except the oil and whisk well.   Grease your Crock Pot with the oil, add the eggs and potato mix, spread, put the lid on and cook on Low for 6 hours.   Divide everything between plates and serve.
Nutrition Info:calories 261, fat 6, fiber 6, carbs 16, protein 4

Veggie Hash Brown Mix

Servings: 2   Cooking Time: 6 Hours And 5 Minutes
Ingredients:
- 1 tablespoon olive oil
- ½ cup white mushrooms, chopped
- ½ yellow onion, chopped
- ¼ teaspoon garlic powder
- ¼ cup sour cream
- ¼ teaspoon onion powder
- 10 ounces hash browns
- ¼ cup cheddar cheese, shredded
- Salt and black pepper to the taste
- ½ tablespoon parsley, chopped

Directions:
Heat up a pan with the oil over medium heat, add the onion and mushrooms, stir and cook for 5 minutes.   Transfer this to the Crock Pot, add hash browns and the other ingredients, toss, put the lid on and cook on Low for 6 hours.   Divide between plates and for breakfast.
Nutrition Info:calories 571, fat 35.6, fiber 5.4, carbs 54.9, protein 9.7

Butter Oatmeal

Servings: 4   Cooking Time: 10 Minutes

Ingredients:

1 tablespoon liquid honey	1 teaspoon vanilla extract
1 tablespoon coconut shred	½ cup heavy cream
1 cup of water	1 cup oatmeal
	2 tablespoons butter

Directions:

Put butter, oatmeal, heavy cream, water, vanilla extract, and coconut shred in the Crock Pot. Carefully stir the ingredients and close the lid. Cook the meal on Low for 5 hours.   Then add liquid honey, stir it, and transfer in the serving bowls.

Nutrition Info: Per Serving: 212 calories, 3.1g protein, 19.2g carbohydrates, 13.9g fat, 2.3g fiber, 36mg cholesterol, 51mg sodium, 92mg potassium.

Veggies Casserole

Servings: 8   Cooking Time: 4 Hours

Ingredients:

8 eggs	¾ cup almond milk
4 egg whites	1 teaspoon sweet paprika
2 teaspoons mustard	
A pinch of salt and black pepper	4 bacon strips, chopped
2 red bell peppers, chopped	6 ounces cheddar cheese, shredded
1 yellow onion, chopped	Cooking spray

Directions:

In a bowl, mix the eggs with egg whites, mustard, milk, salt, pepper and sweet paprika and whisk well.   Grease your Crock Pot with cooking spray and spread bell peppers, bacon and onion on the bottom.   Add mixed eggs, sprinkle cheddar all over, cover and cook on Low for 4 hours.   Divide between plates and serve for breakfast.

Nutrition Info:calories 262, fat 6, fiber 3, carbs 15, protein 7

Mixed Egg And Sausage Scramble

Servings: 6   Cooking Time: 6 Hours

Ingredients:

12 eggs	1 cup milk
14 ounces sausages, sliced	1 teaspoon basil, dried
16 ounces cheddar cheese, shredded	1 teaspoon oregano, dried
A pinch of salt and black pepper	Cooking spray

Directions:

Grease your Crock Pot with cooking spray, spread sausages on the bottom, crack eggs, add milk, basil, oregano, salt and pepper, whisk a bit, sprinkle cheddar all over, cover and cook on Low for 6 hours.   Divide egg and sausage scramble between plates and serve.

Nutrition Info:calories 267, fat 4, fiber 5, carbs 12, protein 9

Chicken Burrito Bowl

Servings: 6   Cooking Time: 7 Hrs

Ingredients:

10 oz. chicken breast, sliced	1 tsp minced garlic
1 tbsp chili flakes	¼ cup green peas
1 tsp salt	1 cup chicken stock
1 tsp onion powder	½ avocado, pitted and chopped
½ cup white beans, canned	1 tsp ground black pepper

Directions:

Place the chicken breast in the Crock Pot.   Drizzle salt, onion powder, chili flakes, black pepper, and minced garlic on top.   Pour the chicken stock on top of the chicken.   Put the cooker's lid on and set the cooking time to 2 hours on High settings. Now add white beans and green peas to the chicken.   Close the lid again and cook for 5 hours on Low setting.   Shred the slow-cooked chicken and return to the bean's mixture.   Mix well and add chopped avocado.   Serve the burrito with avocado on top.

Nutrition Info: Per Serving: Calories 192, Total Fat 7.7g, Fiber 5g, Total Carbs 15.66g, Protein 16g

Apricots Bread Pudding

Servings: 9   Cooking Time: 5 Hrs

Ingredients:

10 oz. French bread	1 tsp vanilla sugar
6 tbsp dried apricots	½ tsp ground nutmeg
10 oz. milk	
3 eggs, beaten	½ tsp ground cardamom
4 tbsp butter	
½ tsp salt	¼ cup whipped cream
	4 tbsp brown sugar

Directions:

Melt butter by heating in a saucepan then add milk. Cook until warm, then stir in vanilla sugar, salt, ground cardamom, ground nutmeg, and brown sugar.   Continue mixing the milk mixture until sugar is fully dissolved.   Spread French bread and dried apricots in the Crock Pot.   Beat eggs in a bowl and add to the milk mixture.   Stir in cream and mix well until fully incorporated. Pour this milk-cream mixture over the bread and apricots in the Crock Pot.   Put the cooker's lid on and set the cooking time to 5 hours on Low settings.   Serve.

Nutrition Info: Per Serving: Calories 229, Total Fat 11.5g, Fiber 1g, Total Carbs 24.3g, Protein 8g

Creamy Quinoa With Nuts

Servings: 5   Cooking Time: 3 Hours

Ingredients:

1 oz nuts, crushed
2 cup quinoa
1 cup heavy cream
1 cup of water

1 teaspoon salt
¼ teaspoon chili flakes
1 oz Parmesan, grated

Directions:

Put quinoa, heavy cream, water, salt, and chili flakes in the Crock Pot.   Cook the ingredients on High for 3 hours.   Then add grated cheese and crushed nuts.   Stir the meal well and transfer in the serving plates.

Nutrition Info: Per Serving: 385 calories, 12.9g protein, 46g carbohydrates, 17.1g fat, 5.3g fiber, 37mg cholesterol, 570mg sodium, 436mg potassium.

Pumpkin And Berries Bowls

Servings: 2   Cooking Time: 4 Hours

Ingredients:

½ cup coconut cream
1 and ½ cups pumpkin, peeled and cubed
2 tablespoons maple syrup

1 cup blackberries
¼ teaspoon nutmeg, ground
½ teaspoon vanilla extract

Directions:

In your Crock Pot, combine the pumpkin with the berries, cream and the other ingredients, toss, put the lid on and cook on Low for 4 hours.   Divide into bowls and serve for breakfast!

Nutrition Info:calories 120, fat 2, fiber 2, carbs 4, protein 2

Leek Eggs

Servings: 4   Cooking Time: 2.5 Hours

Ingredients:

10 oz leek, sliced
4 eggs, beaten
½ teaspoon cumin seeds

1 teaspoon olive oil
3 oz Cheddar cheese, shredded

Directions:

Mix leek with olive oil and eggs.   Then transfer the mixture in the Crock Pot.   Sprinkle the egg mixture with Cheddar cheese and cumin seeds. Close the lid and cook the meal on High for 2.5 hours.

Nutrition Info: Per Serving: 203 calories, 11.9g protein, 10.8g carbohydrates, 12.9g fat, 1.3g fiber, 186mg cholesterol, 208mg sodium, 212mg potassium

Feta And Eggs Muffins

Servings: 2   Cooking Time: 6 Hours

Ingredients:

2 eggs, beaten
2 teaspoons cream cheese
1 oz fresh cilantro, chopped

1 oz feta, crumbled
½ teaspoon chili powder
1 teaspoon butter, melted

Directions:

Mix all ingredients and pour in the silicone muffin molds.   After this, transfer the muffin molds in the Crock Pot.   Cook the breakfast on Low for 6 hours.

Nutrition Info: Per Serving: 134 calories, 8.2g protein, 1.9g carbohydrates, 10.6g fat, 0.6g fiber, 185mg cholesterol, 256mg sodium, 159mg potassium

Eggs And Sausage Casserole

Servings: 4   Cooking Time: 8 Hours

Ingredients:

8 eggs, whisked
1 yellow onion, chopped
1 pound pork sausage, chopped
2 teaspoons basil, dried

1 tablespoon garlic powder
Salt and black pepper to the taste
1 yellow bell pepper, chopped
1 teaspoon olive oil

Directions:

Grease your Crock Pot with the olive oil, add eggs, onion, pork sausage, basil, garlic powder, salt, pepper and yellow bell pepper, toss, cover and cook on Low for 8 hours.   Slice, divide between plates and serve for breakfast.

Nutrition Info:calories 301, fat 4, fiber 4, carbs 14, protein 7

Smoked Salmon Omelet

Servings: 4   Cooking Time: 2 Hours

Ingredients:

4 oz smoked salmon, sliced
1 teaspoon ground coriander

5 eggs, beaten
1 teaspoon butter, melted

Directions:

Brush the Crock Pot bottom with melted butter. Then mix eggs with ground coriander and pour the liquid in the Crock Pot.   Add smoked salmon and close the lid.   Cook the omelet on High for 2 hours.

Nutrition Info: Per Serving: 120 calories, 12.1g protein, 0.4g carbohydrates, 7.7g fat, 0g fiber, 214mg cholesterol, 651mg sodium, 124mg potassium

Chia Oatmeal

Servings: 2   Cooking Time: 8 Hours

Ingredients:

2 cups almond milk
1 cup steel cut oats
2 tablespoons butter, soft

½ teaspoon almond extract
2 tablespoons chia seeds

Directions:

In your Crock Pot, mix the oats with the chia seeds and the other ingredients, toss, put the lid on and cook on Low for 8 hours.   Stir the oatmeal one more time, divide into bowls and serve.

Nutrition Info:calories 812, fat 71.4, fiber 9.4, carbs 41.1, protein 11

Bacon Cider Muffins

Servings: 9   Cooking Time: 4.5 Hrs
Ingredients:
- 1 cup flour
- 6 tbsp butter
- 3 eggs
- 1 tsp salt
- ½ tbsp apple cider vinegar
- 1 tsp baking powder
- 5 oz. bacon, chopped

Directions:
Whisk butter with apple cider vinegar, flour, baking powder, and salt in a bowl.   Take a non-skillet and toss in bacon.   Stir cook until crispy and crunchy then transfer it to the butter mixture. Beat eggs with the bacon-mixture and liquid in the bigger bowl to form a batter   Layer the muffin tins with paper cups.   Divide the eggs batter into the muffin cups.   Pour 1 cup water into the base of your Crock Pot and place the muffin tray in it. Put the cooker's lid on and set the cooking time to 4 hours 30 minutes on High settings.   Serve.
Nutrition Info: Per Serving: Calories 211, Total Fat 15.7g, Fiber 1g, Total Carbs 12.13g, Protein 6g

Breakfast Muffins

Servings: 4   Cooking Time: 3 Hours
Ingredients:
- 7 eggs, beaten
- 1 bell pepper, diced
- ½ teaspoon salt
- ½ teaspoon cayenne pepper
- 2 tablespoons almond meal
- 1 teaspoon avocado oil

Directions:
Brush the muffin molds with avocado oil.   In the mixing bowl, mix eggs, bell pepper, salt, cayenne pepper, and almond meal.   Pour the muffin mixture in the muffin molds and transfer in the Crock Pot.   Cook the muffins on high for 3 hours.
Nutrition Info: Per Serving: 139 calories, 10.7g protein, 3.7g carbohydrates, 9.4g fat, 0.9g fiber, 286mg cholesterol, 399mg sodium, 189mg potassium

Peppers And Eggs Mix

Servings: 2   Cooking Time: 4 Hours
Ingredients:
- 4 eggs, whisked
- ½ teaspoon coriander, ground
- ½ teaspoon rosemary, dried
- 2 spring onions, chopped
- 1 red bell pepper, cut into strips
- 1 green bell pepper, cut into strips
- 1 yellow bell pepper, cut into strips
- ¼ cup heavy cream
- ½ teaspoon garlic powder
- A pinch of salt and black pepper
- 1 teaspoon sweet paprika
- Cooking spray

Directions:
Grease your Crock Pot with the cooking spray, and mix the eggs with the coriander, rosemary and the other ingredients into the pot.   Put the lid on, cook on Low for 4 hours, divide between plates and serve for breakfast.
Nutrition Info:calories 172, fat 6, fiber 3, carbs 6, protein 7

Chicken- Pork Meatballs

Servings: 8   Cooking Time: 7 Hrs
Ingredients:
- 1 cup bread crumbs
- 2 tbsp sour cream
- 9 oz. ground chicken
- 7 oz. ground pork
- 1 tsp onion powder
- 1 onion, chopped
- 1 tsp ketchup
- ¼ tsp olive oil

Directions:
Thoroughly mix ground chicken, onion powder, sour cream, ground pork, ketchup, and onion in a large bowl.   Add breadcrumbs to bind this mixture well.   Make small meatballs out of this mixture and roll them in extra breadcrumbs. Brush the base of your Crock Pot with olive oil. Gently place the chicken-pork meatballs in the Crock Pot.   Put the cooker's lid on and set the cooking time to 7 hours on Low settings.   Serve warm.
Nutrition Info: Per Serving: Calories 116, Total Fat 5g, Fiber 0g, Total Carbs 4.08g, Protein 14g

Carrot Oatmeal

Servings: 4   Cooking Time: 6 Hours
Ingredients:
- 1 cup oatmeal
- 1 cup carrot, shredded
- 1 tablespoon raisins
- 1 tablespoon maple syrup
- 2 cups of water
- 1 teaspoon butter

Directions:
Put all ingredients in the Crock Pot.   Close the lid and cook the oatmeal on low for 6 hours. Carefully mix the cooked meal.
Nutrition Info: Per Serving: 117 calories, 3g protein, 21.7g carbohydrates, 2.g fat, 2.8g fiber, 3mg cholesterol, 31mg sodium, 191mg potassium

Cream Grits

Servings: 2   Cooking Time: 5 Hours
Ingredients:
- ½ cup grits
- ½ cup heavy cream
- 1 cup of water
- 1 tablespoon cream cheese

Directions:
Put grits, heavy cream, and water in the Crock Pot. Cook the meal on LOW for 5 hours.   When the grits are cooked, add cream cheese and stir carefully.   Transfer the meal in the serving bowls.
Nutrition Info: Per Serving: 151 calories, 1.6g protein, 6.9g carbohydrates, 13.2g fat, 1g fiber, 47mg cholesterol, 116mg sodium, 33mg potassium.

Breakfast Potatoes

Servings: 8   Cooking Time: 4 Hours
Ingredients:

- 3 potatoes, peeled and cubed
- 1 green bell pepper, chopped
- 1 red bell pepper, chopped
- 1 yellow onion, chopped
- 1 and ½ cups cheddar cheese, shredded
- ¼ teaspoon oregano, dried
- 12 ounces smoked chicken sausage, sliced
- ½ cup sour cream
- ¼ teaspoon basil, dried
- 10 ounces cream of chicken soup
- 2 tablespoons parsley, chopped
- Salt and black pepper to the taste

Directions:
In your Crock Pot, mix potatoes with red bell pepper, green bell pepper, sausage, onion, oregano, basil, cheese, salt, pepper and cream of chicken, cover and cook on Low for 4 hours.   Add parsley, divide between plates and serve for breakfast.
Nutrition Info:calories 320, fat 5, fiber 7, carbs 10, protein 5

Crockpot Fisherman's Eggs

Servings: 2   Cooking Time: 3 Hours
Ingredients:

- 1 can organic sardines in olive oil
- 2 organic eggs
- ½ cup arugula, rinsed and drained
- ½ of artichoke hearts, chopped
- Salt and pepper to taste

Directions:
Put the sardines in the bottom of the CrockPot. Break the eggs on top of the sardines and add the arugula and artichokes on top.   Season with salt and pepper to taste.   Close the lid and cook on high for 2 hours or on low for 3 hours.
Nutrition Info: Calories per serving:315; Carbohydrates: 3.5g; Protein: 28g; Fat:20.6 g; Sugar: 0g; Sodium: 491mg; Fiber: 1.3g

Turkey Omelet

Servings: 4   Cooking Time: 5 Hours
Ingredients:

- ½ teaspoon garlic powder
- 6 oz ground turkey
- 4 eggs, beaten
- 1 tablespoon coconut oil
- ½ teaspoon salt
- ¼ cup milk

Directions:
Mix milk with salt, eggs, and garlic powder. Then add ground turkey.   Grease the Crock Pot bowl bottom with coconut oil.   Put the egg mixture in the Crock Pot, flatten it, and close the lid.   Cook the omelet on Low for 5 hours.
Nutrition Info: Per Serving: 184 calories, 17.7g protein, 1.3g carbohydrates, 12.8g fat, 0g fiber, 208mg cholesterol, 405mg sodium, 186mg potassium

Morning Ham Muffins

Servings: 4   Cooking Time: 2.5 Hours
Ingredients:

- 4 eggs, beaten
- 3 oz Mozzarella, shredded
- 3 oz ham, chopped
- 1 teaspoon olive oil
- 1 teaspoon dried parsley
- ½ teaspoon salt

Directions:
Mix eggs with dried parsley, salt, and ham.   Add mozzarella and stir the muffin mixture carefully. Sprinkle the silicone muffin molds with olive oil. After this, pour the egg and ham mixture in the muffin molds and transfer in the Crock Pot. Cook the muffins on High for 2.hours.
Nutrition Info: Per Serving: 168 calories, 15.1g protein, 1.9g carbohydrates, 11.1g fat, 0.3g fiber, 187mg cholesterol, 757mg sodium, 122mg potassium

Fried Apple Slices

Servings: 6   Cooking Time: 6 Hours 10 Minutes
Ingredients:

- 1 teaspoon ground cinnamon
- 3 tablespoons cornstarch
- 3 pounds Granny Smith apples
- ¼ teaspoon nutmeg, freshly grated
- 1 cup sugar, granulated
- 2 tablespoons butter

Directions:
Put the apple slices in the crock pot and stir in nutmeg, cinnamon, sugar and cornstarch.   Top with butter and cover the lid.   Cook on LOW for about 6 hours, stirring about halfway.   Dish out to serve hot.
Nutrition Info: Calories: 234 Fat: 4.1g Carbohydrates: 52.7g

Breakfast Banana Bread

Servings: 4   Cooking Time: 4 Hours
Ingredients:

- 2 eggs
- 1 cup sugar
- 2 cups flour
- 1 teaspoon baking powder
- ½ cup butter
- 3 bananas, mashed
- ½ teaspoon baking soda

Directions:
In a bowl, mix butter with sugar and eggs and whisk well.   Add baking soda, baking powder, flour and bananas, stir really well and pour into a bread pan that fits your Crock Pot.   Put the pan into your Crock Pot, cover and cook on Low for 4 hours.   Slice and serve for breakfast.
Nutrition Info:calories 261, fat 9, fiber 6, carbs 20, protein 16

Sausage Pie(2)

Servings: 4   Cooking Time: 3 Hours
Ingredients:
- ½ cup flour
- ¼ cup skim milk
- 1 teaspoon baking powder
- 1 teaspoon salt
- ½ teaspoon chili flakes
- 4 sausages, chopped
- 1 egg, beaten
- Cooking spray

Directions:
Mix flour with skin milk and baking powder. Then add salt, chili flakes, and egg. Stir the mixture until smooth. You will get the batter.   Spray the Crock Pot with cooking spray from inside.   Then pour the batter in the Crock Pot.   Add chopped sausages and close the lid.   Cook the pie on High for 3 hours.
Nutrition Info: Per Serving: 171 calories, 8.7g protein, 13.4g carbohydrates, 8.9g fat, 0.5g fiber, 64mg cholesterol, 809mg sodium, 262mg potassium

Vanilla Quinoa

Servings: 2   Cooking Time: 4 Hours
Ingredients:
- ½ cup quinoa
- 1 teaspoon vanilla extract
- 2 cups of milk
- 1 tablespoon butter

Directions:
Put quinoa, milk, and vanilla extract in the Crock Pot.   Cook it for 4 hours on Low.   Then add butter and stir the quinoa carefully.
Nutrition Info: Per Serving: 335 calories, 14.1g protein, 39.5g carbohydrates, 13.3g fat, 3g fiber, 35mg cholesterol, 158mg sodium, 384mg potassium.

Raspberry Chia Porridge

Servings: 4   Cooking Time: 4 Hours
Ingredients:
- 1 cup raspberry
- 3 tablespoons maple syrup
- 1 cup chia seeds
- 4 cups of milk

Directions:
Put chia seeds and milk in the Crock Pot and cook the mixture on low for 4 hours.   Meanwhile, mix raspberries and maple syrup in the blender and blend the mixture until smooth.   When the chia porridge is cooked, transfer it in the serving bowls and top with blended raspberry mixture.
Nutrition Info: Per Serving: 315 calories, 13.1g protein, 37.7g carbohydrates, 13.9g fat, 11.7g fiber, 20mg cholesterol, 121mg sodium, 332mg potassium

Bacon Potatoes

Servings: 4   Cooking Time: 5 Hours
Ingredients:
- 4 russet potatoes
- 1 teaspoon dried thyme
- 4 teaspoons olive oil
- 4 bacon slices

Directions:
Cut the potatoes into halves and sprinkle with dried thyme and olive oil.   After this, cut every bacon slice into halves.   Put the potatoes in the Crock Pot bowl and top with bacon slices.   Close the lid and cook them for 5 hours on High.
Nutrition Info: Per Serving: 290 calories, 10.6g protein, 33.9g carbohydrates, 12.8g fat, 5.2g fiber, 21mg cholesterol, 452mg sodium, 976mg potassium.

Ham Pockets

Servings: 4   Cooking Time: 1 Hour
Ingredients:
- 4 pita bread
- ½ cup Cheddar cheese, shredded
- 4 ham slices
- 1 tablespoon mayonnaise
- 1 teaspoon dried dill

Directions:
Mix cheese with mayonnaise and dill.   Then fill the pita bread with sliced ham and cheese mixture. Wrap the stuffed pitas in the foil and place it in the Crock Pot.   Cook them on High for 1 hour.
Nutrition Info: Per Serving: 283 calories, 13.7g protein, 35.7g carbohydrates, 9.1g fat, 1.7g fiber, 32mg cholesterol, 801mg sodium, 175mg potassium.

Carrots Oatmeal

Servings: 2   Cooking Time: 8 Hours
Ingredients:
- ½ cup old fashioned oats
- 2 carrots, peeled and grated
- ½ teaspoon cinnamon powder
- 1 cup almond milk
- 2 tablespoons brown sugar
- ¼ cup walnuts, chopped
- Cooking spray

Directions:
Grease your Crock Pot with cooking spray, add the oats, milk, carrots and the other ingredients, toss, put the lid on and cook on Low for 8 hours. Divide the oatmeal into bowls and serve.
Nutrition Info:calories 590, fat 40.7, fiber 9.1, carbs 49.9, protein 12

Cranberry Maple Oatmeal

Servings: 2   Cooking Time: 6 Hours
Ingredients:
- 1 cup almond milk
- ½ cup steel cut oats
- ½ teaspoon vanilla extract
- ½ cup cranberries
- 1 tablespoon maple syrup
- 1 tablespoon sugar

Directions:
In your Crock Pot, mix the oats with the berries, milk and the other ingredients, toss, put the lid on and cook on Low for 6 hours.   Divide into bowls and serve for breakfast.
Nutrition Info:calories 200, fat 5, fiber 7, carbs 14, protein 4

Sausage And Eggs Mix

Servings: 2   Cooking Time: 8 Hours And 10 Minutes

Ingredients:

4 eggs, whisked
1 red onion, chopped
¼ teaspoon rosemary, dried
½ teaspoon turmeric powder
½ pound pork sausage, sliced
½ tablespoon garlic powder
1 teaspoon basil, dried
A pinch of salt and black pepper
Cooking spray

Directions:

Grease a pan with the cooking spray, heat it up over medium-high heat, add the onion and the pork sausage, toss and cook for   minutes.   Transfer this to the Crock Pot, also add the eggs mixed with the remaining ingredients, toss everything, put the lid on and cook on Low for 8 hours.   Divide between plates and serve right away for breakfast.

Nutrition Info:calories 271, fat 7, fiber 8, carbs 20, protein 11

Chicken Frittata

Servings: 2   Cooking Time: 3 Hours

Ingredients:

½ cup chicken, cooked and shredded
1 teaspoon mustard
1 tablespoon mayonnaise
2 bacon slices, cooked and crumbled
1 tomato, chopped
4 eggs
1 small avocado, pitted, peeled and chopped
Salt and black pepper to the taste

Directions:

In a bowl, mix the eggs with salt, pepper, chicken, avocado, tomato, bacon, mayo and mustard, toss, transfer to your Crock Pot, cover and cook on Low for 3 hours.   Divide between plates and serve for breakfast

Nutrition Info:calories 300, fat 32, fiber 6, carbs 15, protein 25

Cheddar Eggs

Servings: 4   Cooking Time: 2 Hours

Ingredients:

1 teaspoon butter, softened
4 eggs
½ teaspoon salt
1/3 cup Cheddar cheese, shredded

Directions:

Grease the Crock Pot bowl with butter and crack the eggs inside.   Sprinkle the eggs with salt and shredded cheese.   Close the lid and cook on High for 2 hours.

Nutrition Info: Per Serving: 109 calories, 7.9g protein, 0.5g carbohydrates, 8.5g fat, 0g fiber, 176mg cholesterol, 418mg sodium, 69mg potassium.

Salami Eggs

Servings: 4   Cooking Time: 2.5 Hours

Ingredients:

4 oz salami, sliced
1 teaspoon butter, melted
4 eggs
1 tablespoon chives, chopped

Directions:

Pour the melted butter in the Crock Pot.   Crack the eggs inside.   Then top the eggs with salami and chives.   Close the lid and cook them on High for 2.5 hours.

Nutrition Info: Per Serving: 146 calories, 9.1g protein, 0.9g carbohydrates, 11.6g fat, 0g fiber, 186mg cholesterol, 392mg sodium, 115mg potassium

Breakfast Rice Pudding

Servings: 4   Cooking Time: 4 Hours

Ingredients:

1 cup coconut milk
2 cups water
1 cup almond milk
½ cup raisins
1 cup brown rice
2 teaspoons vanilla extract
2 tablespoons flaxseed
1 teaspoon cinnamon powder
2 tablespoons coconut sugar
Cooking spray

Directions:

Grease your Crock Pot with the cooking spray, add coconut milk, water, almond milk, raisins, rice, vanilla, flaxseed and cinnamon, cover, cook on Low for 4 hours, stir, divide into bowls, sprinkle coconut sugar all over and serve.

Nutrition Info:calories 213, fat 3, fiber 6, carbs 10, protein 4

Squash Butter

Servings: 4   Cooking Time: 2 Hours

Ingredients:

1 cup butternut squash puree
4 tablespoons applesauce
1 teaspoon allspices
2 tablespoons butter
1 teaspoon cornflour

Directions:

Put all ingredients in the Crock Pot and mix until homogenous.   Then close the lid and cook the butter on High for   hours.   Transfer the cooked squash butter in the plastic vessel and cool it well.

Nutrition Info: Per Serving: 78 calories, 0.2g protein, 6.3g carbohydrates, 5.8g fat, 0.8g fiber, 15mg cholesterol, 44mg sodium, 20mg potassium

Celery Stalk Muffins

Servings: 4   Cooking Time: 3 Hours

Ingredients:

4 teaspoons flour
1 egg, beaten
2 tablespoons cream cheese
½ teaspoon baking powder
4 oz celery stalk, diced
1 teaspoon cayenne pepper
2 oz Cheddar cheese, shredded

Directions:

Mix flour with eggs, cream cheese, baking powder, and cayenne pepper.   Then add cheese and celery stalk. Stir the mixture with the help of the spoon. After this, put it in the muffin molds and transfer in the Crock Pot.   Cook the muffins on High for 3 hours.

Nutrition Info: Per Serving: 106 calories, 5.8g protein, 3.8g carbohydrates, 7.7g fat, 0.7g fiber, 61mg cholesterol, 142mg sodium, 184mg potassium

Chocolate Breakfast Bread

Servings: 2   Cooking Time: 3 Hours
Ingredients:

Cooking spray	2 eggs, whisked
1 cup almond flour	1 tablespoon butter
½ teaspoon baking soda	½ tablespoon milk
½ teaspoon cinnamon powder	½ teaspoon vanilla extract
1 tablespoon avocado oil	½ cup dark chocolate, melted
2 tablespoons maple syrup	2 tablespoons walnuts, chopped

Directions:
In a bowl, mix the flour with the baking soda, cinnamon, oil and the other ingredients except the cooking spray and stir well.   Grease a loaf pan that fits the Crock Pot with the cooking spray, pour the bread batter into the pan, put the pan in the Crock Pot after you've lined it with tin foil, put the lid on and cook on High for 3 hours.   Cool the sweet bread down, slice, divide between plates and serve for breakfast.
Nutrition Info: calories 200, fat 3, fiber 5, carbs 8, protein 4

Ham Stuffed Peppers

Servings: 3   Cooking Time: 4 Hrs
Ingredients:

3 bell peppers, halved and deseeded	½ cup milk
Salt and black pepper to the taste	½ cup ham, chopped
4 eggs	¼ cup spinach, chopped
2 tbsp green onions, chopped	¾ cup cheddar cheese, shredded

Directions:
Beat eggs with green onion, salt, black pepper, spinach, milk, half of the cheese and ham in a medium bowl.   Cover the base of your Crock Pot with aluminum foil.   Divide the egg-spinach mixture into the bell pepper halves.   Place these stuffed pepper halves in the Crock Pot.   Drizzle the cheese over the bell peppers.   Put the cooker's lid on and set the cooking time to 4 hours on Low settings.   Serve warm.   Devour.
Nutrition Info: Per Serving: Calories 162, Total Fat 4g, Fiber 1g, Total Carbs 6g, Protein 11g

Sage Chicken Strips

Servings: 6   Cooking Time: 4 Hours
Ingredients:

½ cup coconut cream	1 teaspoon ground black pepper
1-pound chicken fillet, cut into the strips	1 teaspoon dried sage
2 tablespoons cornflour	2 tablespoons sour cream

Directions:
Sprinkle the chicken strips with ground black pepper, dried sage, and sour cream.   Then coat every chicken strip in the cornflour and arrange it in the Crock Pot.   Top the chicken with coconut cream and close the lid.   Cook the chicken strips on High for hours.
Nutrition Info: Per Serving: 208 calories, 22.7g protein, 3.5g carbohydrates, 11.3g fat, 0.8g fiber, 69mg cholesterol, 70mg sodium, 255mg potassium.

Oats Craisins Granola

Servings: 8   Cooking Time: 2 Hrs
Ingredients:

5 cups old-fashioned rolled oats	½ cup peanut butter
1/3 cup coconut oil	1 tbsp vanilla
2/3 cup honey	2 tsp cinnamon powder
½ cup almonds, chopped	1 cup craisins
	Cooking spray

Directions:
Toss oats with honey, oil, craisins, cinnamon, vanilla, peanut butter, and almonds in the Crock Pot.   Put the cooker's lid on and set the cooking time to hours on High settings.   Serve.
Nutrition Info: Per Serving: Calories 200, Total Fat 3g, Fiber 6g, Total Carbs 9g, Protein 4g

Saucy Sriracha Red Beans

Servings: 5   Cooking Time: 6 Hrs
Ingredients:

1 cup red beans, soaked and drained	1 chili pepper, sliced
3 chicken stock	1 tsp sriracha
3 tbsp tomato paste	1 tbsp butter
1 onion, sliced	1 tsp turmeric
1 tsp salt	1 cup green peas

Directions:
Spread the red beans in the Crock Pot.   Add turmeric, salt, and chicken stock on its top.   Put the cooker's lid on and set the cooking time to 4 hours on High settings.   Toss the sliced onion with Sriracha, butter, chili pepper, and sriracha in a separate bowl.   Spread this onion-pepper mixture over the cooked beans in the Crock Pot.   Cover the beans again and slow cook for another 1 hour on Low setting.   Serve after a gentle stir.
Nutrition Info: Per Serving: Calories 190, Total Fat 3.1g, Fiber 8g, Total Carbs 31.6g, Protein 11g

Strawberry Yogurt Oatmeal

Servings: 8   Cooking Time: 8 Hrs
Ingredients:

6 cups of water	1 tsp cinnamon powder
2 cups of milk	
2 cups steel-cut oats	2 cups strawberries, halved
1 cup Greek yogurt	
	1 tsp vanilla extract

Directions:
Add oats, milk, cinnamon, yogurt, water, vanilla, and strawberries to the Crock Pot.   Put the cooker's lid on and set the cooking time to 8 hours on Low settings.   Serve.
Nutrition Info: Per Serving: Calories 200, Total Fat 4g, Fiber 6g, Total Carbs 8g, Protein 4g

Dates Quinoa

Servings: 4   Cooking Time: 3 Hours
Ingredients:

1 cup quinoa
4 medjol dates, chopped
3 cups milk
1 apple, cored and chopped
¼ cup pepitas

2 teaspoons cinnamon powder
1 teaspoon vanilla extract
¼ teaspoon nutmeg, ground

Directions:
In your Crock Pot, mix quinoa with dates, milk, apple, pepitas, cinnamon, nutmeg and vanilla, stir, cover and cook on High for 3 hours.   Stir again, divide into bowls and serve.
Nutrition Info:calories 241, fat 4, fiber 4, carbs 10, protein 3

Mushroom Quiche

Servings: 2   Cooking Time: 6 Hours
Ingredients:

2 cups baby Bella mushrooms, chopped
½ cup cheddar cheese, shredded
4 eggs, whisked
½ cup heavy cream
1 tablespoon basil, chopped

2 tablespoons chives, chopped
A pinch of salt and black pepper
½ cup almond flour
¼ teaspoons baking soda
Cooking spray

Directions:
In a bowl, mix the eggs with the cream, flour and the other ingredients except the cooking spray and stir well.   Grease the Crock Pot with the cooking spray, pour the quiche mix, spread well, put the lid on and cook on High for 6 hours.   Slice the quiche, divide between plates and serve for breakfast.
Nutrition Info:calories 211, fat 6, fiber 6, carbs 6, protein 10

Apricot Butter

Servings: 4   Cooking Time: 7 Hours
Ingredients:

1 cup apricots, pitted, chopped
1 teaspoon ground cinnamon

3 tablespoons butter
1 teaspoon brown sugar

Directions:
Put all ingredients in the Crock Pot and stir well Close the lid and cook them on Low for 7 hours. Then blend the mixture with the help of the immersion blender and cool until cold.
Nutrition Info: Per Serving: 99 calories, 0.6g protein, 5.5g carbohydrates, 8.9g fat, 1.1g fiber, 23mg cholesterol, 62mg sodium, 106mg potassium.

Italian Style Scrambled Eggs

Servings: 4   Cooking Time: 4 Hours
Ingredients:

4 eggs, beaten
3 oz Mozzarella, shredded
1 teaspoon Italian seasonings

¼ cup milk
¼ teaspoon salt
1 teaspoon butter, melted

Directions:
Mix eggs with milk, Italian seasonings, and salt. Pour butter and milk mixture in the Crock Pot and close the lid.   Cook the meal on high for 1 hour. Then open the lid and scramble the eggs.   After this, top the meal with cheese and cook the eggs on low for 3 hours more.
Nutrition Info: Per Serving: 143 calories, 12.1g protein, 2g carbohydrates, 9.7g fat, 0g fiber, 180mg cholesterol, 351mg sodium, 69mg potassium.

Carrot Pudding

Servings: 4   Cooking Time: 5 Hours
Ingredients:

3 cups carrot, shredded
1 tablespoon potato starch
4 cups of milk

3 tablespoons maple syrup
1 teaspoon ground cinnamon

Directions:
Mix potato starch with milk and pour the liquid in the Crock Pot.   Add ground cinnamon, maple syrup, and carrot.   Close the lid and cook the pudding on Low for 5 hours.
Nutrition Info: Per Serving: 206 calories, 8.7g protein, 33.1g carbohydrates, 5g fat, 2.3g fiber, 20mg cholesterol, 173mg sodium, 437mg potassium

Peppers, Kale And Cheese Omelet

Servings: 4   Cooking Time: 3 Hours
Ingredients:

1 teaspoon olive oil
7 ounces roasted red peppers, chopped
6 ounces baby kale
Salt and black pepper to the taste

6 ounces feta cheese, crumbled
¼ cup green onions, sliced
7 eggs, whisked

Directions:
In a bowl, mix the eggs with cheese, kale, red peppers, green onions, salt and pepper, whisk well, pour into the Crock Pot after you've greased it with the oil, cover, cook on Low for 3 hours, divide between plates and serve right away.
Nutrition Info:calories 231, fat 7, fiber 4, carbs 7, protein 14

Corn Casserole

Servings: 6   Cooking Time: 8 Hours
Ingredients:

1 cup sweet corn kernels	2 tablespoons cream cheese
1 chili pepper, chopped	5 oz ham, chopped
1 tomato, chopped	1 teaspoon garlic powder
1 cup Mozzarella, shredded	2 eggs, beaten

Directions:
Mix sweet corn kernels, with chili pepper, tomato, and ham.   Add minced garlic and stir the ingredients.   Transfer it in the Crock Pot and flatten gently.   Top the casserole with eggs, cream cheese, and Mozzarella.   Cook the casserole on LOW for 8 hours.
Nutrition Info: Per Serving: 110 calories, 8.3g protein, 7.2g carbohydrates, 5.8g fat, 1g fiber, 74mg cholesterol, 449mg sodium, 159mg potassium.

Cheesy Eggs

Servings: 2   Cooking Time: 3 Hours
Ingredients:

4 eggs, whisked	2 ounces feta cheese, crumbled
¼ cup spring onions, chopped	A pinch of salt and black pepper
1 tablespoon oregano, chopped	Cooking spray
1 cup milk	

Directions:
In a bowl, combine the eggs with the spring onions and the other ingredients except the cooking spray and whisk.   Grease your Crock Pot with cooking spray, add eggs mix, stir , put the lid on and cook on Low for 3 hours.   Divide between plates and serve for breakfast.
Nutrition Info:calories 214, fat 4, fiber 7, carbs 18, protein 5

Salmon Frittata

Servings: 3   Cooking Time: 3 Hours And 40 Minutes
Ingredients:

4 eggs, whisked	Salt and black pepper to the taste
½ teaspoon olive oil	4 ounces smoked salmon, chopped
2 tablespoons green onions, chopped	

Directions:
Drizzle the oil in your Crock Pot, add eggs, salt and pepper, whisk, cover and cook on Low for 3 hours. Add salmon and green onions, toss a bit, cover, cook on Low for 40 minutes more and divide between plates.   Serve right away for breakfast.
Nutrition Info:calories 220, fat 10, fiber 2, carbs 15, protein 7

Tomato Eggs

Servings: 4   Cooking Time: 2.5 Hours
Ingredients:

2 cups tomatoes, chopped	1 teaspoon olive oil
	½ teaspoon ground

¼ cup tomato juice	black pepper
1 onion, diced	4 eggs

Directions:
Pour olive oil in the Crock Pot.   Add onion, tomato juice, and tomatoes.   Close the lid and cook the mixture on High for 1 hour.   Then mix the tomato mixture and crack the eggs inside. Close the lid and cook them on High for 1.hours more.
Nutrition Info: Per Serving: 103 calories, 6.8g protein, 7.2g carbohydrates, 5.8g fat, 1.8g fiber, 164mg cholesterol, 108mg sodium, 350mg potassium

Breakfast Sausage & Cauliflower

Servings: 6 (serving Size Is 6.2 Ounces)
Cooking Time: 7 Hours And 15 Minutes
Ingredients:

10 eggs	¼ cup milk
1 lb. breakfast sausage, chopped	1 ½ cups cheddar cheese, shredded
1 head cauliflower, shredded	Salt and pepper to taste
½ teaspoon mustard	Olive oil

Directions:
Whisk together milk, mustard, eggs, salt, and pepper in a mixing bowl.   Grease Crock-Pot with olive oil.   Place one layer of sausage on the bottom, then cheese, and season with salt and pepper.   Repeat layer.   Pour egg mixture over all ingredients.   Cover and cook on LOW for 6-7 hours or until eggs are set.   Serve hot.
Nutrition Info: Calories: 324.42, Total Fat: 18.01 g, Saturated Fat: 6.96 g, Cholesterol: 259.93 mg, Sodium: 988.86 mg, Potassium: 222.34 mg, Total Carbohydrates: 7.23 g, Fiber: 3.08 g, Sugar: 1.77 g, Protein: 32.48 g

Parmesan Quinoa

Servings: 2   Cooking Time: 6 Hours
Ingredients:

1 cup quinoa	½ cup parmesan, grated
2 cups veggie stock	
1 tablespoon chives, chopped	¼ cup heavy cream
1 carrot, peeled and grated	Salt and black pepper to the taste
	Cooking spray

Directions:
Grease your Crock Pot with the cooking spray, add the quinoa mixed with the stock and the other ingredients except the parmesan and the cream, toss, put the lid on and cook on High for 3 hours. Add the remaining ingredients, toss the mix again, cook on High for 3 more hours, divide into bowls and serve for breakfast.
Nutrition Info:calories 261, fat 6, fiber 8, carbs 26, protein 11

Zucchini Carrot Oatmeal

Servings: 4   Cooking Time: 8 Hrs

Ingredients:
- ½ cup steel cut oats
- 1 carrot, grated
- 1 and ½ cups of coconut milk
- A pinch of cloves, ground
- ¼ zucchini, grated
- A pinch of nutmeg, ground
- ½ tsp cinnamon powder
- 2 tbsp brown sugar
- ¼ cup pecans, chopped

Directions:
Toss oats with milk, carrot, cloves, zucchini, cinnamon, nutmeg, and sugar in the Crock Pot. Put the cooker's lid on and set the cooking time to 8 hours on Low settings.   Divide the oatmeal in the serving bowls.   Garnish with pecans.   Serve.
Nutrition Info: Per Serving: Calories 251, Total Fat 6g, Fiber 8g, Total Carbs 19g, Protein 6g

Shredded Chicken Muffins

Servings: 4   Cooking Time: 2.5 Hours

Ingredients:
- 6 oz chicken fillet, boiled
- 4 eggs, beaten
- 1 teaspoon salt
- 1 teaspoon ground black pepper
- 1 teaspoon olive oil

Directions:
Shred the chicken fillet with the help of the fork and mix with eggs, salt, and ground black pepper. Then brush the muffin molds with olive oil and transfer the shredded chicken mixture inside. Put the muffins in the Crock Pot.   Close the lid and cook them on High for 2.5 hours.
Nutrition Info: Per Serving: 155 calories, 17.9g protein, 0.7g carbohydrates, 8.7g fat, 0.1g fiber, 202mg cholesterol, 680mg sodium, 169mg potassium

Raisins And Rice Pudding

Servings: 4   Cooking Time: 6 Hours

Ingredients:
- 1 cup long-grain rice
- 2.5 cups organic almond milk
- 2 tablespoons cornstarch
- 1 teaspoon vanilla extract
- 2 tablespoons raisins, chopped

Directions:
Put all ingredients in the Crock Pot and carefully mix.   Then close the lid and cook the pudding for 6 hours on Low.
Nutrition Info: Per Serving: 238 calories, 4.1g protein, 49.4g carbohydrates, 1.9g fat, 0.8g fiber, 0mg cholesterol, 91mg sodium, 89mg potassium

Radish Bowl

Servings: 4   Cooking Time: 1.5 Hours

Ingredients:
- 1 tablespoon dried dill
- 1 tablespoon olive oil
- 2 cups radish, halved
- 4 eggs, beaten
- ¼ teaspoon salt
- ¼ cup milk

Directions:
Mix radish with dried dill, olive oil, salt, and milk and transfer in the Crock Pot.   Cook the radish on High for 30 minutes.   Then shake the vegetables well and add eggs. Mix the mixture gently and close the lid.   Cook the meal on High for 1 hour.
Nutrition Info: Per Serving: 112 calories, 6.6g protein, 3.5g carbohydrates, 8.3g fat, 1g fiber, 165mg cholesterol, 240mg sodium, 229mg potassium

Mexican Egg Bake

Servings: 8   Cooking Time: 2 Hours And 15 Minutes

Ingredients:
- Cooking spray
- 10 eggs
- 12 oz. Monterey Jack, shredded
- 1 cup half and half
- 1 garlic clove, minced
- ½ tsp chili powder
- A pinch of salt and black pepper
- 10 oz. taco sauce
- 4 oz. canned green chilies, chopped
- 8 corn tortillas

Directions:
Beat eggs with 8 oz. cheese, half and half, black pepper, salt, green chilies, chili powder, and garlic in a bowl.   Coat the base of your Crock Pot with cooking spray.   Pour the egg-cheese mixture into the cooker.   Put the cooker's lid on and set the cooking time to 2 hours on Low settings.   Now top the egg with remaining cheese and taco sauce. Cover again and cook for 15 minutes on the low setting.   Serve warm with a tortilla.
Nutrition Info: Per Serving: Calories 312, Total Fat 4g, Fiber 8g, Total Carbs 12g, Protein 5g

Apple Cinnamon Granola

Servings: 6   Cooking Time: 4 Hrs

Ingredients:
- 2 green apples, peeled, cored and sliced
- ½ cup granola
- ½ cup bran flakes
- ¼ cup apple juice
- 1/8 cup maple syrup
- 1 tsp cinnamon powder
- 2 tbsp soft butter
- ½ tsp nutmeg, ground

Directions:
Toss the apples with granola, bran flakes, maple syrup, apple juice, butter, cinnamon, nutmeg, and butter in a large bowl.   Spread this apple crumble into the base of your Crock Pot.   Put the cooker's lid on and set the cooking time to 4 hours on Low settings.   Serve and devour.
Nutrition Info: Per Serving: Calories 363, Total Fat 5g, Fiber 6g, Total Carbs 20g, Protein 6g

Leek Bake

Servings: 3   Cooking Time: 8 Hours
Ingredients:
- 2 cups leek, chopped
- 3 oz Cheddar cheese, shredded
- ¼ cup ground chicken
- 1 teaspoon dried thyme
- ½ cup chicken stock

Directions:
Pour the chicken stock in the Crock Pot.   Put the leek in the chicken stock and sprinkle it with dried thyme and ground chicken.   Then top the chicken with Cheddar cheese and close the lid.   Cook the leek bake on low for 8 hours.
Nutrition Info: Per Serving: 175 calories, 11.5g protein, 9.1g carbohydrates, 10.6g fat, 1.2g fiber, 40mg cholesterol, 325mg sodium, 168mg potassium.

Mushroom Casserole

Servings: 2   Cooking Time: 5 Hours
Ingredients:
- ½ cup mozzarella, shredded
- 2 eggs, whisked
- ½ tablespoon balsamic vinegar
- ½ tablespoon olive oil
- 4 ounces baby kale
- 1 red onion, chopped
- ¼ teaspoon oregano
- ½ pound white mushrooms, sliced
- Salt and black pepper to the taste
- Cooking spray

Directions:
In a bowl, mix the eggs with the kale, mushrooms and the other ingredients except the cheese and cooking spray and stir well.   Grease your Crock Pot with cooking spray, add the mushroom mix, spread, sprinkle the mozzarella all over, put the lid on and cook on Low for 5 hours.   Divide between plates and serve for breakfast.
Nutrition Info: calories 216, fat 6, fiber 8, carbs 12, protein 4

Leek Casserole

Servings: 2   Cooking Time: 4 Hours
Ingredients:
- 1 cup leek, chopped
- Cooking spray
- ½ cup mozzarella, shredded
- 1 garlic clove, minced
- 4 eggs, whisked
- 1 cup beef sausage, chopped
- 1 tablespoon cilantro, chopped

Directions:
Grease the Crock Pot with the cooking spray and mix the leek with the mozzarella and the other ingredients inside.   Toss, spread into the pot, put the lid on and cook on Low for 4 hours.   Divide between plates and serve for breakfast.
Nutrition Info: calories 232, fat 4, fiber 8, carbs 17, protein 4

Egg Scramble

Servings: 4   Cooking Time: 2.5 Hours
Ingredients:
- 4 eggs, beaten
- 1 tablespoon butter, melted
- 2 oz Cheddar cheese, shredded
- ¼ teaspoon cayenne pepper
- 1 teaspoon ground paprika

Directions:
Mix eggs with butter, cheese, cayenne pepper, and ground paprika.   Then pour the mixture in the Crock Pot and close the lid.   Cook it on high for 2 hours.   Then open the lid and scramble the eggs. Close the lid and cook the meal on high for 30 minutes.
Nutrition Info: Per Serving: 147 calories, 9.2g protein, 0.9g carbohydrates, 12g fat, 0.2g fiber, 186mg cholesterol, 170mg sodium, 88mg potassium.

Coconut Oatmeal

Servings: 6   Cooking Time: 5 Hours
Ingredients:
- 2 cups oatmeal
- 2 cups of coconut milk
- 1 cup of water
- 2 tablespoons coconut shred
- 1 tablespoon maple syrup

Directions:
Put all ingredients in the Crock Pot and carefully mix.   Then close the lid and cook the oatmeal on low for 5 hours.
Nutrition Info: Per Serving: 313 calories, 5.4g protein, 25.8g carbohydrates, 22.5g fat, 4.8g fiber, 0mg cholesterol, 16mg sodium, 316mg potassium

Cherries And Cocoa Oats

Servings: 2   Cooking Time: 7 Hours
Ingredients:
- 1 cup almond milk
- 1 tablespoon cocoa powder
- ½ cup cherries, pitted
- ½ cup steel cut oats
- 2 tablespoons sugar
- ¼ teaspoon vanilla extract

Directions:
In your Crock Pot, mix the almond milk with the cherries and the other ingredients, toss, put the lid on and cook on Low for 7 hours.   Divide into bowls and serve for breakfast.
Nutrition Info: calories 150, fat 1, fiber 2, carbs 6, protein 5

Mexican Eggs

Servings: 8   Cooking Time: 2 Hours And 15 Minutes
Ingredients:
- Cooking spray
- 10 eggs
- 12 ounces Monterey jack, shredded
- ½ teaspoon chili powder
- 1 garlic clove, minced
- 1 cup half and half
- A pinch of salt and black pepper
- 10 ounces taco sauce
- 4 ounces canned green chilies, chopped
- 8 corn tortillas

Directions:
In a bowl, mix the eggs with half and half, 8 ounces of cheese, salt, pepper, chili powder, green chilies and garlic and whisk everything.   Grease your Crock Pot with cooking spray, add eggs mix, cover and cook on Low for hours.   Spread taco sauce and the rest of the cheese all over, cover and cook on Low for 15 minutes more.   Divide eggs on tortillas, wrap and serve for breakfast.
Nutrition Info: calories 312, fat 4, fiber 8, carbs 12, protein 5

Greek Breakfast Casserole

Servings: 4   Cooking Time: 4 Hours
Ingredients:

12 eggs, whisked
Salt and black pepper to the taste
½ cup milk
1 red onion, chopped
1 cup baby bell mushrooms, sliced
½ cup sun-dried tomatoes
1 teaspoon garlic, minced
2 cups spinach
½ cup feta cheese, crumbled

Directions:
In a bowl, mix the eggs with salt, pepper and milk and whisk well.   Add garlic, onion, mushrooms, spinach and tomatoes, toss well, pour this into your Crock Pot, sprinkle cheese all over, cover and cook on Low for 4 hours.   Slice, divide between plates and serve for breakfast.
Nutrition Info: calories 325, fat 7, fiber 7, carbs 27, protein 18

Walnut And Cheese Balls

Servings: 5   Cooking Time: 1.5 Hours
Ingredients:

1 cup walnuts, grinded
2 eggs, beaten
3 oz Parmesan, grated
¼ cup breadcrumbs
2 tablespoons coconut oil, melted

Directions:
Mix grinded walnuts and breadcrumbs.   Then add eggs and Parmesan.   Carefully mix the mixture and make the medium size balls from them.   Then pour melted coconut oil in the Crock Pot.   Add walnuts balls. Arrange them in one layer and close the lid.   Cook the balls on high for 1 hour.   Then flip them on another side and cook for 30 minutes more.
Nutrition Info: Per Serving: 303 calories, 14.4g protein, 7.1g carbohydrates, 25.9g fat, 1.9g fiber, 78mg cholesterol, 223mg sodium, 165mg potassium

Breakfast Casserole

Servings: 5   Cooking Time: 7 Hours
Ingredients:

1 cup Cheddar cheese, shredded
1 potato, peeled, diced
½ cup carrot, grated
1 teaspoon ground turmeric
½ teaspoon cayenne pepper
5 eggs, beaten
5 oz ham, chopped
½ cup bell pepper, chopped

Directions:
Make the layer from potato in the Crock Pot mold. Then put the layer of carrot over the potatoes. Sprinkle the vegetables with ground turmeric and cayenne pepper.   Then add ham and bell pepper. Pour the beaten eggs over the casserole and top

with shredded cheese.   Cook the meal on LOW for 7 hours.
Nutrition Info: Per Serving: 237 calories, 16.8g protein, 10g carbohydrates, 14.4g fat, 1.7g fiber, 204mg cholesterol, 582mg sodium, 378mg potassium.

Spinach Frittata(2)

Servings: 2   Cooking Time: 5 Hours And 10 Minutes
Ingredients:

Cooking spray
1 cup cherry tomatoes, halved
3 spring onions, chopped
3 ounces roasted red peppers, drained and chopped
1 cup baby spinach
2 ounces mozzarella, shredded
4 eggs, whisked
½ teaspoon allspice, ground
A pinch of salt and black pepper

Directions:
Grease a pan with the cooking spray, heat up over medium heat, add the spring onions and roasted peppers and cook for   minutes.   Transfer the mix to the Crock Pot, add the eggs mixed with the rest of the ingredients, toss, spread into the pot, put the lid on and cook on Low for 5 hours.   Divide the frittata between plates and serve.
Nutrition Info: calories 251, fat 4, fiber 6, carbs 12, protein 5

Nutmeg Squash Oatmeal

Servings: 6   Cooking Time: 8 Hrs
Ingredients:

½ cup almonds, soaked for 12 hours in water and drained
½ cup walnuts, chopped
2 apples, peeled, cored and cubed
1 butternut squash, peeled and cubed
½ tsp nutmeg, ground
1 tsp cinnamon powder
1 tbsp sugar
1 cup milk

Directions:
Toss almond with apples, walnuts, nutmeg, sugar, squash, and cinnamon in the base of your Crock Pot.   Pour in milk and give it a gentle stir.   Put the cooker's lid on and set the cooking time to 8 hours on Low settings.   Serve.
Nutrition Info: Per Serving: Calories 178, Total Fat 7g, Fiber 7g, Total Carbs 9g, Protein 4g

Beef Meatloaf

Servings: 2   Cooking Time: 4 Hours

Ingredients:

- 1 red onion, chopped
- 1 pound beef stew meat, ground
- ½ teaspoon chili powder
- 1 egg, whisked
- ½ teaspoon sweet paprika
- 2 tablespoons white flour
- ½ teaspoon olive oil
- ½ teaspoon oregano, chopped
- ½ tablespoon basil, chopped
- A pinch of salt and black pepper
- ½ teaspoon marjoram, dried

Directions:

In a bowl, mix the beef with the onion, chili powder and the other ingredients except the oil, stir well and shape your meatloaf.   Grease a loaf pan that fits your Crock Pot with the oil, add meatloaf mix into the pan, put it in your Crock Pot, put the lid on and cook on Low for 4 hours.   Slice and serve for breakfast.

Nutrition Info:calories 200, fat 6, fiber 12, carbs 17, protein 10

Cranberry Quinoa

Servings: 4   Cooking Time: 2 Hours

Ingredients:

- 3 cups coconut water
- 1 teaspoon vanilla extract
- 1 cup quinoa
- 1/8 cup almonds, sliced
- 3 teaspoons honey
- 1/8 cup coconut flakes
- ¼ cup cranberries, dried

Directions:

In your Crock Pot, mix coconut water with vanilla, quinoa, honey, almonds, coconut flakes and cranberries, toss, cover and cook on High for 2 hours.   Divide quinoa mix into bowls and serve.

Nutrition Info:calories 261, fat 7, fiber 8, carbs 18, protein

Broccoli Quiche

Servings: 8   Cooking Time: 5 Hours

Ingredients:

- 1 cup broccoli, chopped
- ½ cup fresh cilantro, chopped
- ¼ cup Mozzarella, shredded
- 2 tablespoons oatmeal
- 1 teaspoon olive oil
- 8 eggs, beaten
- 1 teaspoon ground paprika

Directions:

Brush the Crock Pot bowl with olive oil.   In the mixing bowl mix oatmeal, eggs, and ground paprika.   Pour the mixture in the Crock Pot. Add all remaining ingredients, gently stir the mixture.   Close the lid and cook the quiche for hours on High.

Nutrition Info: Per Serving: 80 calories, 6.3g protein, 2.2g carbohydrates, 5.3g fat, 0.6g fiber, 164mg cholesterol, 71mg sodium, 111mg potassium.

Broccoli Casserole

Servings: 2   Cooking Time: 6 Hours

Ingredients:

- 2 eggs, whisked
- 1 cup broccoli florets
- ½ teaspoon coriander, ground
- ½ teaspoon rosemary, dried
- ½ teaspoon turmeric powder
- ½ teaspoon mustard powder
- 2 cups hash browns
- A pinch of salt and black pepper
- 1 small red onion, chopped
- ½ red bell pepper, chopped
- 1 ounce cheddar cheese, shredded
- Cooking spray

Directions:

Grease your Crock Pot with the cooking spray, and spread hash browns, broccoli, bell pepper and the onion on the bottom of the pan.   In a bowl, mix the eggs with the coriander and the other ingredients, whisk and pour over the broccoli mix in the pot.   Put the lid on, cook on Low for 6 hours, divide between plates and serve for breakfast.

Nutrition Info:calories 261, fat 7, fiber 8, carbs 20, protein 11

Artichoke Frittata

Servings: 4   Cooking Time: 3 Hours

Ingredients:

- 14 ounces canned artichokes hearts, drained and chopped
- 12 ounces roasted red peppers, chopped
- 8 eggs, whisked
- ¼ cup green onions, chopped
- 4 ounces feta cheese, crumbled
- Cooking spray

Directions:

Grease your Crock Pot with cooking spray and add artichokes, roasted peppers and green onions. Add eggs, sprinkle cheese all over, cover and cook on Low for 3 hours.   Divide frittata between plates and serve.

Nutrition Info:calories 232, fat 7, fiber 9, carbs 17, protein 6

Apple Spread

Servings: 2   Cooking Time: 4 Hours

Ingredients:

- 2 apples, cored, peeled and pureed
- ½ cup coconut cream
- 2 tablespoons apple cider
- 2 tablespoons sugar
- ¼ teaspoon cinnamon powder
- ½ teaspoon lemon juice
- ¼ teaspoon ginger, grated

Directions:

In your Crock Pot, mix the apple puree with the cream, sugar and the other ingredients, whisk, put the lid on and cook on High for 4 hours.   Blend using an immersion blender, cool down and serve for breakfast.

Nutrition Info:calories 172, fat 3, fiber 3, carbs 8, protein 3

Herbed Pork Meatballs

Servings: 9   Cooking Time: 4 Hrs

Ingredients:

2 lb. ground pork
1 tbsp dried parsley
1 tsp dried dill
1 tsp paprika
1 tsp salt
1 egg
1 tbsp semolina

½ cup tomato juice
3 tbsp flour
1 tbsp minced garlic
1 tsp onion powder
1 tsp sugar
1 tsp chives
1 oz. bay leaves

Directions:

Beat egg in a bowl then stir in ground pork, parsley, dill, salt, paprika, garlic, semolina, and onion powder in a large bowl.   Make medium-sized meatballs out of this mixture.   Cover the base of your Crock Pot with a parchment sheet.   Place the meatballs in the cooker.   Now mix tomato juice, flour, bay leaf, sugar and chives in a separate bowl.   Pour this mixture over the meatballs. Put the cooker's lid on and set the cooking time to 4 hours on Low settings.   Serve the meatballs with their sauce.

Nutrition Info: Per Serving: Calories 344, Total Fat 22.4g, Fiber 1g, Total Carbs 6.87g, Protein 28g

Peas And Rice Bowls

Servings: 2   Cooking Time: 6 Hours

Ingredients:

¼ cup peas
1 cup wild rice
2 cups veggie stock
1 tablespoon dill, chopped
3 spring onions, chopped
½ teaspoon coriander, ground

¼ cup heavy cream
½ teaspoon allspice, ground
A pinch of salt and black pepper
¼ cup cheddar cheese, shredded
1 teaspoon olive oil

Directions:

Grease the Crock Pot with the oil, add the rice, peas, stock and the other ingredients except the dill and heavy cream, stir, put the lid on and cook on Low for 3 hours.   Add the remaining ingredients, stir the mix, put the lid back on, cook on Low for 3 more hours, divide into bowls and serve for breakfast.

Nutrition Info: calories 442, fat 13.6, fiber 6.8, carbs 66, protein 17.4

Lunch & Dinner Recipes

Autumnal Stew

Servings: 6   Cooking Time: 6 1/4 Hours

Ingredients:

4 cups butternut squash cubes	2 ripe tomatoes, peeled and diced
1 shallot, chopped	1/4 teaspoon cumin powder
2 garlic cloves, chopped	1 pinch chili powder
2 red apples, peeled and diced	1/2 cup tomato sauce
1 celery stalk, sliced	1/2 cup vegetable stock
1 carrot, sliced	Salt and pepper to taste

Directions:
Combine all the ingredients in your Crock Pot. Add salt and pepper to taste and cook on low settings for 6 hours.   Serve the stew warm and fresh.

Turnip And Beans Casserole

Servings: 4   Cooking Time: 6 Hours

Ingredients:

½ cup turnip, chopped	¼ cup potato, chopped 1 carrot, diced
1 teaspoon chili powder	1 cup red kidney beans, canned
¼ cup of coconut milk	½ cup Cheddar cheese, shredded
1 teaspoon coconut oil	

Directions:
Grease the Crock Pot bottom with coconut oil. Then put the turnip and potato inside.   Sprinkle the vegetables with chili powder and coconut mil. After this, top the with red kidney beans and Cheddar cheese.   Close the lid and cook the casserole on Low for 6 hours.

Nutrition Info: Per Serving: 266 calories, 14.5g protein, 31.4g carbohydrates, 10g fat, 7.9g fiber, 15mg cholesterol, 113mg sodium, 742mg potassium.

Quinoa Black Bean Chili

Servings: 6   Cooking Time: 6 1/4 Hours

Ingredients:

1/2 cup quinoa, rinsed	1 1/2 cups vegetable stock
1 can (15 oz.) black beans, drained	1/4 teaspoon chili powder
1 can fire roasted tomatoes	1/4 teaspoon cumin powder
1 sweet onion, chopped	Salt and pepper to taste
2 garlic cloves, chopped	

Directions:
Combine the quinoa, black beans, tomatoes, onion, garlic and stock, as well as chili powder and cumin powder.   Season with salt and pepper and cook on low settings for 6 hours.   Serve the chili warm.

Collard Greens Stew

Servings: 6   Cooking Time: 6 1/4 Hours

Ingredients:

1 tablespoon olive oil	1/2 cup tomato sauce
2 garlic cloves, chopped	1 bunch collard greens, shredded
1 cup dried black beans, rinsed	Salt and pepper to taste
2 cups vegetable stock	1 tablespoon chopped cilantro for serving

Directions:
Combine all the ingredients in your crock pot, adding salt and pepper as needed.   Cook on low settings for 6 hours.   Serve the stew warm and fresh or chilled.

Button Mushroom Beef Stew

Servings: 6   Cooking Time: 6 1/2 Hours

Ingredients:

2 pounds beef roast, cubed	1 can fire roasted tomatoes
1 tablespoon all-purpose flour	1 pound button mushrooms
2 tablespoons canola oil	1 cup beef stock
2 carrots, diced	2 bay leaves
1 celery root, peeled and diced	1 red chili, chopped
	Salt and pepper to taste

Directions:
Season the beef with salt and pepper and sprinkle it with flour.   Heat the oil in a frying pan and add the beef. Cook for a few minutes until golden then transfer in your Crock Pot.   Add the rest of the ingredients and adjust the taste with salt and pepper.   Cover and cook on low settings for 6 hours.   Serve the stew warm or chilled.

Carne Guisada

Servings: 8   Cooking Time: 6 1/2 Hours

Ingredients:

3 pounds beef chuck roast, cut into small cubes	2 shallots, chopped
	1/4 teaspoon chili powder
2 red bell peppers, cored and diced	1/2 teaspoon cumin powder
3 garlic cloves, minced	1 1/2 cups beef stock
4 medium size potatoes, peeled and cubed	1 cup tomato sauce
	Salt and pepper to taste

Directions:
Combine the chuck roast, bell peppers, shallots, garlic, tomatoes, chili powder, cumin powder, stock and tomato sauce in your crock pot.   Season with salt and pepper as needed and cook on low settings for 6 hours.   The carne guisada is best served in burritos or tortillas.

Madras Lentils

Servings: 6   Cooking Time: 4 1/4 Hours
Ingredients:

1 cup dried red lentils, rinsed	3 garlic cloves, chopped
1/2 cup brown lentils, rinsed	1/2 teaspoon cumin powder
1 cup tomato sauce	1/2 teaspoon dried oregano
2 cups vegetable stock	Salt and pepper to taste
1 large potato, peeled and cubed	1/2 cup coconut milk
1 shallot, chopped	

Directions:
Mix the lentils, tomato sauce, stock, potato, shallot, garlic, cumin powder, oregano and coconut milk in your Crock Pot.   Add salt and pepper to taste and cook over low settings for 4 hours.   Serve the lentils warm or store them in an airtight container in the freezer until needed.

Chicken And Cabbage Mix

Servings: 6   Cooking Time: 5 Hours And 20 Minutes
Ingredients:

6 garlic cloves, minced	2 teaspoons sugar
4 scallions, sliced	1 teaspoon ginger, minced
1 cup veggie stock	2 pounds chicken thighs, skinless and boneless
1 tablespoon olive oil	
1 tablespoon soy sauce	2 cups cabbage, shredded

Directions:
In your Crock Pot, mix stock with oil, scallions, garlic, sugar, soy sauce, ginger and chicken, stir, cover and cook on Low for 5 hours.   Transfer chicken to plates, add cabbage to the Crock Pot, cover, cook on High for   minutes more, add next to the chicken and serve for lunch.
Nutrition Info: calories 240, fat 3, fiber 4, carbs 14, protein 10

Vegetarian Bolognese Sauce

Servings: 10   Cooking Time: 8 1/4 Hours
Ingredients:

12 oz. firm tofu, crumbled	1 parsnip, grated
2 tablespoons olive oil	1 teaspoon dried oregano
2 large onions, chopped	2 tablespoons tomato paste
6 garlic cloves, minced	1 can (15 oz.) diced tomatoes
2 celery stalks, diced	1 cup vegetable stock
2 carrots, grated	Salt and pepper to taste
1 teaspoon dried basil	1 bay leaf
	2 tablespoons lemon juice

Directions:
Heat the oil in a skillet and add the tofu. Cook for a few minutes until golden then transfer in your Crock Pot.   Add the remaining ingredients and adjust the taste with salt and pepper.   Cook on low settings for 8 hours.   Serve the Bolognese sauce fresh or freeze it in individual portions in airtight containers.

Apple And Onion Lunch Roast

Servings: 8   Cooking Time: 5 Hours
Ingredients:

1 beef sirloin roast, halved	1/2 teaspoon Worcestershire sauce
Salt and black pepper to the taste	1 yellow onion, cut into medium wedges
1 cup water	2 tablespoons water
1/2 teaspoon soy sauce	2 tablespoons cornstarch
1 apple, cored and quartered	1/8 teaspoon browning sauce
1/4 teaspoon garlic powder	Cooking spray

Directions:
Grease a pan with the cooking spray, heat it up over medium-high heat, add roast, brown it for a few minutes on each side and transfer to your Crock Pot.   Add salt, pepper, soy sauce, garlic powder, Worcestershire sauce, onion and apple, cover and cook on Low for 6 hours.   Transfer cooking juices from the Crock Pot to a pan, heat it up over medium heat, add cornstarch, water and browning sauce, stir well, cook for a few minutes and take off heat.   Slice roast, divide between plates, drizzle sauce all over and serve for lunch.
Nutrition Info: calories 242, fat 8, fiber 1, carbs 8, protein 34

Lime Bean Stew

Servings: 8   Cooking Time: 6 1/4 Hours
Ingredients:

2 cups dried lime beans	1 cup diced tomatoes
2 carrots, sliced	1 cup tomato sauce
2 celery stalks, sliced	2 cups vegetable stock
1 head cauliflower, cut into florets	1 bay leaf
1 teaspoon grated ginger	1 thyme sprig
	Salt and pepper to taste

Directions:
Combine the beans, carrots, celery, cauliflower, ginger, tomatoes, tomato sauce, stock, salt and pepper, as well as bay leaf and thyme in your crock pot.   Season with salt and pepper as needed and cook on low settings for 6 hours.   The stew is best served warm.

Red Wine Braised Oxtail

Servings: 4   Cooking Time: 6 1/4 Hours
Ingredients:

2 pounds oxtails, sliced	1 parsnip, sliced
2 tablespoons olive oil	2 cups cherry tomatoes, halved
1 large onion, sliced	1 orange, juiced
4 garlic cloves, chopped	1 bay leaf
1 carrot, sliced	1 rosemary sprig
	Salt and pepper to taste

Directions:
Heat the oil in a skillet and add the oxtails. Fry on each side until golden then transfer in your crock pot.   Add the remaining ingredients and season with salt and pepper.   Cook on low settings for 6 hours and serve the dish warm.

Banana Chicken Curry

Servings: 6   Cooking Time: 7 1/4 Hours
Ingredients:

2 pounds chicken drumsticks
1 jalapeno pepper, chopped
1 1/2 cups diced tomatoes
1 large onion, chopped
4 garlic cloves, chopped
1 teaspoon cumin powder
1 banana, sliced
1 teaspoon curry powder
1/4 cup dry white wine
1 bay leaf
1 lemongrass stalk, crushed
1 cup coconut milk
Salt and pepper to taste

Directions:
Combine the chicken, jalapeno, banana, tomatoes, onion, garlic, spices, wine, bay leaf, lemongrass and coconut milk in a Crock Pot.   Add salt and pepper to taste and cook on low settings for 7 hours. Serve the curry warm or chilled.

White Bean Casoulet

Servings: 6   Cooking Time: 6 1/2 Hours
Ingredients:

2 tablespoons olive oil
1 large onion, chopped
2 carrots, diced
2 garlic cloves, chopped
2 cans white beans, drained
1 parsnip, diced
1 cup vegetable stock
1 thyme sprig
1 1/2 cups diced tomatoes
1 bay leaf
Salt and pepper to taste

Directions:
Heat the oil in a skillet and add the onion, carrot and garlic. Sauté for 2 minutes until softened and translucent then transfer in your Crock Pot.   Add the remaining ingredients and cook on low settings for 6 hours.   Serve the cassoulet warm.

Spiced Pork Belly

Servings: 6   Cooking Time: 7 1/4 Hours
Ingredients:

3 pounds piece of pork belly
1 tablespoon cumin powder
1 tablespoon brown sugar
1 teaspoon chili powder
1 teaspoon grated ginger
1 tablespoon molasses
2 garlic cloves, minced
1 tablespoon soy sauce
1/2 cup white wine

Directions:
Mix the cumin powder, sugar, chili powder, ginger, molasses, garlic and soy sauce in a bowl.   Spread this mixture over the pork belly and rub it well into the skin and meat.   Place the belly in your crock pot and add the wine.   Cook on low settings for 7 hours.   Serve the belly warm with your favorite side dish.

Jamaican Jerk Chicken

Servings: 4   Cooking Time: 7 1/2 Hours
Ingredients:

4 chicken breasts
2 tablespoons jerk seasoning
2 tablespoons olive oil
1/2 cup chicken stock
1/4 cup brewed coffee
1 jalapeno pepper, chopped
Salt and pepper to taste

Directions:
Season the chicken with salt, pepper and jerk seasoning.   Combine the seasoned chicken, stock and coffee, as well as jalapeno pepper in your Crock Pot.   Cover with a lid and cook on low settings for 7 hours.   Serve the chicken warm and fresh.

Creamy Chicken And Mushroom Pot Pie

Servings: 6   Cooking Time: 6 1/4 Hours
Ingredients:

4 cups sliced cremini mushrooms
4 carrots, sliced
2 chicken breasts, cubed
1 large onion, chopped
1 cup frozen peas
1 cup vegetable stock
Salt and pepper to taste
1/2 teaspoon dried thyme
1 sheet puff pastry

Directions:
Combine the mushrooms, carrots, chicken, onion, peas, stock and thyme in your crock pot.   Add salt and pepper to taste then top with the puff pastry.   Cover with a lid and cook on low settings for 6 hours.   Serve the pot pie warm and fresh.

Honey Sesame Glazed Chicken

Servings: 4   Cooking Time: 6 1/4 Hours
Ingredients:

4 chicken breasts
3 tablespoons honey
1/2 teaspoon red pepper flakes
2 garlic cloves, minced
1 teaspoon grated ginger
2 tablespoons soy sauce
1/4 cup ketchup
1/4 cup chicken stock
2 tablespoons sesame seeds
1 teaspoon sesame oil

Directions:
Combine the chicken and the remaining ingredients in your crock pot.   Cover with a lid and cook on low settings for 6 hours.   Serve the chicken warm with your favorite side dish.

Chicken Tacos

Servings: 16   Cooking Time: 5 Hours
Ingredients:

2 mangos, peeled and chopped
2 tomatoes, chopped
1 and ½ cups pineapple chunks
2 small green bell peppers, chopped
1 tablespoon lime juice
2 green onions, chopped
1 red onion, chopped
1 teaspoon sugar
4 pounds chicken breast halves, skinless
Salt and black pepper to the taste
32 taco shells, warm
¼ cup cilantro, chopped
¼ cup brown sugar

Directions:
In a bowl, mix mango with pineapple, red onion, tomatoes, bell peppers, green onions and lime juice and toss.   Put chicken in your Crock Pot, add salt, pepper and sugar and toss.   Add mango mix, cover and cook on Low for 5 hours.   Transfer chicken to a cutting board, cool it down, discard bones and shred meat.   Divide meat and mango mix between taco shells and serve them for lunch.
Nutrition Info:calories 246, fat 7, fiber 2, carbs 25, protein 21

Cheesy Chicken Burrito Filling

Servings: 6   Cooking Time: 6 1/4 Hours
Ingredients:

1 1/2 pounds ground chicken
2 tablespoons canola oil
1 can (15 oz.) diced tomatoes
2 cups chicken stock
1 teaspoon chili powder
1 cup brown rice
1 can (15 oz.) black beans, drained
1 can (10 oz.) sweet corn, drained
Salt and pepper to taste
1 1/2 cups grated Cheddar

Directions:
Heat the canola oil in a skillet and add the chicken. Cook for a few minutes, stirring often, then transfer in your crock pot.   Add the rest of the ingredients, finishing with grated cheese.   Season with salt and pepper as needed and cook on low settings for 6 hours.   Serve the dish warm and fresh.

Rich Stout Beef Casserole

Servings: 8   Cooking Time: 8 1/4 Hours
Ingredients:

4 pounds beef roast, cubed
2 tablespoons canola oil
6 bacon slices, chopped
4 garlic cloves, minced
1 celery stalk,
1 cup finely chopped mushrooms
1 1/2 cups brown stout
2 tablespoons tomato paste
1 teaspoon dried thyme
1/2 teaspoon chili
chopped
2 shallots, finely chopped
powder
Salt and pepper to taste

Directions:
Heat the canola oil in your crock pot and add the beef and bacon. Cook for a few minutes until golden then transfer in your crock pot.   Add the rest of the ingredients and adjust the taste with salt and pepper.   Cook the beef on low settings for 8 hours.   Serve the roast warm with your favorite side dish.

Butter Buckwheat

Servings: 4   Cooking Time: 4 Hours
Ingredients:

2 tablespoons butter
1 cup buckwheat
2 cups chicken stock
½ teaspoon salt

Directions:
Mix buckwheat with salt and transfer in the Crock Pot.   Add chicken stock and close the lid.   Cook the buckwheat on High for 4 hours.   Then add butter, carefully mixture the buckwheat, and transfer in the bowls.
Nutrition Info: Per Serving: 202 calories, 6g protein, 30.8g carbohydrates, 7.5g fat, 4.3g fiber, 15mg cholesterol, 714mg sodium, 205mg potassium.

Red Chile Pulled Pork

Servings: 8   Cooking Time: 7 1/4 Hours
Ingredients:

4 pounds pork roast
2 red chilis, seeded and chopped
1 large onion, chopped
1 cup tomato sauce
1 cup red salsa
Salt and pepper to taste

Directions:
Combine all the ingredients in your Crock Pot. Add salt and pepper to fit your taste and cook under the lid on low settings for 7 hours.   When done, shred the pork into fine threads using two forks.   Serve the pork warm and fresh or re-heat it later.

Lemon Roasted Pork Tenderloin

Servings: 6   Cooking Time: 7 1/4 Hours
Ingredients:

2 pounds pork tenderloin
1 lemon, sliced
1 teaspoon black pepper kernels
1 cup canola oil
1 cup vegetable stock
Salt and pepper to taste

Directions:
Combine all the ingredients in your Crock Pot. Add enough salt and pepper and cook on low settings for 7 hours.   Slice the pork and serve it warm.

Low-carb Meatballs

Servings: 4   Cooking Time: 4 Hours 10 Minutes

Ingredients:

1 pound pork, minced
1 pound beef, minced
½ large onion
2 tablespoons olive oil
2 eggs
½ cup Parmesan cheese, shredded
3 garlic cloves, minced

Directions:

Put olive oil, onions and garlic in a pan and sauté for about 3 minutes.   Transfer the onion mixture to a bowl and add the remaining ingredients. Make small-sized meatballs out of this mixture. Arrange these meatballs in a crockpot and cook, covered on LOW for about hours.   Dish out in a bowl and serve hot.

Nutrition Info: Calories: 521 Fat: 23.3g Carbohydrates: 3.2g

Rice And Chorizo Bowl

Servings: 5   Cooking Time: 3 Hours

Ingredients:

8 oz chorizo, sliced
2 oz green chiles, canned, chopped
1 garlic clove, diced
½ cup white rice
1.5 cup chicken stock
1 teaspoon avocado oil

Directions:

Put rice in the Crock Pot.   Add chicken stock, garlic, chiles, and chicken stock.   Close the lid and cook the rice on high for hours.   Meanwhile, heat the avocado oil in the skillet.   Add chorizo and roast it for 2 minutes per side on medium heat. When the rice is cooked, transfer it in the bowls and top with roasted chorizo.

Nutrition Info: Per Serving: 283 calories, 12.5g protein, 16.9g carbohydrates, 17.8g fat, 0.3g fiber, 40mg cholesterol, 836mg sodium, 212mg potassium.

Provence Summer Veggie Stew

Servings: 8   Cooking Time: 6 1/2 Hours

Ingredients:

1 cup frozen pearl onions
3 large carrots, sliced
1 cup frozen corn
1 cup frozen green peas
1 cup vegetable stock
2 ripe tomatoes, peeled and cubed
2 zucchinis, cubed
1 teaspoon herbs de Provence
1 can (15 oz.) chickpeas, drained
Salt and pepper to taste
Cooked white rice for serving

Directions:

Combine the onions, carrots, corn, green peas, stock, zucchinis, tomatoes, herbs, chickpeas, salt and pepper in your crock pot.   Add salt and pepper to taste and cook on low settings for 6 hours.   Serve the stew fresh over cooked white rice or simple.

Beef Three Bean Casserole

Servings: 8   Cooking Time: 6 1/4 Hours

Ingredients:

1 pound ground beef
4 bacon slices, chopped
2 tablespoons canola oil
1 can (15 oz.) black beans, drained
1 can (15 oz.) red beans, drained
1 can (15 oz.) kidney beans, drained
2 carrots, diced
1 celery stalk, diced
4 garlic cloves, chopped
1 tablespoon molasses
1/4 teaspoon cayenne pepper
1 cup beef stock
1/4 cup tomato paste
Salt and pepper to taste
1 1/2 cups grated Cheddar

Directions:

Heat the oil in a frying pan and add the beef and bacon. Cook for 5 minutes, stirring often then transfer the mixture in your Crock Pot.   Add the beans, carrots, celery, garlic, molasses, cayenne, stock and tomato paste, as well as salt and pepper. Top with Cheddar and cook on low settings for 6 hours.   The casserole is best served warm.

Beef Strips With Egg Noodles

Servings: 6   Cooking Time: 5 1/4 Hours

Ingredients:

1 1/2 pounds beef roast, cut into thin strips
2 tablespoons peanut oil
2 red bell peppers, cored and sliced
1/2 teaspoon grated ginger
1/2 teaspoon chili powder
2 tablespoons soy sauce
1 shallot, sliced
1/2 cup tomato sauce
1 teaspoon Worcestershire sauce
1 teaspoon orange zest
1/4 cup fresh orange juice
Salt and pepper to taste
Cooked egg noodles for serving

Directions:

Heat the peanut oil in a frying pan. Add the beef roast and cook for 5 minutes on all sides then transfer in your crock pot.   Add the shallot, bell peppers, ginger, chili powder, soy sauce, tomato sauce, Worcestershire sauce, orange zest, orange juice, salt and pepper.   Cover the pot and cook on low settings for 5 hours.   Serve the beef and the sauce warm over egg noodles.

Savory Chowder

Servings: 6   Cooking Time: 6 Hours 20 Minutes

Ingredients:

¼ cup red onions, chopped
2 cups cauliflower, chopped
¼ teaspoon thyme
2 teaspoons parsley
1 cup organic chicken broth
1 can clams
1 pint half-and-half
2 slices bacon, cooked
1 teaspoon salt
1 garlic clove, minced
1/8 teaspoon pepper

Directions:

Put all the ingredients in a crock pot and stir well. Cover and cook on LOW for about 6 hours.   Ladle out in a bowl and serve hot.

Nutrition Info: Calories: 169 Fat: 12.2g Carbohydrates: 9.2g

Tomato Sauce Pork Roast

Servings: 4   Cooking Time: 3 1/4 Hours
Ingredients:
- 2 pounds pork roast, cubed
- 2 tablespoons canola oil
- 1/2 cup tomato sauce
- 1/2 cup chicken stock
- 2 tablespoons tomato paste
- 1/4 teaspoon cayenne pepper
- Salt and pepper to taste

Directions:
Combine all the ingredients in your Crock Pot. Add salt and pepper to taste and cook on high settings for 3 hours.   Serve the pork roast warm and fresh with your favorite side dish.

Fajitas

Servings: 8   Cooking Time: 3 Hours
Ingredients:
- 1 and ½ pounds beef sirloin, cut into thin strips
- 2 tablespoons lemon juice
- 2 tablespoons olive oil
- 1 garlic clove, minced
- 1 and ½ teaspoon cumin, ground
- Salt and black pepper to the taste
- ½ teaspoon chili powder
- A pinch of red pepper flakes, crushed
- 1 red bell pepper, cut into thin strips
- 1 yellow onion, cut into thin strips
- 8 mini tortillas

Directions:
Heat up a pan with the oil over medium-high heat, add beef strips, brown them for a few minutes and transfer to your Crock Pot.   Add lemon juice, garlic, cumin, salt, pepper, chili powder and pepper flakes to the Crock Pot as well, cover and cook on High for hours.   Add bell pepper and onion, stir and cook on High for 1 more hour.   Divide beef mix between your mini tortillas and serve for lunch.
Nutrition Info: calories 220, fat 9, fiber 2, carbs 14, protein 20

Classic Osso Buco

Servings: 4   Cooking Time: 7 1/4 Hours
Ingredients:
- 4 veal shanks
- 2 tablespoons all-purpose flour
- 2 tablespoon butter
- 2 red onions, chopped
- 1 can (15 oz.) diced tomatoes
- 1/4 cup red wine
- 1 teaspoon dried thyme
- 1/4 teaspoon cayenne pepper
- 1/2 teaspoon garlic powder
- Salt and pepper to taste

Directions:
Season the veal shanks with salt and pepper and sprinkle them with flour.   Melt the butter in a frying pan and add the veal shanks. Cook on all sides until golden.   Mix the remaining ingredients in your crock pot then place the veal shanks on top.   Cover with a lid and cook on low settings for 7 hours.   Serve the osso bucco and the sauce formed in the pot warm and fresh.

Paste Veggie Stew

Servings: 8   Cooking Time: 6 1/4 Hours
Ingredients:
- 1 large onion, chopped
- 1 celery stalk, sliced
- 2 garlic cloves, chopped
- 1/2 head cauliflower, cut into florets
- 1 cup diced tomatoes
- 2 cups chopped green beans
- 1 cup green peas
- 1/2 teaspoon dried oregano
- 1/2 teaspoon dried basil
- 1 cup short pasta of your choice
- 2 cups vegetable stock
- Salt and pepper to taste

Directions:
Combine the onion, celery, cauliflower and the remaining ingredients in your crock pot.   Add salt and pepper to taste and cook on low settings for 6 hours.   Serve the stew warm and fresh.

Roasted Bell Pepper Pork Stew

Servings: 6   Cooking Time: 5 1/4 Hours
Ingredients:
- 2 pounds pork tenderloin, cubed
- 2 tablespoons canola oil
- 1 jar roasted bell pepper, drained and chopped
- 4 garlic cloves, chopped
- 1 large onion, chopped
- 1/2 teaspoon red pepper flakes
- 1 cup chicken stock
- 1 cup tomato sauce
- Salt and pepper to taste

Directions:
Heat the oil in a skillet and add the pork. Cook for a few minutes on all sides until golden. Transfer in your Crock Pot.   Add the rest of the ingredients and adjust the taste with salt and pepper.   Cover the pot with its lid and cook on low settings for 5 hours.   Serve the stew warm or chilled.

Adobo Chicken With Bok Choy

Servings: 4   Cooking Time: 6 1/2 Hours
Ingredients:
- 4 chicken breasts
- 4 garlic cloves, minced
- 1 sweet onion, chopped
- 2 tablespoons soy sauce
- 1 tablespoon brown sugar
- 1 teaspoon paprika
- 1 cup chicken stock
- 1 head bok choy, shredded

Directions:
Mix the chicken, garlic, onion, soy sauce, brown sugar, paprika and stock in your crock pot.   Cook on low settings for 4 hours then add the bok choy and continue cooking for additional hours.   Serve the chicken and bok choy warm.

Shrimp Stew(1)

Servings: 8   Cooking Time: 4 Hours And 30 Minutes

Ingredients:

29 ounces canned tomatoes, chopped	1 tablespoon red vinegar
2 yellow onions, chopped	2 tablespoons olive oil
2 celery ribs, chopped	3 pounds shrimp, peeled and deveined
½ cup fish stock	6 ounces canned clams
4 garlic cloves, minced	2 tablespoons cilantro, chopped

Directions:

In your Crock Pot, mix tomatoes with onion, celery, stock, vinegar and oil, stir, cover and cook on Low for 4 hours.   Add shrimp, clams and cilantro, stir, cover, cook on Low for 30 minutes more, divide into bowls and serve for lunch.

Nutrition Info: calories 255, fat 4, fiber 3, carbs 14, protein 26

Sauerkraut Cumin Pork

Servings: 6   Cooking Time: 6 1/4 Hours

Ingredients:

1 1/2 pounds pork shoulder, cubed	2 carrots, grated
1 1/2 pounds sauerkraut, shredded	1/4 teaspoon red pepper flakes
1 large onion, chopped	1 cup chicken stock
1 1/2 teaspoons cumin seeds	1 bay leaf
	Salt and pepper to taste

Directions:

Combine all the ingredients in your crock pot. Add enough salt and pepper and cook on low settings for 6 hours.   Serve the pork and sauerkraut warm and fresh.

Indian Spiced Lentils

Servings: 6   Cooking Time: 6 1/4 Hours

Ingredients:

2 garlic cloves, chopped	1/4 teaspoon chili powder
1 sweet onion, chopped	1/2 teaspoon turmeric powder
2 tablespoons olive oil	1/2 teaspoon garam masala
1 cup red lentils, rinsed	2 cups vegetable stock
1 sweet potato, peeled and cubed	1/2 teaspoon grated ginger
1/2 teaspoon cumin powder	Salt and pepper to taste
1 cup tomato sauce	

Directions:

Combine the lentils and the remaining ingredients in your Crock Pot.   Add salt and pepper to taste

and cook on low settings for 6 hours.   Serve the lentils warm.

Red Salsa Chicken

Servings: 8   Cooking Time: 8 1/4 Hours

Ingredients:

8 chicken thighs	1/2 cup chicken stock
2 cups red salsa	Salt and pepper to taste
1 cup grated Cheddar cheese	

Directions:

Combine the chicken with the salsa and stock in your Crock Pot.   Add the cheese and cook on low settings for 8 hours.   Serve the chicken warm with your favorite side dish.

Cuban Flank Steaks

Servings: 6   Cooking Time: 8 1/4 Hours

Ingredients:

6 beef flank steaks	2 red onions, sliced
1 teaspoon cumin seeds	1 cup beef stock
1 teaspoon chili powder	1 chipotle pepper, chopped
1 teaspoon dried oregano	2 limes, juiced
	Salt and pepper to taste

Directions:

Combine the steaks in your Crock Pot and add salt and pepper.   Cover and cook for 8 hours on low settings.   Serve the steaks warm.

Old Fashioned Beef Stew

Servings: 6   Cooking Time: 7 1/4 Hours

Ingredients:

1 1/2 pounds beef roast, cubed	1 onion, chopped
2 tablespoons all-purpose flour	2 parsnips, sliced
2 tablespoons canola oil	4 potatoes, peeled and cubed
1 celery stalk, sliced	1 cup diced tomatoes
4 large carrots, sliced	1 1/2 cups beef stock
	Salt and pepper to taste
	1 bay leaf
	1 thyme sprig

Directions:

Heat the oil in a frying pan. Sprinkle the meat with flour and place it in the hot oil. Fry on all sides until golden then transfer in your Crock Pot.   Add the rest of the ingredients and season with salt and pepper.   Cook on low settings for 7 hours. Serve the stew warm and fresh.

Salmon And Cilantro Sauce

Servings: 4   Cooking Time: 2 Hours And 30 Minutes

Ingredients:

2 garlic cloves, minced
4 salmon fillets, boneless
¾ cup cilantro, chopped
3 tablespoons lime juice
1 tablespoon olive oil
Salt and black pepper to the taste

Directions:

Grease your Crock Pot with the oil, add salmon fillets inside skin side down, also add garlic, cilantro, lime juice, salt and pepper, cover and cook on Low for 2 hours and 30 minutes.   Divide salmon fillets on plates, drizzle the cilantro sauce all over and serve for lunch.

Nutrition Info: calories 200, fat 3, fiber 2, carbs 14, protein 8

Carne Adovada

Servings: 6   Cooking Time: 6 Hours 20 Minutes

Ingredients:

12 hot New Mexico red chili pods
1 teaspoon ground cumin
3 cups chicken broth
2 garlic cloves, minced
½ teaspoon salt
1/8 cup canola oil
2 pounds boneless pork shoulder, chunked
1 teaspoon Mexican oregano

Directions:

Put canola oil and pork shoulder in a pan over medium heat and cook for about 2 minutes on each side.   Transfer to a crock pot and stir in the remaining ingredients.   Cover and cook on LOW for about 6 hours.   Dish out and serve hot.

Nutrition Info: Calories: 280 Fat: 10.6g Carbohydrates: 1.2g

Sweet Potato Stew

Servings: 8   Cooking Time: 8 Hours

Ingredients:

1 yellow onion, chopped
½ cup red beans, dried
2 red bell peppers, chopped
2 tablespoons ginger, grated
4 garlic cloves, minced
2 pounds sweet, peeled and cubed
14 ounces canned tomatoes, chopped
3 cups chicken stock
2 jalapeno peppers, chopped
Salt and black pepper to the taste
½ teaspoon cumin, ground
½ teaspoon coriander, ground
¼ teaspoon cinnamon powder
¼ cup peanuts, roasted and chopped
Juice of ½ lime

Directions:

In your Crock Pot, mix onion with red beans, red bell peppers, ginger, garlic, potatoes, stock, tomatoes, jalapenos, salt, pepper, cumin, coriander and cinnamon, stir, cover and cook on Low for 8 hours.   Divide into bowls, divide peanuts on top, drizzle lime juice and serve for lunch.

Nutrition Info: calories 259, fat 8, fiber 7, carbs 42, protein 8

Barley And Bean Tacos

Servings: 10   Cooking Time: 6 1/4 Hours

Ingredients:

1 red onion, chopped
1 cup frozen corn
1 can (15 oz.) black beans, drained
1 cup fire roasted tomatoes
2 cups vegetable stock
1/2 teaspoon cumin powder
1 cup pearl barley
1/2 teaspoon chili powder
Salt and pepper to taste
10-14 taco shells
1/2 cup chopped cilantro for serving
2 limes for serving

Directions:

Combine the onion, corn, black beans, tomatoes, pearl barley, stock, cumin powder and chili powder in your crock pot.   Add salt and pepper to taste and cook on low settings for 6 hours.   When done, spoon the mixture into taco shells and top with chopped cilantro.   Drizzle with lime juice and serve fresh.

Pumpkin Apple Stew

Servings: 6   Cooking Time: 6 1/2 Hours

Ingredients:

4 cups pumpkin cubes
2 red apples, peeled and cubed
1/2 cinnamon stick
2 tablespoons olive oil
2 shallots, chopped
2 garlic cloves, chopped
2 ripe tomatoes, peeled and diced
1/4 cup red wine
1 cup vegetable stock
Salt and pepper to taste
1 bay leaf
1 thyme sprig

Directions:

Combine the pumpkin cubes, apples, cinnamon stick, olive oil, shallots, garlic and the remaining ingredients.   Season with salt and pepper to taste and cook on low settings for 6 hours.   Serve the stew warm and fresh or chilled.

Multigrain Chicken Pilaf

Servings: 8   Cooking Time: 6 1/2 Hours

Ingredients:

2 chicken breasts, cubed
1/2 cup wild rice
1/2 cup pearl barley
1 leek, sliced
2 garlic cloves, chopped
1 cup frozen edamame
1 cup green peas
1 sweet potato, peeled and cubed
2 cups vegetable stock
Salt and pepper to taste
1/2 teaspoon dried sage
1/2 teaspoon dried oregano
1 tablespoon chopped parsley for serving

Directions:

Combine the chicken, wild rice, pearl barley, leek, garlic, edamame, green peas, sweet potatoes, stock, sage and oregano in your crock pot.   Add salt and pepper to taste and cook on low settings for 6 hours.   When done, stir in the parsley and serve the pilaf warm and fresh.

Chicken Layered Potato Casserole

Servings: 8   Cooking Time: 6 1/2 Hours

Ingredients:

2 pounds potatoes, peeled and sliced	1/2 teaspoon garlic powder
2 chicken breasts, cut into thin strips	1/4 teaspoon onion powder
1/4 teaspoon chili powder	1 cup heavy cream
1/4 teaspoon cumin powder	1 1/2 cups whole milk
	Salt and pepper to taste

Directions:
Combine the cream, milk, chili powder, cumin powder, garlic powder and onion powder.   Layer the potatoes and chicken in your Crock Pot.   Pour the milk mix over the potatoes and chicken, seasoning with salt and pepper.   Cook on low settings for 6 hours.   Serve the casserole warm or chilled.

Broccoli With Peanuts

Servings: 6   Cooking Time: 2 1/4 Hours

Ingredients:

2 heads broccoli, cut into florets	2 tablespoons olive oil
1 cup raw peanuts, chopped	1 lemon, juiced
4 garlic cloves, chopped	1 tablespoons soy sauce
1 shallot, sliced	Salt and pepper to taste

Directions:
Combine the broccoli, peanuts, garlic, shallot, olive oil, lemon juice and soy sauce in your Crock Pot. Add salt and pepper to taste and cook the dish on high settings for hours.   Serve the dish warm and fresh.

Deviled Chicken

Servings: 4   Cooking Time: 6 1/4 Hours

Ingredients:

4 chicken breasts	4 garlic cloves, minced
1 cup tomato sauce	
1/2 cup hot sauce	Salt and pepper to taste
2 tablespoons butter	

Directions:
Combine all the ingredients in your crock pot. Add salt and pepper and cover with a lid.   Cook on low settings for 6 hours.   Serve the chicken warm and fresh.

Sour Cream Pork Chops

Servings: 6   Cooking Time: 6 1/4 Hours

Ingredients:

6 pork chops, bone in	2 tablespoons chopped parsley
1 cup sour cream	
1/2 cup chicken stock	Salt and pepper to taste
2 green onions, chopped	

Directions:
Combine the pork chops, sour cream, stock, onions and parsley in your crock pot.   Add salt and pepper to taste and cook on low settings for 6 hours.   Serve the pork chops warm and fresh, topped with plenty of sauce.

Beef Zucchini Stew

Servings: 6   Cooking Time: 2 3/4 Hours

Ingredients:

1 pound ground beef	3 zucchinis, sliced
2 tablespoons canola oil	1/2 cup beef stock
	2 bay leaves
1 leek, sliced	1/4 teaspoon paprika
2 garlic cloves, minced	1/4 teaspoon cumin seeds
1 can fire roasted tomatoes	Salt and pepper to taste

Directions:
Heat the oil in a skillet or frying pan and add the beef. Cook for a few minutes, stirring often, then transfer in your crock pot.   Add the rest of the ingredients in a Crock Pot.   Adjust the taste with salt and pepper and cook on high settings for 2 1/2 hours.   Serve the stew warm and fresh.

Seafood Soup

Servings: 2   Cooking Time: 8 Hours

Ingredients:

2 cups chicken stock	Salt and black pepper to the taste
1 cup coconut milk	
1 sweet potato, cubed	½ pounds salmon fillets, skinless, boneless cubed
½ yellow onion, chopped	
1 bay leaf	12 shrimp, peeled and deveined
1 carrot, peeled and sliced	
½ tablespoon thyme, dried	1 tablespoon chives, chopped

Directions:
In your Crock Pot, mix the carrot with the sweet potato, onion and the other ingredients except the salmon, shrimp and chives, toss, put the lid on and cook on Low for 6 hours.   Add the rest of ingredients, toss, put the lid on and cook on Low for more hours.   Divide the soup into bowls and serve for lunch.

Nutrition Info: calories 354, fat 10, fiber 4, carbs 17, protein 12

French Style Braised Beef Sirloin

Servings: 8   Cooking Time: 8 1/4 Hours

Ingredients:

4 pounds beef sirloin	2 carrots, sliced
1 cup dry white wine	1 celery stalk, sliced
4 large onions, sliced	1 cup beef stock
6 garlic cloves, chopped	1 thyme sprig
	1 rosemary sprig
1/2 pound button mushrooms	Salt and pepper to taste

Directions:
Combine the wine, onions, garlic, mushrooms, carrots, celery stalk, beef stock, thyme and rosemary sprig in your crock pot.   Season the beef with salt and pepper and place in the pot. Cover with its lid and cook on low settings for 8 hours.   When done, slice the beef and serve it warm.

Balsamic Vegetable Sauce

Servings: 8   Cooking Time: 6 1/2 Hours

Ingredients:

1 large onion, chopped
4 garlic cloves, chopped
2 red bell peppers, cored and diced
2 cans (15 oz. each) diced tomatoes
2 cups vegetable stock
10 oz. soy crumbles
2 tablespoons balsamic vinegar
1/2 teaspoon dried basil
1/2 teaspoon dried oregano
Salt and pepper to taste

Directions:
Combine all the ingredients in your crock pot. Season with salt and pepper as needed and cook on low settings for 6 hours.   Serve the sauce warm and fresh or freeze it into individual portions for later.

Shrimp Stew(2)

Servings: 2   Cooking Time: 3 Hours

Ingredients:

1 garlic clove, minced
1 red onion, chopped
1 cup canned tomatoes, crushed
1 cup veggie stock
½ teaspoon turmeric powder
1 pound shrimp, peeled and deveined
½ teaspoon coriander, ground
½ teaspoon thyme, dried
½ teaspoon basil, dried
A pinch of salt and black pepper
A pinch of red pepper flakes

Directions:
In your Crock Pot, mix the onion with the garlic, shrimp and the other ingredients, toss, put the lid on and cook on High for 3 hours.   Divide the stew into bowls and serve.
Nutrition Info:calories 313, fat 4.2, fiber 2.5, carbs 13.2, protein 53.3

Vegetarian Jambalaya

Servings: 6   Cooking Time: 6 1/2 Hours

Ingredients:

1 tablespoon olive oil
2 shallots, chopped
2 garlic cloves, chopped
8 oz. seaman, cubed
1 red bell pepper, cored and diced
1 celery stalk, sliced
2 cups vegetable stock
1 teaspoon miso paste
1 teaspoon Cajun seasoning
1 cup white rice
1/2 teaspoon turmeric powder
Salt and pepper to taste

Directions:
Heat the oil in a skillet and add the shallots and garlic. Sauté for 2 minutes until softened then transfer in your Crock Pot.   Add the remaining ingredients and season with salt and pepper as needed. Cook on low settings for 6 hours and serve the dish warm and fresh.

Worcestershire Beef Mix

Servings: 2   Cooking Time: 8 Hours

Ingredients:

1 pound beef stew meat, cubed
1 teaspoon chili powder
Salt and black pepper to the taste
1 cup beef stock
1 and ½ tablespoons Worcestershire sauce
1 teaspoon garlic, minced
2 ounces cream cheese, soft
Cooking spray

Directions:
Grease your Crock Pot with the cooking spray, and mix the beef with the stock and the other ingredients inside.   Put the lid on, cook on Low for 8 hours, divide between plates and serve.
Nutrition Info:calories 372, fat 6, fiber 9, carbs 18, protein 22

Beef Salsa Chili

Servings: 8   Cooking Time: 7 1/2 Hours

Ingredients:

2 pounds beef roast, cubed
2 tablespoons canola oil
2 red onions, chopped
2 garlic cloves, chopped
2 carrots, diced
2 red bell peppers, cored and diced
1 leek, sliced
1 1/2 cups red salsa
1 bay leaf
1 teaspoon cumin seeds
1 teaspoon chili powder
2 cups dried black bean
4 cups chicken stock or water
Salt and pepper to taste

Directions:
Heat the oil in a skillet or frying pan and add the beef. Cook for a few minutes until golden brown then transfer in your crock pot.   Add the rest of the ingredients and season with salt and pepper. Cook on low settings for 7 hours.   The chili is best served warm, but it can also be re-heated.

Garlicky Butter Roasted Chicken

Servings: 8   Cooking Time: 8 1/4 Hours

Ingredients:

1/4 cup butter, softened
6 garlic cloves, minced
2 tablespoons chopped parsley
1 whole chicken
1 teaspoon dried sage
Salt and pepper to taste
1/2 cup chicken stock

Directions:
Mix the butter, garlic, parsley, sage, salt and pepper in your crock pot.   Place the chicken on your working board and carefully lift up the skin on its breast and thighs, stuffing that space with the butter mixture.   Place the chicken in your crock pot.   Add the stock and cook on low settings for 8 hours.   Serve the chicken fresh with your favorite side dish.

38

Pork Chili

Servings: 2   Cooking Time: 10 Hours

Ingredients:

- 1 pound pork stew meat, cubed
- 1 red onion, sliced
- 1 carrot, sliced
- 1 teaspoon sweet paprika
- 1/2 teaspoon cumin, ground
- 1 cup tomato paste
- 1 cup veggie stock
- 2 tablespoons chili powder
- 2 teaspoons cayenne pepper
- 1 tablespoon red pepper flakes
- A pinch of salt and black pepper
- 1 red bell pepper, chopped
- 1 yellow bell pepper, chopped
- 1 tablespoon chives, chopped

Directions:

In your Crock Pot, mix the pork meat with the onion, carrot and the other ingredients, toss, put the lid on and cook on Low for   hours.   Divide the mix into bowls and serve.

Nutrition Info:calories 261, fat 7, fiber 4, carbs 8, protein 18

Sweet Glazed Chicken Drumsticks

Servings: 4   Cooking Time: 5 1/4 Hours

Ingredients:

- 2 pounds chicken drumsticks
- 1 teaspoon grated ginger
- 2 tablespoons soy sauce
- 2 tablespoons brown sugar
- 1 cup pineapple juice
- 1/4 teaspoon chili powder
- 2 green onions, chopped
- 1/4 cup chicken stock
- White rice for serving

Directions:

Combine the drumsticks, ginger, pineapple juice, soy sauce, brown sugar, chili, stock and green onions in your crock pot.   Add salt and pepper to taste and cook on low settings for 5 hours.   Serve the dish warm, over cooked white rice.

Pesto Pork Shanks

Servings: 2   Cooking Time: 7 Hours

Ingredients:

- 1 and 1/2 pounds pork shanks
- 1 tablespoon olive oil
- 2 tablespoons basil pesto
- 1 red onion, sliced
- 1 cup beef stock
- 1/2 cup tomato paste
- 4 garlic cloves, minced
- 1 tablespoon oregano, chopped
- Zest and juice of 1 lemon
- A pinch of salt and black pepper

Directions:

In your Crock Pot, mix the pork shanks with the oil, pesto and the other ingredients, toss, put the lid on and cook on Low for 7 hours.   Divide everything between plates and serve for lunch.

Nutrition Info:calories 372, fat 7, fiber 5, carbs 12, protein 37

Barley Saute

Servings: 2   Cooking Time: 8 Hours

Ingredients:

- 1/4 cup barley
- 1 teaspoon dried thyme
- 1/2 cup tomatoes, chopped
- 1/2 cup ground pork
- 1 jalapeno pepper, diced
- 3 cups of water

Directions:

Put barley, ground pork, and tomatoes in the Crock Pot.   Sprinkle the ingredients with dried thyme and jalapeno pepper.   Add water and close the lid.   Cook the saute for 8 hours on low.

Nutrition Info: Per Serving: 325 calories, 23.5g protein, 19.4g carbohydrates, 7g fat, 4.9g fiber, 74mg cholesterol, 73mg sodium, 517mg potassium.

Veggie Chickpea Curry

Servings: 6   Cooking Time: 6 1/4 Hours

Ingredients:

- 1 cup dried chickpeas, rinsed
- 1 large onion, chopped
- 1 carrot, sliced
- 1 teaspoon grated ginger
- 2 garlic cloves, chopped
- 2 potatoes, peeled and diced
- 1 red bell pepper, cored and diced
- 1 teaspoon curry
- 1 poblano pepper, chopped
- 1 cup fire roasted tomatoes
- 2 cups vegetable stock
- Salt and pepper to taste
- 1 bay leaf
- Chopped cilantro for serving

Directions:

Combine all the ingredients in your Crock Pot. Add salt and pepper to taste and cook the curry on low settings for 6 hours.   The curry is best served warm, topped with chopped cilantro.

Mediterranean Crock Pot Stew

Servings: 6   Cooking Time: 6 1/2 Hours

Ingredients:

- 2 tablespoons olive oil
- 1 large onion, chopped
- 2 carrots, sliced
- 2 red bell peppers, cored and diced
- 2 ripe tomatoes, peeled and diced
- 4 sun-dried tomatoes, chopped
- 2 zucchinis, cubed
- 1/2 cup pitted black olives
- 2 tablespoons tomato paste
- 1 tablespoon lemon juice
- 1 1/2 cups vegetable stock
- Salt and pepper to taste
- 2 tablespoons pesto sauce for serving

Directions:

Heat the oil in a skillet and stir in the onion, carrots and bell peppers and cook for 5 minutes.
Transfer in your Crock Pot and add the remaining ingredients, seasoning with salt and pepper to taste.   Cook on low settings for 6 hours.   Serve the stew warm and fresh.

Vegetarian Fajitas

Servings: 8   Cooking Time: 6 1/4 Hours

Ingredients:

4 heirloom tomatoes, peeled and diced
4 oz. green chilies, chopped
2 red bell peppers, cored and diced
1 small onion, chopped
1 teaspoon cumin powder
1/4 teaspoon chili powder
1/2 teaspoon dried oregano
1/2 cup vegetable stock
1 can (15 oz.) kidney beans, drained
Salt and pepper to taste
Flour tortillas for serving

Directions:

Combine the tomatoes, green chilies, bell peppers, onion, cumin powder, chili powder, oregano, stock and beans in your Crock Pot.   Add salt and pepper to taste and cook on low settings for 6 hours.   Serve the dish warm, wrapped in flour tortillas.

Sriracha Style Corned Beef

Servings: 6   Cooking Time: 5 1/4 Hours

Ingredients:

2 pounds corned beef
1/4 cup low sodium soy sauce
2 tablespoons brown sugar
4 garlic cloves, chopped
1/2 teaspoon onion powder
1 tablespoon Sriracha
1 teaspoon sesame oil
1 tablespoon rice vinegar
2 shallots, sliced
1/2 cup beef stock
Salt and pepper to taste

Directions:

Mix the soy sauce, sugar, garlic, onion powder, Sriracha, sesame oil, vinegar, stock and shallots in your crock pot.   Place the beef in the pot and coat it well with the sauce.   Add salt and pepper if needed and cook on low settings for 5 hours.   Serve the beef sliced and warm with your favorite side dish.

Crock Pot Jambalaya

Servings: 8   Cooking Time: 6 1/2 Hours

Ingredients:

2 tablespoons olive oil
8 oz. firm tofu, cubed
1 large onion, chopped
2 red bell peppers, cored and diced
2 garlic cloves, chopped
1/2 teaspoon Cajun seasoning
2 ripe tomatoes, peeled and diced
1/2 head cauliflower, cut into florets
1 large sweet potato, peeled and cubed
1 tablespoon tomato paste
1 1/4 cups vegetable stock
Salt and pepper to taste

Directions:

Heat the oil in a skillet and add the tofu. Cook on low settings for a few minutes until golden brown. Transfer in your Crock Pot and add the rest of the ingredients, adjusting the taste with salt and pepper.   Cook on low settings for 6 hours. Serve the jambalaya warm and fresh.

Cider Braised Chicken

Servings: 8   Cooking Time: 8 1/4 Hours

Ingredients:

1 whole chicken, cut into smaller pieces
Salt and pepper to taste
1 teaspoon dried thyme
Salt to taste
1 teaspoon dried oregano
1 teaspoon cumin powder
1 1/2 cups apple cider

Directions:

Season the chicken with salt, thyme, oregano and cumin powder and place it in your crock pot.   Add the apple cider and cook on low settings for 8 hours.   Serve the chicken warm with your favorite side dish.

Sesame Salmon Bowls

Servings: 2   Cooking Time: 3 Hours

Ingredients:

2 salmon fillets, boneless and roughly cubed
1 cup cherry tomatoes, halved
3 spring onions, chopped
1 cup baby spinach
1/2 cup chicken stock
Salt and black pepper to the taste
2 tablespoons balsamic vinegar
2 tablespoons lemon juice
1 teaspoon sesame seeds

Directions:

In your Crock Pot, mix the salmon with the cherry tomatoes, spring onions and the other ingredients, toss gently, put the lid on and cook on Low for 3 hours.   Divide everything into bowls and serve.

Nutrition Info: calories 230, fat 4, fiber 2, carbs 7, protein 6

Creamy Salsa Verde Chicken

Servings: 6   Cooking Time: 4 1/4 Hours

Ingredients:

2 pounds chicken breast, cubed
1 jar salsa verde
1 cup cream cheese
2 tablespoons chopped cilantro
1/4 cup chicken stock
Salt and pepper to taste
1 ripe avocado for serving
1 lime for serving

Directions:

Combine the chicken, salsa verde, cream cheese, cilantro, stock, salt and pepper in a crock pot. Cover with a lid and cook on low settings for 4 hours.   Serve the chicken warm, topped with sliced or cubed avocado and a drizzle of lime juice.

Mushroom Stroganoff

Servings: 6   Cooking Time: 6 1/4 Hours

Ingredients:

1 1/2 pounds mushrooms, sliced
2 tablespoons all-purpose flour
4 garlic cloves, chopped
2 tablespoons olive oil
1 onion, chopped
1/2 teaspoon smoked paprika
1 cup half and half
1/2 cup vegetable stock
Salt and pepper to taste

Directions:

Heat the oil in a skillet. Add the onion and garlic and cook for 2 minutes then transfer in your Crock Pot.   Sprinkle the mushrooms with flour and coat them well. Place in your Crock Pot.   Add the remaining ingredients and season with salt and pepper.   Cook on low settings for 6 hours. Serve the stroganoff warm.

Broccoli Rice Pilaf

Servings: 4   Cooking Time: 2 1/4 Hours

Ingredients:

1 head broccoli, cut into florets
1 shallot, chopped
2/3 cup white rice
1 cup vegetable stock
1 cup water
Salt and pepper to taste
1/2 teaspoon dried oregano

Directions:

Combine all the ingredients in your crock pot. Add salt and pepper to taste and cook the pilaf on high settings for hours.   The pilaf is best served warm and fresh.

Roasted Beef And Cauliflower

Servings: 2   Cooking Time: 8 Hours

Ingredients:

1 pound beef chuck roast, sliced
1 cup cauliflower florets
½ cup tomato sauce
½ cup veggie stock
½ tablespoon olive oil
2 garlic cloves, minced
½ carrot, roughly chopped
1 celery rib, roughly chopped
A pinch of salt and black pepper to the taste
1 tablespoon parsley, chopped

Directions:

In your Crock Pot, mix the roast with the cauliflower, tomato sauce and the other ingredients, toss, put the lid on and cook on Low for 8 hours.   Divide between plates and serve.

Nutrition Info:calories 340, fat 5, fiber 7, carbs 18, protein 22

Red Wine Vegetable Stew

Servings: 8   Cooking Time: 6 1/2 Hours

Ingredients:

2 tablespoons olive oil
1 large onion, chopped
2 garlic cloves, minced
2 large carrots, sliced
2 sweet potatoes, peeled and cubed
2 red potatoes, peeled and cubed
2 parsnips, diced
1 cup diced tomatoes
4 Portobello mushrooms, sliced
1/2 cup red wine
1 1/2 cups vegetable stock
1 bay leaf
1 thyme sprig
Salt and pepper to taste

Directions:

Heat the oil in a skillet and add the onion and garlic. Cook for 2 minutes until softened then transfer in your Crock Pot.   Add the remaining ingredients and season with salt and pepper. Cook on low settings for 6 hours.   Serve the stew warm and fresh.

Red Wine Braised Pork Ribs

Servings: 8   Cooking Time: 8 1/4 Hours

Ingredients:

5 pounds pork short ribs
4 tablespoons brown sugar
2 tablespoons olive oil
1 teaspoon chili powder
1 tablespoon molasses
1 teaspoon cumin powder
1 teaspoon dried thyme
1 teaspoon salt
1 cup BBQ sauce
1 cup red wine

Directions:

Mix the brown sugar, molasses, olive oil, chili powder, cumin powder, thyme and salt in a bowl. Spread this mixture over the pork ribs and rub the meat well with the spice. Place in your crock pot. Add the BBQ sauce and red wine and cook on low settings for 8 hours.   Serve the pork ribs warm.

Cumin Rice

Servings: 6   Cooking Time: 3.5 Hours

Ingredients:

2 cups long-grain rice
1 teaspoon cumin seeds
5 cups chicken stock
1 teaspoon olive oil
1 tablespoon cream cheese

Directions:

Heat the olive oil in the skillet.   Add cumin seeds and roast them for 3 minutes.   Then transfer the roasted cumin seeds in the Crock Pot.   Add rice and chickens tock. Gently stir the ingredients. Close the lid and cook the rice on high for 3.hours. Then add cream cheese and stir the rice well.

Nutrition Info: Per Serving: 247 calories, 5.2g protein, 50.1g carbohydrates, 2.3g fat, 0.8g fiber, 2mg cholesterol, 645mg sodium, 91mg potassium.

Creamy Chicken

Servings: 6   Cooking Time: 8 Hours And 30 Minutes

Ingredients:

10 ounces canned cream of chicken soup	3 tablespoons flour
	1 celery rib, chopped
Salt and black pepper to the taste	½ cup green bell pepper, chopped
A pinch of cayenne pepper	¼ cup yellow onion, chopped
1 pound chicken breasts, skinless, boneless and cubed	10 ounces peas
	2 tablespoons pimientos, chopped

Directions:
In your Crock Pot, mix cream of chicken with salt, pepper, cayenne and flour and whisk well.   Add chicken, celery, bell pepper and onion, toss, cover and cook on Low for 8 hours.   Add peas and pimientos, stir, cover and cook on Low for minutes more.   Divide into bowls and serve for lunch.
Nutrition Info: calories 200, fat 3, fiber 4, carbs 16, protein 17

Milky Semolina

Servings: 2   Cooking Time: 1 Hour

Ingredients:

¼ cup semolina	1 ½ cup milk
1 teaspoon vanilla extract	1 teaspoon sugar

Directions:
Put all ingredients in the Crock Pot.   Close the lid and cook the semolina on high for 1 hour.   When the meal is cooked, carefully stir it and cool it to room temperature.
Nutrition Info: Per Serving: 180 calories, 8.7g protein, 26.5g carbohydrates, 4g fat, 0.8g fiber, 15mg cholesterol, 87mg sodium, 147mg potassium.

Five Spice Marinated Tofu

Servings: 6   Cooking Time: 8 1/4 Hours

Ingredients:

18 oz. firm tofu, cubed	1 teaspoon grated ginger
1/4 cup soy sauce	1 teaspoon five spices powder
1 teaspoon sesame oil	
2 garlic cloves, minced	1 cup vegetable stock

Directions:
Combine all the ingredients in your crock pot. Cover and cook on low settings for 8 hours. Serve the tofu warm or chilled.

Creamy Polenta

Servings: 4   Cooking Time: 2.5 Hours

Ingredients:

1 cup polenta	1 cup heavy cream
3 cups of water	1 teaspoon salt

Directions:

Put all ingredients in the Crock Pot.   Close the lid and cook them on High for 5 hours.   When the polenta is cooked, stir it carefully and transfer it in the serving plates.
Nutrition Info: Per Serving: 242 calories, 3.5g protein, 31.3g carbohydrates, 11.4g fat, 1g fiber, 41mg cholesterol, 600mg sodium, 24mg potassium.

Chickpeas Stew(2)

Servings: 2   Cooking Time: 6 Hours

Ingredients:

½ tablespoon olive oil	1 red onion, chopped
2 garlic cloves, minced	½ cup chicken stock
	1 bay leaf
1 red chili pepper, chopped	½ teaspoon coriander, ground
¼ cup carrots, chopped	A pinch of red pepper flakes
6 ounces canned tomatoes, chopped	½ tablespoon parsley, chopped
6 ounces canned chickpeas, drained	Salt and black pepper to the taste

Directions:
In your Crock Pot, mix the chickpeas with the onion, garlic and the other ingredients, toss, put the lid on and cook on Low for 6 hours.   Divide into bowls and serve.
Nutrition Info: calories 462, fat 7, fiber 9, carbs 30, protein 17

Bacon Chicken Stew

Servings: 6   Cooking Time: 6 1/2 Hours

Ingredients:

6 chicken thighs	1 cup green peas
6 bacon slices, chopped	2 cups sliced mushrooms
1 sweet onion, chopped	1/4 cup dry white wine
2 garlic cloves, chopped	1 cup vegetable stock
2 large carrots, sliced	1/2 cup heavy cream
2 celery stalk, sliced	Salt and pepper to taste
	1 thyme sprig
	1 rosemary sprig

Directions:
Heat a skillet over medium flame. Add the bacon and cook until crisp.   Transfer the bacon in your crock pot and add the remaining ingredients. Season with salt and pepper and cook on low settings for 6 hours.   Serve the chicken warm.

Cabbage Rice Beef Stew

Servings: 6   Cooking Time: 6 1/2 Hours

Ingredients:

1 pound beef roast, cut into thin strips	1 cup white rice
2 tablespoons canola oil	1 cup beef stock
1 head green cabbage, shredded	1/4 cup water
	2 tablespoons tomato paste
1 large onion, chopped	1/2 teaspoon cumin seeds
1 large carrot, grated	1/2 teaspoon chili powder
2 ripe tomatoes, peeled and diced	Salt and pepper to taste

Directions:

Heat the oil in a frying pan and add the beef. Sauté for a few minutes on all sides then transfer in your crock pot.   Add the cabbage, onion, carrot, tomatoes, rice, stock, water, tomato paste, cumin seeds and chili powder in your cooker as well. Adjust the taste with salt and pepper and cook on low settings for 6 hours.   The stew is best served warm.

Beef Stew(2)

Servings: 2   Cooking Time: 6 Hours And 10 Minutes

Ingredients:

1 tablespoon olive oil	½ cup beef stock
1 red onion, chopped	2 tablespoons balsamic vinegar
1 carrot, peeled and sliced	
1 pound beef meat, cubed	2 garlic cloves, minced
½ cup canned tomatoes, chopped	½ cup black olives, pitted and sliced
2 tablespoons tomato sauce	1 tablespoon rosemary, chopped
	Salt and black pepper to the taste

Directions:

Heat up a pan with the oil over medium-high heat, add the meat, brown for   minutes and transfer to your Crock Pot.   Add the rest of the ingredients, toss, put the lid on and cook on High for 6 hours. Divide between plates and serve right away!

Nutrition Info:calories 370, fat 14, fiber 6, carbs 26, protein 38

Rice And Corn Bowl

Servings: 5   Cooking Time: 3 Hours

Ingredients:

1 cup basmati rice	1 cup corn kernels
1.5 cup vegetable stock	1 teaspoon hot sauce
	2 tablespoons butter

Directions:

Put corn kernels and rice in the Crock Pot.   Add vegetable stock and cook the meal on high for 3 hours.   Then open the lid, add hot sauce and butter.   Carefully stir the meal and transfer in the bowls.

Nutrition Info: Per Serving: 205 calories, 3.7g protein, 36g carbohydrates, 5.8g fat, 1.3g fiber,

12mg cholesterol, 281mg sodium, 128mg potassium.

Chunky Pasta Sauce

Servings: 8   Cooking Time: 8 1/4 Hours

Ingredients:

1 can (15 oz.) black beans, drained	1 celery stalk, sliced
	1 teaspoon cumin powder
1 can (15 oz.) kidney beans	1 teaspoon dried oregano
2 cups tomato sauce	
1 cup fire roasted tomatoes	1 cup vegetable stock
	Salt and pepper to taste
1 cup frozen corn	
1 cup green peas	

Directions:

Combine all the ingredients in your crock pot. Add salt and pepper to taste and cook on low settings for 8 hours.   Serve the sauce right away or freeze it into individual portions for later serving.

Creamy Mushroom Stew

Servings: 6   Cooking Time: 6 1/4 Hours

Ingredients:

1 pound cremini mushrooms, sliced	2 shallots, chopped
2 tablespoons all-purpose flour	4 garlic cloves, chopped
2 tablespoons olive oil	1 cup whole milk
	1/2 cup cream cheese
1/4 cup vegetable stock	Salt and pepper to taste

Directions:

Sprinkle the mushrooms with flour. Heat the oil in a skillet and add the mushrooms. Sauté on each side until golden then transfer the mushrooms in your Crock Pot.   Add the remaining ingredients and adjust the taste with salt and pepper.   Cook on low settings for 6 hours.   Serve the stew warm.

Mango Chicken Sauté

Servings: 6   Cooking Time: 2 3/4 Hours

Ingredients:

2 chicken breasts, cut into thin strips	1 chipotle pepper, chopped
2 tablespoons canola oil	1/2 teaspoon cumin powder
1 large sweet onion, sliced	1/4 teaspoon grated ginger
4 garlic cloves, chopped	1 can fire roasted tomatoes
1 large mango, peeled and cubed	Salt and pepper to taste
1 cup chicken stock	

Directions:

Heat the canola oil in your crock pot and add the chicken. Cook on all sides for a few minutes until golden brown.   Transfer the chicken in your crock pot.   Add the rest of the ingredients and cover the pot with a lid.   Cook the chicken sauté on high settings for 2 1/2 hours.   Serve the dish warm and fresh.

Vegetable Medley Stew

Servings: 10   Cooking Time: 6 1/2 Hours

Ingredients:

2 tablespoons olive oil
1 sweet onion, chopped
4 garlic cloves, chopped
1/2 head cauliflower, cut into florets
2 red bell peppers, cored and diced
1 carrot, sliced
1 parsnip, cubed
1 zucchini, cubed
1 cup cherry tomatoes, halved
1/2 cup tomato sauce
2 cups vegetable stock
1 bay leaf
Salt and pepper to taste

Directions:

Heat the oil in a skillet and add the onion and garlic. Cook for 2 minutes until softened then transfer in your Crock Pot.   Add the remaining ingredients and add salt and pepper to taste. Cook on low settings for 6 hours.   Serve the stew warm and fresh.

Bbq Tofu

Servings: 4   Cooking Time: 2 1/4 Hours

Ingredients:

4 thick slices firm tofu
1 shallot, sliced
2 garlic cloves, minced
1 teaspoon Worcestershire sauce
1 cup BBQ sauce
1/4 teaspoon cumin powder
1 pinch cayenne pepper
1 thyme sprig

Directions:

Combine the shallot, garlic, BBQ sauce, Worcestershire sauce, cumin powder, cayenne pepper and thyme in your Crock Pot.   Add the tofu and coat it well.   Cover the pot with its lid and cook on high settings for 2 hours.   Serve the tofu warm with your favorite side dish.

Spinach Bean Casserole

Servings: 8   Cooking Time: 6 1/2 Hours

Ingredients:

2 bacon slices, chopped
2 sweet onions, chopped
1 carrot, diced
1 celery stalk, sliced
4 garlic cloves, chopped
2 tablespoons tomato paste
1/2 cup tomato sauce
1/2 teaspoon dried sage
1 1/2 cups dried black beans, rinsed
2 cups vegetable stock
2 cups water
4 cups fresh spinach, shredded
1 bay leaf
Salt and pepper to taste

Directions:

Heat a skillet over medium flame and add the bacon. Cook until crisp then stir in the onions and garlic. cook for 2 minutes until softened. Transfer in your Crock Pot and add the remaining ingredients.   Season with salt and pepper to taste and cook on low settings for 6 hours.   Serve the stew warm and fresh.

Cauliflower Lentil Stew

Servings: 6   Cooking Time: 6 1/4 Hours

Ingredients:

1 shallot, chopped
2 garlic cloves, chopped
1 celery stalk, sliced
1 carrot, sliced
1 small head cauliflower, cut into florets
1/2 cup red lentils, rinsed
2 cups vegetable stock
1 cup diced tomatoes
1 bay leaf
1/4 teaspoon cumin powder
1 pinch cayenne pepper
Salt and pepper to taste

Directions:

Combine all the ingredients in your Crock Pot. Add salt and pepper to taste and cook on low settings for 6 hours.   When done, serve the stew warm and fresh.

Tofu Chickpea Curry

Servings: 6   Cooking Time: 6 1/2 Hours

Ingredients:

12 oz. firm tofu, cubed
2 tablespoons olive oil
1 teaspoon curry powder
1 large onion, chopped
2 garlic cloves, chopped
2 cups cauliflower florets
1 large sweet potato, peeled and cubed
1 can (15 oz.) chickpeas, drained
1 cup diced tomatoes
1 cup coconut milk
1 cup vegetable stock
1 kaffir lime leaf
1 teaspoon grated ginger
Salt and pepper to taste

Directions:

Heat the oil in a skillet and add the tofu. Cook on all sides until golden and crusty.   Sprinkle with curry powder and fry just 1 additional minute. Transfer in your Crock Pot.   Add the remaining ingredients and season well.   Cook on low settings for 6 hours.   Serve the curry warm.

Pumpkin Chili

Servings: 6   Cooking Time: 5 Hours

Ingredients:

1 cup pumpkin puree
30 ounces canned kidney beans, drained
30 ounces canned roasted tomatoes, chopped
2 cups water
1 cup red lentils, dried
1 cup yellow onion, chopped
1 jalapeno pepper, chopped
1 tablespoon chili powder
1 tablespoon cocoa powder
½ teaspoon cinnamon powder
2 teaspoons cumin, ground
A pinch of cloves, ground
Salt and black pepper to the taste
2 tomatoes, chopped

Directions:

In your Crock Pot, mix pumpkin puree with kidney beans, roasted tomatoes, water, lentils, onion, jalapeno, chili powder, cocoa, cinnamon, cumin, cloves, salt and pepper, stir, cover and cook on High for 5 hours.   Divide into bowls, top with chopped tomatoes and serve for lunch.

Nutrition Info: calories 266, fat 6, fiber 4, carbs 12, protein 4

Chicken Pilaf

Servings: 3   Cooking Time: 6 Hours
Ingredients:
- ½ cup basmati rice
- 2 cups of water
- 5 oz chicken fillet, chopped
- 1 teaspoon chili powder
- ½ teaspoon salt

Directions:
Put the rice and chicken fillet in the Crock Pot. Add chili powder, salt, and water. Carefully stir the ingredients and close the lid.   Cook the pilaf on Low for 6 hours.
Nutrition Info: Per Serving: 205 calories, 16g protein, 25.1g carbohydrates, 3.9g fat, 0.7g fiber, 42mg cholesterol, 443mg sodium, 169mg potassium.

Creamy Brisket

Servings: 2   Cooking Time: 8 Hours
Ingredients:
- 1 tablespoon olive oil
- 1 shallot, chopped
- 2 garlic cloves, mined
- Salt and black pepper to the taste
- 1 pound beef brisket
- ¼ cup beef stock
- 3 tablespoons heavy cream
- 1 tablespoon parsley, chopped

Directions:
In your Crock Pot, mix the brisket with the oil and the other ingredients, toss, put the lid on and cook on Low for 8 hours.   Transfer the beef to a cutting board, slice, divide between plates and serve with the sauce drizzled all over.
Nutrition Info:calories 400, fat 10, fiber 4, carbs 15, protein 20

Creamy Chickpea Stew

Servings: 6   Cooking Time: 6 1/2 Hours
Ingredients:
- 1 cup dried chickpeas, rinsed
- 2 cups grated butternut squash
- 1/2 teaspoon cumin seeds
- 1 cup diced tomatoes
- 1/4 teaspoon mustard seeds
- 2 cups vegetable stock
- 1 bay leaf
- Salt and pepper to taste

Directions:
Combine the chickpeas, butternut squash, cumin seeds, mustard seeds, stock, tomatoes and bay leaf. Season with salt and pepper and cook on low settings for 6 hours.   Serve the stew warm and fresh.

Chicken Thighs Mix

Servings: 6   Cooking Time: 6 Hours
Ingredients:
- 1 and ½ tablespoon olive oil
- 2 yellow onions, chopped
- 2 and ½ pounds chicken thighs, skinless and boneless

- 1 teaspoon cinnamon powder
- ¼ teaspoon cloves, ground
- ¼ teaspoon allspice, ground
- Salt and black pepper to the taste
- A pinch of saffron
- A handful pine nuts
- A handful mint, chopped

Directions:
In a bowl, mix oil with onions, cinnamon, allspice, cloves, salt, pepper and saffron, whisk and transfer to your Crock Pot.   Add the chicken, toss well, cover and cook on Low for 6 hours.   Sprinkle pine nuts and mint on top before serving,
Nutrition Info:calories 223, fat 3, fiber 2, carbs 6, protein 13

Roasted Rosemary Pork And Potatoes

Servings: 6   Cooking Time: 6 1/2 Hours
Ingredients:
- 2 pounds pork roast, cubed
- 3 large carrots, sliced
- 1 1/2 pounds potatoes, peeled and cubed
- 1 celery root, peeled and cubed
- 2 rosemary sprigs
- Salt and pepper to taste
- 1 cup chicken stock

Directions:
Combine the pork roast, carrots, celery, potatoes, rosemary and stock in your crock pot.   Add salt and pepper and cook on low settings for 6 hours. Serve the dish warm and fresh.

Spinach Chicken

Servings: 6   Cooking Time: 6 1/2 Hours
Ingredients:
- 6 chicken thighs, boneless
- 2 tablespoons canola oil
- 1/4 cup chopped cilantro
- 1/4 cup chopped parsley
- 3 cups fresh spinach, shredded
- 1 cup vegetable stock
- 2 potatoes, peeled and cubed
- Salt and pepper to taste
- 1/4 teaspoon cumin powder
- 1/4 teaspoon chili powder
- 1/4 teaspoon all-spice powder

Directions:
Combine the chicken and canola oil in a skillet and fry the chicken on all sides until golden.   Transfer the chicken in your crock pot and add the remaining ingredients, including the spices, salt and pepper.   Cook on low settings for 6 hours. Serve the chicken warm and fresh, although it tastes great chilled as well.

Dinner Millet Bowl

Servings: 5   Cooking Time: 8 Hours
Ingredients:

- 2 cups whole-grain millet
- 2 cups chicken stock
- 3 cups of water
- 1 teaspoon butter
- 1 teaspoon salt
- ¼ cup pomegranate seeds
- 1 cup sauerkraut

Directions:
Mix water with chicken stock and pour the liquid in the Crock Pot.   Add salt and millet and cook the ingredients on low for 8 hours.   Then mix the cooked millet with butter and pomegranate seeds. Transfer the millet in the bowls and top with sauerkraut.

Nutrition Info: Per Serving: 323 calories, 9.4g protein, 61g carbohydrates, 4.4g fat, 7.7g fiber, 2mg cholesterol, 972mg sodium, 212mg potassium.

Honey Orange Glazed Tofu

Servings: 4   Cooking Time: 4 1/4 Hours
Ingredients:

- 12 oz. firm tofu, cubed
- 1 tablespoon grated ginger
- 1 garlic clove, minced
- 1 orange, zested and juiced
- 2 tablespoons soy sauce
- 1 teaspoon Worcestershire sauce
- 1/4 cup vegetable stock

Directions:
Combine all the ingredients in your Crock Pot. Cover and cook on low settings for 4 hours.   The tofu is best served warm with your favorite side dish.

Apple Cherry Pork Chops

Servings: 6   Cooking Time: 3 1/4 Hours
Ingredients:

- 6 pork chops
- 4 red, tart apples, cored and sliced
- 1 cup frozen sour cherries
- 1/2 cup apple cider vinegar
- 1/2 cup tomato sauce
- 1 onion, chopped
- 1 garlic clove, minced
- 1 bay leaf
- Salt and pepper to taste

Directions:
Combine the pork chops, apples, sour cherries, tomato sauce, onion, garlic and bay leaf in your Crock Pot.   Add salt and pepper to taste and cook on high settings for 3 hours.   Serve the pork chops warm and fresh.

Chicken Sweet Potato Stew

Servings: 6   Cooking Time: 3 1/4 Hours
Ingredients:

- 2 chicken breasts, cubed
- 2 tablespoons butter
- 2 shallots, chopped
- 1/2 teaspoon garlic powder
- 1 pinch cinnamon powder
- 2 pounds sweet potatoes, peeled and cubed
- 1/2 teaspoon cumin powder
- 1 1/2 cups vegetable stock
- Salt and pepper to taste

Directions:
Combine the chicken, butter and shallots in your crock pot. Cook for 5 minutes then transfer in your crock pot.   Add the sweet potatoes, cumin powder, garlic and cinnamon, as well as stock, salt and pepper.   Cook on high settings for hours. Serve the stew warm or chilled.

Creamy Lentil Stew

Servings: 8   Cooking Time: 7 1/4 Hours
Ingredients:

- 1 cup red lentils
- 1 large sweet potato, peeled and diced
- 1 carrot, diced
- 2 ripe tomatoes, peeled and diced
- 2 cups vegetable stock
- 1/2 teaspoon cumin seeds
- 1/2 red chili, chopped
- Salt and pepper to taste
- 1 bay leaf

Directions:
Combine all the ingredients in your crock pot. Add salt and pepper to taste and cook on low settings for 7 hours.   Serve the stew warm and fresh.

Layered Carrot Pudding

Servings: 6   Cooking Time: 6 1/4 Hours
Ingredients:

- 6 large carrots, finely sliced
- 2 sweet onions, sliced
- 1 pinch nutmeg
- 4 eggs, beaten
- 1 cup whole milk
- Salt and pepper to taste
- 1 cup grated Cheddar

Directions:
Layer the carrots and onions in your crock pot. Season with salt, pepper and nutmeg.   Mix the eggs with milk and pour over the carrots.   Top with grated cheese and cook on low settings for 6 hours.   Serve the pudding warm and fresh, although it tastes great chilled as well.

Ginger Glazed Tofu

Servings: 6   Cooking Time: 2 1/4 Hours
Ingredients:

- 12 oz. firm tofu, cubed
- 1 tablespoon hot sauce
- 1 teaspoon grated ginger
- 2 tablespoons soy sauce
- 1/2 cup vegetable stock

Directions:
Season the tofu with hot sauce, ginger and soy sauce. Place the tofu in your crock pot.   Add the stock and cook on high settings for hours.   Serve the tofu warm with your favorite side dish.

Pork And Tomatoes Mix

Servings: 2   Cooking Time: 8 Hours

Ingredients:

1 and ½ pounds pork stew meat, cubed
1 cup cherry tomatoes, halved
1 tablespoon rosemary, chopped
½ teaspoon sweet paprika
1 cup tomato paste
½ teaspoon coriander, ground
A pinch of salt and black pepper
1 tablespoon chives, chopped

Directions:

In your Crockpot, combine the meat with the tomatoes, tomato paste and the other ingredients, toss, put the lid on and cook on Low for 8 hours. Divide between plates and serve for lunch.

Nutrition Info:calories 352, fat 8, fiber 4, carbs 10, protein 27

Arroz Con Pollo

Servings: 8   Cooking Time: 6 1/4 Hours

Ingredients:

1 cup wild rice
1 cup green peas
2 celery stalks, sliced
1 onion, chopped
2 ripe tomatoes, peeled and diced
1 cup sliced mushrooms
1 red chili, chopped
2 cups vegetable stock
4 chicken breasts, halved
Salt and pepper to taste
1 thyme sprig
1 rosemary sprig

Directions:

Combine the rice, green peas, celery, onion, red chili, tomatoes, mushrooms, stock and chicken in your crock pot.   Add the thyme sprig, rosemary, salt and pepper and cook the dish on low settings for 6 hours.   Serve the dish warm and fresh.

Refried Red Kidney Beans

Servings: 4   Cooking Time: 6 Hours

Ingredients:

2 cups red kidney beans, soaked
1 cayenne pepper, chopped
½ teaspoon garlic powder
1 teaspoon onion powder
8 cups of water
1 teaspoon coconut oil

Directions:

Put all ingredients in the Crock Pot.   Cook the mixture for 6 hours on high.   Then transfer the cooked bean mixture in the blender and pulse for 15 seconds.   Transfer the meal in the bowls

Nutrition Info: Per Serving: 324 calories, 20.9g protein, 57.4g carbohydrates, 2.2g fat, 14.2g fiber, 0mg cholesterol, 26mg sodium, 1274mg potassium.

Mixed Lentil Spicy Stew

Servings: 8   Cooking Time: 6 1/4 Hours

Ingredients:

1/2 cup red lentils
1/2 cup brown lentils
1/2 cup green lentils
1 large onion, finely chopped
2 carrots, diced
2 cups cauliflower florets
1/2 teaspoon cumin seeds
1/2 teaspoon mustard seeds
1 celery stalk, diced
1/2 teaspoon fennel seeds
1 bay leaf
1 thyme sprig
1/4 teaspoon chili powder
1/2 teaspoon ground ginger
Salt and pepper to taste

Directions:

Combine the lentils, onion, carrots, celery, cauliflower florets, seeds, spices, salt and pepper in your crock pot.   Cook on low settings for 6 hours and serve the stew warm and fresh.

Paprika Pork And Chickpeas

Servings: 2   Cooking Time: 10 Hours

Ingredients:

1 red onion, sliced
1 pound pork stew meat, cubed
1 cup canned chickpeas, drained
1 cup beef stock
½ teaspoon sweet paprika
1 cup tomato paste
½ teaspoon turmeric powder
A pinch of salt and black pepper
1 tablespoon hives, chopped

Directions:

In your Crock Pot, mix the onion with the meat, chickpeas, stock and the other ingredients, toss, put the lid on and cook on Low for   hours.   Divide the mix between plates and serve for lunch.

Nutrition Info:calories 322, fat 6, fiber 6, carbs 9, protein 22

Oregano Wild Rice

Servings: 6   Cooking Time: 4 Hours

Ingredients:

2 cups wild rice
1 teaspoon dried oregano
½ teaspoon dried marjoram
5 cups chicken stock
1 tablespoon butter
½ teaspoon ground black pepper

Directions:

Put the wild rice in the Crock Pot.   Add chicken stock, dried oregano, dried marjoram, and ground black pepper.   Close the lid and cook the rice on high for 4 hours.   Then add butter and stir the rice well.

Nutrition Info: Per Serving: 281 calories, 13g protein, 47.3g carbohydrates, 4.9g fat, 3.5g fiber, 11mg cholesterol, 304mg sodium, 445mg potassium.

Beef Stew(1)

Servings: 5   Cooking Time: 7 Hours And 30 Minutes

Ingredients:

2 potatoes, peeled and cubed	3 bay leaves
1 pound beef stew meat, cubed	Salt and black pepper to the taste
11 ounces tomato juice	½ teaspoon chili powder
14 ounces beef stock	½ teaspoon thyme, dried
2 celery ribs, chopped	1 tablespoon water
2 carrots, chopped	2 tablespoons cornstarch
1 yellow onion, chopped	½ cup peas
	½ cup corn

Directions:
In your Crock Pot, mix potatoes with beef, tomato juice, stock, ribs, carrots, bay leaves, onion, salt, pepper, chili powder and thyme, stir, cover and cook on Low for 7 hours.   Add cornstarch mixed with water, peas and corn, stir, cover and cook on Low for 30 minutes more.   Divide into bowls and serve for lunch.
Nutrition Info:calories 273, fat 7, fiber 6, carbs 30, protein 22

Mediterranean Beef Brisket

Servings: 8   Cooking Time: 7 1/2 Hours

Ingredients:

4 pounds beef brisket	4 garlic cloves, chopped
1 can (15 oz.) diced tomatoes	1 rosemary sprig
1/2 cup dry red wine	1 thyme sprig
1/2 cup pitted Kalamata olives, sliced	Salt and pepper to taste

Directions:
Mix the tomatoes, red wine, Kalamata olives, garlic, thyme sprig and rosemary sprig in your crock pot. Add salt and pepper to taste and cover with a lid. Cook on low settings for 7 hours.   Serve the beef brisket and the sauce warm or chilled.

Beef Soup

Servings: 2   Cooking Time: 5 Hours

Ingredients:

1 pound beef stew meat, cubed	½ tablespoon oregano, dried
3 cups beef stock	¼ teaspoon chili pepper
½ cup tomatoes, cubed	2 tablespoon tomato paste
1 red onion, chopped	1 jalapeno, chopped
1 green bell pepper, chopped	1 tablespoon cilantro, chopped
1 carrot, cubed	
A pinch of salt and black pepper	

Directions:
In your Crock Pot, mix the beef with the stock, tomatoes and the other ingredients, toss, put the lid on and cook on Low for 5 hours.   Divide the soup into bowls and serve for lunch.

Nutrition Info:calories 391, fat 6, fiber 7, carbs 8, protein 27

Pizza Pork Chops

Servings: 6   Cooking Time: 6 1/2 Hours

Ingredients:

6 pork chops	1/2 cup pitted black olives, sliced
2 red bell peppers, cored and sliced	2 cups shredded mozzarella
1 1/2 cups tomato sauce	Salt and pepper to taste
1 teaspoon dried oregano	

Directions:
Place the pork chops in your Crock Pot.   Top with tomato sauce, oregano, black olives, salt and pepper.   Cover with a layer of shredded mozzarella and cook on low settings for 6 hours. Serve the dish preferably warm while the cheese is still gooey.

Puttanesca Pizza

Servings: 6   Cooking Time: 2 1/2 Hours

Ingredients:

Dough:	1/4 cup Kalamata olives, pitted and sliced
2 cups all-purpose flour	
1 teaspoon active dry yeast	1/4 cup green olives, sliced
1 cup warm water	1 tablespoon capers, chopped
1/4 teaspoon salt	
2 tablespoons olive oil	1/2 teaspoon dried basil
Topping:	1/2 teaspoon dried oregano
1/2 cup crushed fire roasted tomatoes	

Directions:
To make the dough, combine all the ingredients in a bowl and knead for a few minutes in a bowl. Roll the dough into a round that fits in your Crock Pot.   Top with tomatoes, olives, capers and dried herbs.   Cook on high settings for 1 1/2 hours. Serve the pizza warm.

Beef And Cabbage

Servings: 2   Cooking Time: 8 Hours

Ingredients:

1 pound beef stew meat, cubed	1 cup tomato paste
1 cup green cabbage, shredded	½ teaspoon sweet paprika
1 cup red cabbage, shredded	1 tablespoon chives, chopped
1 carrot, grated	A pinch of salt and black pepper
½ cup water	

Directions:
In your Crock Pot, mix the beef with the cabbage, carrot and the other ingredients, toss, put the lid on and cook on Low for 8 hours.   Divide the mix between plates and serve for lunch.
Nutrition Info:calories 251, fat 6, fiber 7, carbs 12, protein 6

Mustard Baked Potatoes

Servings: 6   Cooking Time: 4 1/4 Hours
Ingredients:

3 pounds potatoes, peeled and cubed	1/2 teaspoon cumin seeds
1 tablespoon Dijon mustard	4 garlic cloves, minced
1/4 cup vegetable stock	1/2 teaspoon salt

Directions:
Combine all the ingredients in your Crock Pot. Mix well until evenly coated.   Cover with a lid and cook on low settings for 4 hours.   Serve the potatoes warm.

Beer Braised Beef

Servings: 6   Cooking Time: 8 1/4 Hours
Ingredients:

1/2 pound baby carrots	2 pounds beef sirloin
2 large potatoes, peeled and cubed	4 garlic cloves, chopped
1 celery stalk, sliced	1 thyme sprig
1 large sweet onion, chopped	1 cup dark beer
	1/4 cup beef stock
	Salt and pepper to taste

Directions:
Mix all the ingredients in your crock pot, adding salt and pepper to taste.   Cover the pot with its lid and cook on low settings for 8 hours.   Serve the beef and veggies warm and fresh.

Basmati Rice With Artichoke Hearts

Servings: 5   Cooking Time: 6 Hours
Ingredients:

4 artichoke hearts, canned, chopped	1/2 cup of coconut milk
1 cup Arborio rice	1 teaspoon coconut oil
1 tablespoon apple cider vinegar	1 onion, sliced
2 cups of water	1 oz Parmesan, grated

Directions:
Put rice in the Crock Pot. Add coconut milk and water.   Close the lid and cook the mixture on low for 6 hours.   Meanwhile, melt the coconut oil. Add onion and roast it for 2 minutes.   Then stir it well, add apple cider vinegar, and artichoke hearts. Roast the ingredients for 3 minutes.   When the rice is cooked, transfer it in the plates and top with roasted artichoke mixture and Parmesan.
Nutrition Info: Per Serving: 289 calories, 9.4g protein, 47.5g carbohydrates, 8.3g fat, 9g fiber, 4mg cholesterol, 185mg sodium, 606mg potassium.

Beef Roast Au Jus

Servings: 8   Cooking Time: 10 1/4 Hours
Ingredients:

4 pounds rump roast	1 teaspoon garlic powder
1 tablespoon ground	

black pepper
1 tablespoon smoked paprika
1 teaspoon chili powder

1 teaspoon mustard seeds
1 cup water
Salt and pepper to taste

Directions:
Mix the black pepper, paprika, chili powder, garlic powder, mustard seeds, salt and pepper in a bowl. Spread this mixture over the beef and rub it well into the meat.   Place the beef on your crock pot and add the water.   Cover with its lid and cook on low settings for 10 hours.   Serve the beef roast sliced and warm.

Chicken Drumsticks And Buffalo Sauce

Servings: 2   Cooking Time: 8 Hours
Ingredients:

1 pound chicken drumsticks	2 tablespoons honey
2 tablespoons buffalo wing sauce	1 teaspoon lemon juice
1/2 cup chicken stock	Salt and black pepper to the taste

Directions:
In your Crock Pot, mix the chicken with the sauce and the other ingredients, toss, put the lid on and cook on Low for 8 hours.   Divide everything between plates and serve.
Nutrition Info:calories 361, fat 7, fiber 8, carbs 18, protein 22

Bbq Beef Brisket

Servings: 8   Cooking Time: 6 1/4 Hours
Ingredients:

2 tablespoons brown sugar	4 pounds beef brisket
1 teaspoon cumin powder	1 teaspoon salt
1 teaspoon smoked paprika	1/4 cup apple cider vinegar
1 teaspoon chili powder	1/2 cup beef stock
1 teaspoon celery seeds	1 cup ketchup
	1 tablespoon Worcestershire sauce
	2 tablespoons soy sauce

Directions:
Mix the sugar, cumin powder, paprika, chili powder, celery seeds and salt in a bowl. Spread the mix over the brisket and rub it well into the meat. Combine the vinegar, stock, ketchup, Worcestershire sauce and soy sauce in your crock pot.   Add the beef and cook on low settings for 6 hours.   Serve the beef brisket sliced and warm.

Shrimp Gumbo

Servings: 2   Cooking Time: 2 Hours

Ingredients:

1 pound shrimp, peeled and deveined
½ pound pork sausage, sliced
1 red onion, chopped
½ green bell pepper, chopped
1 red chili pepper, minced
½ teaspoon cumin, ground
½ teaspoon coriander, ground
Salt and black pepper to the taste
1 cup tomato sauce
½ cup chicken stock
½ tablespoon Cajun seasoning
½ teaspoon oregano, dried

Directions:

In your Crock Pot, mix the shrimp with the sausage, onion and the other ingredients, toss, put the lid on and cook on High for 2 hours.   Divide into bowls and serve.

Nutrition Info: calories 721, fat 36.7, fiber 3.7, carbs 18.2, protein 76.6

Rich Chicken Rice Stew

Servings: 8   Cooking Time: 6 1/2 Hours

Ingredients:

3 chicken breasts, cubed
2 tablespoons butter
1 cup white rice
1/2 pound button mushrooms
1 shallot, chopped
1 garlic clove, chopped
1 cup green peas
2 carrots, sliced
2 cups vegetable stock
1/2 cup cream cheese
1 thyme sprig
Salt and pepper to taste

Directions:

Melt the butter in a skillet and add the chicken. Cook on all sides until golden then transfer in your Crock Pot.   Add the rest of the ingredients and season with salt and pepper.   Cook on low settings for 6 hours.   The stew is best served warm.

Turkey Collard Greens

Servings: 4   Cooking Time: 5 Hours 20 Minutes

Ingredients:

1 bunch collard greens, woody stems removed and thinly sliced
½ teaspoon red pepper flakes
1 scoop stevia
1 pound smoked turkey wings, chopped in half
2 teaspoons Frank's hot pepper sauce
1 teaspoon kosher salt
2 tablespoons olive oil
½ teaspoon black pepper
½ cup chicken broth

Directions:

Put the collard greens into the crockpot along with rest of the ingredients.   Stir thoroughly and cover

the lid.   Cook on HIGH for about 5 hours and dish out into a serving bowl to serve.

Nutrition Info: Calories: 115 Fat: 10.4g Carbohydrates: 1.9g

Boston Baked Beans

Servings: 8   Cooking Time: 6 1/4 Hours

Ingredients:

1 pound dried kidney beans
2 tablespoons molasses
1 teaspoon mustard seeds
1 teaspoon Worcestershire sauce
2 tablespoons brown sugar
1 cup water
1 large onion, chopped
2 cups vegetable stock
1/2 teaspoon celery seeds
1/2 teaspoon cumin seeds
1 bay leaf
Salt and pepper to taste

Directions:

Combine the kidney beans, molasses, mustard seeds, Worcestershire sauce, brown sugar, onion and stock in your Crock Pot.   Season with salt and pepper and add the celery seeds, cumin seeds, water and bay leaf.   Cook on low settings for 6 hours.   Serve the beans warm and fresh.

Turkey Chili

Servings: 8   Cooking Time: 4 Hours

Ingredients:

1 red bell pepper, chopped
2 pounds turkey meat, ground
28 ounces canned tomatoes, chopped
1 green bell pepper, chopped
4 tablespoons tomato paste
1 red onion, chopped
1 tablespoon oregano, dried
3 tablespoon chili powder
3 tablespoons cumin, ground
Salt and black pepper to the taste

Directions:

Heat up a pan over medium-high heat, add turkey, brown it for a few minutes, transfer to your Crock Pot, add red and green bell pepper, onion, tomatoes, tomato paste, chili powder, oregano, cumin, salt and black pepper to the taste, stir, cover and cook on High for 4 hours.   Divide into bowls and serve for lunch.

Nutrition Info: calories 225, fat 6, fiber 4, carbs 15, protein 18

Bacon Potato Stew

Servings: 6   Cooking Time: 6 1/2 Hours
Ingredients:

1 cup diced bacon	2 sweet potatoes,
1 large onion,	peeled and cubed
chopped	1/2 teaspoon cumin
2 carrots, diced	seeds
1 celery stalk, diced	1/2 teaspoon chili
2 red bell peppers,	powder
cored and diced	1 cup diced tomatoes
1 pound Yukon gold	Salt and pepper to
potatoes, peeled and	taste
cubed	2 cups chicken stock

Directions:
Heat a skillet and add the bacon. Cook until crisp then transfer in your Crock Pot.   Add the rest of the ingredients and adjust the taste with salt and pepper.   Cook on low settings for 6 hours. Serve the stew warm and fresh.

Creamy Chicken Soup

Servings: 6   Cooking Time: 6 Hours
Ingredients:

2 chicken breasts,	4 ounces cream
skinless and boneless	cheese, soft
1 cup yellow corn	1 yellow onion,
1 cup peas	chopped
1 celery stalk,	4 cups chicken stock
chopped	2 teaspoons garlic
1 cup carrots,	powder
chopped	3 cups heavy cream
2 gold potatoes,	Salt and black pepper
cubed	to the taste

Directions:
In your Crock Pot, mix chicken with corn, peas, carrots, potatoes, celery, cream cheese, onion, garlic powder, stock, heavy cream, salt and pepper, stir, cover and cook on Low for 6 hours.   Transfer chicken to a cutting board, shred meat usingforks, return to the Crock Pot, stir, ladle soup into bowls and serve for lunch.
Nutrition Info:calories 300, fat 6, fiber 5, carbs 20, protein 22

Navy Bean Stew

Servings: 10   Cooking Time: 10 1/4 Hours
Ingredients:

4 pounds pork	1 cup dried red beans,
shoulder, cubed	rinsed
1/2 cup diced bacon	1 can fire roasted
2 celery stalks, sliced	tomatoes
2 carrots, sliced	2 chipotle peppers,
2 large onions,	chopped
chopped	1 cup chicken stock
1 pound dried navy	Salt and pepper to
beans, rinsed	taste

Directions:
Combine the pork shoulder, celery, bacon, carrots, onions, navy beans, red beans, tomatoes, chipotle peppers and stock in your crock pot.   Add salt and pepper according to your taste and cook on low settings for 10 hours.   Serve the stew warm and fresh.

Turmeric Chicken Stew

Servings: 6   Cooking Time: 6 1/2 Hours
Ingredients:

2 chicken breasts,	2 red bell peppers,
cubed	cored and diced
1 teaspoon turmeric	1 cup tomato sauce
powder	1 cup coconut milk
2 tablespoons canola	1 cup chicken stock
oil	2 cups fresh spinach,
1/2 head cauliflower,	shredded
cut into florets	Salt and pepper to
1 can (15 oz.)	taste
chickpeas, drained	

Directions:
Season the chicken with salt, pepper and turmeric powder.   Heat the canola oil in a skillet and add the chicken. Cook for a few minutes on all sides until golden.   Transfer in your Crock Pot then add the remaining ingredients.   Season with salt and pepper and cook on low settings for 6 hours. Serve the dish warm and fresh.

Chicken Stew

Servings: 6   Cooking Time: 8 Hours
Ingredients:

32 ounces chicken	1 cup lentils
stock	1 carrot, chopped
3 spicy chicken	2 garlic cloves,
sausage links, cooked	minced
and sliced	1 celery rib, chopped
28 ounces canned	½ teaspoon thyme,
tomatoes, chopped	dried
1 yellow onion,	Salt and black pepper
chopped	to the taste

Directions:
In your Crock Pot, mix stock with sausage, tomatoes, onion, lentils, carrot, garlic, celery, thyme, salt and pepper, stir, cover and cook on Low for 8 hours.   Divide into bowls and serve for lunch.
Nutrition Info:calories 231, fat 4, fiber 12, carbs 31, protein 15

Caramelized Onion Beef Pot Roast

Servings: 8   Cooking Time: 8 1/2 Hours
Ingredients:

4 pounds beef roast	1 celery root, peeled
4 large onions, sliced	and cubed
3 tablespoons canola	2 large potatoes,
oil	peeled and cubed
4 garlic cloves,	1 cup beef stock
chopped	1/2 cup water
2 carrots, sliced	Salt and pepper to
	taste

Directions:
Heat the oil in a frying pan and add the onions. Cook for   minutes until golden brown, slightly caramelized.   Transfer in your Crock Pot and add the rest of the ingredients.   Season with enough salt and pepper and cook on low settings for 8 hours.   Serve the pot roast warm.

Fennel Infused Pork Ham

Servings: 8   Cooking Time: 6 1/4 Hours

Ingredients:

4-5 pounds piece of pork ham
2 fennel bulbs, sliced
1 orange, zested and juiced
1/2 cup white wine
1 cup chicken stock
2 bay leaves
1 thyme sprig
Salt and pepper to taste

Directions:

Combine the fennel, orange zest, orange juice, white wine, chicken stock, bay leaves and thyme in your crock pot.   Add salt and pepper and place the ham on top.   Cook on low settings for 6 hours.   Slice and serve the ham warm.

Beef Stroganoff

Servings: 6   Cooking Time: 6 1/4 Hours

Ingredients:

1 1/2 pounds beef stew meat, cubed
1 large onion, chopped
4 garlic cloves, minced
1/2 cup water
1 tablespoon Worcestershire sauce
1 cup cream cheese
Salt and pepper to taste
Cooked pasta for serving

Directions:

Mix all the ingredients in a crock pot.   Add salt and pepper to taste and cook on low settings for 6 hours.   Serve the stroganoff warm and serve it with cooked pasta of your choice.

Beef And Veggie Stew

Servings: 8   Cooking Time: 6 Hours And 30 Minutes

Ingredients:

3 potatoes, cubed
1 and ½ pound beef chuck roast, boneless and cubed
10 ounces canned tomato soup
1 and ½ cup baby carrots
3 and ¾ cups water
1 yellow onion, chopped
1 celery rib, chopped
2 tablespoons Worcestershire sauce
1 garlic clove, minced
Salt and black pepper to the taste
1 teaspoon sugar
2 cups peas
¼ cup cornstarch

Directions:

In your Crock Pot, mix potatoes with beef cubes, tomato soup, baby carrots, 3 cups water, celery, onion, Worcestershire sauce, garlic, salt, pepper and sugar, stir, cover and cook on Low for 6 hours. Add cornstarch mixed with the rest of the water and the peas, stir, cover and cook on Low for 30 minutes more.   Divide into bowls and serve for lunch.

Nutrition Info:calories 287, fat 4, fiber 5, carbs 31, protein 20

Whole Roasted Cauliflower

Servings: 4   Cooking Time: 6 1/4 Hours

Ingredients:

1 head cauliflower
1/4 teaspoon garlic powder
1/4 teaspoon onion powder
1/2 teaspoon dried thyme
1 cup tomato sauce
1/4 teaspoon salt
1 pinch cayenne pepper
1/2 cup vegetable stock

Directions:

Place the cauliflower in your Crock Pot. Combine the remaining ingredients in a bowl and pour this mixture over the cauliflower.   Cover with a lid and cook on low settings for 6 hours. Serve the cauliflower warm and fresh.

Orange Glazed Chicken

Servings: 6   Cooking Time: 6 1/4 Hours

Ingredients:

6 chicken thighs
1 orange, zested and juiced
2 tablespoons olive oil
2 sweet onions, sliced
1 tablespoon cornstarch
1 cup vegetable stock
1 tablespoon balsamic vinegar
1/2 teaspoon Worcestershire sauce
1/4 teaspoon cumin powder
Salt and pepper to taste

Directions:

Combine the chicken, orange zest, orange juice, olive oil, onions, stock, cornstarch, balsamic vinegar, Worcestershire sauce and cumin powder in your crock pot.   Add salt and pepper to taste and cook the chicken on low settings for 6 hours. Serve the chicken warm and fresh.

Sweet Farro

Servings: 3   Cooking Time: 6 Hours

Ingredients:

½ cup farro
2 cups of water
½ cup heavy cream
2 tablespoons dried cranberries
2 tablespoons sugar

Directions:

Chop the cranberries and put in the Crock Pot. Add water, heavy cream, sugar, and farro.   Mix the ingredients with the help of the spoon and close the lid.   Cook the farro on low for 6 hours.

Nutrition Info: Per Serving: 208 calories, 5.1g protein, 31g carbohydrates, 7.4g fat, 2.2g fiber, 27mg cholesterol, 32mg sodium, 24mg potassium.

Bbq Chicken Thighs

Servings: 6   Cooking Time: 5 Hours

Ingredients:

6 chicken thighs, skinless and boneless
1 yellow onion, chopped
½ teaspoon poultry seasoning
14 ounces canned tomatoes, chopped
8 ounces tomato sauce
½ cup bbq sauce

1 teaspoon garlic powder
¼ cup orange juice
½ teaspoon hot pepper sauce
¾ teaspoon oregano, dried
Salt and black pepper to the taste

Directions:

In your Crock Pot, mix chicken with onion, poultry seasoning, tomatoes, tomato sauce, bbq sauce, garlic powder, orange juice, pepper sauce, oregano, salt and pepper, toss, cover and cook on Low for 5 hours.   Divide between plates and serve with the sauce drizzled on top.

Nutrition Info: calories 211, fat 9, fiber 2, carbs 12, protein 23

Ricotta Veggie Lasagna

Servings: 8   Cooking Time: 6 1/2 Hours

Ingredients:

2 large zucchinis, finely sliced
10 oz. frozen spinach, thawed and drained
2 cups chopped cauliflower florets

2 cups ricotta cheese
2 cups tomato sauce
2 cups shredded mozzarellas
Salt and pepper to taste

Directions:

Mix the ricotta, spinach and cauliflower florets in your Crock Pot. Add salt and pepper to taste. Layer the zucchinis, ricotta filling and tomato sauce in your crock pot.   Top with mozzarella cheese and cook on low settings for 6 hours.   Serve the lasagna warm and fresh.

Spicy Vegetarian Chili

Servings: 8   Cooking Time: 6 1/2 Hours

Ingredients:

2 tablespoons olive oil
2 shallots, chopped
4 garlic cloves, chopped
2 cups cauliflower florets

1 zucchini, cubed
2 red bell peppers, cored and diced
1 celery stalk, diced
1 teaspoon chili powder
1 cup tomato sauce

1 can (15 oz.) chickpeas, drained
1 can (15 oz.) black beans, drained
1 can fire toasted tomatoes
1 cup canned corn, drained

2 cups vegetable stock
1 bay leaf
Salt and pepper to taste
Sour cream for serving

Directions:

Heat the oil in a skillet and add the shallots and garlic. Cook for a few minutes until softened then transfer in your Crock Pot.   Add the remaining ingredients and adjust the taste with salt and pepper.   Cook on low settings for 6 hours. Serve the chili warm, topped with sour cream.

Chunky Beef Pasta Sauce

Servings: 8   Cooking Time: 6 1/2 Hours

Ingredients:

2 pounds beef sirloin, cut into thin strips
1 carrot, diced
2 garlic cloves, chopped
1 can (28 oz.) diced tomatoes

1 celery stalk, diced
2 cups sliced mushrooms
1/4 cup red wine
1 cup tomato sauce
1 bay leaf
Salt and pepper to taste

Directions:

Combine the beef sirloin, carrot, celery, garlic, tomatoes, mushrooms, red wine, tomato sauce and bay leaf in your Crock Pot.   Add enough salt and pepper and cover with its lid.   Cook on low settings for 6 hours.   Serve the sauce right away with cooked pasta or freeze it into individual portions to serve later.

Spicy Hot Chicken Thighs

Servings: 8   Cooking Time: 8 1/4 Hours

Ingredients:

8 chicken thighs
1/4 cup hot sauce
2 tablespoons butter
1/2 teaspoon garlic powder
1/2 cup tomato sauce

1/2 cup vegetable stock
1/2 teaspoon cumin powder
Salt and pepper to taste

Directions:

Combine the chicken thighs with the rest of the ingredients, including salt and pepper in your crock pot.   Cover with a lid and cook on low settings for 8 hours.   Serve the chicken thighs warm and fresh.

Soups & Stews Recipes

Roasted Garlic Soup

Servings: 6   Cooking Time: 3 ½ Hours

Ingredients:

1 tablespoon extra-virgin olive oil
2 bulbs of garlic
3 shallots, chopped
6 cups gluten-free vegetable broth

1 large head of cauliflower, chopped, about 5 cups
Fresh ground pepper to taste
Sea salt to taste

Directions:

Preheat oven to 400° Fahrenheit.   Peel the outer layers off garlic bulbs.   Cut about 4 inch off the top of the bulbs, place into foil pan.   Coat bulbs with olive oil, and cook in oven for 35 minutes.   Once cooked, allow them to cool.   Squeeze the garlic out of the bulbs into your food processor.   Meanwhile, in a pan, sauté remaining olive oil and chopped shallots over medium-high heat for about 6 minutes.   Add other ingredients to saucepan, cover and reduce heat to a simmer for 20 minutes or until the cauliflower is softened.   Add the mixture to food processor and puree until smooth.   Add mix to Crock Pot, cover with lid, and cook on LOW for 3 ½ hours.   Serve hot.

Nutrition Info: Calories: 73, Total Fat: 2.4 g, Sodium: 1201 mg, Carbs: 11.3 g, Dietary Fiber: 2.1 g, Net Carbs: 2.1 g, Sugars: 4.1 g, Protein: 2.1 g

Pumpkin Stew With Chicken

Servings: 2   Cooking Time: 4 Hours

Ingredients:

½ cup pumpkin, chopped
6 oz chicken fillet, cut into strips
¼ cup coconut cream

1 tablespoon curry powder
½ teaspoon ground cinnamon
1 onion, chopped

Directions:

Mix pumpkin with chicken fillet strips in the mixing bowl.   Add curry powder, coconut cream, ground cinnamon, and onion.   Mix the stew ingredients and transfer them in the Crock Pot. Cook the meal on high for hours.

Nutrition Info: Per Serving: 291 calories, 16.2g protein, 25g carbohydrates, 15.8g fat, 5.7g fiber, 40mg cholesterol, 586mg sodium, 336mg potassium.

Grits Potato Soup

Servings: 6   Cooking Time: 6 1/4 Hours

Ingredients:

4 bacon slices, chopped
1/2 cup grits
2 cups chicken stock
4 cups water
1 1/2 pounds

1 carrot, diced
1 parsnip, diced
1 cup diced tomatoes
1/2 teaspoon dried thyme
1/2 teaspoon dried

potatoes, peeled and cubed
1/2 celery stalk, sliced

oregano
Salt and pepper to taste

Directions:

Cook the bacon until crisp in a skillet or pan. Transfer in your Crock Pot and add the remaining ingredients.   Cook the soup on low settings, adjusting the taste with salt and pepper as needed. The soup is done in about 6 hours.   Serve warm.

Curried Turkey Soup

Servings: 8   Cooking Time: 6 1/2 Hours

Ingredients:

2 tablespoons olive oil
1 1/2 pounds turkey breast, cubed
1 sweet onion, chopped
1 celery stalk, sliced
2 garlic cloves, chopped

2 carrots, diced
1 teaspoon grated ginger
1 cup coconut milk
3 cups chicken stock
1 cup water
1 tablespoon curry powder
Salt and pepper to taste

Directions:

Heat the oil in a skillet and stir in the turkey. Cook on all sides for a few minutes until golden then transfer in your Crock Pot.   Add the carrots, onion, celery, garlic, ginger, coconut milk, stock, water and curry powder.   Season with salt and pepper and cook on low settings for 6 hours. Serve the soup warm.

Shredded Beef Soup

Servings: 8   Cooking Time: 8 1/2 Hours

Ingredients:

1 1/2 pounds beef roast
1 sweet onion, chopped
2 garlic cloves, chopped
2 carrots, sliced
2 celery stalks, sliced
2 red bell peppers, cored and diced
1/2 teaspoon cumin powder

1/2 teaspoon dried oregano
1/2 teaspoon dried basil
1/2 teaspoon chili powder
2 cups chicken stock
5 cups water
2 jalapenos, chopped
1 cup fire roasted tomatoes
Salt and pepper to taste

Directions:

Combine the onion, garlic, carrots, celery, bell peppers, cumin powder, oregano, basil, chili powder, stock and water in your Crock Pot.   Add the jalapenos and tomatoes, as well as salt and pepper then place the beef in the center of the cooker, making sure it's covered in liquid.   Cook on low settings for 8 hours.   When done, shred the beef into fine threads and serve the soup warm.

Fish Sweet Corn Soup

Servings: 6   Cooking Time: 2 1/4 Hours

Ingredients:

2 bacon slices, chopped	2 potatoes, peeled and diced
1 sweet onion, chopped	1 pound haddock fillets, cubed
2 cups milk	Salt and pepper to taste
2 cups frozen sweet corn	

Directions:

Cook the bacon in a skillet and transfer in your Crock Pot.   Add the remaining ingredients and season with salt and pepper.   cook on high settings for 2 hours.   Serve the soup warm.

Roasted Bell Pepper Quinoa Soup

Servings: 6   Cooking Time: 6 1/2 Hours

Ingredients:

1 shallot, chopped	1 cup water
1 garlic clove, chopped	1/2 teaspoon dried oregano
4 roasted red bell peppers, chopped	1/2 teaspoon dried basil
1/2 cup tomato paste	1 pinch cayenne pepper
2 cups vegetable stock	Salt and pepper to taste
1/2 cup red quinoa, rinsed	

Directions:

Combine the shallot, garlic, bell peppers, tomato paste, stock and water in your Crock Pot.   Add the quinoa, herbs and spices, as well as salt and pepper to taste and cover with a lid.   Cook on low settings for 6 hours.   Serve the soup warm or chilled.

Roasted Chicken Stock

Servings: 10   Cooking Time: 9 Hours

Ingredients:

1 whole chicken, cut into smaller pieces	2 onions, halved
2 carrots, cut in half	10 cups water
1 parsnip	1 bay leaf
1 celery root, peeled and sliced	1 rosemary sprig
	1 thyme sprig
	Salt and pepper to taste

Directions:

Season the chicken with salt and pepper and place it in a baking tray. Roast in the preheated oven at 400F for 40 minutes.   Transfer the chicken in your Crock Pot and add the remaining ingredients. Season with salt and pepper and cook on low settings for 8 hours.   Use the stock right away or store in the fridge or freezer.

Two-fish Soup

Servings: 8   Cooking Time: 6 1/4 Hours

Ingredients:

1 tablespoon canola oil	1 cup diced tomatoes
1 sweet onion, chopped	1 lemon, juiced
1 red bell pepper, cored and diced	3 salmon fillets, cubed
1 chipotle pepper, chopped	3 cod fillets, cubed
1 carrot, diced	2 tablespoons chopped parsley
1 celery stalk, diced	Salt and pepper to taste

Directions:

Heat the canola oil in a skillet and add the onion. Sauté for 2 minutes until softened.   Transfer the onion in a Crock Pot and stir in the remaining ingredients.   Add salt and pepper to taste and cook on low settings for 6 hours.   Serve the soup warm.

Jamaican Stew

Servings: 8   Cooking Time: 1 Hour

Ingredients:

1 tablespoon coconut oil	1-pound salmon fillet, chopped
1 teaspoon garlic powder	1 teaspoon ground coriander
½ cup bell pepper, sliced	½ teaspoon ground cumin
½ cup heavy cream	

Directions:

Put the coconut oil in the Crock Pot.   Then mix the salmon with ground cumin and ground coriander and put in the Crock Pot.   Add the layer of bell pepper and sprinkle with garlic powder.   Add heavy cream and close the lid. Cook the stew on High for 1 hour.

Nutrition Info: Per Serving: 120 calories, 11.3g protein, 1.1g carbohydrates, 8g fat, 6.9g fiber, 35mg cholesterol, 28mg sodium, 244mg potassium.

French Stew

Servings: 4   Cooking Time: 6 Hours

Ingredients:

1 zucchini, cubed	1 eggplant, cubed
1 cup tomatoes, canned	7 oz beef sirloin, chopped
1 teaspoon dried oregano	1 teaspoon ground black pepper
3 oz Provolone cheese, chopped	3 cups of water

Directions:

Put chopped beef sirloin in the Crock Pot.   Add water, ground black pepper, dried oregano, and tomatoes.   Cook the ingredients on High for 4 hours.   Then add zucchini, eggplant, and all remaining ingredients.   Close the lid and cook the stew on high for 2 hours.

Nutrition Info: Per Serving: 214 calories, 22.7g protein, 11.2g carbohydrates, 9.2g fat, 5.4g fiber, 59mg cholesterol, 234mg sodium, 741mg potassium.

White Chicken Chili Soup

Servings: 8   Cooking Time: 7 1/2 Hours

Ingredients:

1 pound ground chicken	2 cans (15 oz.) white beans, drained
2 tablespoons olive oil	2 cups chicken stock
1 yellow bell pepper, cored and diced	3 cups water
2 carrots, diced	1/2 teaspoon chili powder
1 celery stalk, diced	Salt and pepper to taste
1 parsnip, diced	

Directions:

Heat the oil in a skillet and stir in the chicken. Cook for 5 minutes, stirring often, then transfer the meat in your Crock Pot.   Add the remaining ingredients and season with salt and pepper. Cover the pot and cook on low settings for 7 hours. Serve the soup either warm or chilled.

Orange Sweet Potato Soup

Servings: 8   Cooking Time: 3 1/2 Hours

Ingredients:

2 tablespoons olive oil	2 oranges, juiced
1 shallot, chopped	2 cups chicken stick
2 carrots, sliced	1 bay leaf
1/2 celery stalk	1/2 cinnamon stalk
2 large sweet potatoes, peeled and cubed	Salt and pepper to taste
1 teaspoon orange zest	1 teaspoon pumpkin seeds oil
	2 tablespoons pumpkin seeds

Directions:

Heat the olive oil in a skillet and add the shallot and carrots. Sauté for 5 minutes then transfer in your Crock Pot.   Add the celery stalk, potatoes, orange juice, orange zest, stock, bay leaf, cinnamon, salt and pepper.   Cook the soup on high settings for 2 hours then on low settings for 1 additional hour.   When done, remove the bay leaf and cinnamon stick and puree the soup with an immersion blender.   To serve, pour the soup into bowls and top with pumpkin seeds drizzle of pumpkin seed oil. Serve right away.

Herbed Spinach Lentil Soup

Servings: 8   Cooking Time: 3 1/4 Hours

Ingredients:

1 cup green lentils, rinsed	2 cups chicken stock
1 celery stalk, sliced	6 cups water
1 carrot, sliced	1 bay leaf
1 sweet onion, chopped	1 thyme sprig
2 sweet potatoes, peeled and cubed	Salt and pepper to taste
	4 cups fresh spinach, shredded

Directions:

Combine the lentils, celery, carrot, onion, potatoes, stock and water in your Crock Pot.   Add the bay leaf and thyme and season with salt and pepper. Cook on high settings for 2 hours then add the spinach and cook one more hour.   Serve the soup warm or chilled.

Mixed Bean Vegetarian Soup

Servings: 8   Cooking Time: 4 1/4 Hours

Ingredients:

1 tablespoon olive oil	1 carrot, diced
1 sweet onion, chopped	1 can (15 oz.) white bean, drained
1 garlic clove, chopped	1 can (15 oz.) cannellini beans, drained
1 celery stalk, sliced	1 cup diced tomatoes
1 red bell pepper, cored and diced	2 cups water
1/2 teaspoon chili powder	Salt and pepper to taste
1/2 teaspoon cumin powder	2 tablespoons chopped cilantro
2 cups vegetable stock	1 lime, juiced
	1 avocado, peeled and sliced

Directions:

Heat the oil in a skillet and add the onion, carrot, garlic and celery. Cook for 5 minutes until softened. Transfer in your Crock Pot and stir in the remaining ingredients, except the cilantro, lime and avocado.   Adjust the taste with salt and pepper and cook on low settings for 4 hours. When done, pour the soup into serving bowls and top with cilantro and avocado.   Drizzle with lime juice and serve right away.

Lemony Salmon Soup

Servings: 6   Cooking Time: 4 1/4 Hours

Ingredients:

1 shallot, chopped	1/2 teaspoon dried basil
1 garlic clove, chopped	2 cups milk
1 celery stalk, sliced	2 cups water
1 carrot, sliced	1 lemon, juiced
1 parsnip, sliced	1 teaspoon lemon zest
1 red bell pepper, cored and diced	1 pound salmon fillets, cubed
1/2 teaspoon dried oregano	Salt and pepper to taste

Directions:

Combine the shallot, garlic, celery, carrot, parsnip and bell pepper in your Crock Pot.   Add the dried herbs, milk, water, lemon juice and lemon zest and cook for 1 hour on high settings.   Add the fish and season with salt and pepper.   Cook for 3 additional hours on low settings.   Serve the soup warm or chilled.

Crock-pot Chicken Parmesan Soup

Servings: 4   Cooking Time: 7 Hours

Ingredients:

1 green bell pepper, chopped	5 cups chicken broth
4 garlic cloves, minced	2 teaspoons oregano, fresh, chopped
½ medium white onion, chopped	1 teaspoon sea salt
1 can (14.5-ounces) crushed tomatoes	½ teaspoon black pepper
½ lb. chicken breasts, raw, boneless, skinless	¼ teaspoon red pepper flakes
½ cup Parmesan cheese, shredded	4-ounces (uncooked) dry penne pasta
2 tablespoons basil, fresh, chopped	2 tablespoons unsalted butter
	Chopped parsley for garnish

Directions:

In a Crock-Pot, stir together bell pepper, onion, tomatoes, garlic, chicken, broth, ½ cup cheese, basil, oregano, salt, black pepper, and red pepper flakes.   Cover and cook on LOW for 7 hours.   Remove chicken about six hours into cooking time and shred it up on a cutting board, then add it back to Crock-Pot, along with penne pasta.   Resume cooking. Serve garnished with parsley and Parmesan cheese.

Nutrition Info: Calories: 247, Total Fat: 7.3 g, Saturated Fat: 3.5 g, Sodium 378 mg, Carbs: 23 g, Fiber: 4.8 g, Sugars: 5.1 g, Protein: 22.5 g

Spiced Lasagna Soup

Servings: 6   Cooking Time: 6 Hours

Ingredients:

2 sheets of lasagna noodles, crushed	2 cups ground beef
1 oz Parmesan, grated	6 cups beef broth
1 teaspoon ground turmeric	½ cup tomatoes, chopped
1 yellow onion, diced	1 tablespoon dried basil

Directions:

Roast the ground beef in the hot skillet for 4 minutes. Stir it constantly and transfer in the Crock Pot.   Add turmeric, onion, tomatoes, basil, and beef broth.   Stir the soup, add lasagna noodles, and close the lid.   Cook the soup on High for 6 hours.   Top the cooked soup with Parmesan.

Nutrition Info: Per Serving: 208 calories, 17.8g protein, 14.6g carbohydrates, 8.3g fat, 0.7g fiber, 40mg cholesterol, 840mg sodium, 390mg potassium.

Creamy Cauliflower Soup

Servings: 6   Cooking Time: 3 1/4 Hours

Ingredients:

1 tablespoon canola oil	1 head cauliflower, cut into florets
1 sweet onion,	1 can condensed
chopped	cream of chicken soup
2 garlic cloves, chopped	Salt and pepper to taste
2 medium size potatoes, peeled and cubed	1/2 cup water
	1/2 cup grated Parmesan cheese

Directions:

Heat the oil in a skillet and add the onion. Cook for 2 minutes then transfer the onion in your Crock Pot.   Add the remaining ingredients, except the cheese, and season with salt and pepper.   Cook on high settings for hours.   When done, puree the soup with an immersion blender.   Serve the soup warm.

Comforting Chicken Soup

Servings: 8   Cooking Time: 8 1/2 Hours

Ingredients:

1 whole chicken, cut into pieces	8 cups water
2 carrots, cut into sticks	6 oz. egg noodles
1 celery stalk, sliced	2 garlic cloves, chopped
4 potatoes, peeled and cubed	Salt and pepper to taste
	1 whole onion
	1 bay leaf

Directions:

Combine all the ingredients in your Crock Pot. Add salt and pepper to taste and cook on low settings for 8 hours.   Serve the soup warm.

Spicy Chili Soup With Tomatillos

Servings: 8   Cooking Time: 8 1/2 Hours

Ingredients:

1/2 pound beef roast, cubed	1 can fire roasted tomatoes
10 oz. canned tomatillos, rinsed, drained and chopped	1 cup beef stock
	4 cups water
1 dried ancho chili, seeded and chopped	Salt and pepper to taste
1 jalapeno pepper, chopped	1 bay leaf
	1 thyme sprig
1 can (15 oz.) black beans, drained	Chopped cilantro and sour cream for serving

Directions:

Combine the beef roast, tomatillos, ancho chili, jalapeno pepper and black beans in your Crock Pot. Add the tomatoes, beef stock, water, salt and pepper, as well as bay leaf and thyme sprig.   Cook on low settings for 8 hours.   The soup is best served warm, topped with chopped cilantro and a dollop of sour cream.

Beef Barley Soup

Servings: 8   Cooking Time: 14 Hours 20 Minutes

Ingredients:

2 tablespoons butter
¼ cup onions
3 cups water
16 oz round beef steak
½ cup barley
½ teaspoon black pepper
2 cups beef broth

1 cup celery, diced
¼ tablespoon dried basil
¼ teaspoon savory, ground
1 cup carrots, chopped
¾ fl oz red wine

Directions:
Put water, beef steaks, barley and beef broth in the one pot crock pot and cover the lid.   Cook on LOW for about 13 hours and add the remaining ingredients.   Cover and cook on LOW for 1 more hour.   Dish out to serve hot.

Nutrition Info: Calories: 210 Fat: 9g Carbohydrates: 10.9g

Vegan Grain-free Cream Of Mushroom Soup

Servings: 2   Cooking Time: 4 Hours

Ingredients:

2 cups cauliflower florets
1 teaspoon onion powder
1 ½ cups white mushrooms, diced

1 2/3 cups unsweetened almond milk
¼ teaspoon Himalayan rock salt
½ yellow onion, diced

Directions:
Place onion powder, milk, cauliflower, salt, and pepper in a pan, cover and bring to a boil over medium heat. Reduce heat to low and simmer for 8 minutes or until cauliflower is softened. Then, puree mixture in food processor. In a pan, add oil, mushrooms, and onions, heat over high heat for about 8 minutes. Add mushrooms and onion mix to cauliflower mixture in Crock-Pot. Cover and cook on LOW for 4 hours. Serve hot.

Nutrition Info: Calories: 95, Total Fat: 4 g, Sodium: 475 mg, Carbs: 12.3 g, Dietary Fiber: 4.4 g, Net Carbs: 7.9 g, Sugars: 4.9 g, Protein: 4.9 g

Celery Soup With Ham

Servings: 8   Cooking Time: 5 Hours

Ingredients:

8 oz ham, chopped
1 teaspoon white pepper
½ teaspoon cayenne pepper

8 cups chicken stock
2 cups celery stalk, chopped
½ cup corn kernels

Directions:
Put all ingredients in the Crock Pot and gently stir. Close the lid and cook the soup on High for 5 hours.

When the soup is cooked, cool it to the room temperature and ladle into the bowls.

Nutrition Info: Per Serving: 69 calories, 5.9g protein, 4.6g carbohydrates, 3.2g fat, 1.1g fiber, 16mg cholesterol, 1155mg sodium, 193mg potassium.

Creamy Tortellini Soup

Servings: 6   Cooking Time: 6 1/4 Hours

Ingredients:

1 shallot, chopped
1 garlic clove, chopped
1/2 pound mushrooms, sliced
1 can condensed cream of mushroom soup
2 cups chicken stock
1 cup water

1/2 teaspoon dried oregano
1/2 teaspoon dried basil
1 cup evaporated milk
7 oz. cheese tortellini
Salt and pepper to taste

Directions:
Combine the shallot, garlic, mushrooms, cream of mushroom soup, stock, water, dried herbs and milk in your Crock Pot.   Add the cheese tortellini and season with salt and pepper.   Cook on low settings for 6 hours.   Serve the soup warm.

Moroccan Lentil Soup

Servings: 6   Cooking Time: 6 1/4 Hours

Ingredients:

1 large sweet onion, chopped
2 garlic cloves, chopped
2 tablespoons olive oil
2 carrots, diced
1 cup chopped cauliflower
1/2 teaspoon cumin powder
1/4 teaspoon turmeric powder

1 parsnip, diced
1/2 teaspoon ground coriander
2 cups water
3 cups chicken stock
1 cup red lentils
2 tablespoons tomato paste
2 tablespoons lemon juice
Salt and pepper to taste

Directions:
Heat the oil in a skillet and stir in the onion, garlic, carrots and parsnip. Cook for 5 minutes then transfer in your Crock Pot.   Stir in the cauliflower, cumin powder, turmeric and coriander, as well as water, stock, lentils and tomato paste. Add the lemon juice, salt and pepper and cook on low settings for 6 hours.   Serve the soup warm or chilled.

58

Sweet Corn Chowder

Servings: 8   Cooking Time: 6 1/4 Hours

Ingredients:

2 shallots, chopped	1 can (15 oz.) sweet
4 medium size	corn, drained
potatoes, peeled and	2 cups chicken stock
cubed1	2 cups water
1 celery stalk, sliced	Salt and pepper to
	taste

Directions:

Combine the shallot, potatoes, celery, corn, stock and water in a Crock Pot.   Add salt and pepper to taste and cook on low settings for 6 hours.   When done, remove a few tablespoons of corn from the pot then puree the remaining soup in the pot. Pour the soup into serving bowls and top with the reserved corn.   Serve warm.

Beef Cabbage Soup

Servings: 8   Cooking Time: 7 1/2 Hours

Ingredients:

1 pound beef roast,	1 can (15 oz.) diced
cubed	tomatoes
2 tablespoons olive	2 cups beef stock
oil	2 cups water
1 sweet onion,	1/2 teaspoon cumin
chopped	seeds
1 carrot, grated	Salt and pepper to
1 small cabbage head,	taste
shredded	

Directions:

Heat the oil in a skillet and add the beef roast. Cook for 5-6 minutes on all sides then transfer the meat in your Crock Pot.   Add the remaining ingredients and season with salt and pepper. Cook on low settings for 7 hours.   Serve the cabbage soup warm.

Shrimp Soup

Servings: 6   Cooking Time: 6 1/4 Hours

Ingredients:

2 tablespoons olive	1 pinch chili powder
oil	4 medium size
1 large sweet onion,	tomatoes, peeled and
chopped	diced
1 fennel bulb, sliced	1 bay leaf
4 garlic cloves,	1/2 pound cod fillets,
chopped	cubed
1 cup dry white wine	1/2 pound fresh
1/2 cup tomato sauce	shrimps, peeled and
2 cup water	deveined
1 teaspoon dried	Salt and pepper to
oregano	taste
1 teaspoon dried basil	1 lime, juiced

Directions:

Heat the oil in a skillet and stir in the onion, fennel and garlic. Sauté for 5 minutes until softened. Transfer the mixture in your Crock Pot and stir in the wine, tomato sauce, water, oregano, basil, chili powder, tomatoes and bay leaf.   Cook on high settings for 1 hour then add the cod and shrimps, as well as lime juice, salt and pepper and continue

cooking on low settings for 5 additional hours. Serve the soup warm or chilled.

Peas & Mushroom Soup (crock-pot)

Servings: 4 (13.5 Ounces)   Cooking Time: 7 Hours And 5 Minutes

Ingredients:

3 cups Cremini	4 cups water
mushrooms, thinly	2 tablespoons wine
sliced	vinegar
1 cup peas, fresh or	1 teaspoon chili paste
frozen	2 teaspoons sesame
4 garlic cloves,	oil
minced	Salt and black
2 tablespoons ginger,	pepper, to taste
fresh, grated	Parmesan cheese,
2 tablespoons tamari	freshly grated
(or soy sauce)	

Directions:

Place all the ingredients in Crock-Pot. Cover and cook on LOW for 7 hours or on HIGH for 4 hours. When ready sprinkle with grated cheese. Serve hot.

Nutrition Info: Calories: 215.83 , Total Fat: 3.11 g, Saturated Fat: 0.44 g, Cholesterol: 0 mg, Sodium: 286.92 mg, Potassium: 806.92 mg, Total Carbohydrates: 18 g, Fiber: 13.47 g, Sugar: 2.58 g, Protein: 14.97 g

Ground Beef Stew

Servings: 5   Cooking Time: 7 Hours

Ingredients:

1 cup bell pepper,	2 cups ground beef
diced	1 cup tomatoes,
1 teaspoon minced	chopped
garlic	1 teaspoon salt
1 teaspoon dried	3 cups of water
rosemary	

Directions:

Put all ingredients in the Crock Pot and stir them. Close the lid and cook the stew on Low for 7 hours.

Nutrition Info: Per Serving: 135 calories, 18.6g protein, 3.5g carbohydrates, 4.8g fat, 0.9g fiber, 55mg cholesterol, 524mg sodium, 419mg potassium.

Curried Corn Chowder

Servings: 8   Cooking Time: 8 1/4 Hours

Ingredients:

1 sweet onion,	2 cups chicken stock
chopped	1/2 chili pepper,
2 garlic cloves,	chopped
chopped	1 1/2 cups whole milk
1 can (15 oz.) sweet	Salt and pepper to
corn, drained	taste
2 large potatoes,	1/4 teaspoon cumin
peeled and cubed	seeds

Directions:

Combine the onion, garlic, stock, sweet corn, potatoes and chili pepper in your Crock Pot.   Add the remaining ingredients and season with salt and pepper.   Cook on low settings for 8 hours. Serve the soup warm and fresh.

Garlicky Chicken Soup

Servings: 6   Cooking Time: 6 1/4 Hours

Ingredients:

1 large chicken breast (bone in)	1 parsnip, diced
1 cup chicken stock	Salt and pepper to taste
6 cups water	1 cup sour cream
2 carrots, diced	2 egg yolks
1 sweet onion, chopped	4 garlic cloves, minced
1/2 celery root, peeled and diced	2 tablespoons chopped parsley

Directions:

Combine the chicken breast, stock, water, carrots, onion, parsnip and celery in your Crock Pot.   Add salt and pepper to taste and cook on low settings for 6 hours.   When done, remove the chicken breast and place aside.   In a small bowl, mix the sour cream, egg yolks and garlic then pour this mixture over the hot soup. Mix well and stir in the parsley.   Remove the meat off the bone and shred it finely. Add it into the soup.   Serve the soup right away.

Chicken Tortellini Clear Soup

Servings: 8   Cooking Time: 8 1/2 Hours

Ingredients:

1 whole chicken, cut into smaller pieces	8 cups water
1 carrot, halved	10 oz. cheese tortellini
1 celery stalk, halved	Salt and pepper to taste
1 parsnip, halved	

Directions:

Combine the chicken, carrot, celery, parsnip and water in your Crock Pot.   Add salt and pepper to taste and cook on low settings for 6 hours.   When done, remove and discard the carrot, celery and parsnip then shred the meat off the bone and place it back in the cooker.   Add the tortellini and cook on high settings for 2 additional hours.   Serve the soup warm and fresh.

Ham Bone Cabbage Soup

Servings: 8   Cooking Time: 7 1/4 Hours

Ingredients:

1 ham bone	1 can diced tomatoes
1 sweet onion, chopped	2 cups beef stock
1 mediums size cabbage head, shredded	Salt and pepper to taste
	1 bay leaf
2 tablespoons tomato paste	1 thyme sprig
	1 lemon, juiced

Directions:

Combine the ham bone, onion, cabbage, tomato paste, tomatoes, stock, bay leaf and thyme sprig in your Crock Pot.   Add salt and pepper to taste and cook on low settings for 7 hours.   When done, stir in the lemon juice and serve the soup warm.

Beef Bacon Barley Soup

Servings: 8   Cooking Time: 8 1/2 Hours

Ingredients:

4 bacon slices, chopped	1 cup frozen sweet corn
1 pound beef steak,	1 cup fire roasted
cubed	tomatoes
1/2 teaspoon smoked paprika	1/2 cup pearl barley, rinsed
1 medium onion, chopped	4 cups water
4 small potatoes, peeled and cubed	1/2 teaspoon dried basil
1 cup baby carrots, halved	1/2 teaspoon dried oregano
2 cups beef stock	Salt and pepper to taste

Directions:

Heat a skillet over medium flame and add the bacon. Cook until crisp then stir in the beef. Cook on all sides until golden for about 5 minutes.   Transfer in your Crock Pot.   Add the remaining ingredients and season with salt and pepper.   Cook the soup on low settings for 8 hours.   Serve the soup warm.

Three Cheese Broccoli Soup

Servings: 6   Cooking Time: 2 1/2 Hours

Ingredients:

2 tablespoons butter	10 oz. broccoli florets
1 sweet onion, chopped	Salt and pepper to taste
1 garlic clove, chopped	1 cup grated Cheddar cheese
1 tablespoon all-purpose flour	1 cup grated Monterey Jack
1 1/2 cups evaporated milk	1/2 cup grated Parmesan
4 cups chicken stock	

Directions:

Heat the butter in a skillet and stir in the onion and garlic. Sauté for 2 minutes until softened then add the flour and cook additional minute.   Transfer the mixture in your Crock Pot and add the milk, stock, broccoli and cheeses.   Season with salt and pepper if needed and cook on high settings for 2 hours.   Serve the soup warm.

Sausage Bean Soup

Servings: 8   Cooking Time: 3 1/4 Hours

Ingredients:

2 bacon slices, chopped	1 carrot, diced
1 sweet onion, chopped	1 parsnip, diced
	1 celery stalk, sliced
1 garlic clove, chopped	1 can diced tomatoes
1/2 teaspoon dried rosemary	1 can (15 oz.) white beans, drained
1/2 teaspoon dried thyme	2 cups chicken stock
	4 cups water
4 pork sausages, sliced	Salt and pepper to taste

Directions:

Heat a skillet over medium flame and stir in the bacon. Sauté for 2-3 minutes until crisp.   Transfer the bacon in your Crock Pot.   Add the remaining ingredients and season with salt and pepper.   Cook the soup on high settings for 3 hours.   The soup is best served warm, but it tastes great chilled as well.

Pumpkin Hearty Soup

Servings: 10   Cooking Time: 6 1/4 Hours

Ingredients:

2 tablespoons olive oil
2 shallots, chopped
2 garlic cloves, chopped
1 red chili, seeded and chopped
1/4 teaspoon grated ginger
2 tablespoons tomato paste
1 can diced tomatoes
1 can (15 oz.) black beans, drained
2 cups pumpkin cubes
2 cups water
3 cups vegetable stock
1 bay leaf
Salt and pepper to taste
1/2 cinnamon stick
1/4 teaspoon cumin powder

Directions:
Heat the oil in a skillet or saucepan and add the shallots, garlic, red chili and ginger. Cook for 3-4 minutes then transfer in your Crock Pot.   Add the tomato paste, tomatoes, black beans and pumpkin, as well as the water, stock, bay leaf, cinnamon and cumin.   Adjust the taste with salt and cook on low settings for 6 hours.   Serve the soup warm and fresh.

Chicken Wild Rice Soup

Servings: 6   Cooking Time: 6 1/2 Hours

Ingredients:

3/4 cup wild rice, rinsed
1 pound chicken breasts, cubed
2 celery stalk, sliced
1 sweet onion, chopped
2 carrots, sliced
6 cups chicken stock
1/2 teaspoon dried oregano
1 tablespoon butter
1/2 cup half and half
Salt and pepper to taste

Directions:
Combine all the ingredients in your Crock Pot. Add salt and pepper to taste and cook on low settings for 6 hours.   When done, serve the soup warm and fresh.

Tomato And Turkey Chili

Servings: 6   Cooking Time: 7 Hours

Ingredients:

1-pound turkey fillet, chopped
2 cup tomatoes, chopped
1 jalapeno pepper, chopped
1 onion, diced
1 cup chicken stock

Directions:
Put turkey and tomatoes in the Crock Pot.   Add jalapeno pepper, onion, and chicken stock.   Close the lid and cook the chili on low for 7 hours.
Nutrition Info: Per Serving: 164 calories, 22.7g protein, 4.3g carbohydrates, 5.8g fat, 1.2g fiber, 67mg cholesterol, 196mg sodium, 360mg potassium.

Light Minestrone Soup

Servings: 4   Cooking Time: 4 Hours

Ingredients:

1 cup green beans, chopped
1 small zucchini, chopped
1/4 cup garbanzo beans
5 cups chicken stock
1 teaspoon curry powder
2 tablespoons tomato paste
1/2 cup ground pork

Directions:
Put all ingredients in the Crock Pot bowl.   Close the lid and cook the soup on High for 4 hours.
Nutrition Info: Per Serving: 195 calories, 14.6g protein, 13.3g carbohydrates, 9.8g fat, 3.9g fiber, 37mg cholesterol, 999mg sodium, 493mg potassium.

Minestrone Soup

Servings: 6   Cooking Time: 6 1/2 Hours

Ingredients:

1 shallot, chopped
1 garlic clove, chopped
1 celery stalk, sliced
1 red bell pepper, cored and diced
1 carrot, diced
2 potatoes, peeled and diced
1 cup diced tomatoes
1 teaspoon Italian herbs
2 cups chicken stock
4 cups water
1 cup short pasta of your choice
Salt and pepper to taste

Directions:
Combine all the ingredients in your Crock Pot. Add salt and pepper to taste and cook on low settings for 6 hours.   Serve the soup warm or chilled.

Swedish Split Pea Soup

Servings: 8   Cooking Time: 6 1/4 Hours

Ingredients:

2 cups yellow split peas, rinsed
4 cups chicken stock
4 cups water
1 large sweet onion, chopped
2 carrots, diced
1 celery stalk, diced
2 cups diced ham
1/2 teaspoon dried oregano
1/2 teaspoon dried marjoram
Salt and pepper to taste

Directions:
Combine the split peas, stock, water, onion, carrots and celery stalk in your Crock Pot.   Add the ham, herbs, salt and pepper and cook on low settings for 6 hours.   Serve the soup warm.

Lentil Soup With Garlic Topping

Servings: 8   Cooking Time: 6 1/2 Hours

Ingredients:

Soup:
1/2 cup red lentils, rinsed
1/2 cup green lentils, rinsed
1 shallot, chopped
1 celery stalk, sliced
1 carrot, diced
1 red bell pepper, cored and diced
1/2 cup tomato sauce
1 bay leaf
2 cups water
2 cups chicken stock
Salt and pepper to taste
Topping:
3 garlic cloves, chopped
2 tablespoons chopped parsley
2 tomatoes, peeled and diced
Salt and pepper to taste
1 tablespoon olive oil

Directions:
To make the soup, combine all the ingredients in your Crock Pot.   Add salt and pepper to taste and cook on low settings for 6 hours.   For the topping, mix the garlic, parsley, tomatoes, salt, pepper and olive oil in a bowl.   Pour the warm soup into serving bowls and top with the tomato and garlic topping.   Serve right away.

Lobster Stew

Servings: 4   Cooking Time: 1 Hour

Ingredients:

7 oz lobster tail, peeled, chopped
3 tomatoes, chopped
1 onion, roughly chopped
1 cup fish stock
½ teaspoon dried lemongrass
2 tablespoons cream cheese

Directions:
Put all ingredients in the Crock Pot and gently stir. Close the lid and cook the stew on High for 1 hour.
Nutrition Info: Per Serving: 100 calories, 12.2g protein, 6.3g carbohydrates, 2.8g fat, 1.7g fiber, 78mg cholesterol, 352mg sodium, 464mg potassium.

Barley Stew

Servings: 4   Cooking Time: 9 Hours

Ingredients:

½ cup barley
4 cups chicken stock
1 cup zucchini, chopped
1 tablespoon tomato paste
½ carrot, diced
1 teaspoon salt

Directions:
Put all ingredients in the Crock Pot and carefully stir.   Cook the stew on low for 9 hours.
Nutrition Info: Per Serving: 102 calories, 4.1g protein, 20.1g carbohydrates, 1.2g fat, 4.6g fiber, 0mg cholesterol, 1360mg sodium, 258mg potassium.

Tuscan White Bean Soup

Servings: 6   Cooking Time: 6 1/2 Hours

Ingredients:

1 cup dried white beans
1 bay leaf
2 cups spinach,
2 cups chicken stock
4 cups water
1 carrot, diced
1 celery stalk, diced
4 garlic cloves, chopped
2 tablespoons tomato paste
shredded
Salt and pepper to taste
1 teaspoon dried oregano
1 teaspoon dried basil
1/2 lemon, juiced

Directions:
Combine the beans, stock, water, carrot, celery, garlic and tomato paste in your Crock Pot.   Add the bay leaf, dried herbs and lemon juice, as well as salt and pepper.   Cook on low settings for 4 hours then add the spinach and cook for 2 additional hours on low settings.   Serve the soup warm or chilled.

Beef Chili

Servings: 8   Cooking Time: 3 Hours 15 Minutes

Ingredients:

29 ounces canned diced tomatoes, not drained
3 tablespoons chili powder
1 yellow onion, chopped
2 pounds lean ground beef
¼ cup tomato paste
½ cup saltine cracker crumbs, finely ground
1 jalapeno, minced
3 garlic cloves, minced
2 (16-ounce) cans red kidney beans, rinsed and drained
1 teaspoon Kosher salt
1 teaspoon ground cumin
1 teaspoon black pepper

Directions:
Cook onions and beef over medium high heat in a pot until brown.   Transfer to the crock pot along with the rest of the ingredients.   Cover and cook on HIGH for about hours and dish out to serve.
Nutrition Info: Calories: 638 Fat: 9.1g Carbohydrates: 78.9g

Cheesy Broccoli Soup

Servings: 8   Cooking Time: 4 1/4 Hours

Ingredients:

1 shallot, chopped
2 garlic cloves, chopped
2 tablespoons olive oil
1 head broccoli, cut into florets
1 large potato, peeled and cubed
1 can condensed chicken soup
2 cups water1/2 teaspoon dried oregano
1 cup grated Cheddar soup
Salt and pepper to taste

Directions:
Heat the olive oil in a skillet and stir in the shallot and garlic. Cook for 2 minutes until softened. Transfer the shallot and garlic in your Crock Pot and add the remaining ingredients.   Cook on low settings for 4 hours then puree the soup with an immersion blender.   Serve the soup warm.

Chicken Sausage Rice Soup

Servings: 6   Cooking Time: 6 1/4 Hours

Ingredients:

2 fresh chicken sausages, sliced
1 shallot, chopped
1 carrot, sliced
1 celery stalk, sliced
1 yellow bell pepper, cored and diced
1 cup diced tomatoes
2 large potatoes, peeled and cubed
1/4 cup jasmine rice
2 cups chicken stock
4 cups water
Salt and pepper to taste

Directions:

Combine the chicken, shallot and the rest of the ingredients in your Crock Pot.   Add salt and pepper to taste and cook on low settings for 6 hours.   The soup is best served warm.

Chicken, Corn And Bean Stew

Servings: 10   Cooking Time: 5 Hours 15 Minutes

Ingredients:

3 pounds chicken tenders
1 cup Parmesan cheese, shredded
1 can seasoned diced tomatoes
1 can chili beans
1 can corn, drained

Directions:

Arrange chicken at the bottom of a crockpot and stir in the remaining ingredients.   Cover and cook on HIGH for about 5 hours.   Sprinkle with Parmesan cheese and dish out to serve.

Nutrition Info: Calories: 338 Fat: 14g Carbohydrates: 5.9g

Creamy Leek And Potato Soup

Servings: 6   Cooking Time: 6 1/4 Hours

Ingredients:

2 tablespoons olive oil
2 leeks, sliced
1 tablespoon all-purpose flour
2 cups chicken stock
2 cups water
4 large potatoes, peeled and cubed
Salt and pepper to taste
1/2 cup heavy cream
1 thyme sprig

Directions:

Heat the oil in a skillet and add the leeks. Sauté for 5 minutes until softened. Add the flour and cook for additional minute.   Transfer the mixture in your Crock Pot and add the remaining ingredients, except the cream.   Cook on low settings for 6 hours.   When done, remove the thyme sprig, add the cream and puree the soup with an immersion blender.   Serve the soup warm or chilled.

Fennel Stew

Servings: 6   Cooking Time: 5 Hours

Ingredients:

1-pound beef sirloin, chopped
1 cup fennel bulb,
1 yellow onion, chopped
1 tablespoon dried
chopped
3 cups of water
dill
1 teaspoon olive oil

Directions:

Roast beef sirloin in the skillet for 2 minutes per side.   Then transfer the meat in the Crock Pot. Add olive oil, a fennel bulb, water, onion, and dried dill.   Close the lid and cook the stew on high for 5 hours.

Nutrition Info: Per Serving: 160 calories, 23.4g protein, 3.1g carbohydrates, 5.6g fat, 0.9g fiber, 68mg cholesterol, 63mg sodium, 410mg potassium.

Butternut Squash Creamy Soup

Servings: 6   Cooking Time: 4 1/4 Hours

Ingredients:

1 sweet onion, chopped
2 garlic cloves, chopped
2 tablespoons olive oil
2 parsnips, cubed
2 cups butternut squash cubed
1 celery root, peeled and cubed
1 potato, peeled and cubed
3 cups water
2 cups chicken stock
Salt and pepper to taste
1 pinch cayenne pepper
1/4 teaspoon cumin powder

Directions:

Heat the oil in a skillet and stir in the onion and garlic. Sauté for 2-3 minutes until softened then transfer in your Crock Pot.   Add the remaining ingredients then season with salt and pepper. Cook the soup on low settings for 4 hours.   When done, remove the lid and puree the soup with an immersion blender.   Serve the soup warm.

Zucchini Soup

Servings: 6   Cooking Time: 2 1/4 Hours

Ingredients:

1 pound Italian sausages, sliced
2 celery stalks, sliced
2 zucchinis, cubed
2 large potatoes, peeled and cubed
2 yellow bell peppers, cored and diced
2 carrots, sliced
1 shallot, chopped
3 cups water
2 cups vegetable stock
1/2 teaspoon dried oregano
1/2 teaspoon dried basil
1/4 teaspoon garlic powder
Salt and pepper to taste
2 tablespoons chopped parsley

Directions:

Combine the sausages, celery stalks, zucchinis, potatoes, bell peppers, carrots, shallot, water, stock and seasoning in your Crock Pot.   Add salt and pepper to taste and cook on high settings for hours. When done, stir in the parsley and serve the soup warm.

Garlicky Spinach Soup With Herbed Croutons

Servings: 6   Cooking Time: 2 1/4 Hours

Ingredients:

1 pound fresh spinach, shredded	2 cups chicken stock
1/2 teaspoon dried oregano	1 lemon, juiced
1 shallot, chopped	1/2 cup half and half
4 garlic cloves, chopped	10 oz. one-day old bread, cubed
1/2 celery stalk, sliced	3 tablespoons olive oil
2 cups water	1 teaspoon dried basil
Salt and pepper to taste	1 teaspoon dried marjoram

Directions:
Combine the spinach, oregano, shallot, garlic and celery in your Crock Pot.   Add the water, stock and lemon juice, as well as salt and pepper to taste and cook on high settings for hours.   While the soup is cooking, place the bread cubes in a large baking tray and drizzle with olive oil. Sprinkle with salt and pepper and cook in the preheated oven at 5F for 10-12 minutes until crispy and golden. When the soup is done, puree it with an immersion blender, adding the half and half while doing so. Serve the soup warm, topped with herbed croutons.

Hot Lentil Soup

Servings: 4   Cooking Time: 24.5 Hours

Ingredients:

1 potato, peeled, diced	1 onion, diced
1 cup lentils	1 teaspoon cayenne pepper
5 cups chicken stock	1 teaspoon olive oil
1 teaspoon chili powder	1 tablespoon tomato paste

Directions:
Roast the onion in the olive oil until light brown and transfer in the Crock Pot.   Add lentils, chicken stock, potato, chili powder, cayenne pepper, and tomato paste.   Carefully stir the soup mixture until the tomato paste is dissolved. Close the lid and cook the soup on High for 5 hours.
Nutrition Info: Per Serving: 242 calories, 14.7g protein, 41.1g carbohydrates, 2.7g fat, 16.7g fiber, 0mg cholesterol, 972mg sodium, 758mg potassium.

Garlic Bean Soup

Servings: 4   Cooking Time: 8 Hours

Ingredients:

1 teaspoon minced garlic	5 cups of water
1 cup celery stalk, chopped	1 teaspoon salt
	1 teaspoon ground paprika
1 cup white beans, soaked	1 tablespoon tomato paste

Directions:
Put all ingredients in the Crock Pot and carefully stir until tomato paste is dissolved.   Then close the lid and cook the soup on low for 8 hours.
Nutrition Info: Per Serving: 178 calories, 12.3g protein, 32.5g carbohydrates, 0.6g fat, 8.5g fiber,

0mg cholesterol, 623mg sodium, 1031mg potassium.

Salmon Fennel Soup

Servings: 6   Cooking Time: 5 1/4 Hours

Ingredients:

1 shallot, chopped	3 salmon fillets, cubed
1 garlic clove, sliced	
1 fennel bulb, sliced	1 lemon, juiced
1 carrot, diced	1 bay leaf
1 celery stalk, sliced	Salt and pepper to taste

Directions:
Combine the shallot, garlic, fennel, carrot, celery, fish, lemon juice and bay leaf in your Crock Pot. Add salt and pepper to taste and cook on low settings for 5 hours.   Serve the soup warm.

Roasted Tomato Soup

Servings: 6   Cooking Time: 5 Hours

Ingredients:

2 pounds heirloom tomatoes, halved	2 cups vegetable stock
2 red onions, halved	1 cup water
4 garlic cloves	1 carrot, sliced
1 teaspoon dried oregano	1/2 celery root, peeled and cubed
2 tablespoons olive oil	Salt and pepper to taste

Directions:
Combine the tomatoes, red onions, garlic and oregano in a baking tray lined with parchment paper.   Season with salt and pepper and roast in the preheated oven at 400F for 30 minutes. Transfer the vegetables and juices in your Crock Pot.   Add the remaining ingredients and cook on low settings for hours.   When done, puree the soup with an immersion blender.   The soup can be served warm or chilled.

White Mushroom Soup

Servings: 6   Cooking Time: 8 Hours

Ingredients:

9 oz white mushrooms, chopped	6 chicken stock
1 teaspoon dried cilantro	1 teaspoon butter
	1 cup potatoes, chopped
1/2 teaspoon ground black pepper	1/2 carrot, diced

Directions:
Melt butter in the skillet.   Add white mushrooms and roast them for 5 minutes on high heat. Stir the mushrooms constantly.   Transfer them in the Crock Pot.   Add chicken stock, cilantro, ground black pepper, and potato.   Add carrot and close the lid.   Cook the soup on low for 8 hours.
Nutrition Info: Per Serving: 44 calories, 2.5g protein, 6.7g carbohydrates, 1.4g fat, 1.2g fiber, 2mg cholesterol, 776mg sodium, 271mg potassium.

Chicken Chickpea Soup

Servings: 8   Cooking Time: 6 1/4 Hours

Ingredients:

1/4 pound dried chickpeas, rinsed	2 garlic cloves, chopped
2 chicken breasts, cubed	1 leek, sliced
1 chorizo link, sliced	2 cups chicken stock
2 tablespoons canola oil	6 cups water
2 carrots, diced	1/2 teaspoon dried marjoram
1 celery stalk	Salt and pepper to taste
1 pound potatoes, peeled and cubed	2 tablespoons chopped cilantro

Directions:

Heat the oil in a skillet and add the chicken and chorizo. Sauté for 5 minutes on all sides then transfer in your Crock Pot.   Add the carrots, celery, potatoes, garlic, leek, stock, water and marjoram, as well as salt and pepper.   Cook on low settings for 6 hours.   When done, stir in the cilantro and serve the soup warm.

Chicken Bacon Orzo Soup

Servings: 6 (1.7 Ounces Per Serving)   Cooking Time: 5 Hours

Ingredients:

5 slices of bacon	½ cup orzo
2 cups yellow onion, diced	1 ½ teaspoons sea salt
2 cloves garlic, minced	½ teaspoon fresh ground pepper
1 cup carrots, diced	Parsley, fresh, chopped to taste
1 cup celery, diced	
6 cups chicken stock	

Directions:

Cook bacon in pan over medium-high heat until crisp.   Place bacon on plate lined with paper towels.   Save 2 tablespoons of fat from pan.   Add the garlic, celery, carrots, onions to the pan with a pinch of salt.   Cook the veggies over medium heat for several minutes, stirring periodically.   Place chicken breasts in Crock-Pot and cover with veggies and chicken stock.   Cover and cook over LOW heat for 5 hours.   Halfway through cooking time, take out chicken, shred it up, and then place back in Crock-Pot along with orzo.   Garnish each bowl of soup with diced bacon and fresh parsley.   Serve hot.

Nutrition Info: Calories: 507, Total Fat: 7 g, Saturated Fat: 1 g, Sodium: 220 mg, Carbs: 87 g, Fiber: 23 g, Sugars: 10 g, Protein: 28.3 g

Chicken Rice Soup

Servings: 8   Cooking Time: 7 1/4 Hours

Ingredients:

2 chicken breasts, cubed	2 carrots, diced
2 tablespoons canola oil	1 parsnip, diced
	1 can diced tomatoes
	2 cups water

2 red bell peppers, cored and diced	2 cups chicken stock
1 celery stalk, sliced	2/3 cup white rice, rinsed
1 sweet onion, chopped	Salt and pepper to taste

Directions:

Heat the canola oil in a skillet and stir in the chicken. Cook for 5 minutes on all sides until golden.   Transfer the chicken in a Crock Pot and stir in the remaining ingredients.   Add salt and pepper to taste and cook on low settings for 7 hours.   Serve the soup warm or re-heat it when needed.

Smoked Sausage Lentil Soup

Servings: 6   Cooking Time: 6 1/4 Hours

Ingredients:

2 links smoked sausages, sliced	1/2 teaspoon smoked paprika
1 sweet onion, chopped	1 bay leaf
2 carrots, diced	1 thyme sprig
1 cup red lentils	1 lemon, juiced
1/2 cup green lentils	1 cup fire roasted tomatoes
2 cups chicken stock	Salt and pepper to taste
2 cups water	

Directions:

Combine the sausages with the remaining ingredients in your Crock Pot.   Add salt and pepper to taste and cover with a lid.   Cook on low settings for 6 hours.   The soup can be served both warm and chilled.

Chorizo Soup

Servings: 6   Cooking Time: 5 Hours

Ingredients:

9 oz chorizo, chopped	1 zucchini, chopped
7 cups of water	½ cup spinach, chopped
1 cup potato, chopped	
1 teaspoon minced garlic, chopped	1 teaspoon salt

Directions:

Put the chorizo in the skillet and roast it for 2 minutes per side on high heat.   Then transfer the chorizo in the Crock Pot.   Add water, potato, minced garlic, zucchini, spinach, and salt.   Close the lid and cook the soup on high for 5 hours. Then cool the soup to the room temperature.

Nutrition Info: Per Serving: 210 calories, 11g protein, 4.3g carbohydrates, 16.4g fat, 0.7g fiber, 37mg cholesterol, 927mg sodium, 326mg potassium.

Italian Barley Soup

Servings: 8   Cooking Time: 6 1/4 Hours

Ingredients:

2 tablespoons olive oil	1 celery stalk, diced
1 shallot, chopped	1 teaspoon dried oregano
1 garlic clove, chopped	1 teaspoon dried basil
1 carrot, diced	2/3 cup pearl barley
2 red bell peppers, cored and diced	3 cups water
2 tomatoes, peeled and diced	2 cups fresh spinach, chopped
2 cups vegetable stock	1 lemon, juiced
	Salt and pepper to taste

Directions:
Heat the oil in a skillet and stir in the shallot, garlic, carrot and celery, as well as bell peppers.   Cook for 5 minutes just until softened then transfer in your Crock Pot. You can skip this step, but sautéing the vegetables first improves the taste.   Add the remaining ingredients to the pot and season with salt and pepper.   Cook on low settings for 6 hours.   The soup is great served either warm or chilled.

Vegetable Chickpea Soup

Servings: 6   Cooking Time: 6 1/2 Hours

Ingredients:

2/3 cup dried chickpeas, rinsed	1 shallot, chopped
2 cups chicken stock	1 red bell pepper, cored and diced
4 cups water	1 potato, peeled and diced
1 celery stalk, sliced	1 tablespoon lemon juice
1 carrot, diced	Salt and pepper to taste
2 ripe tomatoes, peeled and diced	

Directions:
Combine all the ingredients in your Crock Pot. Add salt and pepper to taste and cook on low settings for 6 hours.   Serve the soup warm and fresh.

Orange Salmon Soup

Servings: 8   Cooking Time: 2 1/4 Hours

Ingredients:

1 sweet onion, chopped	1 cup diced tomatoes
1 garlic clove, chopped	2 cups vegetable stock
1 celery stalk, sliced	3 cups water
1 small fennel bulb, sliced	1 lemon, juiced
3 salmon fillets, cubed	1 orange, juiced
	1/2 teaspoon grated orange zest
	Salt and pepper to taste

Directions:
Combine the onion, garlic, celery, fennel bulb, tomatoes, salmon, stock and water in your Crock Pot.   Add the remaining ingredients and season with salt and pepper.   Cook on high settings for 2 hours.   Serve the soup warm or chilled.

Chicken Gnocchi Soup

Servings: 8   Cooking Time: 6 1/4 Hours

Ingredients:

1 sweet onion, chopped	2 carrots, sliced
1 garlic clove, chopped	8 oz. gnocchi
8 chicken thighs, without skin	1 can condensed cream of mushroom soup
1 celery stalk, sliced	2 cups chicken stock
1 cup frozen green peas	3 cups water
	1 thyme sprig
	1 rosemary sprig
	Salt and pepper to taste

Directions:
Combine the onion, garlic, chicken thighs, carrots, celery, peas and gnocchi in your Crock Pot.   Add the mushroom soup, stock, water, thyme and rosemary and season with salt and pepper.   Cook on low settings for 6 hours.   The soup is best served warm.

Crab Stew

Servings: 4   Cooking Time: 5 Hours

Ingredients:

8 oz crab meat, chopped	½ cup mango, chopped
1 teaspoon dried lemongrass	1 potato, peeled chopped
1 teaspoon ground turmeric	1 cup of water
	½ cup of coconut milk

Directions:
Put all ingredients in the Crock Pot.   Gently stir them with the help of the spoon and close the lid. Cook the stew on low for 5 hours.   Then leave the cooked stew for 10-15 minutes to rest.
Nutrition Info: Per Serving: 167 calories, 8.9g protein, 13.6g carbohydrates, 8.3g fat, 2.1g fiber, 30mg cholesterol, 364mg sodium, 310mg potassium.

Three Bean Soup

Servings: 10   Cooking Time: 4 1/2 Hours

Ingredients:

2 tablespoons olive oil	2 carrots, diced
2 sweet onions, chopped	1 can (15 oz.) pinto beans, drained
2 garlic cloves, minced	2 cups chicken stock
2 red bell peppers, cored and diced	4 cups water
1 can (15 oz.) black beans, drained	1 cup diced tomatoes
1 can (15 oz.) kidney beans, drained	Salt and pepper to taste
	1 lime, juiced
	1/2 cup sour cream
	2 tablespoons chopped parsley

Directions:
Heat the oil in a skillet and stir in the onions, garlic, peppers and carrot. Sauté for 5 minutes. Transfer the mixture in your Crock Pot and stir in the beans, stock, water, tomatoes, salt and pepper. Cook on low settings for 4 hours.   When done, add the lime juice.   Pour the soup in serving bowls and top with sour cream and parsley.   The soup is best served warm or cold.

Okra Vegetable Soup

Servings: 8   Cooking Time: 7 1/4 Hours

Ingredients:

1 pound ground beef	2 potatoes, peeled
2 tablespoons canola	and cubed
oil	1/2 cup sweet corn,
2 shallots, chopped	drained
1 carrot, sliced	Salt and pepper to
1 can fire roasted	taste
tomatoes, chopped	2 cups water
2 cups chopped okra	2 cups chicken stock
1/2 cup green peas	1 lemon, juiced

Directions:
Heat the oil in a skillet and stir in the beef. Cook for a few minutes then transfer the meat in your Crock Pot.   Add the shallots, carrot, tomatoes, okra, peas, potatoes, corn, water and stock, as well as lemon juice, salt and pepper.   Cook the soup on low settings for 7 hours.   Serve the soup warm and fresh.

Smoked Sausage Cabbage Soup

Servings: 8   Cooking Time: 7 1/4 Hours

Ingredients:

4 smoked sausage	2 cups chicken stock
links, sliced	4 cups water
2 sweet onions,	1/4 teaspoon cumin
chopped	seeds
1 head green cabbage,	1/4 teaspoon chili
shredded	powder
1 cup fire roasted	Salt and pepper to
tomatoes	taste
1 thyme sprig	

Directions:
Combine the sausage links, onions, cabbage, tomatoes, thyme sprig, stock, water, cumin seeds and chili powder in your Crock Pot.   Add salt and pepper to taste and cook on low settings for 7 hours.   Serve the soup warm.

Black Bean Mushroom Soup

Servings: 8   Cooking Time: 6 1/2 Hours

Ingredients:

2 garlic cloves,	1 shallot, chopped
chopped	4 cups water
1 can (15 oz.) black	1/2 teaspoon mustard
beans, drained	seeds
1/2 pound	1/2 teaspoon cumin
mushrooms, sliced	seeds
1 can fire roasted	Salt and pepper to
tomatoes	taste
2 cups vegetable	2 tablespoons
stock	chopped parsley

Directions:
Combine the shallot, garlic and black beans with the mushrooms, tomatoes, stock, water and seeds in your Crock Pot.   Add salt and pepper to taste and cook on low settings for 6 hours.   When done, add the parsley and serve the soup warm.

Ham And Sweet Potato Soup

Servings: 6   Cooking Time: 3 1/2 Hours

Ingredients:

1 1/2 cups diced ham	1 parsnip, diced
1 sweet onion,	2 cups chicken stock
chopped	2 cups water
1 carrot, diced	1 bay leaf
1 celery stalk, diced	1 thyme sprig
2 large sweet	Salt and pepper to
potatoes, peeled and	taste
cubed	

Directions:
Combine all the ingredients in your Crock Pot. Add salt and pepper to taste and cook on high settings for 3 hours.   Serve the soup warm and fresh.

Indian Cauliflower Creamy Soup

Servings: 8   Cooking Time: 6 1/2 Hours

Ingredients:

2 tablespoons olive	2 medium size
oil	potatoes, peeled and
1 sweet onion,	cubed
chopped	2 cups vegetable
1 celery stalk, sliced	stock
2 garlic cloves,	2 cups water
chopped	1/4 teaspoon cumin
1 tablespoon red	powder
curry paste	1 pinch red pepper
1 cauliflower head,	flakes
cut into florets	Salt and pepper to
	taste

Directions:
Heat the oil in a skillet and stir in the onion, celery and garlic. Sauté for 2 minutes until softened. Transfer the mix in your Crock Pot.   Add the remaining ingredients and cook on low settings for 6 hours.   When done, puree the soup with an immersion blender and serve it warm.

Kielbasa Kale Soup

Servings: 8   Cooking Time: 6 1/4 Hours

Ingredients:

1 pound kielbasa	1/2 pound kale,
sausages, sliced	shredded
1 sweet onion,	2 cups chicken stock
chopped	2 cups water
1 carrot, diced	1/2 teaspoon dried
1 parsnip, diced	oregano
1 red bell pepper,	1/2 teaspoon dried
cored and diced	basil
1 can (15 oz.) white	Salt and pepper to
beans, drained	taste
1 cup diced tomatoes	

Directions:
Combine the kielbasa sausages, onion, carrot, parsnip, bell pepper, white beans, tomatoes and kale in a Crock Pot.   Add the remaining ingredients and season with salt and pepper. Cook on low settings for 6 hours.   Serve the soup warm or chilled.

Chicken Taco Soup

Servings: 8   Cooking Time: 6 1/2 Hours

Ingredients:

4 chicken breasts, cut into strips	1/2 cup canned corn, drained
1 large onion, chopped	1 cup dark beer
2 garlic cloves, chopped	1 tablespoon Taco seasoning
1 can (15 oz.) pinto beans, drained	2 cups chicken stock
1 can (15 oz.) black beans, drained	4 cups water
1 cup diced tomatoes	Salt and pepper to taste
	Tortilla chips for serving

Directions:
Combine the chicken, onion, garlic, beans and tomatoes in your Crock Pot.   Add the corn, beer, seasoning, stock and water then season with salt and pepper.   Cook the soup on low settings for 6 hours.   Serve the soup warm, topped with tortilla chips.

Southwestern Turkey Stew

Servings: 6   Cooking Time: 7 Hours 15 Minutes

Ingredients:

½ cup red kidney beans	½ medium onion, diced
½ cup corn	½ cup sour cream
2 cups diced canned tomatoes	½ cup cheddar cheese, shredded
15 oz ground turkey	
1 cup red bell peppers, sliced	1 garlic clove, minced
	1½ medium red potatoes, cubed

Directions:
Put all the ingredients in a bowl except sour cream and cheddar cheese.   Transfer into the crock pot and cook on LOW for about 7 hours.   Stir in the sour cream and cheddar cheese.   Dish out in a bowl and serve hot.
Nutrition Info: Calories: 332 Fat: 15.5g Carbohydrates: 17.1g Protein: 27.7g

Summer Squash Chickpea Soup

Servings: 6   Cooking Time: 2 1/2 Hours

Ingredients:

1 sweet onion, chopped	3 cups water
1 garlic clove, chopped	1 cup diced tomatoes
1 carrot, diced	1 bay leaf
1 celery stalk, sliced	1 thyme sprig
2 summer squashes, cubed	Salt and pepper to taste
1 can (15 oz.) chickpeas, drained	1 lemon, juiced
2 cups chicken stock	1 tablespoon chopped cilantro
	1 tablespoon chopped parsley

Directions:
Combine the onion, garlic, celery, carrot, summer squash, chickpeas, stock and water in your Crock Pot.   Add the tomatoes, bay leaf, thyme, salt and pepper and cook on high settings for hours.

When done, stir in the lemon juice, parsley and cilantro and serve the soup warm.

Russet Potato Soup

Servings: 6   Cooking Time: 7 Hours

Ingredients:

1 cup onion, diced	5 cups of water
2 cups russet potatoes, chopped	1 garlic clove
1 teaspoon dried parsley	½ cup carrot, grated
	1 oz Parmesan, grated
	1 cup heavy cream

Directions:
Put the onion in the Crock Pot.   Add water, potatoes, parsley, peeled garlic clove, carrot, and heavy cream.   Close the lid and cook the soup on low for 7 hours.   When the time is finished, mash the soup gently with the help of the potato mash. Add Parmesan and stir the soup.
Nutrition Info: Per Serving: 131 calories, 3.1g protein, 11.5g carbohydrates, 8.5g fat, 1.9g fiber, 31mg cholesterol, 68mg sodium, 281mg potassium.

Haddock Stew

Servings: 6   Cooking Time: 3 Hours

Ingredients:

2 teaspoons tomato paste	½ cup clam juice
2 celery stalks, chopped	14 oz haddock fillet, chopped
½ teaspoon ground coriander	1 cup of water
	1 teaspoon butter

Directions:
Melt the butter in the skillet and add chopped fish fillets.   Roast them for 1 minute per side and transfer in the Crock Pot.   Add celery stalk, ground coriander, clam juice, and tomato paste. Then add water and close the lid.   Cook the stew on high for 3 hours.   Carefully stir the stew before serving.
Nutrition Info: Per Serving: 92 calories, 16.3g protein, 2.7g carbohydrates, 1.3g fat, 0.2g fiber, 51mg cholesterol, 142mg sodium, 315mg potassium.

Mexican Style Stew

Servings: 6   Cooking Time: 6 Hours

Ingredients:

1 cup corn kernels	4 cups chicken stock
1 cup green peas	1 teaspoon dried cilantro
¼ cup white rice	
1 teaspoon taco seasoning	1 tablespoon butter

Directions:
Put butter and wild rice in the Crock Pot.   Then add corn kernels, green peas, chicken stock, taco seasoning, and dried cilantro.   Close the lid and cook the stew on Low for 6 hours.
Nutrition Info: Per Serving: 97 calories, 3.2g protein, 15.6g carbohydrates, 2.7g fat, 2g fiber, 5mg cholesterol, 599mg sodium, 148mg potassium.

Potato Kielbasa Soup

Servings: 8   Cooking Time: 6 1/4 Hours

Ingredients:

1 pound kielbasa sausages, sliced	2 large potatoes, peeled and cubed
1 sweet onion, chopped	2 cups chicken stock
2 carrots, diced	3 cups water
1 parsnip, diced	1/2 pound fresh spinach, shredded
1 garlic clove, chopped	1 lemon, juiced
2 red bell peppers, cored and diced	Salt and pepper to taste

Directions:

Combine the sausages, onion, carrots, parsnip, garlic, potatoes and bell peppers in your Crock Pot. Stir in the stock, water, spinach and lemon juice then add salt and pepper to taste.   Cook on low settings for 6 hours.   Serve the soup warm or chilled.

Butternut Squash Chili

Servings: 4   Cooking Time: 3.5 Hours

Ingredients:

1 cup butternut squash, chopped	1 teaspoon smoked paprika
2 tablespoons pumpkin puree	½ teaspoon chili flakes
½ cup red kidney beans, canned	1 tablespoon cocoa powder
½ teaspoon salt	2 cups chicken stock

Directions:

Mix cocoa powder with chicken stock and stir it until smooth.   Then pour the liquid in the Crock Pot.   Add all remaining ingredients and carefully mix the chili.   Close the lid and cook the chili on high for 3.5 hours.

Nutrition Info: Per Serving: 105 calories, 6.3g protein, 20.2g carbohydrates, 0.8g fat, 5g fiber, 0mg cholesterol, 678mg sodium, 506mg potassium.

Chunky Mushroom Soup

Servings: 8   Cooking Time: 8 1/2 Hours

Ingredients:

1 sweet onion, chopped	1 zucchini, cubed
1 garlic clove, chopped	2 tomatoes, peeled and diced
1 yellow bell pepper, cored and diced	2 cups vegetable stock
2 tablespoons olive oil	3 cups water
1 pound fresh mushrooms, chopped	1/2 cup tomato sauce
2 large potatoes, peeled and cubed	Salt and pepper to taste
	1 lemon, juiced
	1 tablespoon chopped dill

Directions:

Heat the oil in a skillet and stir in the onion, garlic and bell pepper. Sauté for 5 minutes until softened then transfer in your Crock Pot.   Add the mushrooms, zucchini, potatoes, tomatoes, stock, water and tomato sauce then season with salt and pepper.   Cook on low settings for 8 hours. When done, add the lemon juice and chopped dill and serve the soup warm or chilled.

Lima Bean Soup

Servings: 8   Cooking Time: 7 1/4 Hours

Ingredients:

2 bacon slices, chopped	1 can diced tomatoes
4 cups frozen lima beans	2 cups vegetable stock
2 shallots, chopped	3 cups water
2 carrots, diced	1 bay leaf
2 potatoes, peeled and cubed	Salt and pepper to taste
1 celery stalk, sliced	1 tablespoon chopped cilantro

Directions:

Combine the bacon, lima beans, shallots, carrots, potatoes, celery and tomatoes in a Crock Pot. Add the remaining ingredients, except cilantro and season with salt and pepper.   Cook on low settings for 7 hours.   When done, stir in the chopped cilantro and serve the soup warm.

Light Zucchini Soup

Servings: 4   Cooking Time: 30 Minutes

Ingredients:

1 large zucchini	4 cups beef broth
1 white onion, diced	½ teaspoon dried rosemary
1 teaspoon dried thyme	

Directions:

Pour the beef broth in the Crock Pot.   Add onion, dried thyme, and dried rosemary.   After this, make the spirals from the zucchini with the help of the spiralizer and transfer them in the Crock Pot. Close the lid and cook the sou on High for 30 minutes.

Nutrition Info: Per Serving: 64 calories, 6.2g protein, 6.5g carbohydrates, 1.6g fat, 1.6g fiber, 0mg cholesterol, 773mg sodium, 462mg potassium.

Mixed Veggies Coconut Soup

Servings: 8   Cooking Time: 7 1/2 Hours

Ingredients:

1 sweet onion, chopped	1/2 head cauliflower, cut into florets
2 garlic cloves, chopped	1/2 teaspoon cumin powder
1 teaspoon grated ginger	1/4 teaspoon chili powder
2 tablespoons red curry paste	1 cup coconut milk
2 tablespoons olive oil	3 cups vegetable stock
2 large sweet potatoes, peeled and cubed	Salt and pepper to taste
	1/2 lemongrass stalk

Directions:

Heat the oil in a skillet or saucepan and add the onion, garlic, ginger and curry paste.   Cook for a few minutes until softened then transfer in your Crock Pot.   Add the cauliflower, sweet potatoes, cumin powder, chili powder and coconut milk, as well as stock and lemongrass.   Season with salt and pepper and cook on low settings for 7 hours. When done, remove the lemongrass stalk and puree the soup in a blender or use an immersion blender instead.   Serve the soup warm.

Quinoa Soup With Parmesan Topping

Servings: 6   Cooking Time: 3 1/2 Hours

Ingredients:

2 chicken breasts, cubed	1 sweet onion, chopped
2 tablespoons olive oil	1 garlic clove, chopped
2/3 cup quinoa, rinsed	2 cups chicken stock
1/2 teaspoon dried oregano	4 cups water
1/2 teaspoon dried basil	Salt and pepper to taste
1 cup diced tomatoes	1 cup grated Parmesan for serving

Directions:

Heat the oil in a skillet and add the chicken. Cook on all sides until golden brown then transfer the chicken in your Crock Pot.   Add the remaining ingredients, except the Parmesan, and cook on high settings for 3 hours.   When done, pour the soup into serving bowls and top with grated Parmesan before serving.

Asparagus Crab Soup

Servings: 6   Cooking Time: 2 1/4 Hours

Ingredients:

1 tablespoon olive oil	1 cup green peas
1 shallot, chopped	1 cup chicken stock
1 celery stalk, sliced	2 cups water
1 bunch asparagus, trimmed and chopped	Salt and pepper to taste
	1 can crab meat, drained

Directions:

Heat the oil in a skillet and add the shallot and celery. Sauté for 2 minutes until softened then transfer in your Crock Pot.   Add the asparagus, green peas, stock and water and season with salt and pepper.   Cook on high settings for 2 hours. When done, puree the soup with an immersion blender until creamy.   Pour the soup into serving bowls and top with crab meat.   Serve the soup right away.

Curried Vegetable Soup

Servings: 10   Cooking Time: 6 1/2 Hours

Ingredients:

1 sweet onion, finely chopped	1/2 head cabbage, shredded
4 garlic cloves, chopped	2 tomatoes, peeled and diced
2 tablespoons olive oil	2 tablespoons red curry paste
1 teaspoon grated ginger	2 cups vegetable stock
1/2 head cauliflower, cut into florets	4 cups water
2 large potatoes, peeled and cubed	1/2 lemongrass talk, crushed
1 cup green peas	Salt and pepper to taste

Directions:

Heat the olive oil in a skillet and stir in the onion and garlic. Cook for 2 minutes then add the ginger and curry paste. Sauté for 2 additional minutes then transfer in your Crock Pot.   Add the cauliflower, potatoes, cabbage, tomatoes, green peas, stock and water, as well as the lemongrass stalk.   Season with salt and pepper and cook on low settings for 6 hours.   Serve the soup warm.

Mussel Stew

Servings: 4   Cooking Time: 55 Minutes

Ingredients:

1-pound mussels	1 eggplant, chopped
2 garlic cloves, diced	1 cup coconut cream
1 teaspoon smoked paprika	1 tablespoon sesame seeds
½ teaspoon chili powder	1 teaspoon tomato paste

Directions:

Put all ingredients from the list above in the Crock Pot and gently stir.   Close the lid and cook the mussel stew for 55 minutes on High.

Nutrition Info: Per Serving: 283 calories, 16.7g protein, 16g carbohydrates, 18.3g fat, 6g fiber, 32mg cholesterol, 341mg sodium, 832mg potassium.

Moroccan Lamb Soup

Servings: 6   Cooking Time: 7 1/2 Hours

Ingredients:

1 pound lamb shoulder	3 cups water
1 teaspoon turmeric powder	1 cup canned chickpeas, drained
1/2 teaspoon cumin powder	1 thyme sprig
1/2 teaspoon chili powder	1/2 teaspoon dried sage
2 tablespoons canola oil	1/2 teaspoon dried oregano
2 cups chicken stock	Salt and pepper to taste
1 cup fire roasted tomatoes	1 lemon, juiced

Directions:

Sprinkle the lamb with salt, pepper, turmeric, cumin powder and chili powder.   Heat the oil in a skillet and add the lamb. Cook on all sides for a few minutes then transfer it in a Crock Pot.   Add the remaining ingredients and season with salt and pepper.   Cook the soup on low settings for 7 hours.   Serve the soup warm.

Leek Potato Soup

Servings: 8   Cooking Time: 6 1/2 Hours

Ingredients:

4 leeks, sliced	3 cups water
1 tablespoon olive oil	1 bay leaf
4 bacon slices, chopped	Salt and pepper to taste
1 celery stalk, sliced	1/4 teaspoon cayenne pepper
4 large potatoes, peeled and cubed	1/4 teaspoon smoked paprika
2 cups chicken stock	1 thyme sprig
	1 rosemary sprig

Directions:

Heat the oil in a skillet and add the bacon. Cook until crisp then stir in the leeks.   Sauté for 5 minutes until softened then transfer in your Crock Pot.   Add the remaining ingredients and cook on low settings for about 6 hours.   Serve the soup warm.

Spiced Creamy Pumpkin Soup

Servings: 6   Cooking Time: 5 1/4 Hours

Ingredients:

1 shallot, chopped	2 cups water
2 carrots, sliced	1 thyme sprig
2 garlic cloves, chopped	Salt and pepper to taste
2 tablespoons olive oil	1/2 cinnamon stick
1 medium sugar pumpkin, peeled and cubed	1 star anise
	1/2 teaspoon cumin powder
2 cups chicken stock	1/4 teaspoon chili powder

Directions:

Combine the shallot, carrots, garlic and olive oil in a skillet. Cook for 5 minutes until softened. Transfer in your Crock Pot and add the remaining ingredients, including the spices.   Cook on low settings for 5 hours then remove the cinnamon, thyme sprig and star anise and puree the soup with an immersion blender.   The soup can be served either warm or chilled.

Lentil Stew

Servings: 4   Cooking Time: 6 Hours

Ingredients:

2 cups chicken stock	1 eggplant, chopped
½ cup red lentils	1 cup of water
1 tablespoon tomato paste	1 teaspoon Italian seasonings

Directions:

Mix chicken stock with red lentils and tomato paste.   Pour the mixture in the Crock Pot.   Add eggplants and Italian seasonings.   Cook the stew on low for 6 hours.

Nutrition Info: Per Serving: 125 calories, 7.8g protein, 22.4g carbohydrates, 1.1g fat, 11.5g fiber, 1mg cholesterol, 392mg sodium, 540mg potassium.

Ginger Fish Stew

Servings: 5   Cooking Time: 6 Hours

Ingredients:

1 oz fresh ginger, peeled, chopped	1 teaspoon fish sauce
1 cup baby carrot	½ teaspoon ground nutmeg
1-pound salmon fillet, chopped	½ cup green peas
	3 cups of water

Directions:

Put all ingredients in the Crock Pot bowl.   Gently stir the stew ingredients and close the lid.   Cook the stew on low for 6 hours.

Nutrition Info: Per Serving: 159 calories, 19.1g protein, 7.7g carbohydrates, 6.1g fat, 2g fiber, 40mg cholesterol, 153mg sodium, 506mg potassium.

Poultry Recipes

Simple Buttered Rosemary Chicken Breasts

Servings: 4   Cooking Time: 6 Hours

Ingredients:

4 boneless chicken breasts	5 tablespoons butter
Salt and pepper to taste	1 tablespoon parsley
	1 teaspoon rosemary

Directions:

Melt the butter in the skillet.   Season chicken with salt and pepper to taste. Brown all sides of the chicken for 3 minutes.   Transfer into the crockpot and sprinkle with parsley and rosemary. Cook on low for 6 hours or on high for 5 hours.

Nutrition Info: Calories per serving: 459; Carbohydrates: 1.17g; Protein: 61.6g; Fat: 21.5g; Sugar: 0g; Sodium: 527mg; Fiber: 0.6g

Saucy Chicken Thighs

Servings: 6   Cooking Time: 5 Hrs And 20 Minutes

Ingredients:

6 garlic cloves, minced	1 tsp ginger, minced
4 scallions, sliced	2 lbs. chicken thighs, skinless and boneless
1 cup veggie stock	2 cups cabbage, shredded
1 tbsp olive oil	
2 tsp sugar	
1 tbsp soy sauce	

Directions:

Add stock along with other ingredients except cabbage to the Crock Pot.   Put the cooker's lid on and set the cooking time to 5 hours on Low settings.   Toss in cabbage and cook for another minutes on the low setting.   Serve warm.

Nutrition Info: Per Serving: Calories 240, Total Fat 3g, Fiber 4g, Total Carbs 14g, Protein 10g

Mexican Chicken

Servings: 2   Cooking Time: 6 Hours

Ingredients:

½ cup sweet pepper, sliced	2 chicken thighs, skinless, boneless
1 teaspoon cayenne pepper	½ cup salsa verde
1 red onion, sliced	1 cup of water

Directions:

Pour water in the Crock Pot.   Add salsa verde and onion.   Then add cayenne pepper and chicken thighs.   Cook the mixture on High for 3 hours. After this, add sweet pepper and cook the meal on Low for 3 hours.

Nutrition Info: Per Serving: 327 calories, 44g protein, 10.5g carbohydrates, 11.3g fat, 2.1g fiber, 130mg cholesterol, 477mg sodium, 510mg potassium.

Pineapple Chicken

Servings: 4   Cooking Time: 8 Hours

Ingredients:

12 oz chicken fillet	1 tablespoon butter, softened
1 cup pineapple, canned, chopped	1 teaspoon ground black pepper
½ cup Cheddar cheese, shredded	¼ cup of water

Directions:

Grease the Crock Pot bowl bottom with softened butter.   Then cut the chicken fillet into servings and put in the Crock Pot in one layer.   After this, top the chicken with ground black pepper, water, pineapple, and Cheddar cheese.   Close the lid and cook the meal on Low for 8 hours.

Nutrition Info: Per Serving: 266 calories, 28.4g protein, 5.9g carbohydrates, 13.9g fat, 0.7g fiber, 98mg cholesterol, 183mg sodium, 273mg potassium.

Latin Chicken

Servings: 6   Cooking Time: 5 Hours

Ingredients:

6 oz. sweet pepper, julienned	½ cup salsa verde
1 tsp salt	¼ cup sweet corn, frozen
1 tsp chili flakes	
21 oz. chicken thighs	2 cups of water
1 onion, cut into petals	1 peach, pitted, chopped
1 tsp garlic powder	1 tsp canola oil

Directions:

Add chicken, salsa verde, and all other ingredients to the Crock Pot.   Put the cooker's lid on and set the cooking time to 5 hours on High settings. Serve warm.

Nutrition Info: Per Serving: Calories: 182, Total Fat: 9.2g, Fiber: 1g, Total Carbs: 7.35g, Protein: 18g

Crockpot Roasted Chicken

Servings: 8   Cooking Time: 8 Hours

Ingredients:

2 tablespoons olive oil	8 chicken breasts, skin and bones removed
1 cup parsley leaves, chopped	Salt and pepper to taste
5 cloves of garlic, sliced	

Directions:

Place foil in the bottom of the crockpot.   Pour the olive oil.   Season the chicken breasts with parsley leaves, garlic, salt and pepper.   Place in the crockpot and give a good mix.   Close the lid and cook on low for 8 hours and on high for 6 hours.

Nutrition Info: Calories per serving: 526; Carbohydrates: 1.6g; Protein: 60.9g; Fat: 30.3g; Sugar: 0g; Sodium: 536mg; Fiber:0.7 g

Cilantro Lime Chicken

Servings: 3   Cooking Time: 8 Hours
Ingredients:

3 chicken breasts, bones and skin removed	6 cloves of garlic, minced
Juice from 3 limes, freshly squeezed	1 teaspoon cumin
	¼ cup cilantro

Directions:
Place all ingredients in the crockpot.   Give a stir to mix everything.   Close the lid and cook on low for 8 hours or on high for 6 hours.
Nutrition Info: Calories per serving: 522; Carbohydrates: 6.1g; Protein: 61.8g; Fat: 27.1g; Sugar: 2.3g; Sodium: 453mg; Fiber: 1.2g

Chicken Minestrone

Servings: 4   Cooking Time: 3.5 Hours
Ingredients:

10 oz chicken fillet, sliced	2 cup of water
1 cup tomatoes, chopped	1 teaspoon ground cumin
1 teaspoon chili powder	1 cup swiss chard, chopped
1 teaspoon ground paprika	¼ cup red kidney beans, canned

Directions:
Sprinkle the chicken fillet with chili powder, ground paprika, and ground cumin.   Transfer it in the Crock Pot.   Add tomatoes, water, swiss chard, and red kidney beans.   Close the lid and cook the meal on High for 3.5 hours.
Nutrition Info: Per Serving: 189 calories, 23.9g protein, 10g carbohydrates, 5.8g fat, 2.9g fiber, 63mg cholesterol, 95mg sodium, 505mg potassium.

Lemongrass Chicken Thighs

Servings: 6   Cooking Time: 4 Hours
Ingredients:

6 chicken thighs	1 teaspoon salt
1 tablespoon dried sage	2 tablespoons sesame oil
1 teaspoon ground paprika	1 cup of water

Directions:
Mix dried sage with salt, and ground paprika. Then rub the chicken thighs with the sage mixture and transfer in the Crock Pot.   Sprinkle the chicken with sesame oil and water.   Close the chicken on High for hours.
Nutrition Info: Per Serving: 320 calories, 42.3g protein, 0.4g carbohydrates, 15.4g fat, 0.3g fiber, 130mg cholesterol, 514mg sodium, 367mg potassium.

Paella

Servings: 6   Cooking Time: 4 Hours
Ingredients:

12 oz chicken fillet, chopped	2 cups chicken stock
4 oz chorizo, chopped	1 teaspoon dried cilantro
½ cup white rice	1 teaspoon chili flakes
1 teaspoon garlic, diced	Cooking spray

Directions:
Spray the skillet with cooking spray and put the chorizo inside.   Roast the chorizo for minutes per side and transfer in the Crock Pot.   Then put rice in the Crock Pot.   Then add all remaining ingredients and carefully stir the paella mixture. Cook it on High for 4 hours.
Nutrition Info: Per Serving: 254 calories, 22.3g protein, 13.1g carbohydrates, 11.7g fat, 0.2g fiber, 67mg cholesterol, 538mg sodium, 238mg potassium.

Dill Turkey And Peas

Servings: 2   Cooking Time: 5 Hours
Ingredients:

1 pound turkey breast, skinless, boneless and sliced	A pinch of salt and black pepper
1 cup green peas	1 cup chicken stock
½ cup tomato sauce	1 teaspoon garam masala
½ cup scallions, chopped	1 tablespoon dill, chopped

Directions:
In your Crock Pot, mix the turkey with the peas, tomato sauce and the other ingredients, toss, put the lid on and cook on High for 5 hours.   Divide the mix into bowls and serve right away.
Nutrition Info: calories 326, fat 4.6, fiber 6.6, carbs 26.7, protein 44.6

Jalapeno Chicken Wings

Servings: 6   Cooking Time: 3 Hours
Ingredients:

5 jalapenos, minced	½ cup tomato juice
2-pounds chicken wings, skinless	1 teaspoon salt
	¼ cup of water

Directions:
Mix minced jalapenos with tomato juice, salt, and water.   Pour the liquid in the Crock Pot.   Add chicken wings and close the lid.   Cook the meal on High for 3 hours.
Nutrition Info: Per Serving: 294 calories, 44.1g protein, 1.6g carbohydrates, 11.3g fat, 0.4g fiber, 135mg cholesterol, 573mg sodium, 439mg potassium.

Chicken And Mango Mix

Servings: 2   Cooking Time: 5 Hours
Ingredients:

- 1 pound chicken breast, skinless, boneless and sliced
- 1 cup mango, peeled and cubed
- 4 scallions, chopped
- 1 tablespoon avocado oil
- ½ teaspoon chili powder
- ½ teaspoon rosemary, dried
- 1 cup chicken stock
- 1 tablespoon sweet paprika
- A pinch of salt and black pepper
- 1 tablespoon chives, chopped

Directions:
In your Crock Pot, mix the chicken with the mango, scallions, chili powder and the other ingredients, toss, put the lid on and cook on Low for 5 hours. Divide the mix between plates and serve.
Nutrition Info:calories 263, fat 8, fiber 2, carbs 7, protein 12

Turkey With Rice

Servings: 2   Cooking Time: 7 Hours
Ingredients:

- 1 pound turkey breasts, skinless, boneless and cubed
- 1 cup wild rice
- 1 tablespoon cilantro, chopped
- 1 tablespoon oregano, chopped
- 2 tablespoons green onions, chopped
- 2 cups chicken stock
- ½ teaspoon coriander, ground
- ½ teaspoon rosemary, dried
- ½ teaspoon turmeric powder
- A pinch of salt and black pepper

Directions:
In your Crock Pot, mix the turkey with the rice, stock and the other ingredients, toss, put the lid on and cook on Low for 7 hours.   Divide everything between plates and serve.
Nutrition Info:calories 232, fat 12, fiber 2, carbs 6, protein 15

Chicken Stuffed With Plums

Servings: 6   Cooking Time: 4 Hours
Ingredients:

- 6 chicken fillets
- 1 cup plums, pitted, sliced
- 1 cup of water
- 1 teaspoon salt
- 1 teaspoon white pepper

Directions:
Beat the chicken fillets gently and rub with salt and white pepper.   Then put the sliced plums on the chicken fillets and roll them.   Secure the chicken rolls with toothpicks and put in the Crock Pot. Add water and close the lid.   Cook the meal on High for 4 hours.   Then remove the chicken from the Crock Pot, remove the toothpicks and transfer in the serving plates.

Nutrition Info: Per Serving: 283 calories, 42.4g protein, 1.6g carbohydrates, 10.9g fat, 0.2g fiber, 130mg cholesterol, 514mg sodium, 377mg potassium.

Peppercorn Chicken Thighs

Servings: 6   Cooking Time: 4 Hrs
Ingredients:

- 5 lbs. chicken thighs
- Salt and black pepper to the taste
- 1 tsp black peppercorns
- ½ cup white vinegar
- 4 garlic cloves, minced
- 3 bay leaves
- ½ cup of soy sauce

Directions:
Add chicken, peppercorns, and all other ingredients to the Crock Pot.   Put the cooker's lid on and set the cooking time to 4 hours on High settings.   Discard the bay leaves.   Serve warm.
Nutrition Info: Per Serving: Calories: 430, Total Fat: 12g, Fiber: 3g, Total Carbs: 10g, Protein: 36g

Italian Style Tenders

Servings: 4   Cooking Time: 3 Hours
Ingredients:

- 12 oz chicken fillet
- 1 tablespoon Italian seasonings
- ½ cup of water
- 1 tablespoon olive oil
- 1 teaspoon salt

Directions:
Cut the chicken into tenders and sprinkle with salt and Italian seasonings.   Then heat the oil in the skillet.   Add chicken tenders and cook them on high heat for 1 minute per side.   Then put the chicken tenders in the Crock Pot.   Add water and close the lid.   Cook the chicken for 3 hours on High.
Nutrition Info: Per Serving: 202 calories, 24.6g protein, 0.4g carbohydrates, 10.8g fat, 0g fiber, 75mg cholesterol, 657mg sodium, 209mg potassium.

Chicken With Peach And Orange Sauce

Servings: 8   Cooking Time: 6 Hours
Ingredients:

- 6 chicken breasts, skinless and boneless
- 15 ounces canned peaches and their juice
- 12 ounces orange juice
- 2 tablespoons lemon juice
- 1 teaspoon soy sauce

Directions:
In your Crock Pot, mix chicken with orange juice, lemon juice, peaches and soy sauce, toss, cover and cook on Low for 6 hours.   Divide chicken breasts on plates, drizzle peach and orange sauce all over and serve.
Nutrition Info:calories 251, fat 4, fiber 6, carbs 18, protein 14

Crockpot Kalua Chicken

Servings: 4   Cooking Time: 8 Hours

Ingredients:

2 pounds chicken thighs, bones and skin removed	1 tablespoon liquid smoke
1 tablespoon salt	¼ cup water

Directions:
Place all ingredients in the CrockPot.   Close the lid and cook on high for 6 hours or on low for 8 hours.   Once cooked, serve with organic sour cream, avocado slices, and cilantro if desired.
Nutrition Info: Calories per serving: 501; Carbohydrates: 0.6g; Protein: 37.8g; Fat: 36.4g; Sugar: 0g; Sodium: 930mg; Fiber: 0g

Chicken And Cabbage Bowl

Servings: 4   Cooking Time: 7 Hours

Ingredients:

1-pound chicken fillet, sliced	1 teaspoon dried rosemary
1 cup white cabbage, shredded	1 teaspoon salt
1 tablespoon tomato paste	1 teaspoon dried dill
	2 cups of water

Directions:
Mix water with tomato paste and whisk until smooth.   Pour the liquid in the Crock Pot.   Add cabbage, chicken fillet, and all remaining ingredients.   Close the lid and cook the meal on Low for 7 hours.   When the meal is cooked, transfer it in the serving bowls.
Nutrition Info: Per Serving: 225 calories, 33.3g protein, 2.1g carbohydrates, 8.5g fat, 0.8g fiber, 101mg cholesterol, 690mg sodium, 358mg potassium.

Chicken And Sauce(1)

Servings: 8   Cooking Time: 4 Hours

Ingredients:

1 whole chicken, cut into medium pieces	1 teaspoon cinnamon powder
1 tablespoon olive oil	Salt and black pepper to the taste
1 and ½ tablespoons lemon juice	
1 cup chicken stock	1 tablespoon sweet paprika
1 tablespoon cilantro, chopped	1 teaspoon onion powder

Directions:
In your Crock Pot, mix chicken with oil, lemon juice, stock, cilantro, cinnamon, salt, pepper, paprika and onion powder, stir, cover and cook on High for 4 hours.   Divide chicken between plates and serve with cooking sauce drizzled on top.
Nutrition Info:calories 261, fat 4, fiber 6, carbs 12, protein 22

Tomato Chicken Sausages

Servings: 4   Cooking Time: 2 Hours

Ingredients:

1-pound chicken sausages	1 cup tomato juice
1 tablespoon dried sage	1 teaspoon salt
	1 teaspoon olive oil

Directions:
Heat the olive oil in the skillet well.   Add chicken sausages and roast them for 1 minute per side on high heat.   Then transfer the chicken sausages in the Crock Pot.   Add all remaining ingredients and close the lid.   Cook the chicken sausages on High for 2 hours.
Nutrition Info: Per Serving: 236 calories, 15.3g protein, 10.5g carbohydrates, 13.7g fat, 1.1g fiber, 0mg cholesterol, 1198mg sodium, 145mg potassium.

Asparagus Chicken Salad

Servings: 4   Cooking Time: 4 Hours

Ingredients:

12 oz chicken fillet	1 tablespoon lemon juice
7 oz asparagus, chopped, boiled	1 teaspoon cayenne pepper
2 tablespoons mayonnaise	1 cup of water

Directions:
Put the chicken in the Crock Pot. Add water and close the lid.   Cook the chicken on high for 4 hours.   Then shred it and mix with chopped asparagus.   Add lemon juice, cayenne pepper, and mayonnaise.   Mix the salad.
Nutrition Info: Per Serving: 203 calories, 25.8g protein, 4g carbohydrates, 8.9g fat, 1.2g fiber, 78mg cholesterol, 127mg sodium, 321mg potassium.

Thyme Chicken

Servings: 6   Cooking Time: 6 Hours

Ingredients:

1 whole chicken	2 carrots, chopped
5 thyme springs, chopped	1 yellow onion, chopped
2 celery stalks, chopped	A pinch of white pepper
3 garlic cloves, minced	Juice of 1 lemon

Directions:
Put half of the thyme, garlic, celery, onion and carrots in your Crock Pot, add the chicken on top and season with a pinch of white pepper.   Add the rest of the thyme, onion, garlic, celery and carrots on top, drizzle the lemon juice, cover and cook on Low for 6 hours.   Divide chicken between plates and serve.
Nutrition Info:calories 230, fat 4, fiber 2, carbs 16, protein 6

Slow Cooked Chicken

Servings: 8   Cooking Time: 8 Hours

Ingredients:

1 big chicken	A pinch of sea salt
1 garlic head, peeled	Black pepper to the
1 yellow onion, chopped	taste
1 lemon, sliced	1 teaspoon thyme, dried
1 tablespoons sweet paprika	2 carrots, chopped

Directions:

Stuff your chicken with half of the garlic and with half of the lemon slices and rub with salt, pepper, thyme and paprika both outside and inside.   Put the carrots on the bottom of your Crock Pot, add the rest of the garlic, onion and lemon slices, place the bird on top, cover and cook on Low for 8 hours. Transfer chicken to a platter, carve and serve with a side salad.

Nutrition Info: calories 200, fat 4, fiber 3, carbs 8, protein 16

Chinese Duck

Servings: 6   Cooking Time: 8 Hours

Ingredients:

1 duck, chopped in medium pieces	2 cups chicken stock
1 celery stalk, chopped	Salt and black pepper to the taste
2 carrots, chopped	1 tablespoon ginger, grated

Directions:

In your Crock Pot, mix duck with celery, carrots, stock, salt, pepper and ginger, stir, cover and cook on Low for 8 hours.   Divide duck, ginger sauce between plates, and serve.

Nutrition Info: calories 200, fat 3, fiber 6, carbs 19, protein 17

Turkey Breast And Cranberries

Servings: 6   Cooking Time: 6 Hours

Ingredients:

6 pound turkey breast, skin and bone in	½ cup balsamic vinegar
4 cups cranberries, rinsed	½ cup maple syrup
3 apples, peeled, cored and sliced	A pinch of sea salt Black pepper to the taste

Directions:

Put the turkey breast in your Crock Pot, add cranberries, apple slices, a pinch of salt, black pepper, vinegar and maple syrup, toss a bit, cover and cook on Low for 6 hours.   Slice turkey breast and divide between plates, mash cranberries and apples a bit, add them on top of the meat and serve right away.

Nutrition Info: calories 360, fat 4, fiber 3, carbs 9, protein 20

Butterychicken Wings

Servings: 6   Cooking Time: 5 Hours

Ingredients:

14 oz. chicken wings	1 tsp olive oil
1 tsp onion powder	1 tbsp flour
1 tsp chili flakes	¼ cup milk
1 tsp garlic powder	1 tsp salt
1 tsp cilantro	1 tbsp heavy cream
1/3 cup butter, melted	1 egg, beaten

Directions:

Add chicken wings, butter, onion powder, salt, garlic powder, cilantro, olive oil, and chili flakes to the Crock Pot.   Mix well to coat the chicken wings with the spices.   Put the cooker's lid on and set the cooking time to 2 hours on High settings. Beat egg with olive oil, milk, flour, and cream in a mixer.   Pour this cream mixture over the cooked chicken.   Put the cooker's lid on and set the cooking time to 3 hours on Low settings.   Serve warm.

Nutrition Info: Per Serving: Calories: 225, Total Fat: 16.2g, Fiber: 0g, Total Carbs: 2.64g, Protein: 17g

Turkey And Corn

Servings: 2   Cooking Time: 7 Hours

Ingredients:

1 red onion	1 cup heavy cream
1 cup corn	½ cup chicken stock
1 pound turkey breasts, skinless, boneless and cubed	½ teaspoon rosemary, dried
2 tablespoons olive oil	A pinch of salt and black pepper
1 tablespoon cumin, ground	1 tablespoon cilantro, chopped

Directions:

In your Crock Pot, mix the turkey with the corn, onion and the other ingredients, toss, put the lid on and cook on Low for 7 hours.   Divide everything into bowls and serve.

Nutrition Info: calories 214, fat 14, fiber 2, carbs 6, protein 15

Duck With Potatoes

Servings: 4   Cooking Time: 6 Hrs

Ingredients:

1 duck, cut into small chunks	4 garlic cloves, minced
Salt and black pepper to the taste	4 tbsp sugar
1 potato, cut into cubes	4 tbsp soy sauce
1-inch ginger root, sliced	2 green onions, chopped
	4 tbsp sherry wine
	¼ cup of water

Directions:

Add duck pieces, garlic and all other ingredients to the Crock Pot.   Put the cooker's lid on and set the cooking time to 6 hours on Low settings.   Serve warm.

Nutrition Info: Per Serving: Calories: 245, Total Fat: 12g, Fiber: 1g, Total Carbs: 6g, Protein: 16g

Chicken And Green Onion Sauce

Servings: 4   Cooking Time: 4 Hours
Ingredients:

2 tablespoons butter, melted
4 chicken breast halves, skinless and boneless
4 green onions, chopped
Salt and black pepper to the taste
8 ounces sour cream

Directions:
In your Crock Pot, mix chicken with melted butter, green onion, salt, pepper and sour cream, cover and cook on High for 4 hours.   Divide chicken between plates, drizzle green onions sauce all over and serve.
Nutrition Info:calories 200, fat 7, fiber 2, carbs 11, protein 20

Carrot Meatballs

Servings: 6   Cooking Time: 6 Hours
Ingredients:

1 cup carrot, shredded
14 oz ground chicken
1 teaspoon cayenne pepper
½ cup of water
1 tablespoon butter
1 teaspoon salt
1 teaspoon ground cumin

Directions:
Mix carrot with ground chicken   Then add cayenne pepper, salt, and ground cumin.   After this, make the small meatballs and put them in the Crock Pot.   Add water and butter.   Close the lid and cook the meatballs on low for 6 hours.
Nutrition Info: Per Serving: 152 calories, 19.4g protein, 2.1g carbohydrates, 7g fat, 0.6g fiber, 64mg cholesterol, 472mg sodium, 232mg potassium.

Beer Chicken

Servings: 4   Cooking Time: 6 Hours
Ingredients:

4 chicken thighs, skinless, boneless
1 tablespoon garlic, diced
1 teaspoon coriander seeds
1 cup beer
1 teaspoon chili flakes
1 tablespoon soy sauce

Directions:
Mix beer with garlic, coriander seeds, chili flakes, and soy sauce.   Put the chicken thighs in the beer mixture and leave for 10-15 minutes to marinate. After this, transfer the mixture in the Crock Pot. Cook the chicken on low for 6 hours.
Nutrition Info: Per Serving: 308 calories, 42.9g protein, 3.1g carbohydrates, 10.8g fat, 0.1g fiber, 130mg cholesterol, 354mg sodium, 389mg potassium.

Garlic Pulled Chicken

Servings: 4   Cooking Time: 4 Hours
Ingredients:

1-pound chicken breast, skinless, boneless
2 cups of water
1 tablespoon minced garlic
½ cup plain yogurt

Directions:
Put the chicken breast in the Crock Pot.   Add minced garlic and water.   Close the lid and cook the chicken on High for 4 hours.   Then drain water and shred the chicken breast.   Add plain yogurt and stir the pulled chicken well.
Nutrition Info: Per Serving: 154 calories, 25.9g protein, 2.9g carbohydrates, 3.2g fat, 0g fiber, 74mg cholesterol, 83mg sodium, 501mg potassium.

Banana Chicken

Servings: 6   Cooking Time: 9 Hours
Ingredients:

2 bananas, chopped
2-pound whole chicken
1 tablespoon taco seasonings
1 tablespoon olive oil
½ cup of soy sauce
½ cup of water

Directions:
Fill the chicken with bananas and secure the whole. Then rub the chicken with taco seasonings and brush with olive oil.   After this, pour water and soy sauce in the Crock Pot.   Add chicken and close the lid.   Cook it on Low for 9 hours.
Nutrition Info: Per Serving: 360 calories, 45.5g protein, 11.9g carbohydrates, 13.7g fat, 1.2g fiber, 135mg cholesterol, 1469mg sodium, 555mg potassium.

Buffalo Chicken Tenders

Servings: 4   Cooking Time: 3.5 Hours
Ingredients:

12 oz chicken fillet
3 tablespoons buffalo sauce
½ cup of coconut milk
1 jalapeno pepper, chopped

Directions:
Cut the chicken fillet into tenders and sprinkle the buffalo sauce.   Put the chicken tenders in the Crock Pot.   Add coconut milk and jalapeno pepper.   Close the lid and cook the meal on high for 3.5 hours.
Nutrition Info: Per Serving: 235 calories, 25.3g protein, 2.4g carbohydrates, 13.5g fat, 1g fiber, 76mg cholesterol, 318mg sodium, 293mg potassium.

Orange Chicken(2)

Servings: 4   Cooking Time: 7 Hours
Ingredients:

1-pound chicken fillet, roughly chopped
4 oranges, peeled, chopped
1 cup of water
1 teaspoon peppercorns
1 onion, diced

Directions:
Put chicken and oranges in the Crock Pot.   Add water, peppercorns, and onion.   Close the lid and cook the meal on Low for 7 hours.
Nutrition Info: Per Serving: 314 calories, 34.9g protein, 24.5g carbohydrates, 8.7g fat, 5.2g fiber, 101mg cholesterol, 101mg sodium, 656mg potassium.

Mustard Chicken

Servings: 4   Cooking Time: 6 Hours
Ingredients:

1 tablespoon avocado oil	1 tablespoon mustard
1-pound chicken breast, skinless, boneless and roughly cubed	1 teaspoon chili flakes
	2 tablespoons apple cider vinegar
	1 garlic clove, peeled
½ cup of water	

Directions:
Mix avocado oil with mustard, chili flakes, and apple cider vinegar.   Mix the chicken with mustard mixture and transfer it in the Crock Pot. Add water and garlic clove.   Cook the chicken on low for 6 hours.
Nutrition Info: Per Serving: 150 calories, 24.8g protein, 1.5g carbohydrates, 4.1g fat, 0.6g fiber, 73mg cholesterol, 60mg sodium, 459mg potassium.

Cinnamon And Cumin Chicken Drumsticks

Servings: 4   Cooking Time: 6 Hours
Ingredients:

8 chicken drumsticks	1 onion, peeled, chopped
1 teaspoon cumin seeds	1 teaspoon salt
1 teaspoon ground cinnamon	2 cups of water

Directions:
Put all ingredients in the Crock Pot and carefully mix.   Close the lid and cook the chicken on low for 6 hours.
Nutrition Info: Per Serving: 170 calories, 25.g protein, 3.3g carbohydrates, 5.4g fat, 1g fiber, 81mg cholesterol, 661mg sodium, 237mg potassium.

Turkey In Pomegranate Juice

Servings: 4   Cooking Time: 7 Hours
Ingredients:

1-pound turkey fillet, sliced	1 teaspoon cornstarch
½ cup pomegranate juice	1 teaspoon dried thyme
1 tablespoon maple syrup	1 teaspoon butter
	¼ cup of water

Directions:
Pour water and pomegranate juice in the Crock Pot. Add cornstarch and whisk the mixture until smooth.   Then add all remaining ingredients and close the lid.   Cook the meal on Low for 7 hours.
Nutrition Info: Per Serving: 150 calories, 23.6g protein, 8.8g carbohydrates, 1.5g fat, 0.1g fiber, 61mg cholesterol, 266mg sodium, 88mg potassium.

Tomato Chicken

Servings: 4   Cooking Time: 9 Hours
Ingredients:

1 lb. chicken wings	1 tsp salt
1 cup canned tomatoes, diced	1 tsp ground cinnamon
½ cup fresh tomatoes	1 cup onion
1 cup fresh parsley	1 tbsp olive oil
	1 tbsp red pepper

Directions:

Blend tomatoes in a blender then add parsley, salt, red pepper, and onion.   Puree this mixture again then pour it into the Crock Pot.   Add chicken wings to the cooker.   Put the cooker's lid on and set the cooking time to 8 hours on Low settings. Mix well and serve warm.
Nutrition Info: Per Serving: Calories: 202, Total Fat: 7.7g, Fiber: 2g, Total Carbs: 6.47g, Protein: 26g

Curried Chicken Strips

Servings: 6   Cooking Time: 4 Hrs
Ingredients:

1 tbsp curry paste	2 tbsp maple syrup
11 oz. chicken fillet, cut into strips	1 tsp olive oil
1 tsp salt	3 tbsp sour cream
	½ cup fresh dill
	1 tbsp ground paprika

Directions:
Add chicken strips and all other ingredients in a Crock Pot.   Mix the chicken strips to coat well. Put the cooker's lid on and set the cooking time to hours on High settings.   Serve warm.
Nutrition Info: Per Serving: Calories: 177, Total Fat: 9.1g, Fiber: 2g, Total Carbs: 18.11g, Protein: 6g

Greece Style Chicken

Servings: 6   Cooking Time: 8 Hours
Ingredients:

12 oz chicken fillet, chopped	1 tablespoon cream cheese
1 cup green olives, chopped	½ teaspoon dried thyme
1 cup of water	

Directions:
Put all ingredients in the Crock Pot.   Close the lid and cook the meal on Low for 8 hours.   Then transfer the cooked chicken in the bowls and top with olives and hot liquid from the Crock Pot.
Nutrition Info: Per Serving: 124 calories,16.7g protein, 0.8g carbohydrates, 5.7g fat, 0.3g fiber, 52mg cholesterol, 167mg sodium, 142mg potassium.

Cocoa Chicken

Servings: 8   Cooking Time: 8 Hours
Ingredients:

2 tablespoons cocoa powder	1 cup of water
2-pound chicken breast, skinless, boneless	1 tablespoon tomato paste
	1 teaspoon hot sauce
	½ cup cream

Directions:
Whisk cocoa powder with cream until smooth and pour the liquid in the Crock Pot.   Mix chicken breast with tomato paste and hot sauce and put in the Crock Pot.   Then add water and close the lid. Cook the chicken on low for 8 hours.   Then shred the chicken and serve it with cocoa gravy.
Nutrition Info: Per Serving: 144 calories, 24.5g protein, 1.6g carbohydrates, 3.9g fat, 0.5g fiber, 75mg cholesterol, 82mg sodium, 480mg potassium.

Mushrooms Stuffed With Chicken

Servings: 6   Cooking Time: 3 Hours

Ingredients:

16 ounces button mushroom caps
4 ounces cream cheese
1 teaspoon ranch seasoning mix
4 tablespoons hot sauce
¾ cup blue cheese, crumbled

¼ cup carrot, chopped
¼ cup red onion, chopped
½ cup chicken meat, ground
Salt and black pepper to the taste
Cooking spray

Directions:

In a bowl, mix cream cheese with blue cheese, hot sauce, ranch seasoning, salt, pepper, chicken, carrot and red onion, stir and stuff mushrooms with this mix.   Grease your Crock Pot with cooking spray, add stuffed mushrooms, cover and cook on High for 3 hours.   Divide mushrooms between plates and serve.

Nutrition Info:calories 240, fat 4, fiber 1, carbs 12, protein 7

Chicken And Tomatillos

Servings: 6   Cooking Time: 4 Hours

Ingredients:

1 pound chicken thighs, skinless and boneless
2 tablespoons olive oil
1 yellow onion, chopped
1 garlic clove, minced
4 ounces canned green chilies, chopped
A handful cilantro, chopped
Salt and black pepper to the taste

15 ounces canned tomatillos, chopped
5 ounces canned garbanzo beans, drained
15 ounces rice, cooked
5 ounces tomatoes, chopped
15 ounces cheddar cheese, grated
4 ounces black olives, pitted and chopped

Directions:

In your Crock Pot, mix oil with onions, garlic, chicken, chilies, salt, pepper, cilantro and tomatillos, stir, cover the Crock Pot and cook on High for 3 hours   Take chicken out of the Crock Pot, shred, return to Crock Pot, add rice, beans, cheese, tomatoes and olives, cover and cook on High for 1 more hour.   Divide between plates and serve.

Nutrition Info:calories 300, fat 11, fiber 3, carbs 14, protein 30

Easy Chicken Adobo

Servings: 4   Cooking Time: 4 Hours

Ingredients:

1 teaspoon minced garlic
1 cup onion, chopped
½ teaspoon ground ginger
4 chicken thighs, skinless, boneless

1 tablespoon balsamic vinegar
1 tablespoon soy sauce
½ teaspoon ground black pepper
½ cup of water

Directions:

Put the onion in the Crock Pot.   Then mix soy sauce with balsamic vinegar and minced garlic. Rub the chicken with garlic mixture and put it in the Crock Pot.   Then add ground black pepper, ginger, and water.   Cook the meal on High for 4 hours.

Nutrition Info: Per Serving: 294 calories, 42.9g protein, 3.6g carbohydrates, 10.9g fat, 0.8g fiber, 130g cholesterol, 354mg sodium, 418mg potassium.

Crock Pot Chicken Breasts

Servings: 4   Cooking Time: 4 Hours

Ingredients:

6 chicken breasts, skinless and boneless
Salt and black pepper to the taste
¼ cup jalapenos, chopped
5 bacon slices, chopped

8 ounces cream cheese
¼ cup yellow onion, chopped
½ cup mayonnaise
½ cup parmesan, grated
1 cup cheddar cheese, grated

Directions:

Arrange chicken breasts in your Crock Pot, add salt, pepper, jalapenos, bacon, cream cheese, onion, mayo, parmesan and cheddar, cover and cook on High for 4 hours.   Divide between plates and serve.

Nutrition Info:calories 340, fat 12, fiber 2, carbs 15, protein 20

Spaghetti Chicken Salad

Servings: 6   Cooking Time: 5.5 Hrs

Ingredients:

1 lb. chicken breast
½ cup onion, sliced
6 oz. spaghetti
3 cups chicken stock
1 cup heavy cream
2 tbsp mayo
1 tsp minced garlic
1 tsp paprika
½ tsp salt

½ tsp ground black pepper
1 tsp sesame oil
1 tbsp flax seeds
1 tsp sesame seeds
1 cup lettuce, chopped
2 sweet red peppers, chopped

Directions:

Season the chicken breast with black pepper, salt, and paprika.   Place the chicken breast in the Crock Pot and top it with chicken stock and garlic. Put the cooker's lid on and set the cooking time to 4 hours on High settings.   Remove the slow-cooked chicken and shred with the help of two forks. Return the shreds to the Crock Pot.   Add heavy cream, spaghetti, and sesame seeds to the cooker. Put the cooker's lid on and set the cooking time to 1 hour 30 minutes on High settings.   Stir in sweet pepper, onion, lettuce, and mayonnaise.   Mix well and serve fresh.

Nutrition Info: Per Serving: Calories 312, Total Fat 17.9g, Fiber 2g, Total Carbs 16.37g, Protein 22g

Duck Breast And Veggies

Servings: 2   Cooking Time: 4 Hours

Ingredients:

- 2 duck breasts, skin on and thinly sliced
- 1 tablespoon olive oil
- 1 spring onion stack, chopped
- 2 zucchinis, sliced
- 1 radish, chopped
- 2 green bell peppers, chopped
- Salt and black pepper to the taste

Directions:

In your Crock Pot, mix duck with oil, salt and pepper and toss.   Add zucchinis, onion, radish and bell peppers, cover and cook on High for 4 hours.   Divide everything between plates and serve.

Nutrition Info: calories 450, fat 23, fiber 3, carbs 14, protein 50

Chili Sausages

Servings: 4   Cooking Time: 3 Hours

Ingredients:

- 1-pound chicken sausages, roughly chopped
- ½ cup of water
- 1 tablespoon chili powder
- 1 teaspoon tomato paste

Directions:

Sprinkle the chicken sausages with chili powder and transfer in the Crock Pot.   Then mix water and tomato paste and pour the liquid over the chicken sausages.   Close the lid and cook the meal on High for hours.

Nutrition Info: Per Serving: 221 calories, 15g protein, 8.9g carbohydrates, 12.8g fat, 1.4g fiber, 0mg cholesterol, 475mg sodium, 50mg potassium.

Duck And Mushrooms

Servings: 2   Cooking Time: 6 Hours

Ingredients:

- 1 pound duck leg, skinless, boneless and sliced
- 1 cup white mushrooms, sliced
- ½ teaspoon rosemary, dried
- 1 cup chicken stock
- ½ teaspoon cumin, ground
- ½ cup heavy cream
- 1 tablespoon olive oil
- ¼ cup chives, chopped

Directions:

In your Crock Pot, mix the duck with the stock, mushrooms and the other ingredients, toss, put the lid on and cook on Low for 6 hours.   Divide everything between plates and serve.

Nutrition Info: calories 262, fat 16, fiber 2, carbs 8, protein 16

Pomegranate Turkey

Servings: 4   Cooking Time: 4.5 Hours

Ingredients:

- 1 lb. turkey fillet, diced
- 1 tsp garlic powder
- ¼ cup onion, grated
- ½ cup pomegranate juice
- 2 oz. pomegranate juice
- 1 tbsp soy sauce
- 1 tbsp potato starch
- 1 tsp butter, melted
- 3 tbsp brown sugar
- 1 tsp salt
- 1 tsp ground white pepper

Directions:

Mix turkey with garlic powder, salt, onion, white pepper in a bowl and leave it for   minutes. Transfer the turkey to the Crock Pot along with butter and pomegranate juice.   Put the cooker's lid on and set the cooking time to hours on High settings.   Mix potato starch with soy sauce, 2 oz. pomegranate juice in a bowl.   Pour this mixture into the Crock Pot.   Put the cooker's lid on and set the cooking time to 1.5 hours on High settings. Serve warm.

Nutrition Info: Per Serving: Calories: 676, Total Fat: 52.5g, Fiber: 3g, Total Carbs: 26.15g, Protein: 24g

Oregano Turkey And Tomatoes

Servings: 4   Cooking Time: 7 Hours

Ingredients:

- 1 pound turkey breast, skinless, boneless and sliced
- 1 tablespoon oregano, chopped
- 1 cup chicken stock
- 1 cup cherry tomatoes, halved
- 1 teaspoon turmeric powder
- 2 tablespoons olive oil
- 1 cup scallions, chopped
- 1 teaspoon chili powder
- A pinch of salt and black pepper
- ½ cup tomato sauce

Directions:

In your Crock Pot, mix the turkey with the oregano, stock and the other ingredients, toss, put the lid on and cook on Low for 7 hours.   Divide the mix between plates and serve.

Nutrition Info: calories 162, fat 8, fiber 2, carbs 5, protein 9

Chicken Potato Sandwich

Servings: 4   Cooking Time: 8 Hrs

Ingredients:

- 7 oz. chicken fillet
- 1 tsp cayenne pepper
- 5 oz. mashed potato, cooked
- 6 tbsp chicken gravy
- 4 slices French bread, toasted
- 2 tsp mayo
- 1 cup of water

Directions:

Place the chicken fillet in the Crock Pot and add chicken gravy, water, and cayenne pepper on top. Put the cooker's lid on and set the cooking time to 8 hours on Low settings.   Layer the French bread with mashed potato mixture.   Slice the cooked chicken into strips and return to its gravy.   Mix well, then serve the chicken over the mashed potato.   Serve warm.

Nutrition Info: Per Serving: Calories 314, Total Fat 9.7g, Fiber 3g, Total Carbs 45.01g, Protein 12g

Russian Chicken

Servings: 4 Cooking Time: 4 Hours
Ingredients:

2 tablespoons mayonnaise	1 teaspoon ground black pepper
4 chicken thighs, skinless, boneless	1 teaspoon sunflower oil
1 teaspoon minced garlic	1 teaspoon salt
	½ cup of water

Directions:
In the bowl mix mayonnaise, minced garlic, ground black pepper, salt, and oil.   Then add chicken thighs and mix the ingredients well.   After this, pour water in the Crock Pot. Add chicken thighs mixture.   Cook the meal on High for hours.
Nutrition Info: Per Serving: 319 calories, 42.4g protein, 2.3g carbohydrates, 14.5g fat, 0.2g fiber, 132mg cholesterol, 760mg sodium, 365mg potassium.

Chicken In Apricots

Servings: 4 Cooking Time: 5 Hours
Ingredients:

4 chicken drumsticks	1 teaspoon chili pepper
1 cup of water	
1 teaspoon white pepper	1 cup apricots, pitted, halved
1 teaspoon smoked paprika	1 teaspoon butter

Directions:
Put all ingredients in the Crock Pot and gently stir them.   Close the lid and cook the chicken on low for 5 hours.
Nutrition Info: Per Serving: 108 calories, 13.3g protein, 5g carbohydrates, 3.9g fat, 1.1g fiber, 43mg cholesterol, 46mg sodium, 215mg potassium.

Sesame Chicken Drumsticks

Servings: 4 Cooking Time: 7 Hours
Ingredients:

1-pound chicken drumsticks	1 teaspoon salt
1 teaspoon ground turmeric	1 tablespoon sesame seeds
1 teaspoon chili powder	1 tablespoon olive oil
	1 cup of water

Directions:
Sprinkle the chicken drumsticks with salt, ground turmeric, chili powder, and sesame oil. Mix the chicken well.   Then heat olive oil well and add the chicken drumsticks.   Roast them on high heat for 2 minutes per side.   Transfer the roasted chicken drumsticks in the Crock Pot, add water, and close the lid.   Cook the chicken drumsticks on Low for 7 hours.
Nutrition Info: Per Serving: 239 calories, 31.7g protein, 1.3g carbohydrates, 11.3g fat, 0.6g fiber, 100mg cholesterol, 681mg sodium, 263mg potassium.

Chicken With Green Onion Sauce

Servings: 4 Cooking Time: 4 Hrs
Ingredients:

4 green onions, chopped	2 tbsp butter, melted
4 chicken breast halves, skinless and boneless	Salt and black pepper to the taste
	8 oz. sour cream

Directions:
Add melted butter, chicken, and all other ingredients to the Crock Pot.   Put the cooker's lid on and set the cooking time to 4 hours on High settings.   Serve warm.
Nutrition Info: Per Serving: Calories: 200, Total Fat: 7g, Fiber: 2g, Total Carbs: 11g, Protein: 20g

Curry Chicken Wings

Servings: 4 Cooking Time: 7 Hours
Ingredients:

1-pound chicken wings	½ cup heavy cream
1 teaspoon curry paste	½ teaspoon ground nutmeg
1 teaspoon minced garlic	½ cup of water

Directions:
In the bowl mix curry paste, heavy cream, minced garlic, and ground nutmeg.   Add chicken wings and stir.   Then pour water in the Crock Pot. Add chicken wings with all remaining curry paste mixture and close the lid.   Cook the chicken wings on Low for 7 hours.
Nutrition Info: Per Serving: 278 calories, 33.2g protein, 1.1g carbohydrates, 14.8g fat, 0.1g fiber, 121mg cholesterol, 104mg sodium, 291mg potassium.

Chicken Provolone

Servings: 4 Cooking Time: 8 Hours
Ingredients:

4 chicken breasts, bones and skin removed	8 fresh basil leaves
	4 slices prosciutto
Salt and pepper to taste	4 slices provolone cheese

Directions:
Sprinkle the chicken breasts with salt and pepper to taste.   Place in the crockpot and add the basil leaves, and prosciutto on top.   Arrange the provolone cheese slices on top.   Close the lid and cook on low for 8 hours and on high for 6 hours.
Nutrition Info: Calories per serving: 236; Carbohydrates: 1g; Protein: 33g; Fat: 11g; Sugar:0 g; Sodium: 435mg; Fiber:0 g

Rosemary Chicken

Servings: 2   Cooking Time: 7 Hours
Ingredients:

1 pound chicken thighs, boneless, skinless and sliced
1 tablespoon avocado oil
1 teaspoon cumin, ground

1 tablespoon rosemary, chopped
1 cup chicken stock
A pinch of salt and black pepper
1 tablespoon chives, chopped

Directions:
In your Crock Pot, mix the chicken with the oil, cumin and the other ingredients, toss, put the lid on and cook on Low for 7 hours.   Divide the mix between plates and serve.
Nutrition Info:calories 273, fat 13, fiber 3, carbs 7, protein 17

Chicken Bowl

Servings: 6   Cooking Time: 4 Hours
Ingredients:

1-pound chicken breast, skinless, boneless, chopped
1 cup sweet corn, frozen
1 teaspoon ground paprika

1 teaspoon onion powder
1 cup tomatoes, chopped
1 cup of water
1 teaspoon olive oil

Directions:
Mix chopped chicken breast with ground paprika and onion powder. Transfer it in the Crock Pot. Add water and sweet corn. Cook the mixture on High for 4 hours.   Then drain the liquid and transfer the mixture in the bowl.   Add tomatoes and olive oil. Mix the meal.
Nutrition Info: Per Serving: 122 calories, 17.2g protein, 6.3g carbohydrates, 3g fat, 1.1g fiber, 48mg cholesterol, 45mg sodium, 424mg potassium.

Red Chicken Soup

Servings: 4   Cooking Time: 3 Hours
Ingredients:

3 tablespoons butter, melted
4 ounces cream cheese
2 cups chicken meat, cooked and shredded
1/3 cup red sauce

4 cups chicken stock
Salt and black pepper to the taste
½ cup sour cream
¼ cup celery, chopped

Directions:
In your blender, mix stock with red sauce, cream cheese, butter, salt, pepper and sour cream, pulse well and transfer to your Crock Pot.   Add celery and chicken, stir, cover and cook on High for 3 hours.   Divide into bowls and serve.
Nutrition Info:calories 400, fat 23, fiber 5, carbs 15, protein 30

Lemon Sauce Dipped Chicken

Servings: 11   Cooking Time: 7 Hours
Ingredients:

23 oz. chicken breast, boneless, diced
1 lemon, juiced and zest

1 tbsp flour
1 tsp ground black pepper
1 tsp minced garlic

1 tbsp cornstarch
1 tsp salt
1 cup heavy cream

1 tbsp mustard
3 tbsp lemon juice
1 red onion, chopped

Directions:
Mix lemon juice with salt, garlic, and black pepper in a bowl.   Toss in chicken bread, and onion then mix well. Marinate this chicken for 15 minutes. Transfer the marinated chicken along with lemon marinade to the Crock Pot.   Put the cooker's lid on and set the cooking time to 3 hours on High settings.   Whisk cream with flour, cornstarch, and mustard in a bowl.   Cook this cream mixture in a skillet for 10 minutes then transfer to the Crock Pot.   Put the cooker's lid on and set the cooking time to 4 hours on Low settings.   Serve warm.
Nutrition Info: Per Serving: Calories: 154, Total Fat: 9.6g, Fiber: 0g, Total Carbs: 3.59g, Protein: 13g

Chicken, Peppers And Onions

Servings: 4   Cooking Time: 8 Hours
Ingredients:

1 tablespoon olive oil
½ cup shallots, peeled
½ cup green and red peppers, diced

1-pound boneless chicken breasts, sliced
Salt and pepper to taste

Directions:
Heat oil in a skillet over medium flame.   Sauté the shallots until fragrant and translucent. Allow to cook so that the outer edges of the shallots turn slightly brown.   Transfer into the crockpot. Add the chicken breasts and the peppers.   Season with salt and pepper to taste.   Add a few tablespoons of water.   Close the lid and cook on low for 8 hours or on high for 6 hours.
Nutrition Info: Calories per serving: 179; Carbohydrates: 3.05g; Protein:26.1 g; Fat: 10.4g; Sugar: 0g; Sodium: 538mg; Fiber:2.4 g

Almond-stuffed Chicken

Servings: 6   Cooking Time: 8 Hours
Ingredients:

1/3 cup Boursin cheese or any herbed cheese of your choice
¼ cup slivered almonds, toasted and chopped

1 ½ teaspoons butter
4 boneless chicken breasts, halved
Salt and pepper to taste

Directions:
Line the bottom of the crockpot with foil.   Grease the foil with butter.   In a mixing bowl, mix together the cheese and almonds.   Cut a slit through the chicken breasts to create a pocket. Season the chicken with salt and pepper to taste. Spoon the cheese mixture into the slit on the chicken. Secure the slit with toothpicks.   Place the chicken in the foil-lined crockpot.   Cover with lid and cook on low for hours or on high for 6 hours.
Nutrition Info: Calories per serving: 249; Carbohydrates: 0.9g; Protein: 42.1g; Fat: 10g; Sugar: 0g; Sodium:592 mg; Fiber:0.4 g

Chicken Meatloaf

Servings: 8   Cooking Time: 4 Hours And 20 Minutes

Ingredients:

1 cup marinara sauce
2 pound chicken meat, ground
2 tablespoons parsley, chopped
4 garlic cloves, minced
2 teaspoons onion powder
2 teaspoons Italian seasoning
Salt and black pepper to the taste

Cooking spray
For the filling:
½ cup ricotta cheese
1 cup parmesan, grated
1 cup mozzarella, shredded
2 teaspoons chives, chopped
2 tablespoons parsley, chopped
1 garlic clove, minced

Directions:
In a bowl, mix chicken with half of the marinara sauce, salt, pepper, Italian seasoning, 4 garlic cloves, onion powder and 2 tablespoons parsley and stir well.   In another bowl, mix ricotta with half of the parmesan, half of the mozzarella, chives, 1 garlic clove, salt, pepper and tablespoons parsley and stir well.   Grease your Crock Pot with cooking spray, add half of the chicken mix into the Crock Pot and spread evenly.   Add cheese filling, spread, top with the rest of the meat, spread again, cover and cook on High for hours.   Spread the rest of the marinara sauce, the rest of the parmesan and the mozzarella over the meatloaf, cover Crock Pot and cook on High for 20 minutes more. Leave meatloaf to cool down, slice, divide between plates and serve.

Nutrition Info: calories 273, fat 14, fiber 1, carbs 14, protein 28

Tender Duck Fillets

Servings: 3   Cooking Time: 8 Hours

Ingredients:

1 teaspoon dried rosemary
1 teaspoon ground nutmeg

1 tablespoon butter
9 oz duck fillet
1 cup of water

Directions:
Slice the fillet.   Then melt the butter in the skillet.   Add sliced duck fillet and roast it for 2-minutes per side on medium heat.   Transfer the roasted duck fillet and butter in the Crock Pot. Add dried rosemary, ground nutmeg, and water. Close the lid and cook the meal on Low for 8 hours.

Nutrition Info: Per Serving: 145 calories, 25.2g protein, 0.6g carbohydrates, 4.7g fat, 0.3g fiber, 10mg cholesterol, 158mg sodium, 61mg potassium.

Chicken Pasta Casserole

Servings: 6   Cooking Time: 7 Hours

Ingredients:

1 cup pasta, cooked, chopped
1 cup cream
1 teaspoon cayenne pepper
1 teaspoon salt

½ cup Mozzarella, shredded
12 oz ground chicken
1 teaspoon avocado oil

Directions:
Pour the avocado oil in the Crock Pot.   Then mix ground chicken with salt and cayenne pepper. Put the ground chicken in the Crock Pot and flatten it gently.   After this, add pasta and shredded Mozzarella.   Add cream and close the lid.   Cook the casserole on Low for 7 hours.

Nutrition Info: Per Serving: 167 calories, 18.4g protein, 6.3g carbohydrates, 7.2g fat, 0.1g fiber, 66mg cholesterol, 465mg sodium, 166mg potassium.

Herbed Chicken Salsa

Servings: 4   Cooking Time: 7 Hrs

Ingredients:

4 chicken breasts, skinless and boneless
½ cup veggie stock
Salt and black pepper to the taste
16 oz. salsa
1 and ½ tbsp parsley, dried

1 tsp garlic powder
½ tbsp cilantro, chopped
1 tsp onion powder
½ tbsp oregano, dried
½ tsp paprika, smoked
1 tsp chili powder
½ tsp cumin, ground

Directions:
Add chicken breasts, salsa, and all other ingredients to the Crock Pot.   Put the cooker's lid on and set the cooking time to 7 hours on Low settings.   Serve the chicken with its sauce on top. Devour.

Nutrition Info: Per Serving: Calories 270, Total Fat 4g, Fiber 2g, Total Carbs 14g, Protein 9g

Chicken And Onions Mix

Servings: 2   Cooking Time: 7 Hours

Ingredients:

1 pound chicken breasts, skinless, boneless and cubed
2 red onions, sliced
½ cup chicken stock
½ cup tomato passata
A pinch of salt and black pepper

2 teaspoons olive oil
1 teaspoon black peppercorns, crushed
2 garlic cloves, minced
1 tablespoon chives, chopped

Directions:
Grease the Crock Pot with the oil and mix the chicken with the onions, stock and the other ingredients inside.   Put the lid on, cook on Low for 7 hours, divide between plates and serve.

Nutrition Info: calories 221, fat 14, fiber 3, carbs 7, protein 14

Hot Chicken Wings

Servings: 6   Cooking Time: 4 Hrs
Ingredients:

12 chicken wings, cut into 2 pieces
1 lb. celery, cut into thin matchsticks
¼ cup honey
4 tbsp hot sauce
Salt to the taste
¼ cup tomato puree
1 cup yogurt
1 tbsp parsley, chopped

Directions:
Add chicken, tomato puree, celery, honey, salt, hot sauce, and parsley to the Crock Pot.   Put the cooker's lid on and set the cooking time to 3 hours on High settings.   Stir in yogurt and mix well. Put the cooker's lid on and set the cooking time to 30 minutes on High settings.   Serve warm.
Nutrition Info: Per Serving: Calories: 300, Total Fat: 4g, Fiber: 4g, Total Carbs: 14g, Protein: 22g

Chicken Vegetable Pot Pie

Servings: 8   Cooking Time: 8 Hours
Ingredients:

8 oz. biscuit dough
1 cup sweet corn, frozen
1 cup green peas
11 oz. chicken fillets, chopped
1 cup white onion, chopped
8 oz. chicken creamy soup, canned
1 carrot, chopped
1 tsp onion powder
1 tbsp ground paprika
1 tsp cilantro
½ tsp oregano
1 tsp turmeric
1 tbsp salt
1 tsp butter
1 cup of water

Directions:
Mix the chicken pieces with onion powder, oregano, cilantro, turmeric, and paprika in a Crock Pot.   Stir in green peas, salt, carrot, onion, and sweet corn.   Pour in chicken soup, water, and butter.   Put the cooker's lid on and set the cooking time to 5 hours on High settings.   Spread the biscuit dough and place it over the cooked chicken.   Put the cooker's lid on and set the cooking time to hours on High settings.   Slice and serve.
Nutrition Info: Per Serving: Calories: 283, Total Fat: 10.9g, Fiber: 4g, Total Carbs: 38.42g, Protein: 10g

Garlic Chipotle Lime Chicken

Servings: 6   Cooking Time: 8 Hours
Ingredients:

1 ½ pounds chicken breasts, bones and skin removed
½ cup organic tomato sauce
2 tablespoons olive oil
2 cloves of garlic
2 tablespoons mild green chilies, chopped
1 tablespoon apple cider vinegar
3 tablespoons lime juice
1/3 cup fresh cilantro
1 ½ teaspoon chipotle pepper, chopped
Salt and pepper to taste

Directions:
Place all ingredients in the CrockPot.   Close the lid and cook on high for 5 hours or on low for 8 hours.   Serve with lime wedges.
Nutrition Info: Calories per serving:183; Carbohydrates: 2g; Protein: 22g; Fat: 9g; Sugar: 0g; Sodium: 527mg; Fiber: 1.2g

Mexican Style Chicken Wings

Servings: 4   Cooking Time: 3 Hours
Ingredients:

1 tablespoon Mexican seasonings
2 tablespoon sesame oil
1 tablespoon mayonnaise
1-pound chicken wings, boneless, skinless
1 teaspoon tomato paste
½ cup of water

Directions:
Mix sesame oil with mayonnaise, tomato paste, and Mexican seasonings.   Rub the chicken wings with Mexican seasonings mixture and leave for 10-15 minutes to marinate.   Transfer the marinated chicken wings and all remaining Mexican seasonings mixture in the Crock Pot.   Add water and close the lid.   Cook the chicken wings on High for 3 hours.
Nutrition Info: Per Serving: 297 calories, 33.1g protein, 2.3g carbohydrates, 16.4g fat, 0.1g fiber, 102mg cholesterol, 242mg sodium, 290mg potassium.

Duck And Potatoes

Servings: 4   Cooking Time: 6 Hours
Ingredients:

1 duck, cut into small chunks
Salt and black pepper to the taste
1 potato, cut into cubes
1-inch ginger root, sliced
4 tablespoons sugar
4 garlic cloves, minced
4 tablespoons soy sauce
2 green onions, chopped
4 tablespoons sherry wine
¼ cup water

Directions:
In your Crock Pot mix duck pieces with garlic, ginger, green onions, soy sauce, sugar, wine, a pinch of salt, black pepper, potatoes and water, stir, cover and cook on Low for 6 hours.   Divide between plates and serve right away,
Nutrition Info: calories 245, fat 12, fiber 1, carbs 6, protein 16

Chicken And Beans

Servings: 2   Cooking Time: 7 Hours
Ingredients:

1 cup canned black beans, drained and rinsed
½ cup canned kidney beans, drained and rinsed
1 pound chicken breast, skinless, boneless and cubed
1 red onion, chopped
2 garlic cloves, minced
1 tablespoon olive oil
½ teaspoon sweet paprika
1 tablespoon chili powder
1 cup tomato sauce
A pinch of salt and black pepper
1 tablespoon parsley, chopped

Directions:
In your Crock Pot, mix the chicken with the beans, onion and the other ingredients, toss, put the lid on and cook on Low for 7 hours.   Divide the mix into bowls and serve hot.
Nutrition Info: calories 263, fat 12, fiber 3, carbs 7, protein 15

Turkey Wings And Sauce

Servings: 4   Cooking Time: 8 Hours

Ingredients:

2 tablespoons butter, melted	4 turkey wings
2 tablespoons olive oil	1 yellow onion, roughly chopped
1 and ½ cups cranberries, dried	1 cup walnuts
Salt and black pepper to the taste	1 cup orange juice
	1 bunch thyme, chopped

Directions:

In your Crock Pot mix butter with oil, turkey wings, cranberries, salt, pepper, onion, walnuts, orange juice and thyme, stir a bit, cover and cook on Low for 8 hours.   Divide turkey and orange sauce between plates and serve.

Nutrition Info:calories 300, fat 12, fiber 4, carbs 17, protein 1

Turkey, Tomato And Fennel Mix

Servings: 2   Cooking Time: 7 Hours And 10 Minutes

Ingredients:

1 pound turkey breast, skinless, boneless and cut into strips	½ teaspoon cumin, ground
1 fennel bulb, sliced	½ teaspoon fennel seeds, crushed
1 cup cherry tomatoes, halved	1 tablespoon olive oil
¼ cup chicken stock	1 red onion, chopped
½ cup tomato sauce	A pinch of salt and black pepper
½ teaspoon hot paprika	1 tablespoon cilantro, chopped

Directions:

Heat up a pan with the oil over medium-high heat, add the meat, onion and fennel seeds, stir, brown for   minutes and transfer to the Crock Pot.   Add the rest of the ingredients, toss, put the lid on, cook on Low for 7 hours, divide between plates and serve.

Nutrition Info:calories 231, fat 7, fiber 2, carbs 6, protein 12

Buffalo Chicken

Servings: 12   Cooking Time: 4 Hours

Ingredients:

2 pounds chicken breasts, skinless and boneless	1 cup cayenne sauce
Salt and black pepper to the taste	½ cup chicken stock
2 garlic cloves, minced	½ packet ranch seasoning mix
	1 tablespoon brown sugar

Directions:

In your Crock Pot, mix chicken with salt, pepper, garlic, cayenne sauce, stock, seasoning and sugar, toss, cover and cook on High for 4 hours.   Divide between plates and serve.

Nutrition Info:calories 273, fat 6, fiber 7, carbs 17, protein 2

Chicken With Figs

Servings: 4   Cooking Time: 7 Hours

Ingredients:

5 oz fresh figs, chopped	1 teaspoon peppercorns
14 oz chicken fillet, chopped	1 tablespoon dried dill
1 cup of water	

Directions:

Put all ingredients in the Crock Pot.   Close the lid and cook the meal on Low for 7 hours.

Nutrition Info: Per Serving: 280 calories, 30.1g protein, 23.4g carbohydrates, 7.7g fat, 3.7g fiber, 88mg cholesterol, 93mg sodium, 515mg potassium.

Chicken And Olives

Servings: 2   Cooking Time: 5 Hours

Ingredients:

1 pound chicken breasts, skinless, boneless and sliced	1 tablespoon lime zest, grated
1 cup black olives, pitted and halved	1 teaspoon chili powder
½ cup chicken stock	2 spring onions, chopped
½ cup tomato sauce	1 tablespoon chives, chopped
1 tablespoon lime juice	

Directions:

In your Crock Pot, mix the chicken with the olives, stock and the other ingredients except the chives, toss, put the lid on and cook on High for 5 hours. Divide the mix into bowls, sprinkle the chives on top and serve.

Nutrition Info:calories 200, fat 7, fiber 1, carbs 5, protein 12

Cannellini Chicken

Servings: 4   Cooking Time: 3 Hours

Ingredients:

1 cup cannellini beans, canned	1 teaspoon dried oregano
12 oz chicken fillet, chopped	1 cup of water
1 teaspoon lemon zest, grated	1 tablespoon butter
1 teaspoon salt	1 garlic clove, chopped

Directions:

Put the chopped chicken in the Crock Pot.   Add lemon zest, salt, water, butter, and garlic.   Close the lid and cook the chicken on high for 2 hours. Then add cannellini beans and stir the chicken well. Close the lid and cook the chicken on High for 1 hour.

Nutrition Info: Per Serving: 343 calories, 35.6g protein, 28.2g carbohydrates, 9.6g fat, 11.7g fiber, 83mg cholesterol, 688mg sodium, 866mg potassium.

Chicken Piccata

Servings: 4   Cooking Time: 8 Hours
Ingredients:

4 chicken breasts, skin and bones removed

¼ cup butter, cubed

Salt and pepper to taste

¼ cup chicken broth

1 tablespoon lemon juice

Directions:
Place all ingredients in the crockpot.   Give a good stir to combine everything.   Close the lid and cook on low for 8 hours or on high for 6 hours.
Nutrition Info: Calories per serving: 265; Carbohydrates:2.3 g; Protein:24 g; Fat: 14g; Sugar: 0g; Sodium:442 mg; Fiber:0 g

Moscow Bacon Chicken

Servings: 5   Cooking Time: 7 Hours
Ingredients:

6 oz. Russian dressing

17 oz. chicken thighs

1 tbsp minced garlic

1 tsp ground black pepper

1 tsp onion powder

4 oz. bacon, sliced

1 tsp salt

1 tsp oregano

¼ cup of water

Directions:
Add bacon slices to a skillet and saute until brown from both the sides.   Mix garlic, onion powder, salt, oregano, and black pepper in a bowl.   Rub the chicken with garlic mixture and transfer to the Crock Pot.   Add bacon and all other ingredients to the Crock Pot.   Put the cooker's lid on and set the cooking time to 7 hours on Low settings. Serve warm.
Nutrition Info: Per Serving: Calories: 273, Total Fat: 18.2g, Fiber: 1g, Total Carbs: 9.05g, Protein: 20g

Turkey With Zucchini

Servings: 4   Cooking Time: 8 Hours
Ingredients:

1-pound ground turkey

2 red peppers cut into strips

Salt and pepper to taste

2 green onions, sliced

1 large zucchini, sliced

Directions:
Place the ground turkey and red peppers in the crockpot.   Season with salt and pepper to taste. Close the lid and cook on low for 8 hours or on high for 6 hours.   An hour before the cooking time is done, stir in the green onions and zucchini.   Cook further until the vegetables are soft.
Nutrition Info: Calories per serving: 195; Carbohydrates: 5.7g; Protein: 23.9g; Fat: 9.01g; Sugar: 0.4g; Sodium: 542mg; Fiber: 2.5g

Chicken With Tomatillos

Servings: 6   Cooking Time: 4 Hrs
Ingredients:

1 lb. chicken thighs, skinless and boneless

1 yellow onion, chopped

1 garlic clove, minced

4 oz. canned green chilies, chopped

Handful cilantro, chopped

Salt and black pepper to the taste

2 tbsp olive oil

15 oz. canned tomatillos, chopped

5 oz. canned garbanzo beans, drained

15 oz. rice, cooked

5 oz. tomatoes, chopped

15 oz. cheddar cheese, grated

4 oz. black olives, pitted and chopped

Directions:
Toss onion, chicken, garlic, chilies, salt, black pepper, tomatillos, and cilantro to the Crock Pot. Put the cooker's lid on and set the cooking time to 3 hours on High settings.   Shred the chicken and return to the cooker.   Stir in beans, cheese, rice, olives, and tomatoes.   Put the cooker's lid on and set the cooking time to 1 hour on High settings. Serve.
Nutrition Info: Per Serving: Calories: 300, Total Fat: 11g, Fiber: 3g, Total Carbs: 14g, Protein: 30g

Shredded Soy Lemon Chicken

Servings: 8   Cooking Time: 8 Hours
Ingredients:

2 pounds chicken breasts, bones and skin removed

1 cup water

¼ cup lemon juice

4 cloves of garlic, minced

½ cup soy sauce

1 onion, chopped finely

2 tablespoons sesame oil

Salt and pepper to taste

Directions:
Place all ingredients in the CrockPot.   Close the lid and cook on high for 6 hours or on low for 8 hours.   Once the chicken is very tender, shred the meat using two forks.   Serve with the sauce.
Nutrition Info: Calories per serving: 283; Carbohydrates: 6.8g; Protein: 25.2g; Fat: 18.2g; Sugar: 1.2g; Sodium: 612mg; Fiber: 2.8g

Chicken And Broccoli Casserole

Servings: 4   Cooking Time: 4 Hours
Ingredients:

3 cups cheddar cheese, grated

10 ounces broccoli florets

3 chicken breasts, skinless, boneless, cooked and cubed

1 cup mayonnaise

1 tablespoon olive oil

1/3 cup chicken stock

Salt and black pepper to the taste

Juice of 1 lemon

Directions:
Grease your Crock Pot with the oil and arrange chicken pieces on the bottom.   Spread broccoli florets and then half of the cheese.   In a bowl, mix mayo with stock, salt, pepper and lemon juice. Pour this over chicken, sprinkle the rest of the cheese, cover and cook on High for hours.   Serve hot.

Nutrition Info: calories 320, fat 5, fiber 4, carbs 16, protein 25

Poultry Stew

Servings: 6   Cooking Time: 8 Hours

Ingredients:

3 garlic cloves, peeled and minced

3 carrots, cut into 3 parts

1 lb. chicken fillet, diced

1 lb. duck fillet, diced

1 tbsp smoked paprika

¼ cup of soy sauce

1 tbsp honey

1 tsp nutmeg

1 tsp fresh rosemary

1 tsp black peas

2 cups of water

Directions:

Add chicken, duck, and all other ingredients to the Crock Pot.   Put the cooker's lid on and set the cooking time to 8 hours on Low settings.   Serve warm.

Nutrition Info: Per Serving: Calories: 422, Total Fat: 24.6g, Fiber: 3g, Total Carbs: 27.21g, Protein: 23g

Curry Chicken Strips

Servings: 6   Cooking Time: 3.5 Hours

Ingredients:

1 tablespoon curry paste

1-pound chicken fillet, cut into strips

1 teaspoon olive oil

1 teaspoon liquid honey

1 tablespoon cream cheese

1/3 cup water

Directions:

Mix curry paste with honey, olive oil, and cream cheese,   Then mix the curry mixture with chicken strips and carefully mix.   Put the chicken strips in the Crock Pot, add water, and close the lid.   Cook the meal in High for 3.5 hours.

Nutrition Info: Per Serving: 176 calories, 22.1g protein, 1.7g carbohydrates, 8.4g fat, 0g fiber, 69mg cholesterol, 70mg sodium, 186mg potassium.

Crockpot Yellow Chicken Curry

Servings: 5   Cooking Time: 8 Hours

Ingredients:

1 ½ pounds boneless chicken breasts, cut into chunks

6 cups vegetable broth (made from boiling onions, broccoli, bell pepper, and carrots in 7 cups water)

1 cup coconut milk, unsweetened

1 cup tomatoes, crushed

1 tablespoon cumin

2 teaspoons ground coriander

1 teaspoon turmeric powder

1 thumb-size ginger, sliced

4 cloves of garlic, minced

1 teaspoon cinnamon

½ teaspoon cayenne pepper

Salt to taste

Directions:

Place all ingredients in the CrockPot.   Close the lid and cook on high for 6 hours or on low for 8 hours.

Nutrition Info: Calories per serving: 291; Carbohydrates: 6.1g; Protein: 32.5g; Fat: 15.4g; Sugar: 0.3g; Sodium: 527mg; Fiber: 2.8g

Turkey Soup With Rosemary And Kale

Servings: 6   Cooking Time: 8 Hours

Ingredients:

½ onion, chopped

2 cloves of garlic, minced

Salt and pepper to taste

1-pound turkey meat, cut into bite-sized pieces

1 tablespoon tallow or ghee

4 cups homemade chicken stock

2 sprigs rosemary, chopped

3 cups kale, chopped

Directions:

Place all ingredients except the kale in the CrockPot.   Close the lid and cook on high for 6 hours or on low for 8 hours.   An hour before the cooking time ends, add in the kale.   Close the lid and cook until the kale has wilted.

Nutrition Info: Calories per serving: 867; Carbohydrates: 2.6g; Protein: 151.3g; Fat: 23.6g; Sugar: 0g; Sodium: 1373mg; Fiber: 1.4g

Duck Saute

Servings: 3   Cooking Time: 5 Hours

Ingredients:

8 oz duck fillet, sliced

1 cup of water

1 cup mushrooms, sliced

1 teaspoon salt

1 teaspoon ground black pepper

1 tablespoon olive oil

Directions:

Heat the olive oil in the skillet well.   Add mushrooms and roast them for 3-5 minutes on medium heat.   Transfer the roasted mushrooms in the Crock Pot.   Add duck fillet, and all remaining ingredients.   Close the lid and cook saute for hours on High.

Nutrition Info: Per Serving: 141 calories, 23.1g protein, 1.2g carbohydrates, 5.2g fat, 0.4g fiber, 0mg cholesterol, 893mg sodium, 131mg potassium.

Bacon Chicken

Servings: 4   Cooking Time: 7 Hours

Ingredients:

4 bacon slices, cooked

4 chicken drumsticks

½ cup of water

¼ tomato juice

1 teaspoon salt

½ teaspoon ground black pepper

Directions:

Sprinkle the chicken drumsticks with the salt and ground black pepper.   Then wrap every chicken drumstick in the bacon and arrange it in the Crock Pot.   Add water and tomato juice.   Cook the meal on Low for 7 hours.

Nutrition Info: Per Serving: 184 calories, 19.8g protein, 1.1g carbohydrates, 10.6g fat, 0.1g fiber, 61mg cholesterol, 1099mg sodium, 237mg potassium.

Chicken With Mushroom Sauce

Servings: 4   Cooking Time: 4 Hrs

Ingredients:

8 chicken thighs
Salt and black pepper to the taste
1 yellow onion, chopped
4 bacon strips, cooked and chopped
4 garlic cloves, minced
1 tbsp olive oil
10 oz. cremini mushrooms halved
2 cups white chardonnay wine
1 cup whipping cream
Handful parsley, chopped

Directions:

Add oil, chicken pieces, black pepper, and salt to a pan.   Stir cook the chicken until it turns golden brown.   Transfer the chicken to the Crock Pot and the remaining ingredients.   Put the cooker's lid on and set the cooking time to hours on High settings.   Serve warm.

Nutrition Info: Per Serving: Calories: 340, Total Fat: 10g, Fiber: 7g, Total Carbs: 14g, Protein: 24g

Coca Cola Dipped Chicken

Servings: 4   Cooking Time: 4 Hrs

Ingredients:

1 yellow onion, minced
1 tbsp balsamic vinegar
1 chili pepper, chopped
4 chicken drumsticks
15 oz. coca cola
Salt and black pepper to the taste
2 tbsp olive oil

Directions:

Add chicken to a pan greased with oil and sear it until golden brown from both the sides.   Transfer the chicken to the Crock Pot.   Stir in coca-cola, chili, onion, vinegar, black pepper, and salt to the cooker.   Put the cooker's lid on and set the cooking time to hours on High settings.   Serve warm.

Nutrition Info: Per Serving: Calories: 372, Total Fat: 14g, Fiber: 3g, Total Carbs: 20g, Protein: 15g

Turkey And Okra

Servings: 2   Cooking Time: 5 Hours

Ingredients:

1 pound turkey breasts, skinless, boneless and cubed
1 teaspoon olive oil
½ teaspoon
1 cup okra, halved
1 tablespoon lime zest, grated
½ cup chicken stock
1 tablespoon lime juice
½ teaspoon sweet paprika
coriander, ground
½ teaspoon oregano, dried
1 teaspoon chili powder
A pinch of salt and black pepper
1 tablespoon cilantro, chopped

Directions:

In your Crock Pot, mix the turkey with the okra, lime zest, juice and the other ingredients, toss, put the lid on and cook on High for 5 hours.   Divide everything between plates and serve.

Nutrition Info: calories 162, fat 8, fiber 2, carbs 5, protein 9

Citrus Glazed Chicken

Servings: 4   Cooking Time: 4 Hrs

Ingredients:

2 lbs. chicken thighs, skinless, boneless and cut into pieces
Salt and black pepper to the taste
3 tbsp olive oil
¼ cup flour
For the sauce:
2 tbsp fish sauce
1 and ½ tsp orange extract
1 tbsp ginger, grated
¼ cup of orange juice
2 tsp sugar
1 tbsp orange zest
¼ tsp sesame seeds
2 tbsp scallions, chopped
½ tsp coriander, ground
1 cup of water
¼ tsp red pepper flakes
2 tbsp soy sauce

Directions:

Whisk flour with black pepper, salt, and chicken pieces in a bowl to coat well.   Add chicken to a pan greased with oil and sear it over medium heat until golden brown.   Transfer the chicken to the Crock Pot.   Blend orange juice, fish sauce, soy sauce, ginger, water, coriander, orange extract, and stevia in a blender jug.   Pour this fish sauce mixture over the chicken and top it with orange zest, scallions, sesame seeds, and pepper flakes. Put the cooker's lid on and set the cooking time to 4 hours on High settings.   Serve warm.

Nutrition Info: Per Serving: Calories: 423, Total Fat: 20g, Fiber: 5g, Total Carbs: 12g, Protein: 45g

Fish & Seafood Recipes

Fish Potato Cakes

Servings: 12   Cooking Time: 5 Hrs.

Ingredients:

1 lb. trout, minced	1 egg, beaten
6 oz mashed potato	1 tsp minced garlic
1 carrot, grated	1 onion, grated
½ cup fresh parsley	1 tsp olive oil
1 tsp salt	1 tsp ground black
½ cup panko bread	pepper
crumbs	¼ tsp cilantro

Directions:
Mix minced trout with mashed potatoes, carrot, salt, garlic, cilantro, onion, black pepper, and egg in a bowl.   Stir in breadcrumbs and olive oil, then mix well.   Make 12 balls out of this mixture then flatten the balls.   Place these fish cakes in the insert of Crock Pot.   Put the cooker's lid on and set the cooking time to hours on Low settings. Flip all the fish cakes when cooked halfway through.   Serve warm.
Nutrition Info: Per Serving: Calories: 93, Total Fat: 3.8g, Fiber: 1g, Total Carbs: 5.22g, Protein: 9g

Red Thai Salmon Curry

Servings: 4   Cooking Time: 4 Hours

Ingredients:

2 onions, chopped	1 teaspoon coriander
4 salmon fillets	powder
1 can coconut milk	1 teaspoon cayenne
1 teaspoon coconut	pepper
oil	½ teaspoon cumin
1 tablespoon curry	1 teaspoon cinnamon
powder	2 red bell peppers,
3 curry leaves	julienned

Directions:
Place all ingredients in the CrockPot.   Give a good stir.   Close the lid and cook on high for hours or on low for 4 hours.
Nutrition Info: Calories per serving: 499; Carbohydrates: 5.7g; Protein: 27.6g; Fat: 38.3g; Sugar: 0.8g; Sodium: 891mg; Fiber: 3.2g

Shrimp And Mango Mix

Servings: 2   Cooking Time: 1 Hour

Ingredients:

1 pound shrimp, peeled and deveined	½ teaspoon rosemary, dried
½ cup mango, peeled and cubed	1 tablespoon olive oil
½ cup cherry tomatoes, halved	½ teaspoon chili powder
½ cup shallots, chopped	A pinch of salt and black pepper
1 tablespoon lime juice	1 tablespoon chives, chopped
½ cup chicken stock	

Directions:
In your Crock Pot, mix the shrimp with the mango, tomatoes and the other ingredients, toss, put the lid on and cook on High for hour.   Divide the mix into bowls and serve.

Nutrition Info:calories 210, fat 9, fiber 2, carbs 6, protein 7

Pesto Cod And Tomatoes

Servings: 2   Cooking Time: 3 Hours

Ingredients:

1 pound cod, boneless and roughly cubed	1 cup cherry tomatoes, halved
2 tablespoons basil pesto	1 tablespoon chives, chopped
1 tablespoon olive oil	A pinch of salt and
½ cup veggie stock	black pepper

Directions:
In your Crock Pot, mix the cod with the pesto, oil and the other ingredients, toss, put the lid on and cook on High for 3 hours.   Divide the mix between plates and serve.
Nutrition Info:calories 211, fat 13, fiber 2, carbs 7, protein 11

Fish Corners

Servings: 4   Cooking Time: 3.5 Hours

Ingredients:

7 oz salmon, canned, shredded	1 egg, beaten
¼ onion, diced	1 teaspoon sesame oil
1 teaspoon dried basil	¼ teaspoon chili powder
	4 oz puff pastry

Directions:
Roll up the puff pastry and cut it into squares. After this, mix canned salmon with onion, basil, egg, and chili powder.   Put the salmon mixture in the center of every puff pastry square and roll into the shape of corners.   Then brush the fish corners with sesame oil and put in the Crock Pot. Cook the meal on High for 3.hours.
Nutrition Info: Per Serving: 251 calories, 13.2g protein, 13.6g carbohydrates, 16.1g fat, 0.6g fiber, 63mg cholesterol, 110mg sodium, 236mg potassium

Sweden Fish Casserole

Servings: 4   Cooking Time: 3.5 Hours

Ingredients:

8 oz mackerel fillet, chopped	1 cup of water
3 tablespoons mayonnaise	1 teaspoon ground black pepper
1 tablespoon sesame oil	2 onions, sliced
	2 oz Provolone cheese, grated

Directions:
Brush the Crock Pot bottom with sesame oil. Then mix chopped mackerel with onion and put in the Crock Pot.   Spread the mayonnaise over the fish.   Add grated Provolone cheese, ground black pepper, and water.   Close the lid and cook the casserole on High for 3.hours.
Nutrition Info: Per Serving: 295 calories, 17.9g protein, 8.4g carbohydrates, 21g fat, 1.3g fiber, 55mg cholesterol, 254mg sodium, 335mg potassium

Mackerel Bites

Servings: 4   Cooking Time: 3 Hours
Ingredients:

- 1-pound mackerel fillet, chopped
- 1 tablespoon avocado oil
- 1/3 cup water
- ½ teaspoon ground paprika
- ½ teaspoon ground turmeric

Directions:
In the shallow bowl mix ground paprika with ground turmeric.   Then sprinkle the mackerel fillet with a spice mixture.   Heat the avocado oil in the skillet well.   Add fish and roast it for 1 minute per side on high heat.   Pour water in the Crock Pot.   Add fish and close the lid.   Cook the mackerel bites on High for 3 hours.
Nutrition Info: Per Serving: 304 calories, 27.2g protein, 0.5g carbohydrates, 20.7g fat, 0.3g fiber, 85mg cholesterol, 95mg sodium, 479mg potassium

Almond-crusted Tilapia

Servings: 4   Cooking Time: 4 Hours
Ingredients:

- 2 tablespoons olive oil
- 1 cup chopped almonds
- ¼ cup ground flaxseed
- 4 tilapia fillets
- Salt and pepper to taste

Directions:
Line the bottom of the crockpot with a foil. Grease the foil with the olive oil.   In a mixing bowl, combine the almonds and flaxseed.   Season the tilapia with salt and pepper to taste.   Dredge the tilapia fillets with the almond and flaxseed mixture.   Place neatly in the foil-lined crockpot. Close the lid and cook on high for 2 hours and on low for 4 hours.
Nutrition Info: Calories per serving: 233; Carbohydrates: 4.6g; Protein: 25.5g; Fat: 13.3g; Sugar: 0.4g; Sodium: 342mg; Fiber: 1.9g

Alaska Salmon With Pecan Crunch Coating

Servings: 6   Cooking Time: 6 Hours 30 Minutes
Ingredients:

- ½ cup fresh bread crumbs
- ½ cup pecans, finely chopped
- Salt and black pepper, to taste
- 3 tablespoons butter, melted
- 6 lemon wedges
- 3 tablespoons Dijon mustard
- 5 teaspoons honey
- 6 (4 ounce) salmon fillets
- 3 teaspoons fresh parsley, chopped

Directions:
Season the salmon fillets with salt and black pepper and transfer into the crock pot.   Combine honey, mustard and butter in a small bowl.   Mix together the parsley, pecans and bread crumbs in another bowl.   Brush the salmon fillets with

honey mixture and top with parsley mixture. Cover and cook for about 6 hours on LOW. Garnish with lemon wedges and dish out to serve warm.
Nutrition Info: Calories: 270 Fat: 14.4g Carbohydrates: 12.6g

Shrimp And Baby Carrots Mix

Servings: 2   Cooking Time: 4 Hours And 30 Minutes
Ingredients:

- 1 small yellow onion, chopped
- 2 garlic cloves, minced
- 1 small green bell pepper, chopped
- 8 ounces canned coconut milk
- 3 tablespoons tomato paste
- 15 baby carrots
- ½ teaspoon red pepper, crushed
- ¾ tablespoons curry powder
- ¾ tablespoon tapioca flour
- 1 pound shrimp, peeled and deveined

Directions:
In your food processor, mix onion with garlic, bell pepper, tomato paste, coconut milk, red pepper and curry powder, blend well, add to your Crock Pot, also add baby carrots, stir, cover and cook on Low for 4 hours.   Add tapioca and shrimp, stir, cover and cook on Low for 30 minutes more.   Divide into bowls and serve.
Nutrition Info:calories 230, fat 4, fiber 3, carbs 14, protein 5

Stuffed Mackerel

Servings: 4   Cooking Time: 4.5 Hours
Ingredients:

- ½ cup yams, diced
- 1-pound mackerel, cleaned, trimmed
- 1 teaspoon dried thyme
- 1 teaspoon salt
- 1 tablespoon sour cream
- 1 teaspoon chili powder
- 1 teaspoon olive oil

Directions:
Rub the mackerel with dried thyme, salt, and chili powder.   Then fil it with yams and secure the cut. After this, sprinkle the fish with olive oil and sour cream and wrap in the foil.   Put the fish in the Crock Pot and close the lid.   Cook the fish on high for 4.hours.
Nutrition Info: Per Serving: 336 calories, 27.5g protein, 5.3g carbohydrates, 22.2g fat, 1g fiber, 86mg cholesterol, 685mg sodium, 588mg potassium

Mackerel And Lemon

Servings: 4   Cooking Time: 2 Hours
Ingredients:

4 mackerels	3 ounces
Juice and rind of 1	breadcrumbs
lemon	1 egg, whisked
1 tablespoon chives,	1 tablespoon butter
finely chopped	1 tablespoon
Salt and black pepper	vegetable oil
to the taste	3 lemon wedges

Directions:
In a bowl, mix breadcrumbs with lemon juice, lemon rind, salt, pepper, egg and chives, stir very well and coat mackerel with this mix.   Add the oil and the butter to your Crock Pot and arrange mackerel inside.   Cover, cook on High for 2 hours, divide fish between plates and serve with lemon wedges on the side.
Nutrition Info:calories 200, fat 3, fiber 1, carbs 3, protein 12

Clams In Coconut Sauce

Servings: 2   Cooking Time: 2 Hours
Ingredients:

1 cup coconut cream	1 teaspoon salt
1 teaspoon minced	1 teaspoon ground
garlic	coriander
1 teaspoon chili flakes	8 oz clams

Directions:
Pour coconut cream in the Crock Pot.   Add minced garlic, chili flakes, salt, and ground coriander.   Cook the mixture on high for 1 hour. Then add clams and stir the meal well. Cook it for 1 hour on high more.
Nutrition Info: Per Serving: 333 calories, 3.5g protein, 19.6g carbohydrates, 28.9g fat, 3.1g fiber, 0mg cholesterol, 1592mg sodium, 425mg potassium.

Fish Pie(2)

Servings: 6   Cooking Time: 7 Hours
Ingredients:

7 oz yeast dough	1 onion, diced
1 tablespoon cream	1 teaspoon salt
cheese	1 tablespoon fresh dill
8 oz salmon fillet,	1 teaspoon olive oil
chopped	

Directions:
Brush the Crock Pot bottom with olive oil.   Then roll up the dough and place it in the Crock Pot. Flatten it in the shape of the pie crust.   After this, in the mixing bowl mix cream cheese, salmon, onion, salt, and dill.   Put the fish mixture over the pie crust and cover with foil.   Close the lid and cook the pie on Low for 7 hours.
Nutrition Info: Per Serving: 158 calories, 9.5g protein, 18.6g carbohydrates, 5g fat, 1.3g fiber, 19mg cholesterol, 524mg sodium, 191mg potassium.

Paprika Cod

Servings: 2   Cooking Time: 3 Hours
Ingredients:

1 tablespoon olive oil	¼ cup white wine
1 pound cod fillets,	2 scallions, chopped
boneless	½ teaspoon
1 teaspoon sweet	rosemary, dried
paprika	A pinch of salt and
¼ cup chicken stock	black pepper

Directions:
In your Crock Pot, mix the cod with the paprika, oil and the other ingredients, toss gently, put the lid on and cook on High for 3 hours.   Divide everything between plates and serve.
Nutrition Info:calories 211, fat 8, fiber 4, carbs 8, protein 8

Japanese Pea Shrimp

Servings: 4   Cooking Time: 1 Hr.
Ingredients:

1 lb.'s shrimp, peeled	3 tbsp vinegar
and deveined	¾ cup pineapple
2 tbsp soy sauce	juice
½ lb. pea pods	1 cup chicken stock
	3 tbsp sugar

Directions:
First, place the pea pods and shrimp in the insert of the Crock Pot.   Top the shrimps with the rest of the ingredients.   Put the cooker's lid on and set the cooking time to 1 hour on High settings. Serve warm.
Nutrition Info: Per Serving: Calories: 251, Total Fat: 4g, Fiber: 1g, Total Carbs: 12g, Protein: 30g

Shrimp With Spinach

Servings: 2   Cooking Time: 1 Hour
Ingredients:

1 pound shrimp,	3 scallions, chopped
peeled and deveined	½ teaspoon sweet
1 cup baby spinach	paprika
¼ cup tomato	A pinch of salt and
passata	black pepper
½ cup chicken stock	1 tablespoon chives,
1 tablespoon olive oil	chopped

Directions:
In your Crock Pot, mix the shrimp with the spinach, tomato passata and the other ingredients, toss, put the lid on and cook on High for hour. Divide the mix between plates and serve.
Nutrition Info:calories 200, fat 13, fiber 3, carbs 6, protein 11

Salmon Picatta

Servings: 4   Cooking Time: 3.5 Hours

Ingredients:

4 salmon fillets	1 teaspoon capers
1 tablespoon avocado oil	1 tablespoon flour
½ lemon, sliced	¼ cup chicken stock
1 tablespoon butter	½ teaspoon minced garlic
¼ cup white wine	

Directions:
In the mixing bowl mix minced garlic and butter. Put the mixture in the Crock Pot.   Add chicken stock and flour.   Gently whisk the mixture. Add lemon, white wine, and avocado oil.   Then add salmon fillets and capers.   Close the lid and cook the meal on High for 3.5 hours.
Nutrition Info: Per Serving: 288 calories, 35g protein, 3g carbohydrates, 14.4g fat, 0.4g fiber, 86mg cholesterol, 169mg sodium, 725mg potassium

Cod Fingers

Servings: 5   Cooking Time: 2.5 Hours

Ingredients:

3 cod fillets	½ teaspoon salt
½ cup panko bread crumbs	3 eggs, beaten
	4 tablespoons butter

Directions:
Slice the cod fillet into sticks and sprinkle with salt. Then dip the fish sticks in the eggs and coat well with panko bread crumbs.   Put butter in the Crock Pot and melt it.   Put the fish sticks in the Crock Pot in one layer and close the lid.   Cook them on High for 2.hours.
Nutrition Info: Per Serving: 216 calories, 16.9g protein, 8g carbohydrates, 13g fat, 0.5g fiber, 156mg cholesterol, 456mg sodium, 59mg potassium.

Indian Shrimp

Servings: 2   Cooking Time: 1 Hours

Ingredients:

1 tablespoon olive oil	4 scallions, chopped
1 pound shrimp, peeled and deveined	½ teaspoon turmeric powder
½ teaspoon garam masala	1 tablespoon lime juice
½ teaspoon coriander, ground	½ cup chicken stock
	¼ cup lime leaves, torn

Directions:
In your Crock Pot, mix the shrimp with the oil, scallions, masala and the other ingredients, toss, put the lid on and cook on High for hour.   Divide the mix into bowls and serve.
Nutrition Info:calories 211, fat 12, fiber 3, carbs 6, protein 7

Apricot And Halibut Saute

Servings: 2   Cooking Time: 5 Hours

Ingredients:

6 oz halibut fillet, chopped	1 tablespoon soy sauce
½ cup apricots, pitted, chopped	1 teaspoon ground cumin
½ cup of water	

Directions:
Put all ingredients in the Crock Pot.   Close the lid and cook the fish sauté on Low for 5 hours.
Nutrition Info: Per Serving: 407 calories, 28.7g protein, 5.3g carbohydrates, 28.7g fat, 0.9g fiber, 94mg cholesterol, 619mg sodium, 684mg potassium.

Butter Salmon

Servings: 2   Cooking Time: 1.5 Hours

Ingredients:

8 oz salmon fillet	1 teaspoon dried sage
3 tablespoons butter	¼ cup of water

Directions:
Churn butter with sage and preheat the mixture until liquid.   Then cut the salmon fillets into servings and put in the Crock Pot.   Add water and melted butter mixture.   Close the lid and cook the salmon on High for 1.5 hours.
Nutrition Info: Per Serving: 304 calories, 22.2g protein, 0.2g carbohydrates, 24.3g fat, 0.1g fiber, 96mg cholesterol, 174mg sodium, 444mg potassium.

Teriyaki Tilapia

Servings: 4   Cooking Time: 5 Hours

Ingredients:

1 teaspoon sesame seeds	1 tablespoon avocado oil
¼ cup teriyaki sauce	12 oz tilapia fillet, roughly chopped
¼ cup of water	

Directions:
Mix water with teriyaki sauce, sesame seeds, and avocado oil.   Pour the liquid in the Crock Pot. Add tilapia fillet and close the lid.   Cook the fish on Low for 5 hours.
Nutrition Info: Per Serving: 95 calories, 17.1g protein, 3.2g carbohydrates, 1.6g fat, 0.3g fiber, 41mg cholesterol, 721mg sodium, 55mg potassium

Ginger Tuna

Servings: 2   Cooking Time: 2 Hours

Ingredients:

1 pound tuna fillets, boneless and roughly cubed	Juice of 1 lime
1 tablespoon ginger, grated	¼ cup chicken stock
1 red onion, chopped	1 tablespoon chives, chopped
2 teaspoons olive oil	A pinch of salt and black pepper

Directions:
In your Crock Pot, mix the tuna with the ginger, onion and the other ingredients, toss, put the lid on and cook on High for 2 hours.   Divide the mix into bowls and serve.
Nutrition Info:calories 200, fat 11, fiber 4, carbs 5, protein 12

Sautéed Smelt

Servings: 4   Cooking Time: 4.5 Hours

Ingredients:

1 onion, chopped
1 cup bell pepper, chopped
1 tablespoon coconut oil
1 cup of coconut milk
12 oz smelt fillet, chopped
1 teaspoon ground nutmeg

Directions:

Put all ingredients in the Crock Pot and gently mix with the help of the spoon.   Close the lid and cook the smelt on High for 4.5 hours.

Nutrition Info: Per Serving: 296 calories, 21.2g protein, 8.4g carbohydrates, 20.7g fat, 2.4g fiber, 77mg cholesterol, 76mg sodium, 572mg potassium

Salmon And Relish

Servings: 2   Cooking Time: 2 Hours

Ingredients:

2 medium salmon fillets, boneless
Salt and black pepper to the taste
1 shallot, chopped
1 tablespoon lemon juice
1 big lemon, peeled and cut into wedges
¼ cup olive oil+ 1 teaspoon
2 tablespoons parsley, finely chopped

Directions:

Brush salmon fillets with the olive oil, sprinkle with salt and pepper, put in your Crock Pot, add shallot and lemon juice, cover and cook on High for 2 hours.   Shed salmon and divide into bowls. Add lemon segments to your Crock Pot, also add ¼ cup oil and parsley and whisk well.   Divide this mix over salmon, toss and serve.

Nutrition Info:calories 200, fat 10, fiber 1, carbs 5, protein 20

Mackerel In Wine Sauce

Servings: 4   Cooking Time: 3.5 Hours

Ingredients:

1-pound mackerel
½ cup white wine
1 teaspoon cornflour
1 teaspoon cayenne pepper
1 tablespoon olive oil
½ teaspoon dried rosemary

Directions:

Mix white wine with cornflour and pour it in the Crock Pot.   Then rub the fish with cayenne pepper and dried rosemary.   Sprinkle the fish with olive oil and put it in the Crock Pot.   Close the lid and cook the mackerel on High for 3.5 hours.

Nutrition Info: Per Serving: 356 calories, 27.2g protein, 1.6g carbohydrates, 23.8g fat, 0.2g fiber, 85mg cholesterol, 96mg sodium, 496mg potassium

Shrimp And Sausage Boil

Servings: 4   Cooking Time: 2 Hours And 30 Minutes

Ingredients:

1 and ½ pounds shrimp, head removed
12 ounces Andouille sausage, already cooked and chopped
4 ears of corn, each cut into 3 pieces
1 tablespoon old bay seasoning
Salt and black pepper to the taste
16 ounces beer
1 teaspoon red pepper flakes, crushed
2 sweet onions, cut into wedges
1 pound potatoes, cut into medium chunks
8 garlic cloves, crushed
French baguettes for serving

Directions:

In your Crock Pot mix beer with old bay seasoning, red pepper flakes, salt, black pepper, onions, garlic, potatoes, corn and sausage, cover and cook on High for 2 hours.   Add shrimp, cover, cook on High for 30 minutes more, divide into bowls and serve with French baguettes on the side.

Nutrition Info:calories 261, fat 5, fiber 6, carbs 20, protein 16

Chicken Stuffed Squid

Servings: 4   Cooking Time: 7 Hrs.

Ingredients:

1 lb. squid tubes
2 oz capers
1 cup tomatoes, chopped
1 tsp salt
1 tsp cayenne pepper
1 tsp ground black pepper
1 tsp butter
1 tbsp tomato paste
1 garlic clove, chopped
1 cup chicken stock
6 oz ground chicken
1 tsp cilantro

Directions:

Toss tomatoes with cayenne pepper, salt, black pepper, capers, butter, chicken, cilantro, and garlic in a bowl.   Stuff the squid tubes with chicken mixture.   Place these stuffed tubes in the insert of Crock Pot and top then with tomato paste and stock.   Put the cooker's lid on and set the cooking time to 7 hours on Low settings.   Serve warm.

Nutrition Info: Per Serving: Calories: 216, Total Fat: 7g, Fiber: 1g, Total Carbs: 10.1g, Protein: 28g

Parsley Cod

Servings: 2   Cooking Time: 2 Hours

Ingredients:

1 pound cod fillets, boneless
3 scallions, chopped
2 teaspoons olive oil
1 teaspoon coriander, ground
Juice of 1 lime
Salt and black pepper to the taste
1 tablespoon parsley, chopped

Directions:

In your Crock Pot, mix the cod with the scallions, the oil and the other ingredients, rub gently, put the lid on and cook on High for hour.   Divide everything between plates and serve.

Nutrition Info:calories 200, fat 12, fiber 2, carbs 6, protein 9

Shrimp Salad

Servings: 4   Cooking Time: 1 Hour
Ingredients:

2 tablespoons olive oil	3 tablespoons parsley, chopped
1 pound shrimp, peeled and deveined	2 teaspoons mint, chopped
Salt and black pepper to the taste	1 tablespoon tarragon, chopped
2 tablespoons lime juice	1 tablespoon lemon juice
3 endives, leaves separated	2 tablespoons mayonnaise
1 teaspoon lime zest	½ cup sour cream

Directions:
In a bowl, mix shrimp with salt, pepper and the olive oil, toss to coat and spread into the Crock Pot, Add lime juice, endives, parsley, mint, tarragon, lemon juice, lemon zest, mayo and sour cream, toss, cover and cook on High for 1 hour.   Divide into bowls and serve.
Nutrition Info:calories 200, fat 11, fiber 2, carbs 11, protein 13

Rice Stuffed Squid

Servings: 4   Cooking Time: 3 Hrs.
Ingredients:

3 squids	2 tbsp sake
Tentacles from 1 squid, chopped	4 tbsp soy sauce
1 cup sticky rice	1 tbsp mirin
14 oz. dashi stock	2 tbsp sugar

Directions:
Toss the chopped tentacles with rice and stuff the 3 squids with rice mixture.   Seal the squid using toothpicks then place them in the Crock Pot. Add soy sauce, stock, sugar, sake, and mirin to the squids.   Put the cooker's lid on and set the cooking time to 3 hours on High settings.   Serve warm.
Nutrition Info: Per Serving: Calories: 230, Total Fat: 4g, Fiber: 4g, Total Carbs: 7g, Protein: 11g

Shrimps Boil

Servings: 2   Cooking Time: 45 Minutes
Ingredients:

½ cup of water	1 tablespoon butter
1 tablespoon piri piri sauce	7 oz shrimps, peeled

Directions:
Pour water in the Crock Pot.   Add shrimps and cook them on high for 45 minutes.   Then drain water and transfer shrimps in the skillet.   Add butter and piri piri sauce.   Roast the shrimps for 2-3 minutes on medium heat.
Nutrition Info: Per Serving: 174 calories, 22.7g protein, 1.8g carbohydrates, 7.8g fat, 0.1g fiber, 224mg cholesterol, 285mg sodium, 170mg potassium

Butter Tilapia

Servings: 4   Cooking Time: 6 Hours
Ingredients:

4 tilapia fillets	½ teaspoon ground black pepper
½ cup butter	
1 teaspoon dried dill	

Directions:
Sprinkle the tilapia fillets with dried dill and ground black pepper. Put them in the Crock Pot. Add butter.   Cook the tilapia on Low for 6 hours.
Nutrition Info: Per Serving: 298 calories, 21.3g protein, 0.3g carbohydrates, 24.1g fat, 0.1g fiber, 116mg cholesterol, 204mg sodium, 18mg potassium

Marinara Salmon

Servings: 4   Cooking Time: 3 Hours
Ingredients:

1-pound salmon fillet, chopped	¼ cup fresh cilantro, chopped
½ cup marinara sauce	¼ cup of water

Directions:
Put the salmon in the Crock Pot.   Add marinara sauce, cilantro, and water.   Close the lid and cook the fish on High for hours.
Nutrition Info: Per Serving: 177 calories, 22.6g protein, 4.3g carbohydrates, 7.9g fat, 0.8g fiber, 51mg cholesterol, 179mg sodium, 540mg potassium

Salmon And Strawberries Mix

Servings: 2   Cooking Time: 2 Hours
Ingredients:

1 pound salmon fillets, boneless	4 scallions, chopped
1 cup strawberries, halved	1 teaspoon balsamic vinegar
½ cup orange juice	1 tablespoon chives, chopped
Zest of 1 lemon, grated	A pinch of salt and black pepper

Directions:
In your Crock Pot, mix the salmon with the strawberries, orange juice and the other ingredients, toss, put the lid on and cook on High for 2 hours.   Divide everything into bowls and serve.
Nutrition Info:calories 200, fat 12, fiber 4, carbs 6, protein 8

Mini Fish Balls

Servings: 6   Cooking Time: 2.5 Hours
Ingredients:

4 oz corn kernels, cooked	1 teaspoon ground black pepper
1-pound salmon fillet, minced	½ teaspoon salt
1 tablespoon semolina	1 tablespoon sesame oil
½ zucchini, grated	½ cup of water

Directions:
Mix corn kernels, salmon, semolina, grated zucchini, ground black pepper, and salt in the bowl. Make the small balls.   Then heat the sesame oil well.   Put the small balls in the hot oil and roast for 1.5 minutes per side.   Then arrange the fish balls one-by-one in the Crock Pot.   Add water and close the lid.   Cook the meal on High for 2.5 hours.
Nutrition Info: Per Serving: 218 calories, 18.5g protein, 21.4g carbohydrates, 8.2g fat, 3.1g fiber, 33mg cholesterol, 245mg sodium, 618mg potassium.

Stuffed Squid

Servings: 4   Cooking Time: 3 Hours
Ingredients:

4 squid	4 tablespoons soy
1 cup sticky rice	sauce
14 ounces dashi stock	1 tablespoon mirin
2 tablespoons sake	2 tablespoons sugar

Directions:
Chop tentacles from squid, mix with the rice, stuff each squid with this mix and seal ends with toothpicks.   Place squid in your Crock Pot, add stock, soy sauce, sake, sugar and mirin, stir, cover and cook on High for 3 hours.   Divide between plates and serve.
Nutrition Info:calories 230, fat 4, fiber 4, carbs 7, protein 11

White Fish With Olives Sauce

Servings: 4   Cooking Time: 2 Hrs.
Ingredients:

4 white fish fillets, boneless	1 garlic clove, minced
	A drizzle of olive oil
1 cup olives, pitted and chopped	Salt and black pepper to the taste
1 lb. cherry tomatoes halved	¼ cup chicken stock
A pinch of thyme, dried	

Directions:
Pour the stock into the insert of the Crock Pot. Add fish, tomatoes, olives, oil, black pepper, salt, garlic, and thyme to the stock.   Put the cooker's lid on and set the cooking time to 2 hours on High settings.   Serve warm.
Nutrition Info: Per Serving: Calories: 200, Total Fat: 3g, Fiber: 3g, Total Carbs: 12g, Protein: 20g

Lobster Cheese Soup

Servings: 6   Cooking Time: 3.5 Hrs.
Ingredients:

5 cups fish stock	8 oz lobster tails
1 tbsp paprika	1/3 cup fresh dill, chopped
½ tsp powdered chili	
1 tsp salt	1 tbsp almond milk
6 oz Cheddar cheese, shredded	1 garlic clove, peeled
	3 potatoes, peeled and diced
1 tsp ground white pepper	

Directions:
Add stock, potatoes, paprika, salt, almond milk, garlic cloves, white pepper, powdered chili to the insert of Crock Pot.   Put the cooker's lid on and set the cooking time to hours on High settings. Now add dill, and lobster tails to the cooker.   Put the cooker's lid on and set the cooking time to 1.5 hours on High settings.   Serve warm with shredded cheese on top.
Nutrition Info: Per Serving: Calories: 261, Total Fat: 4.8g, Fiber: 5g, Total Carbs: 37.14g, Protein: 19g

Chili-rubbed Tilapia

Servings: 4   Cooking Time: 4 Hours

Ingredients:

2 tablespoons chili powder	2 tablespoons lemon juice
½ teaspoon garlic powder	2 tablespoons olive oil
1-pound tilapia	

Directions:
Place all ingredients in a mixing bowl. Stir to combine everything.   Allow to marinate in the fridge for at least 30 minutes.   Get a foil and place the fish including the marinade in the middle of the foil.   Fold the foil and crimp the edges to seal.   Place inside the crockpot.   Cook on high for 2 hours or on low for 4 hours.
Nutrition Info: Calories per serving: 183; Carbohydrates: 2.9g; Protein: 23.4g; Fat: 11.3g; Sugar: 0.3g; Sodium: 215mg; Fiber:1.4 g

Rosemary Seabass

Servings: 3   Cooking Time: 4 Hours
Ingredients:

3 seabass fillets	2 teaspoons sesame oil
1 teaspoon dried rosemary	
	½ cup of water
1 carrot, grated	

Directions:
Rub the seabass fillets with dried rosemary and sesame oil.   Then place them in the Crock Pot in one layer.   Top the fillets with grated carrot. Add water and close the lid.   Cook the fish on low for 4 hours.
Nutrition Info: Per Serving: 271 calories, 26.3g protein, 2.3g carbohydrates, 17.2g fat, 1.6g fiber, 0mg cholesterol, 16mg sodium, 69mg potassium.

Cumin Snapper

Servings: 4   Cooking Time: 4 Hours
Ingredients:

1-pound snapper, peeled, cleaned	½ teaspoon salt
	1 teaspoon dried oregano
1 teaspoon ground cumin	
½ teaspoon garlic powder	1 tablespoon sesame oil
	¼ cup of water

Directions:
Cut the snapper into 4 servings.   After this, in the shallow bowl mix ground cumin, salt, garlic powder, and dried oregano.   Sprinkle fish with spices and sesame oil.   Arrange the snapper in the Crock Pot. Add water.   Cook the fish on Low for 4 hours.
Nutrition Info: Per Serving: 183 calories, 29.9g protein, 0.7g carbohydrates, 5.6g fat, 0.3g fiber, 54mg cholesterol, 360mg sodium, 20mg potassium.

Milky Fish

Servings: 6   Cooking Time: 2 Hours

Ingredients:

17 ounces white fish, skinless, boneless and cut into medium chunks
1 yellow onion, chopped
13 ounces potatoes, peeled and cut into chunks

13 ounces milk
Salt and black pepper to the taste
14 ounces chicken stock
14 ounces water
14 ounces half and half

Directions:
In your Crock Pot, mix fish with onion, potatoes, water, milk and stock, cover and cook on High for 2 hours.   Add salt, pepper, half and half, stir, divide into bowls and serve.

Nutrition Info: calories 203, fat 4, fiber 5, carbs 20, protein 15

Caribbean Seasoning Fish Balls

Servings: 4   Cooking Time: 3 Hours

Ingredients:

1 teaspoon Caribbean seasonings
½ teaspoon dried thyme
1 egg, beaten

12 oz salmon fillet, chopped
1 teaspoon sunflower oil
¼ cup of water

Directions:
Mix Caribbean seasonings with dried thyme. Then add chopped salmon and carefully mix. Add egg.   Pour sunflower oil in the Crock Pot. Add water.   Make the fish balls with the help of the spoon and put them in the Crock Pot.   Cook the fish balls on High for 3 hours.

Nutrition Info: Per Serving: 145 calories, 17.9g protein, 1.7g carbohydrates, 0.1g fat, 0.1g fiber, 78mg cholesterol, 161mg sodium, 343mg potassium

Turmeric Mackerel

Servings: 4   Cooking Time: 2.5 Hours

Ingredients:

1-pound mackerel fillet
1 tablespoon ground turmeric

½ teaspoon salt
¼ teaspoon chili powder
½ cup of water

Directions:
Rub the mackerel fillet with ground turmeric and chili powder.   Then put it in the Crock Pot. Add water and salt.   Close the lid and cook the fish on High for 2.5 hours.

Nutrition Info: Per Serving: 304 calories, 27.2g protein, 1.2g carbohydrates, 20.4g fat, 0.4g fiber, 58mg cholesterol, 388mg sodium, 501mg potassium

Italian Barramundi And Tomato Relish

Servings: 4   Cooking Time: 2 Hours

Ingredients:

2 barramundi fillets, skinless
2 teaspoon olive oil
2 teaspoons Italian seasoning
¼ cup green olives, pitted and chopped
¼ cup cherry tomatoes, chopped
¼ cup black olives, chopped

1 tablespoon lemon zest
2 tablespoons lemon zest
Salt and black pepper to the taste
2 tablespoons parsley, chopped
1 tablespoon olive oil

Directions:
Rub fish with salt, pepper, Italian seasoning and 2 teaspoons olive oil and put into your Crock Pot. In a bowl, mix tomatoes with all the olives, salt, pepper, lemon zest and lemon juice, parsley and 1 tablespoon olive oil, toss, add over fish, cover and cook on High for hours.   Divide fish between plates, top with tomato relish and serve.

Nutrition Info: calories 140, fat 4, fiber 2, carbs 11, protein 10

Tomato Fish Casserole

Servings: 2   Cooking Time: 6 Hours

Ingredients:

2 cod fillets
1 cup bell pepper, chopped
1 teaspoon ground cumin

½ cup tomato juice
½ teaspoon salt
1 teaspoon olive oil
½ cup spinach, chopped

Directions:
Slice the cod fillets and sprinkle them with olive oil, salt, and ground cumin.   Put the fish in the Crock Pot.   Top it with bell pepper and spinach. Then add tomato juice and close the lid.   Cook the casserole on Low for 6 hours.

Nutrition Info: Per Serving: 145 calories, 21.5g protein, 7.8g carbohydrates, 3.8g fat, 1.3g fiber, 55mg cholesterol, 824mg sodium, 312mg potassium

Cod Bacon Chowder

Servings: 6   Cooking Time: 3 Hrs

Ingredients:

1 yellow onion, chopped
10 oz. cod, cubed
3 oz. bacon, sliced
1 tsp sage
5 oz. potatoes, peeled and cubed

1 carrot, grated
5 cups of water
1 tbsp almond milk
1 tsp ground coriander
1 tsp salt

Directions:
Place grated carrots and onion in the Crock Pot. Add almond milk, coriander, water, sage, fish, potatoes, and bacon.   Put the cooker's lid on and set the cooking time to hours on High settings. Garnish with chopped parsley.   Serve.

Nutrition Info: Per Serving: Calories 108, Total Fat 4.5g, Fiber 2g, Total Carbs 8.02g, Protein 10g

Chives Mussels

Servings: 2   Cooking Time: 1 Hour
Ingredients:

1 pound mussels, debearded	Juice of 1 lime
½ teaspoon coriander, ground	1 cup tomato passata
½ teaspoon rosemary, dried	¼ cup chicken stock
1 tablespoon lime zest, grated	A pinch of salt and black pepper
	1 tablespoon chives, chopped

Directions:
In your Crock Pot, mix the mussels with the coriander, rosemary and the other ingredients, toss, put the lid on and cook on High for hour. Divide the mix into bowls and serve.
Nutrition Info:calories 200, fat 12, fiber 2, carbs 6, protein 9

Creamy Onion Casserole

Servings: 6   Cooking Time: 3 Hours
Ingredients:

3 white onions, sliced	1 cup cream
1-pound salmon fillet, chopped	¼ cup fresh parsley, chopped
1 teaspoon ground coriander	2 tablespoons breadcrumbs

Directions:
Sprinkle the salmon fillet with ground coriander and coat in the breadcrumbs.   Put the fish in the Crock Pot.   Then top it with sliced onion and fresh parsley.   Add cream and close the lid. Cook the casserole on High for 3 hours.
Nutrition Info: Per Serving: 158 calories, 16g protein, 8.2g carbohydrates, 7.1g fat, 1.4g fiber, 41mg cholesterol, 66mg sodium, 404mg potassium

Indian Fish Curry

Servings: 6   Cooking Time: 2 Hrs.
Ingredients:

6 white fish fillets, cut into medium pieces	6 curry leaves
1 tomato, chopped	1 tbsp ginger, finely grated
14 oz. coconut milk	½ tsp turmeric, ground
2 yellow onions, sliced	2 tsp cumin, ground
2 red bell peppers, cut into strips	Salt and black pepper to the taste
2 garlic cloves, minced	½ tsp fenugreek, ground
1 tbsp coriander, ground	1 tsp hot pepper flakes
	2 tbsp lemon juice

Directions:
Add fish, milk, tomatoes, and rest of the ingredients to the insert of the Crock Pot.   Put the cooker's lid on and set the cooking time to

hours on High settings.   Give it a gentle stir and serve warm.
Nutrition Info: Per Serving: Calories: 231, Total Fat: 4g, Fiber: 6g, Total Carbs: 16g, Protein: 22g

Salmon, Tomatoes And Green Beans

Servings: 2   Cooking Time: 2 Hours
Ingredients:

1 pound salmon fillets, boneless and cubed	1 cup tomato passata
1 cup cherry tomatoes, halved	½ cup chicken stock
1 cup green beans, trimmed and halved	A pinch of salt and black pepper
	1 tablespoon parsley, chopped

Directions:
In your Crock Pot, mix the salmon with the tomatoes, green beans and the other ingredients, toss, put the lid on and cook on High for 2 hours. Divide the mix into bowls and serve.
Nutrition Info:calories 232, fat 7, fiber 3, carbs 7, protein 9

Crockpot Asian Shrimps

Servings: 2   Cooking Time: 3 Hours
Ingredients:

2 tablespoons soy sauce	½ cup chicken stock
½ teaspoon sliced ginger	2 tablespoons sesame oil
½ pound shrimps, cleaned and deveined	2 tablespoons toasted sesame seeds
2 tablespoons rice vinegar	2 tablespoons green onions, chopped

Directions:
Place the chicken stock, soy sauce, ginger, shrimps, and rice vinegar in the CrockPot.   Give a good stir.   Close the lid and cook on high for 2 hours or on low for hours.   Sprinkle with sesame oil, sesame seeds, and chopped green onions before serving.
Nutrition Info: Calories per serving: 352; Carbohydrates: 4.7g; Protein: 30.2g; Fat: 24.3g; Sugar: 0.4g; Sodium: 755mg; Fiber: 2.9g

Cod With Asparagus

Servings: 4   Cooking Time: 2 Hrs
Ingredients:

4 cod fillets, boneless	Salt and black pepper to the taste
1 bunch asparagus	
12 tbsp lemon juice	2 tbsp olive oil

Directions:
Place the cod fillets in separate foil sheets.   Top the fish with asparagus spears, lemon pepper, oil, and lemon juice.   Wrap the fish with its foil sheet then place them in Crock Pot.   Put the cooker's lid on and set the cooking time to 2 hours on High settings.   Unwrap the fish and serve warm.
Nutrition Info: Per Serving: Calories 202, Total Fat 3g, Fiber 6g, Total Carbs 7g, Protein 3g

Mussels Tomato Soup

Servings: 6   Cooking Time: 2 Hrs.

Ingredients:

2 lbs. mussels	2 cup chicken stock
28 oz. canned tomatoes, crushed	1 handful parsley, chopped
28 oz. canned tomatoes, chopped	1 yellow onion, chopped
1 tsp red pepper flakes, crushed	Salt and black pepper to the taste
3 garlic cloves, minced	1 tbsp olive oil

Directions:

Toss mussels with tomatoes, stock, parsley, garlic, pepper flakes, oil, black pepper, salt, and onion in the insert of Crock Pot.   Put the cooker's lid on and set the cooking time to hours on High settings. Serve warm.

Nutrition Info: Per Serving: Calories: 250, Total Fat: 3g, Fiber: 3g, Total Carbs: 8g, Protein: 12g

Tabasco Halibut

Servings: 4   Cooking Time: 2 Hours

Ingredients:

½ cup parmesan, grated	½ teaspoon Tabasco sauce
¼ cup butter, melted	4 halibut fillets, boneless
¼ cup mayonnaise	
2 tablespoons green onions, chopped	Salt and black pepper to the taste
6 garlic cloves, minced	Juice of ½ lemon

Directions:

Season halibut with salt, pepper and some of the lemon juice, place in your Crock Pot, add butter, mayo, green onions, garlic, Tabasco sauce and lemon juice, toss a bit, cover and cook on High for 2 hours.   Add parmesan, leave fish mix aside for a few more minutes, divide between plates and serve.

Nutrition Info:calories 240, fat 12, fiber 1, carbs 15, protein 23

Fish Soufflé(2)

Servings: 4   Cooking Time: 7 Hours

Ingredients:

4 eggs, beaten	¼ cup of coconut milk
8 oz salmon fillet, chopped	2 oz Provolone cheese, grated

Directions:

Mix coconut milk with eggs and pour the liquid in the Crock Pot.   Add salmon and cheese.   Close the lid and cook soufflé for 7 hours on low.

Nutrition Info: Per Serving: 222 calories, 20.5g protein, 1.5g carbohydrates, 15.2g fat, 0.3g fiber, 198mg cholesterol, 212mg sodium, 336mg potassium

Fish Pudding

Servings: 4   Cooking Time: 2 Hours

Ingredients:

1 pound cod fillets, cut into medium pieces	2 eggs, whisked
	2 ounces butter, melted
2 tablespoons parsley, chopped	½ pint milk

4 ounces breadcrumbs	½ pint shrimp sauce
2 teaspoons lemon juice	Salt and black pepper to the taste

Directions:

In a bowl, mix fish with crumbs, lemon juice, parsley, salt and pepper and stir.   Add butter to your Crock Pot, add milk and whisk well.   Add egg and fish mix, stir, cover and cook on High for 2 hours.   Divide between plates and serve with shrimp sauce on top.

Nutrition Info:calories 231, fat 3, fiber 5, carbs 10, protein 5

Basil-parmesan Shrimps

Servings: 4   Cooking Time: 3 Hours

Ingredients:

1 tablespoon grass-fed butter, melted	1 cup grass-fed heavy cream
1-pound shrimps, shelled and deveined	½ cup fresh basil leaves, chopped
2 cloves of garlic, minced	Salt and pepper to taste
2 tablespoons lemon juice, freshly squeezed	1 cup organic parmesan cheese, grated

Directions:

Place butter in the CrockPot. Add in the shrimps, garlic, and lemon juice on top. Mix until combined. Stir in the cream and basil leaves. Season with salt and pepper to taste.   Sprinkle parmesan cheese on top.   Close the lid and cook on high for 2 hours or on low for 3 hours.

Nutrition Info: Calories per serving:428; Carbohydrates: 3g; Protein: 29g; Fat: 33g; Sugar: 0.4g; Sodium: 510mg; Fiber: 0.8g

Jambalaya

Servings: 8   Cooking Time: 4 Hours And 30 Minutes

Ingredients:

1 pound chicken breast, chopped	1 and ½ cups rice
1 pound shrimp, peeled and deveined	2 cups green, yellow and red bell peppers, chopped
2 tablespoons extra virgin olive oil	
1 pound sausage, chopped	3 and ½ cups chicken stock
2 cups onions, chopped	1 tablespoon Creole seasoning
2 tablespoons garlic, chopped	1 tablespoon Worcestershire sauce
	1 cup tomatoes, crushed

Directions:

Add the oil to your Crock Pot and spread.   Add chicken, sausage, onion, rice, garlic, mixed bell peppers, stock, seasoning, tomatoes and Worcestershire sauce, cover and cook on High for 4 hours.   Add shrimp, cover, cook on High for minutes more, divide everything between plates and serve.

Nutrition Info:calories 251, fat 10, fiber 3, carbs 20, protein 25

Seafood Chowder

Servings: 4   Cooking Time: 8 Hours And 30 Minutes

Ingredients:

- 2 cups water
- ½ fennel bulb, chopped
- 2 sweet potatoes, cubed
- 1 yellow onion, chopped
- 2 bay leaves
- 1 tablespoon thyme, dried
- 1 celery rib, chopped
- Salt and black pepper to the taste
- 1 bottle clam juice
- 2 tablespoons tapioca powder
- 1 cup coconut milk
- 1 pounds salmon fillets, cubed
- 5 sea scallops, halved
- 24 shrimp, peeled and deveined
- ¼ cup parsley, chopped

Directions:

In your Crock Pot, mix water with fennel, potatoes, onion, bay leaves, thyme, celery, clam juice, salt, pepper and tapioca, stir, cover and cook on Low for 8 hours.   Add salmon, coconut milk, scallops, shrimp and parsley, cook on Low for 30 minutes more, ladle chowder into bowls and serve.

Nutrition Info:calories 354, fat 10, fiber 2, carbs 10, protein 12

Cardamom Trout

Servings: 4   Cooking Time: 2.5 Hours

Ingredients:

- 1 teaspoon ground cardamom
- 1-pound trout fillet
- 1 teaspoon butter, melted
- 1 tablespoon lemon juice
- ¼ cup of water
- 1.2 teaspoon salt

Directions:

In the shallow bowl mix butter, lemon juice, and salt.   Then sprinkle the trout fillet with ground cardamom and butter mixture.   Place the fish in the Crock Pot and add water.   Cook the meal on High for 2.5 hours.

Nutrition Info: Per Serving: 226 calories, 30.3g protein, 0.4g carbohydrates, 10.6g fat, 0.2g fiber, 86mg cholesterol, 782mg sodium, 536mg potassium.

Turmeric Salmon

Servings: 2   Cooking Time: 2 Hours

Ingredients:

- 1 pound salmon fillets, boneless
- 1 red onion, chopped
- ½ teaspoon turmeric powder
- ½ teaspoon oregano, dried
- ½ cup chicken stock
- 1 teaspoon olive oil
- Salt and black pepper to the taste
- 1 tablespoon chives, chopped

Directions:

In your Crock Pot, mix the salmon with the turmeric, onion and the other ingredients, toss gently, put the lid on and cook on High for 2 hours. Divide the mix between plates and serve.

Nutrition Info:calories 200, fat 12, fiber 3, carbs 6, protein 11

Salmon Salad

Servings: 2   Cooking Time: 3 Hours

Ingredients:

- 1 pound salmon fillets, boneless and cubed
- ¼ cup chicken stock
- 1 zucchini, cut with a spiralizer
- 1 carrot, sliced
- 1 eggplant, cubed
- ½ cup cherry tomatoes, halved
- 1 red onion, sliced
- ½ teaspoon turmeric powder
- ½ teaspoon chili powder
- ½ tablespoon rosemary, chopped
- A pinch of salt and black pepper
- 1 tablespoon chives, chopped

Directions:

In your Crock Pot, mix the salmon with the zucchini, stock, carrot and the other ingredients,, toss , put the lid on and cook on High for 3 hours. Divide the mix into bowls and serve.

Nutrition Info:calories 424, fat 15.1, fiber 12.4, carbs 28.1, protein 49

Braised Salmon

Servings: 4   Cooking Time: 1 Hour

Ingredients:

- 1 cup of water
- 2-pound salmon fillet
- 1 teaspoon salt
- 1 teaspoon ground black pepper

Directions:

Put all ingredients in the Crock Pot and close the lid.   Cook the salmon on High for 1 hour.

Nutrition Info: Per Serving: 301 calories, 44.1g protein, 0.3g carbohydrates, 14g fat, 0.1g fiber, 100mg cholesterol, 683mg sodium, 878mg potassium.

Butter Smelt

Servings: 4   Cooking Time: 6 Hours

Ingredients:

- 16 oz smelt fillet
- 1 teaspoon dried thyme
- 1/3 cup butter
- 1 teaspoon salt

Directions:

Sprinkle the fish with dried thyme and salt and put in the Crock Pot.   Add butter and close the lid. Cook the smelt on Low for 6 hours.

Nutrition Info: Per Serving: 226 calories, 17.2g protein, 0.2g carbohydrates, 17.4g fat, 0.1g fiber, 191mg cholesterol, 750mg sodium, 7mg potassium

Braised Lobster

Servings: 4   Cooking Time: 3 Hours
Ingredients:

2-pound lobster, cleaned   1 teaspoon Italian seasonings

1 cup of water

Directions:
Put all ingredients in the Crock Pot.   Close the lid and cook the lobster in High for 3 hours.
Remove the lobster from the Crock Pot and cool it till room temperature
Nutrition Info: Per Serving: 206 calories, 43.1g protein, 0.1g carbohydrates, 2.2g fat, 0g fiber, 332mg cholesterol, 1104mg sodium, 524mg potassium.

Asian Salmon Mix

Servings: 2   Cooking Time: 3 Hours
Ingredients:

2 medium salmon fillets, boneless   16 ounces mixed broccoli and cauliflower florets

Salt and black pepper to the taste

2 tablespoons soy sauce   2 tablespoons lemon juice

2 tablespoons maple syrup   1 teaspoon sesame seeds

Directions:
Put the cauliflower and broccoli florets in your Crock Pot and top with salmon fillets.   In a bowl, mix maple syrup with soy sauce and lemon juice, whisk well, pour this over salmon fillets, season with salt, pepper, sprinkle sesame seeds on top and cook on Low for 3 hours.   Divide everything between plates and serve.
Nutrition Info:calories 230, fat 4, fiber 2, carbs 12, protein 6

Slow Cooked Haddock

Servings: 4   Cooking Time: 2 Hours
Ingredients:

1 pound haddock   3 teaspoons water

2 tablespoons lemon juice   1 teaspoon dill, chopped

Salt and black pepper to the taste   Cooking spray

2 tablespoons mayonnaise   ½ teaspoon old bay seasoning

Directions:
Spray your Crock Pot with the cooking spray, add lemon juice, water, fish, salt, pepper, mayo, dill and old bay seasoning, cover, cook on High for 2 hours. Divide between plates and serve.
Nutrition Info:calories 274, fat 12, fiber 1, carbs 6, protein 20

Orange Cod

Servings: 4   Cooking Time: 3 Hours
Ingredients:

1-pound cod fillet, chopped   1 cup of water

2 oranges, chopped   1 garlic clove, diced

1 tablespoon maple syrup   1 teaspoon ground black pepper

Directions:
Mix cod with ground black pepper and transfer in the Crock Pot.   Add garlic, water, maple syrup, and oranges.   Close the lid and cook the meal on High for hours.
Nutrition Info: Per Serving: 150 calories, 21.2g protein, 14.8g carbohydrates, 1.2g fat, 2.4g fiber, 56mg cholesterol, 73mg sodium, 187mg potassium.

Basil Cod And Olives

Servings: 2   Cooking Time: 3 Hours
Ingredients:

1 pound cod fillets, boneless   ¼ cup chicken stock

1 cup black olives, pitted and halved   1 red onion, sliced

½ tablespoon tomato paste   1 tablespoon lime juice

1 tablespoon basil, chopped   1 tablespoon chives, chopped

Salt and black pepper to the taste

Directions:
In your Crock Pot, mix the cod with the olives, basil and the other ingredients, toss, put the lid on and cook on Low for 3 hours.   Divide everything between plates and serve.
Nutrition Info:calories 132, fat 9, fiber 2, carbs 5, protein 11

Express Shrimps And Sausage Jambalaya Stew

Servings: 4   Cooking Time: 3 Hours
Ingredients:

1 teaspoon canola oil   1 16-ounce bag frozen bell pepper and onion mix

8 ounces andouille sausage, cut into slices   8 ounces shrimps, shelled and deveined

1 can chicken broth

Directions:
In a skillet, heat the oil and sauté the sausages until the sausages have rendered their fat. Set aside.
Pour the vegetable mix into the crockpot.   Add in the sausages and pour the chicken broth.   Stir in the shrimps last.   Cook on low for 1 hour or on low for 3 hours.
Nutrition Info: Calories per serving: 316; Carbohydrates: 6.3; Protein: 32.1g; Fat: 25.6g; Sugar:0.2 g; Sodium: 425mg; Fiber: 3.2g

Cod And Peas

Servings: 4   Cooking Time: 2 Hours
Ingredients:

- 16 ounces cod fillets
- 1 tablespoon parsley, chopped
- 10 ounces peas
- ½ teaspoon oregano, dried
- 9 ounces wine
- ½ teaspoon paprika
- 2 garlic cloves, chopped
- Salt and pepper to the taste

Directions:
In your food processor mix garlic with parsley, oregano, paprika and wine, blend well and add to your Crock Pot.   Add fish, peas, salt and pepper, cover and cook on High for hours.   Divide into bowls and serve.
Nutrition Info:calories 251, far 2, fiber 6, carbs 7, protein 22

Mustard Salmon Salad

Servings: 4   Cooking Time: 3 Hours
Ingredients:

- 1 cup lettuce, chopped
- 1 cup spinach, chopped
- 2 tablespoons plain yogurt
- 1 tablespoon mustard
- 1 teaspoon olive oil
- 8 oz salmon fillet
- ¼ cup of water
- 1 teaspoon butter

Directions:
Pour water in the Crock Pot.   Add butter and salmon.   Close the lid and cook it on High for hours.   After this, chop the salmon roughly and put it in the salad bowl.   Add chopped spinach and lettuce.   In the shallow bowl mix mustard, plain yogurt, and olive oil. Whisk the mixture. Shake the salmon salad and sprinkle with mustard dressing.
Nutrition Info: Per Serving: 116 calories, 12.4g protein, 2.2g carbohydrates, 6.6g fat, 0.7g fiber, 28mg cholesterol, 44mg sodium, 316mg potassium

Trout Cakes

Servings: 2   Cooking Time: 2 Hours
Ingredients:

- 7 oz trout fillet, diced
- 1 teaspoon dried oregano
- ¼ teaspoon ground black pepper
- 1 tablespoon semolina
- 1 teaspoon cornflour
- 1 egg, beaten
- 1/3 cup water
- 1 teaspoon sesame oil

Directions:
In the bowl mix diced trout, semolina, dried oregano, ground black pepper, and cornflour. Then add egg and carefully mix the mixture. Heat the sesame oil well.   Then make the fish cakes and put them in the hot oil.   Roast them for 1 minute per side and transfer in the Crock Pot. Add water and cook the trout cakes for 2 hours on High.
Nutrition Info: Per Serving: 266 calories, 30g protein, 5.6g carbohydrates, 13.1g fat, 0.7g fiber, 155mg cholesterol, 99mg sodium, 519mg potassium.

Semolina Fish Balls

Servings: 11   Cooking Time: 8 Hrs.
Ingredients:

- 1 cup sweet corn
- 5 tbsp fresh dill, chopped
- 1 tbsp minced garlic
- 7 tbsp bread crumbs
- 2 eggs, beaten
- 10 oz salmon, salmon
- 2 tbsp semolina
- 2 tbsp canola oil
- 1 tsp salt
- 1 tsp ground black pepper
- 1 tsp cumin
- 1 tsp lemon zest
- ¼ tsp cinnamon
- 3 tbsp almond flour
- 3 tbsp scallion, chopped
- 3 tbsp water

Directions:
Mix sweet corn, dill, garlic, semolina, eggs, salt, cumin, almond flour, scallion, cinnamon, lemon zest, and black pepper in a large bowl.   Stir in chopped salmon and mix well.   Make small meatballs out of this fish mixture then roll them in the breadcrumbs.   Place the coated fish ball in the insert of the Crock Pot.   Add canola oil and water to the fish balls.   Put the cooker's lid on and set the cooking time to 8 hours on Low settings.   Serve warm.
Nutrition Info: Per Serving: Calories: 201, Total Fat: 7.9g, Fiber: 2g, Total Carbs: 22.6g, Protein: 11g

Mussels And Sausage Satay

Servings: 4   Cooking Time: 2 Hrs.
Ingredients:

- 2 lbs. mussels, scrubbed and debearded
- 12 oz. amber beer
- 1 tbsp olive oil
- 1 yellow onion, chopped
- 8 oz. spicy sausage
- 1 tbsp paprika

Directions:
Grease the insert of your Crock Pot with oil.   Toss in mussels, beer, onion, sausage, and paprika. Put the cooker's lid on and set the cooking time to 2 hours on High settings.   Discard all the unopened mussels, if any.   Serve the rest and enjoy it.
Nutrition Info: Per Serving: Calories: 124, Total Fat: 3g, Fiber: 1g, Total Carbs: 7g, Protein: 12g

Shrimp And Avocado

Servings: 2   Cooking Time: 1 Hour
Ingredients:

- 1 pound shrimp, peeled and deveined
- 1 cup avocado, peeled, pitted and cubed
- ½ cup chicken stock
- ½ teaspoon sweet paprika
- Juice of 1 lime
- 1 tablespoon olive oil
- 2 tablespoons chili pepper, minced
- A pinch of salt and black pepper
- 1 tablespoon chives, chopped

Directions:
In your Crock Pot, mix the shrimp with the avocado, stock and the other ingredients, toss, put the lid on and cook on High for hour.   Divide the mix into bowls and serve.
Nutrition Info:calories 490, fat 25.4, fiber 5.8, carbs 11.9, protein 53.6

Butter Crab

Servings: 4   Cooking Time: 4.5 Hours
Ingredients:

1-pound crab meat, roughly chopped	1 tablespoon fresh parsley, chopped
3 tablespoons butter	2 tablespoons water

Directions:
Melt butter and pour it in the Crock Pot.   Add water, parsley, and crab meat.   Cook the meal on Low for 4.5 hours.
Nutrition Info: Per Serving: 178 calories, 14.3g protein, 2.1g carbohydrates, 10.7g fat, 0g fiber, 84mg cholesterol, 771mg sodium, 8mg potassium.

Vinaigrette Dipped Salmon

Servings: 6   Cooking Time: 2 Hrs.
Ingredients:

6 salmon steaks	Salt and white pepper to the taste
2 tbsp olive oil	
4 leeks, sliced	1 tsp sherry
2 garlic cloves, minced	1/3 cup dill, chopped
2 tbsp parsley, chopped	For the raspberry vinegar:
1 cup clam juice	2 pints red raspberries
2 tbsp lemon juice	1-pint cider vinegar

Directions:
Mix raspberries with salmon, and vinegar in a bowl.   Cover the raspberry salmon and refrigerate for hours.   Add the raspberry mixture along with the remaining ingredients to the insert of the Crock Pot.   Put the cooker's lid on and set the cooking time to 2 hours on High settings. Serve warm.
Nutrition Info: Per Serving: Calories: 251, Total Fat: 6g, Fiber: 7g, Total Carbs: 16g, Protein: 26g

Flounder Cheese Casserole

Servings: 11   Cooking Time: 6 Hrs.
Ingredients:

8 oz rice noodles	1 cup carrot, cooked
2 cups chicken stock	2 tbsp butter, melted
12 oz flounder fillet, chopped	3 tbsp chives
½ tsp ground black pepper	4 oz shallot, chopped
	7 oz cream cheese
2 sweet peppers, chopped	5 oz Parmesan, shredded
3 sweet potatoes, chopped	½ cup fresh cilantro, chopped
	1 cup of water

Directions:
Brush the insert of your Crock Pot with melted butter.   Place the chopped flounder, carrots, sweet peppers, sweet potatoes, shallots, and chives to the cooker.   Add cilantro, stock, black pepper, cream cheese, and water to the flounder.   Top the flounder casserole with shredded cheese.   Put the cooker's lid on and set the cooking time to 6 hours on Low settings.   Serve warm.

Nutrition Info: Per Serving: Calories: 202, Total Fat: 9.1g, Fiber: 2g, Total Carbs: 19.86g, Protein: 11g

Salmon Pudding

Servings: 4   Cooking Time: 6 Hours
Ingredients:

1-pound salmon fillet, chopped	1 teaspoon coconut oil
½ cup milk	1 teaspoon fish sauce
2 tablespoons breadcrumbs	1 teaspoon salt
	2 eggs, beaten

Directions:
Mix all ingredients in the Crock Pot and close the lid.   Cook the pudding on Low for 6 hours.
Nutrition Info: Per Serving: 220 calories, 26.3g protein, 4.2g carbohydrates, 11.1g fat, 0.2g fiber, 134mg cholesterol, 817mg sodium, 494mg potassium.

Tomato Squid

Servings: 4   Cooking Time: 2 Hours
Ingredients:

1-pound squid tubes, cleaned	1 teaspoon cayenne pepper
1 cup tomatoes, chopped	1 cup of water
½ cup bell pepper, chopped	1 teaspoon avocado oil

Directions:
Chop the squid tube roughly and mix with avocado oil and cayenne pepper.   Put the squid in the Crock Pot.   Add water, bell pepper, and tomatoes.   Close the lid and cook the squid on High for 2 hours.
Nutrition Info: Per Serving: 76 calories, 12.6g protein, 3.2g carbohydrates, 1.8g fat, 0.9g fiber, 351mg cholesterol, 546mg sodium, 148mg potassium.

Creamy Garlic Shrimps With Goat Cheese

Servings: 4   Cooking Time: 3 Hours
Ingredients:

1-pound shrimps, shelled and deveined	1 onion, minced
2 tablespoons butter	1 teaspoon lemon juice
4 cloves of garlic, minced	Salt and pepper to taste
1 teaspoon paprika	¼ cup organic goat cheese
¼ teaspoon cayenne pepper	

Directions:
Place all ingredients in the CrockPot.   Give a good stir.   Close the lid and cook on high for 2 hours or on low for hours.
Nutrition Info: Calories per serving: 512; Carbohydrates: 3.6g; Protein: 59.2g; Fat: 26.8g; Sugar: 1.2g; Sodium: 891mg; Fiber: 1g

Shri Lanka Fish Cutlet

Servings: 14   Cooking Time: 2 Hrs.

Ingredients:

16 oz mackerel fillet, minced	1 tsp salt
1 cup mashed potato	4 oz tomato sauce
1 chili pepper, finely chopped	1 tsp ground thyme
1 cup onion, grated	4 tsp lime juice
1 tsp minced garlic	3 large eggs
¼ tsp ground ginger	1 cup bread crumbs
1 oz curry powder	1 tsp chives
	1 tbsp onion powder

Directions:
Mix mackerel mince with mashed potato, grated onion, ginger, garlic, curry powder, thyme, lime juice, onion powder, and salt in a suitable bowl. Make small round cutlets out of this mixture. Dip the mackerel cutlets in the whisked egg then coat them with breadcrumbs.   Place cutlets in the insert of the Crock Pot and top them with tomato sauce.   Put the cooker's lid on and set the cooking time to 2 hours on High settings.   Serve warm.

Nutrition Info: Per Serving: Calories: 83, Total Fat: 2g, Fiber: 2g, Total Carbs: 7.67g, Protein: 8g

Sriracha Cod

Servings: 4   Cooking Time: 6 Hours

Ingredients:

2 tablespoons sriracha	4 cod fillets
1 tablespoon olive oil	1 teaspoon tomato paste
	½ cup of water

Directions:
Sprinkle the cod fillets with sriracha, olive oil, and tomato paste.   Put the fish in the Crock Pot and add water.   Cook it on Low for 6 hours.

Nutrition Info: Per Serving: 129 calories, 20.1g protein, 1.8g carbohydrates, 4.5g fat, 0.1g fiber, 55mg cholesterol, 125mg sodium, 14mg potassium.

Mustard Garlic Shrimps

Servings: 4   Cooking Time: 2 Hours And 30 Minutes

Ingredients:

1 teaspoon olive oil	1 teaspoon Dijon mustards
3 tablespoons garlic, minced	Salt and pepper to taste
1-pound shrimp, shelled and deveined	Parsley for garnish

Directions:
In a skillet, heat the olive oil and sauté the garlic until fragrant and slightly browned.   Transfer to the crockpot and place the shrimps and Dijon mustard. Stir to combine.   Season with salt and pepper to taste.   Close the lid and cook on low for 2 hours or high for 30 minutes.   Once done, sprinkle with parsley.

Nutrition Info: Calories per serving: 138; Carbohydrates: 3.2g; Protein: 23.8g; Fat: 2.7g; Sugar: 0.5g; Sodium: 535mg; Fiber: 0.9g

Mussels Soup

Servings: 6   Cooking Time: 2 Hours

Ingredients:

2 pounds mussels	2 cup chicken stock
28 ounces canned tomatoes, crushed	1 handful parsley, chopped
28 ounces canned tomatoes, chopped	1 yellow onion, chopped
1 teaspoon red pepper flakes, crushed	Salt and black pepper to the taste
3 garlic cloves, minced	1 tablespoon olive oil

Directions:
In your Crock Pot, mix mussels with canned and crushed tomatoes, stock, pepper flakes, garlic, parsley, onion, salt, pepper and oil, stir, cover and cook on High for 2 hours.   Divide into bowls and serve.

Nutrition Info: calories 250, fat 3, fiber 3, carbs 8, protein 12

Rice Stuffed Trout

Servings: 5   Cooking Time: 4 Hrs.

Ingredients:

16 oz whole trout, peeled	1 tsp ground black pepper
½ cup sweet corn	½ tsp paprika
¼ cup of rice, cooked	1 tbsp olive oil
1 sweet pepper, chopped	1 tbsp sour cream
1 tbsp salt	¼ cup cream cheese
1 tsp thyme	3 lemon wedges
	2 tbsp chives

Directions:
Mix sweet corn, cooked rice, and sweet pepper in a suitable bowl.   Whisk chives, salt, sour cream, olive oil, cream cheese, paprika, thyme, black pepper in a separate bowl.   Place the trout fish in a foil sheet and brush it with a cream cheese mixture.   Stuff the fish with rice mixture and top the fish with lemon wedges.   Wrap the stuffed with the foil sheet.   Put the cooker's lid on and set the cooking time to 4 hours on High settings. Serve warm.

Nutrition Info: Per Serving: Calories: 255, Total Fat: 13.9g, Fiber: 2g, Total Carbs: 13.57g, Protein: 22g

Pangasius With Crunchy Crust

Servings: 2   Cooking Time: 3 Hours

Ingredients:

6 oz pangasius fillet	1/3 cup chicken stock
2 tablespoons breadcrumbs	1 teaspoon salt
1 egg, beaten	1 teaspoon ground black pepper
1 tablespoon flour	

Directions:
Sprinkle the fish fillets with ground black pepper and salt.   Then mix breadcrumbs with flour. After this, dip the fish fillets in the beaten egg and coat in the flour mixture.   Put the fish fillets in the Crock Pot. Add chicken stock and close the lid. Cook the fish on high for 3 hours. Then preheat the skillet well and put the fish fillets inside. Roast them for 2 minutes per side.

Nutrition Info: Per Serving: 119 calories, 12.2g protein, 8.8g carbohydrates, 4.3g fat, 0.7g fiber, 92mg cholesterol, 1508mg sodium, 63mg potassium

Salmon With Almond Crust

Servings: 2   Cooking Time: 2.5 Hours
Ingredients:

8 oz salmon fillet	1 teaspoon butter
2 tablespoons almond flakes	1 teaspoon salt
1 teaspoon ground black pepper	1 egg, beaten
	¼ cup of coconut milk

Directions:
Sprinkle the salmon fillet with ground black pepper and salt.   Then dip the fish in egg and coat in the almond flakes.   Put butter and coconut milk in the Crock Pot.   Then add salmon and close the lid.   Cook the salmon on High for 2.hours.
Nutrition Info: Per Serving: 301 calories, 26.6g protein, 3g carbohydrates, 20.9g fat, 1.5g fiber, 137mg cholesterol, 1262mg sodium, 558mg potassium

Basil Octopus

Servings: 3   Cooking Time: 4 Hours
Ingredients:

12 oz octopus, chopped	1 orange, chopped
1 teaspoon dried basil	½ cup of water
	1 teaspoon butter

Directions:
Put all ingredients in the Crock Pot.   Close the lid and cook the octopus on Low for 4 hours or until it is soft.
Nutrition Info: Per Serving: 226 calories, 34.4g protein, 12.2g carbohydrates, 3.7g fat, 1.5g fiber, 112mg cholesterol, 532mg sodium, 827mg potassium

Cream Cheese Fish Balls

Servings: 4   Cooking Time: 2 Hours
Ingredients:

8 oz salmon fillet, minced	½ teaspoon dried cilantro
1 tablespoon cream cheese	¼ teaspoon garlic powder
2 tablespoons flour	¼ cup fish stock

Directions:
In the mixing bowl mix minced salmon fillet with cream cheese, dried cilantro, garlic powder, and flour.   Make the fish balls and put them in the Crock Pot.   Add fish stock and close the lid. Cook the meal on High for 2 hours.
Nutrition Info: Per Serving: 101 calories, 12g protein, 3.2g carbohydrates, 4.5g fat, 0.1g fiber, 28mg cholesterol, 55mg sodium, 248mg potassium

Bacon-wrapped Shrimps

Servings: 4   Cooking Time: 2 Hours
Ingredients:

2 tablespoons butter, melted	Salt and pepper to taste
30 large shrimps, shelled	15 strips bacon, cut lengthwise
½ teaspoon garlic powder	

Directions:
Line the crockpot bottom with foil.   Pour the butter into the crockpot.   Marinate the shrimps with garlic powder, salt and pepper. Allow to stay in the fridge for   minutes.   Wrap the shrimps with bacon and arrange in the crockpot.   Close the lid and cook on low for 2 hours or on high for 4minutes.   Be sure to flip the shrimps to sear the other side.
Nutrition Info: Calories per serving: 152; Carbohydrates: 3.2g; Protein: 9.5g; Fat: 11.9g; Sugar: 0.5g; Sodium: 492mg; Fiber: 1.7g

Cilantro Salmon

Servings: 4   Cooking Time: 3 Hours
Ingredients:

12 oz salmon fillet	1 teaspoon ground black pepper
1 teaspoon dried cilantro	½ cup of coconut milk
1 tablespoon butter	

Directions:
Toss butter in the skillet and melt it.   Add salmon fillet and sprinkle it with ground black pepper. Roast the salmon on high heat for 1 minute per side.   Then put the fish in the Crock Pot.   Add coconut milk and cilantro.   Cook the fish on high for 3 hours.
Nutrition Info: Per Serving: 208 calories, 17.3g protein, 2g carbohydrates, 15.3g fat, 0.8g fiber, 45mg cholesterol, 63mg sodium, 413mg potassium

Smelt In Avocado Oil

Servings: 4   Cooking Time: 4 Hours
Ingredients:

12 oz smelt fillet	½ teaspoon smoked paprika
1 teaspoon chili powder	4 tablespoons avocado oil
¼ teaspoon ground turmeric	

Directions:
Cut the smelt fillet into 4 servings.   Then sprinkle every fish fillet with chili powder, ground turmeric, and smoked paprika.   Put the fish in the Crock Pot.   Add avocado oil and close the lid.   Cook the fish on Low for 4 hours.
Nutrition Info: Per Serving: 89 calories, 13.1g protein, 1.4g carbohydrates, 3.5g fat, 1g fiber, 112mg cholesterol, 52mg sodium, 66mg potassium

Italian Clams

Servings: 6   Cooking Time: 2 Hours
Ingredients:

½ cup butter, melted	5 garlic cloves, minced
36 clams, scrubbed	1 tablespoon oregano, dried
1 teaspoon red pepper flakes, crushed	2 cups white wine
1 teaspoon parsley, chopped	

Directions:
In your Crock Pot, mix butter with clams, pepper flakes, parsley, garlic, oregano and wine, stir, cover and cook on High for 2 hours.   Divide into bowls and serve.
Nutrition Info: calories 224, fat 15, fiber 2, carbs 7, protein 4

Fish Soufflé(1)

Servings: 4   Cooking Time: 4 Hours

Ingredients:

3 oz white sandwich bread, chopped
1 cup cream
¼ cup Mozzarella, shredded
8 oz salmon, chopped
1 teaspoon ground black pepper
½ cup of water

Directions:

Pour water and cream in the Crock Pot,   Then add salmon and bread.   Top the mixture with Mozzarella and ground black pepper.   Close the lid and cook the soufflé for hours on Low.

Nutrition Info: Per Serving: 181 calories, 13.9g protein, 13.1g carbohydrates, 8.3g fat, 0.4g fiber, 37mg cholesterol, 164mg sodium, 247mg potassium.

Salmon With Green Sauce

Servings: 4   Cooking Time: 2 Hrs And 30 Minutes

Ingredients:

2 garlic cloves, minced
4 salmon fillets, boneless
3 tbsp lime juice
¾ cup cilantro, chopped
1 tbsp olive oil
Salt and black pepper to the taste

Directions:

Coat the base of your Crock Pot with oil.   Place salmon along with all other ingredients in the cooker.   Put the cooker's lid on and set the cooking time to 2 hours minutes on Low settings. Serve warm.

Nutrition Info: Per Serving: Calories 200, Total Fat 3g, Fiber 2g, Total Carbs 14g, Protein 8g

Beef, Pork & Lamb Recipes

Blanked Hot Dogs

Servings: 4   Cooking Time: 4 Hours

Ingredients:

4 mini (cocktail) pork sausages
1 teaspoon cumin seeds
1 tablespoon olive oil
1 egg, beaten
4 oz puff pastry

Directions:

Roll up the puff pastry and cut into strips.   Put the pork sausages on every strip.   Roll the puff pastry and brush with egg.   Then top the blanked hot dogs with cumin seeds.   Brush the Crock Pot with olive oil from inside.   Add the blanked hot dogs and close the lid.   Cook them on high for 4 hours.

Nutrition Info: Per Serving: 225 calories, 4.4g protein, 14.1g carbohydrates, 16.9g fat, 0.6g fiber, 41mg cholesterol, 120mg sodium, 42mg potassium

Flank Steak With Arugula

Servings: 4   Cooking Time: 10 Hours

Ingredients:

1-pound flank steak
1 teaspoon Worcestershire sauce
Salt and pepper to taste
1 package arugula salad mix
2 tablespoon balsamic vinegar

Directions:

Season the flank steak with Worcestershire sauce, salt, and pepper.   Place in the crockpot that has been lined with aluminum foil.   Close the lid and cook on low for 10 hours or on high for 7 hours. Meanwhile, prepare the salad by combining the arugula salad mix and balsamic vinegar. Set aside in the fridge.   Once the steak is cooked, allow to cool before slicing.   Serve on top of the arugula salad.

Nutrition Info: Calories per serving: 452; Carbohydrates: 5.8g; Protein: 30.2g; Fat:29.5g; Sugar: 1.2g; Sodium: 563mg; Fiber:3 g

Nutmeg Lamb And Squash

Servings: 2   Cooking Time: 6 Hours

Ingredients:

1 pound lamb stew meat , roughly cubed
1 cup butternut squash, peeled and cubed
½ teaspoon nutmeg, ground
½ teaspoon chili powder
½ teaspoon coriander, ground
2 teaspoons olive oil
1 cup beef stock
A pinch of salt and black pepper
1 tablespoon cilantro, chopped

Directions:

In your Crock Pot, mix the lamb with the squash, nutmeg and the other ingredients, toss, put the lid on and cook on Low for 6 hours.   Divide the mix between plates and serve.

Nutrition Info:calories 263, fat 12, fiber 4, carbs 7, protein 12

Bbq Ribs

Servings: 4   Cooking Time: 4 Hours

Ingredients:

1-pound pork ribs, roughly chopped
1 teaspoon minced garlic
½ cup BBQ sauce
1 tablespoon olive oil
¼ cup plain yogurt

Directions:

Mix BBQ sauce with plain yogurt and minced garlic and pour it in the Crock Pot.   Then pour olive oil in the skillet and heat well.   Add pork ribs and roast them for minutes per side on high heat. Transfer the pork ribs in the Crock Pot and carefully mix.   Close the lid and cook them on High for 4 hours.

Nutrition Info: Per Serving: 398 calories, 31g protein, 12.6g carbohydrates, 23.9g fat, 0.2g fiber, 118mg cholesterol, 426mg sodium, 430mg potassium

Crockpot Creamy Beef Bourguignon

Servings: 8   Cooking Time: 10 Hours

Ingredients:

3 beef steaks, cut into large chunks
3 tablespoons lard
3 cloves of garlic, minced
1 onion, diced
1 tablespoon organic tomato puree
4 cups white mushrooms, sliced
1 cup homemade chicken stock
Salt and pepper to taste
½ cup heavy cream

Directions:

Place all ingredients except the cream in the CrockPot.   Give a good stir.   Close the lid and cook on high for 8 hours or on low for 10 hours.

Nutrition Info: Calories per serving: 678; Carbohydrates: 4.3g; Protein: 36.7g; Fat: 45g; Sugar: 0g; Sodium: 826mg; Fiber:1.3g

Beef Brisket In Orange Juice

Servings: 4   Cooking Time: 5 Hours

Ingredients:

1 cup of orange juice
2 cups of water
2 tablespoons butter
12 oz beef brisket
½ teaspoon salt

Directions:

Toss butter in the skillet and melt.   Put the beef brisket in the melted butter and roast on high heat for 3 minutes per side.   Then sprinkle the meat with salt and transfer in the Crock Pot.   Add orange juice and water.   Close the lid and cook the meat on High for hours.

Nutrition Info: Per Serving: 237 calories, 26.3g protein, 6.5g carbohydrates, 11.2g fat, 0.1g fiber, 91mg cholesterol, 392mg sodium, 470mg potassium.

Mexican Carne Adovada

Servings: 9   Cooking Time: 12 Hours
Ingredients:

- 3 pounds pork Boston butt
- 2 dried chili peppers, chopped
- 2 ancho peppers, chopped
- 2 guajillo peppers, chopped
- 2 cups homemade beef stock
- 1 onion, chopped
- 6 cloves of garlic, minced
- 1 teaspoon cumin
- 1 teaspoon coriander
- 2 teaspoons apple cider vinegar
- Salt and pepper to taste

Directions:
Place all ingredients in the CrockPot.   Give a good stir.   Close the lid and cook on high for 10 hours or on low for 12 hours.
Nutrition Info: Calories per serving: 453; Carbohydrates: 4.8; Protein: 39.9g; Fat: 28.1g; Sugar: 0.3g; Sodium: 991mg; Fiber: 2.4g

Succulent Pork Ribs

Servings: 4   Cooking Time: 8 Hours
Ingredients:

- 12 oz pork ribs, roughly chopped
- ¼ cup of orange juice
- 1 cup of water
- 1 teaspoon ground nutmeg
- 1 teaspoon salt

Directions:
Pour water and orange juice in the Crock Pot. Then sprinkle the pork ribs with ground nutmeg and salt.   Put the pork ribs in the Crock Pot and close the lid.   Cook the meat on low for 8 hours.
Nutrition Info: Per Serving: 242 calories, 22.7g protein, 1.9g carbohydrates, 15.3g fat, 0.1g fiber, 88mg cholesterol, 633mg sodium, 279mg potassium

Beef And Artichokes

Servings: 2   Cooking Time: 7 Hours
Ingredients:

- 1 tablespoon avocado oil
- 1 pound beef stew meat, cubed
- 1 cup canned artichoke hearts, drained and quartered
- ½ teaspoon chili powder
- 2 scallions, chopped
- A pinch of salt and black pepper
- 1 cup tomato passata
- A pinch of salt and black pepper
- ¼ tablespoon dill, chopped

Directions:
In your Crock Pot, combine the beef with the artichokes and the other ingredients, toss, put the lid on and cook on Low for 7 hours.   Divide the mix between plates and serve.
Nutrition Info:calories 263, fat 14, fiber 5, carbs 7, protein 15

Lamb And Zucchini Mix

Servings: 2   Cooking Time: 4 Hours
Ingredients:

- 1 pound lamb stew meat, ground
- 2 zucchinis, cubed
- 2 teaspoons olive oil
- 1 carrot, peeled and sliced
- 2 tablespoons tomato paste
- ½ cup beef stock
- ½ teaspoon cumin, ground
- 1 tablespoon chives, chopped
- A pinch of salt and black pepper

Directions:
In your Crock Pot, mix the lamb with the zucchinis, oil, carrot and the other ingredients, toss, put the lid on and cook on High for 4 hours.   Divide the mix into bowls and serve hot.
Nutrition Info:calories 254, fat 14, fiber 3, carbs 6, protein 17

Pork Chops Under Peach Blanket

Servings: 4   Cooking Time: 4.5 Hours
Ingredients:

- 4 pork chops
- 2 tablespoons butter, softened
- 1 teaspoon salt
- 1 onion, sliced
- 1 cup of water
- 1 cup peaches, pitted, halved

Directions:
Sprinkle the pork chops with salt.   Grease the Crock Pot bottom with butter.   Put the pork chops inside in one layer.   Then top them with sliced onion and peaches.   Add water and close the lid.   Cook the meal on High for 4.5 hours.
Nutrition Info: Per Serving: 333 calories, 18.7g protein, 6.1g carbohydrates, 25.8g fat, 1.2g fiber, 84mg cholesterol, 681mg sodium, 389mg potassium

London Broil

Servings: 6   Cooking Time: 8 Hours
Ingredients:

- 2-pounds London broil
- 3 garlic cloves, crushed
- 1 onion, sliced
- 3 cups of water
- ¼ cup of soy sauce
- 1 teaspoon ground black pepper

Directions:
Preheat the grill skillet well.   Then put London broil in the hot skillet and roast it on high heat for 3 minutes per side.   After this, transfer the meat in the Crock Pot.   Add all remaining ingredients from the list above.   Close the lid and cook the meal on Low for 8 hours.
Nutrition Info: Per Serving: 74 calories, 9.3g protein, 3.9g carbohydrates, 2.4g fat, 0.6g fiber, 0mg cholesterol, 701mg sodium, 61mg potassium.

Braised Pork Knuckle

Servings: 7   Cooking Time: 10 Hours
Ingredients:

3-pound pork knuckles
1 tablespoon liquid honey
1 cup red wine
2 cups of water
1 teaspoon dried mint
1 teaspoon salt
1 cinnamon stick

Directions:
Put all ingredients in the Crock Pot.   Close the lid and cook the pork knuckle on Low for 10 hours.
Nutrition Info: Per Serving: 412 calories, 60.6g protein, 3.4g carbohydrates, 13g fat, 0g fiber, 179mg cholesterol, 446mg sodium, 770mg potassium

Rosemary Beef

Servings: 2   Cooking Time: 7 Hours
Ingredients:

1 pound beef roast, sliced
1 tablespoon rosemary, chopped
Juice of ½ lemon
1 tablespoon olive oil
½ cup tomato sauce
A pinch of salt and black pepper

Directions:
In your Crock Pot, mix the roast with the rosemary, lemon juice and the other ingredients, toss, put the lid on and cook on Low for 7 hours.   Divide everything between plates and serve.
Nutrition Info:calories 210, fat 5, fiber 3, carbs 8, protein 12

Lamb Meatballs

Servings: 4   Cooking Time: 4 Hours
Ingredients:

2 tablespoons minced onion
9 oz lamb fillet, minced
1 teaspoon Italian seasonings
1 teaspoon flour
1 tablespoon olive oil
½ teaspoon salt
½ cup of water

Directions:
In the bowl mix minced lamb, minced onion, Italian seasonings, flour, and salt.   Make the small meatballs.   After this, preheat the olive oil in the skillet.   Add meatballs and roast them on high heat for 30 seconds per side.   Then transfer the meatballs in the Crock Pot.   Add water and cook the meal on high for 4 hours.
Nutrition Info: Per Serving: 157 calories, 18g protein, 1.1g carbohydrates, 8.6g fat, 0.1g fiber, 58mg cholesterol, 341mg sodium, 223mg potassium.

Hamburger Style Stuffing

Servings: 4   Cooking Time: 3 Hours
Ingredients:

1-pound ground pork
½ cup Cheddar
¼ cup onion, minced
1 cup of water
cheese, shredded
½ cup fresh cilantro, chopped
¼ cup tomato juice
1 bell pepper, diced
1 teaspoon salt

Directions:
Mix ground pork with cilantro, onion, and diced pepper.   Then transfer the mixture in the Crock Pot.   Add all remaining ingredients and mix.   Close the lid and cook the stuffing on High for 3 hours.
Nutrition Info: Per Serving: 235 calories, 33.7g protein, 3.8g carbohydrates, 8.8g fat, 0.7g fiber, 98mg cholesterol, 778mg sodium, 604mg potassium

Cranberry Minced Meat

Servings: 5   Cooking Time: 6 Hours
Ingredients:

¼ cup cranberry sauce
1-pound pork mince
1 tablespoon butter
¼ cup of water
1 teaspoon chili powder
1 teaspoon dried parsley

Directions:
Melt butter and pour in the Crock Pot.   Add pork mince, chili powder, and dried parsley.   Then add water and cranberry sauce. Stir the mixture well.   Close the lid and cook the meal on Low for 6 hours.
Nutrition Info: Per Serving: 274 calories, 0.1g protein, 57.1g carbohydrates, 6g fat, 1.3g fiber, 6mg cholesterol, 22mg sodium, 22mg potassium.

Cider Dipped Pork Roast

Servings: 6   Cooking Time: 8 Hrs.
Ingredients:

1 yellow onion, chopped
2 tbsp sweet paprika
15 oz. canned tomato, roasted and chopped
1 tsp cumin, ground
Salt and black pepper to the taste
1 tsp coconut oil
A pinch of nutmeg, ground
5 lbs. pork roast
Juice of 1 lemon
¼ cup apple cider vinegar

Directions:
Place a suitable pan over medium-high heat and add oil.   Toss in onions and sauté for few minutes until brown.   Transfer the onion to your Crock Pot then add paprika and remaining ingredients.   Put the cooker's lid on and set the cooking time to 8 hours on Low settings.   Slice the meat and serve warm with its sauce.   Enjoy.
Nutrition Info: Per Serving: Calories: 350, Total Fat: 5g, Fiber: 2g, Total Carbs: 13g, Protein: 24g

Beef Saute With Endives

Servings: 4   Cooking Time: 8 Hours

Ingredients:

1-pound beef sirloin, chopped	1 teaspoon peppercorns
3 oz endives, roughly chopped	1 onion, sliced
1 carrot, diced	1 cup of water
	½ cup tomato juice

Directions:

Mix beef with onion, carrot, and peppercorns. Place the mixture in the Crock Pot.   Add water and tomato juice.   Then close the lid and cook it on High for 5 hours.   After this, add endives and cook the meal for 3 hours on Low.

Nutrition Info: Per Serving: 238 calories, 35.4g protein, 6.4g carbohydrates, 7.2g fat, 1.9g fiber, 101mg cholesterol, 175mg sodium, 689mg potassium.

Rosemary And Bacon Pork Chops

Servings: 4   Cooking Time: 4 Hours

Ingredients:

4 pork chops	1 tablespoon olive oil
4 bacon slices	½ cup of water
1 teaspoon dried rosemary	

Directions:

Rub the pork chops with rosemary and olive oil. Then wrap the pork chops in the bacon and put in the hot skillet.   Roast the pork chops for 1 minute per side.   Then transfer them in the Crock Pot. Add water.   Close the lid and cook the meat on High for 4 hours.

Nutrition Info: Per Serving: 390 calories, 25g protein, 0.5g carbohydrates, 31.4g fat, 0.1g fiber, 90mg cholesterol, 496mg sodium, 386mg potassium

Tender Glazed Pork Ribs

Servings: 4   Cooking Time: 7 Hours

Ingredients:

1-pound baby back pork ribs	1 tablespoon tamarind
1 orange, sliced	½ cup apple juice
1 teaspoon liquid honey	1 anise pod
	1 tablespoon tomato sauce

Directions:

Put the baby back ribs in the Crock Pot.   Add tamarind, apple juice, tomato sauce, and anise pod. Then add sliced orange and close the lid.   Cook the pork ribs on low for 6 hours.   Then sprinkle the meat with liquid honey and cook on high for 1 hour.

Nutrition Info: Per Serving: 368 calories, 18.6g protein, 11.7g carbohydrates, 27.2g fat, 1.3g fiber, 90mg cholesterol, 107mg sodium, 140mg potassium

Creamy Lamb

Servings: 2   Cooking Time: 6 Hours

Ingredients:

2 pounds lamb shoulder, cubed	1/3 cup beef stock
1 cup heavy cream	1 red onion, sliced
2 teaspoons avocado oil	A pinch of salt and black pepper
1 teaspoon turmeric powder	1 tablespoon cilantro, chopped

Directions:

In your Crock Pot, mix the lamb with the stock, oil and the other ingredients except the cream, toss, put the lid on and cook on Low for 5 hours.   Add the cream, toss, cook on Low for 1 more hour, divide the mix into bowls and serve.

Nutrition Info:calories 233, fat 7, fiber 2, carbs 6, protein 12

Bbq Meatballs

Servings: 4   Cooking Time: 7 Hours

Ingredients:

3 tablespoons BBQ sauce	3 tablespoons water
10 oz minced pork	1 teaspoon salt
1 garlic clove, diced	1 teaspoon dried cilantro
1 teaspoon chili powder	4 tablespoons coconut oil

Directions:

In the bowl mix minced pork, garlic, chili powder, water, salt, and dried cilantro.   Make the medium size meatballs and arrange them in the Crock Pot in one layer.   Add coconut oil and close the lid. Cook the meatballs on low for 7 hours.   When the meatballs are cooked, brush them gently with BBW sauce.

Nutrition Info: Per Serving: 239 calories, 18.7g protein, 4.9g carbohydrates, 16.2g fat, 0.3g fiber, 52mg cholesterol, 760mg sodium, 339mg potassium.

Beef Heart Saute

Servings: 4   Cooking Time: 6 Hours

Ingredients:

1-pound beef heart, chopped	1 sweet pepper, chopped
1 teaspoon fresh ginger, minced	2 cups tomatoes
2 tablespoons apple cider vinegar	2 tablespoons sunflower oil
1 red onion, chopped	1 cup of water

Directions:

Heat the sunflower oil until hot in the skillet. Add chopped beef heart and roast it for 10 minutes on medium heat.   Then transfer it in the Crock Pot.   Add all remaining ingredients and close the lid.   Cook the saute on low for 6 hours.

Nutrition Info: Per Serving: 289 calories, 33.7g protein, 8.9g carbohydrates, 12.7g fat, 2.1g fiber, 240mg cholesterol, 75mg sodium, 570mg potassium.

Short Ribs With Tapioca Sauce

Servings: 6   Cooking Time: 10 Hrs.
Ingredients:

3 lbs. beef short ribs
1 fennel bulb, cut into wedges
2 yellow onions, cut into wedges
1 cup carrot, sliced
14 oz. canned tomatoes, chopped

1 cup dry red wine
2 tbsp tapioca, crushed
2 tbsp tomato paste
1 tsp rosemary, dried
Salt and black pepper to the taste
4 garlic cloves, minced

Directions:
Add short ribs, onion, and all other ingredients to the insert of Crock Pot.   Put the cooker's lid on and set the cooking time to 10 hours on Low settings.   Serve warm.
Nutrition Info: Per Serving: Calories: 432, Total Fat: 14g, Fiber: 6g, Total Carbs: 25g, Protein: 42g

Beef Pate

Servings: 4   Cooking Time: 4 Hours
Ingredients:

10 oz beef liver
1 onion
2 cups of water

2 tablespoons butter
1 teaspoon salt
1 teaspoon olive oil

Directions:
Dice the onion and roast it with olive oil in the skillet until light brown.   Then pour water in the Crock Pot.   Add liver and cook it on High for 4 hours.   After this, chop the cooked liver and transfer it in the food processor.   Blend it until smooth.   Add butter and roasted onion.   Stir the pate and store it in the fridge for up to 3 days.
Nutrition Info: Per Serving: 196 calories, 19.2g protein, 6.2g carbohydrates, 10.3g fat, 0.6g fiber, 285mg cholesterol, 682mg sodium, 292mg potassium.

Sour Cream Roast

Servings: 4   Cooking Time: 4.5 Hours
Ingredients:

1-pound pork shoulder, boneless, chopped
1 tablespoon lemon zest, grated

4 tablespoons lemon juice
1 cup sour cream
¼ cup of water

Directions:
Sprinkle the pork shoulder with lemon zest and lemon juice.   Transfer the meat in the Crock Pot. Add sour cream and water.   Close the lid and cook it on high for 5 hours.
Nutrition Info: Per Serving: 459 calories, 28.4g protein, 3.1g carbohydrates, 36.4g fat, 0.2g fiber, 127mg cholesterol, 111mg sodium, 480mg potassium

5-ingredients Chili

Servings: 4   Cooking Time: 5 Hours

Ingredients:

½ cup Cheddar cheese, shredded
2 cup tomatoes, chopped

8 oz ground beef
1 teaspoon chili seasonings
½ cup of water

Directions:
Mix the ground beef with chili seasonings and transfer in the Crock Pot.   Add tomatoes and water.   Close the lid and cook the chili on high for hours.   After this, open the lid and mix the chili well. Top it with cheddar cheese and close the lid. Cook the chili on low for 2 hours more.
Nutrition Info: Per Serving: 180 calories, 21.6g protein, 4g carbohydrates, 8.4g fat, 1.1g fiber, 66mg cholesterol, 150mg sodium, 456mg potassium.

Thai Cocoa Pork

Servings: 4   Cooking Time: 7 Hours
Ingredients:

2 tablespoons olive oil
2 pounds pork butt, boneless and cubed
Salt and black pepper to the taste
6 eggs, hard-boiled, peeled and sliced
1 tablespoon cilantro, chopped
1 tablespoon coriander seeds
1 and ½ cup soy sauce

1 tablespoon ginger, grated
1 tablespoon black peppercorns
2 tablespoons garlic, chopped
2 tablespoons five spice powder
2 tablespoons cocoa powder
1 yellow onion, chopped
8 cups water

Directions:
In your Crock Pot, mix oil with pork, salt, pepper, cilantro, coriander, ginger, peppercorns, garlic, five spice, soy sauce, cocoa, onion and water, toss, cover and cook on Low for 7 hours.   Divide stew into bowls, add egg slices on top and serve.
Nutrition Info:calories 400, fat 10, fiber 9, carbs 28, protein 22

Chili Crockpot Brisket

Servings: 4   Cooking Time: 12 Hours
Ingredients:

4 pounds beef brisket
Salt and pepper to taste

1 bottle chili sauce
1 cup onion, chopped
1/8 cup water

Directions:
Place all ingredients in the crockpot.   Give a good stir.   Close the lid and cook on low for 12 hours or on high for 10 hours.
Nutrition Info: Calories per serving: 634; Carbohydrates: 2.1g; Protein: 30.2g; Fat: 45.4g; Sugar:0 g; Sodium: 835mg; Fiber: 1.4g

Honey Beef Sausages

Servings: 4   Cooking Time: 4.5 Hours
Ingredients:

1-pound beef sausages

2 tablespoons of liquid honey

1 teaspoon dried dill

½ teaspoon salt

¼ cup heavy cream

Directions:
In the mixing bowl mix liquid honey with dried dill and salt.   Then add cream and whisk until smooth.   Pour the liquid in the Crock Pot.   Add beef sausages and close the lid.   Cook the meal on High for 4.hours.
Nutrition Info: Per Serving: 507 calories, 15.9g protein, 12.1g carbohydrates, 43.9g fat, 0.1g fiber, 91mg cholesterol, 1207mg sodium, 234mg potassium.

Saucy Beef Cheeks

Servings: 4   Cooking Time: 4 Hrs.
Ingredients:

4 beef cheeks, halved

2 tbsp olive oil

Salt and black pepper to the taste

1 white onion, chopped

4 garlic cloves, minced

2 cup beef stock

5 cardamom pods

1 tbsp balsamic vinegar

3 bay leaves

7 cloves

2 vanilla beans, split

1 and ½ tbsp tomato paste

1 carrot, sliced

Directions:
Add beef cheeks and all remaining ingredients to the insert of your Crock Pot.   Put the cooker's lid on and set the cooking time to 4 hours on High settings.   Mix gently and serve warm.
Nutrition Info: Per Serving: Calories: 321, Total Fat: 5g, Fiber: 7g, Total Carbs: 18g, Protein: 12g

Garlic-parmesan Beef

Servings: 2   Cooking Time: 4 Hours
Ingredients:

1 oz Parmesan, grated

1 carrot, grated

8 oz ground beef

½ cup of water

1 teaspoon olive oil

1 teaspoon chili powder

Directions:
Mix the ground beef with carrot and transfer it in the Crock Pot.   Add olive oil, chili powder, and water.   Close the lid and cook the beef on high for 4 hours.   After this, add parmesan and carefully mix the meal.
Nutrition Info: Per Serving: 293 calories, 39.4g protein, 4.2g carbohydrates, 12.7g fat, 1.2g fiber, 111mg cholesterol, 242mg sodium, 580mg potassium.

Tarragon Pork Chops

Servings: 2   Cooking Time: 6 Hours
Ingredients:

½ pound pork chops

¼ tablespoons olive oil

2 garlic clove, minced

¼ teaspoon chili powder

½ cup beef stock

½ teaspoon coriander, ground

Salt and black pepper to the taste

¼ teaspoon mustard powder

1 tablespoon tarragon, chopped

Directions:
Grease your Crock Pot with the oil and mix the pork chops with the garlic, stock and the other ingredients inside.   Toss, put the lid on, cook on Low for 6 hours, divide between plates and serve with a side salad.
Nutrition Info:calories 453, fat 16, fiber 8, carbs 7, protein 27

Lamb And Potatoes

Servings: 2   Cooking Time: 4 Hours
Ingredients:

1 pound lamb stew meat, roughly cubed

2 sweet potatoes, peeled and cubed

½ cup beef stock

½ teaspoon sweet paprika

½ teaspoon coriander, ground

½ cup tomato sauce

1 tablespoon avocado oil

1 tablespoon balsamic vinegar

1 tablespoon cilantro, chopped

A pinch of salt and black pepper

Directions:
In your Crock Pot, mix the lamb with the potatoes, stock, sauce and the other ingredients, toss, put the lid on and cook on High for 4 hours   Divide everything between plates and serve.
Nutrition Info:calories 253, fat 14, fiber 3, carbs 7, protein 17

Beer Sausages

Servings: 4   Cooking Time: 7 Hours
Ingredients:

1-pound beef sausages

1 teaspoon ground black pepper

3 tablespoons butter

1 teaspoon salt

1 cup beer

Directions:
Toss the butter in the skillet and melt it.   Add beef sausages and roast them on high heat for minutes per side.   Transfer the beef sausages in the Crock Pot.   Add ground black pepper, salt, and beer.   Close the lid and cook the meal on Low for 7 hours.
Nutrition Info: Per Serving: 552 calories, 16.1g protein, 5.5g carbohydrates, 49.8g fat, 0.1g fiber, 103mg cholesterol, 1558mg sodium, 240mg potassium.

Apricot Pork Saute

Servings: 4   Cooking Time: 4 Hours
Ingredients:

12 oz pork loin, cubed
2 cups apricots, pitted, chopped
1 cup of water
1 tablespoon coconut oil
1 teaspoon peppercorns
1 teaspoon ground turmeric
1 teaspoon salt
½ teaspoon smoked paprika

Directions:
Put all ingredients in the Crock Pot.   Carefully mix the saute and close the lid.   Cook the meal on High for 4 hours.
Nutrition Info: Per Serving: 276 calories, 24.4g protein, 9.3g carbohydrates, 15.8g fat, 1.9g fiber, 68mg cholesterol, 637mg sodium, 588mg potassium

Pepsi Pork Tenderloin

Servings: 4   Cooking Time: 6 Hours
Ingredients:

1-pound pork tenderloin
1 teaspoon cumin seeds
1 cup Pepsi
1 teaspoon olive oil
2 tablespoons soy sauce

Directions:
Chop the pork tenderloin roughly and put it in the mixing bowl.   Add cumin seeds, soy sauce, Pepsi, and olive oil. Leave the meat for 30 minutes to marinate.   After this, transfer the meat and all Pepsi liquid in the Crock Pot and close the lid. Cook the meat on low for 6 hours.
Nutrition Info: Per Serving: 179 calories, 30.3g protein, 0.8g carbohydrates, 5.3g fat, 0.1g fiber,83mg cholesterol, 523mg sodium, 514mg potassium

Indian Style Cardamom Pork

Servings: 4   Cooking Time: 6 Hours
Ingredients:

1-pound pork steak, tenderized
1 teaspoon ground cardamom
1 teaspoon chili powder
½ cup of coconut milk
1 teaspoon ground turmeric
1 teaspoon cashew butter
¼ cup of water

Directions:
Cut the pork steak into 4 servings and rub with ground cardamom, chili powder. And ground turmeric.   Place the meat in the Crock Pot. Add cashew butter, water, and coconut milk. Close the lid and cook the pork on high for 6 hours.
Nutrition Info: Per Serving: 295 calories, 21g protein, 7.2g carbohydrates, 21.1g fat, 1.9g fiber, 69mg cholesterol, 569mg sodium, 118mg potassium

Saucy French Lamb

Servings: 4   Cooking Time: 8 Hrs.
Ingredients:

4 lamb chops
1 cup onion, chopped
2 cups canned tomatoes, chopped
1 cup leek, chopped
2 tbsp garlic, minced
1 tsp herbs de Provence
Salt and black pepper to the taste
3 cups of water

Directions:
Add lamb chops, onion, and all other ingredients to the insert of the Crock Pot.   Put the cooker's lid on and set the cooking time to 8 hours on Low settings.   Serve warm.
Nutrition Info: Per Serving: Calories: 430, Total Fat: 12g, Fiber: 8g, Total Carbs: 20g, Protein: 18g

Pesto Beef

Servings: 4   Cooking Time: 8 Hours
Ingredients:

4 teaspoons pesto sauce
4 beef chops
1/3 cup beef broth

Directions:
Rub every beef chop with pesto sauce and arrange in the Crock Pot in one layer.   Then add beef broth and close the lid.   Cook the meal on Low for 8 hours.
Nutrition Info: Per Serving: 246 calories, 17.9g protein, 0.4g carbohydrates, 18.3g fat, 0.1g fiber, 46mg cholesterol, 415mg sodium, 17mg potassium.

Crockpot Cheeseburgers Casserole

Servings: 4   Cooking Time: 8 Hours
Ingredients:

1 white onion, chopped
1 ½ pounds lean ground beef
2 tablespoons mustard
1 teaspoon dried basil leaves
2 cups cheddar cheese

Directions:
Heat skillet over medium flame and sauté both white onions and ground beef for 3 minutes. Continue stirring until lightly brown.   Transfer to the crockpot and stir in mustard and basil leaves. Season with salt and pepper.   Add cheese on top. Close the lid and cook on low for 8 hours and on high for 6 hours.
Nutrition Info: Calories per serving: 472; Carbohydrates: 3g; Protein: 32.7g; Fat: 26.2g; Sugar: 0g; Sodium: 429mg; Fiber: 2.4g

Tender Pork Chops

Servings: 4   Cooking Time: 8 Hours
Ingredients:

2 yellow onions, chopped
6 bacon slices, chopped

½ cup chicken stock
Salt and black pepper to the taste
4 pork chops

Directions:
In your Crock Pot, mix onions with bacon, stock, salt, pepper and pork chops, cover and cook on Low for 8 hours.   Divide pork chops on plates, drizzle cooking juices all over and serve.
Nutrition Info:calories 325, fat 18, fiber 1, carbs 12, protein 36

Beef And Zucchinis Mix

Servings: 2   Cooking Time: 8 Hours
Ingredients:

1 pound beef stew meat, cut into strips
1 tablespoon olive oil
½ teaspoon sweet paprika
½ teaspoon chili powder

¼ cup beef stock
2 small zucchinis, cubed
1 tablespoon balsamic vinegar
1 tablespoon chives, chopped

Directions:
In your Crock Pot, mix the beef with the oil, stock and the other ingredients, toss, put the lid on and cook on Low for 8 hours.   Divide the mix between plates and serve.
Nutrition Info:calories 400, fat 12, fiber 8, carbs 18, protein 20

Ginger Beef Balls

Servings: 4   Cooking Time: 4 Hours
Ingredients:

1 teaspoon ground ginger
1 teaspoon garlic powder
¼ cup butter

1 teaspoon chili flakes
¼ cup of water
12 oz ground beef
1 egg, beaten

Directions:
In the mixing bowl mix ground beef, egg, chili flakes, garlic powder, and ground ginger.   Make the small balls.   After this, melt the butter in the skillet.   Add meatballs and roast them for 3 minutes per side.   Transfer the meatballs in the Crock Pot. Add water and close the lid.   Cook the meatballs on High for 4 hours.
Nutrition Info: Per Serving: 279 calories, 27.5g protein, 0.9g carbohydrates, 17.9g fat, 0.1g fiber, 147mg cholesterol, 154mg sodium, 376mg potassium.

Basil Beef

Servings: 4   Cooking Time: 4 Hours
Ingredients:

1-pound beef loin, chopped
2 tablespoons dried basil

2 tablespoons butter
½ cup of water
1 teaspoon salt

Directions:
Toss the butter in the skillet and melt it.   Then mix the beef loin with dried basil and put in the hot butter.   Roast the meat for 2 minutes per side and transfer in the Crock Pot.   Add salt and water.   Close the lid and cook the beef on high for 4 hours.
Nutrition Info: Per Serving: 220 calories, 21g protein, 1.4g carbohydrates, 13.9g fat, 0g fiber, 76mg cholesterol, 1123mg sodium, 6mg potassium.

Aromatic Meatloaf

Servings: 6   Cooking Time: 6 Hours
Ingredients:

1 potato, grated
1 teaspoon garlic powder
1 onion, minced
10 oz minced beef

1 egg, beaten
1 teaspoon avocado oil
1 cup of water

Directions:
In the mixing bowl, mix grated potato, garlic powder, minced onion, minced beef, and egg. Then brush the meatloaf mold with avocado oil. Place the minced beef mixture inside and flatten it. Then pour the water in the Crock Pot.   Place the mold with meatloaf in water.   Close the lid and cook the meal on High for hours.
Nutrition Info: Per Serving: 130 calories, 16.1g protein, 7.1g carbohydrates, 3.8g fat, 1.1g fiber, 69mg cholesterol, 45mg sodium, 354mg potassium.

Baked Sirloin In Crockpot

Servings: 8   Cooking Time: 12 Hours
Ingredients:

2 pounds sirloin steak, cut into 1-inch pieces
Salt and pepper to taste

1 ½ tablespoons cumin
2 small red onions, cut into wedges
2 red bell peppers, cut into strips

Directions:
Season the steak with cumin, salt, and pepper. Grease a skillet and heat over medium flame. Sear the steak for minutes on each side.   Add the onions and sear until the edges turn brown. Place into the crockpot.   Add a few tablespoons of water.   Close the lid and cook on low for 10 hours or on high for 7 hours.   An hour before the cooking time ends, stir in the red bell peppers. Cook until the bell peppers become soft.
Nutrition Info: Calories per serving: 532; Carbohydrates: 3g; Protein: 34.2g; Fat: 12.6g; Sugar: 0g; Sodium: 613mg; Fiber:1.8 g

Mole Pork Chops

Servings: 3   Cooking Time: 10 Hours
Ingredients:

1 tablespoon butter, melted
3 pork chops, bone in
2 teaspoons paprika
½ teaspoon cocoa powder, unsweetened
Salt and pepper to taste

Directions:
Place the butter into the crockpot.   Season the pork chops with paprika, cocoa powder, salt and pepper.   Arrange in the crockpot.   Close the lid and cook on low for 10 hours or on high for 8 hours.   Halfway through the cooking time, be sure to flip the pork chops.
Nutrition Info: Calories per serving: 579; Carbohydrates: 1.2g; Protein: 41.7g; Fat: 34.7g; Sugar: 0g; Sodium: 753mg; Fiber: 0g

Ground Pork Pie

Servings: 4   Cooking Time: 4.5 Hours
Ingredients:

1 teaspoon tomato paste
1 cup ground pork
1 teaspoon ground black pepper
1 teaspoon salt
1 tablespoon avocado oil
4 oz puff pastry

Directions:
Mix ground pork with salt and ground black pepper.   Then add tomato paste and stir the ingredients well.   Brush the Crock Pot bottom with avocado oil.   Then put the puff pastry inside and flatten it in the shape of the pie crust.   Put the ground pork mixture over the puff pastry, flatten it in one layer and close the lid.   Cook the pie on High for 4.5 hours.
Nutrition Info: Per Serving: 396 calories, 22.3g protein, 13.g carbohydrates, 27.5g fat, 0.8g fiber, 74mg cholesterol, 711mg sodium, 332mg potassium

Crockpot Gingered Pork Stew

Servings: 9   Cooking Time: 12 Hours
Ingredients:

2 tablespoons ground cinnamon
2 tablespoons ground ginger
1 tablespoon ground allspice
1 tablespoon ground nutmeg
1 tablespoon paprika
1 ½ teaspoons ground cloves
3 pounds pork shoulder, cut into cubes
2 cups homemade chicken broth
Salt and pepper to taste

Directions:
Place all ingredients in the CrockPot.   Give a good stir.   Close the lid and cook on high for 10 hours or on low for 12 hours.
Nutrition Info: Calories per serving: 425; Carbohydrates: 4.2g; Protein: 38.7g; Fat: 27.4g; Sugar: 0g; Sodium: 803mg; Fiber: 2.8g

Pork And Eggplant Mix

Servings: 2   Cooking Time: 7 Hours
Ingredients:

1 pound pork stew meat, cubed
1 eggplant, cubed
2 scallions, chopped
2 garlic cloves, minced
½ cup beef stock
¼ cup tomato sauce
1 teaspoon sweet paprika
1 tablespoon chives, chopped

Directions:
In your Crock Pot, mix the pork stew meat with the scallions, eggplant and the other ingredients, toss, put the lid on and cook on Low for 7 hours. Divide the mix between plates and serve right away.
Nutrition Info:calories 287, fat 16, fiber 4, carbs 6, protein 20

Skirt Steak With Red Pepper Sauce

Servings: 4   Cooking Time: 12 Hours
Ingredients:

2 red bell peppers, chopped
2 tablespoons olive oil
1 teaspoon thyme leaves
1-pound skirt steak, sliced into 1 inch thick
Salt and pepper to taste

Directions:
In a food processor, mix together the red bell peppers, olive oil, and thyme leaves. Blend until smooth. Add water to make the mixture slightly runny. Set aside.   Season the skirt steak with salt and pepper.   Place in the crockpot and pour over the pepper sauce.   Add more salt and pepper if desired.   Close the lid and cook on low for 12 hours or on high for 10 hours.
Nutrition Info: Calories per serving: 396; Carbohydrates:4 g; Protein: 32.5g; Fat: 21g; Sugar: 0g; Sodium: 428mg; Fiber: 2.8g

Pork Chops And Peppers

Servings: 4   Cooking Time: 10 Hours
Ingredients:

4 pork chops
1 onion, chopped
2 cups red and green bell peppers
½ cup chicken broth
½ teaspoon thyme leaves

Directions:
Place all ingredients in the crockpot.   Mix to combine all ingredients.   Close the lid and cook on low for 10 hours or on high for 7 hours.
Nutrition Info: Calories per serving: 592; Carbohydrates: 0.5g; Protein: 47.1g; Fat: 39.2g; Sugar: 0g; Sodium:601 mg; Fiber:0 g

Sausage Mix

Servings: 4   Cooking Time: 4 Hours
Ingredients:

1 cup yellow onion, chopped	5 pounds kale, chopped
1 and ½ pound Italian pork sausage, sliced	1 teaspoon garlic, minced
½ cup red bell pepper, chopped	¼ cup red hot chili pepper, chopped
Salt and black pepper to the taste	1 cup water

Directions:
In your Crock Pot, mix onion with sausage, bell pepper, salt, pepper, garlic, chili pepper and water, cover and cook on High for 3 hours.   Add kale, toss a bit, cover and cook on High for 1 more hour. Divide between plates and serve.
Nutrition Info:calories 250, fat 4, fiber 1, carbs 12, protein 20

Lamb And Tomatoes Mix

Servings: 2   Cooking Time: 4 Hours
Ingredients:

1 teaspoon olive oil	1 tablespoon oregano, chopped
1 pound lamb stew meat, cubed	1 cup beef stock
1 cup cherry tomatoes, halved	½ teaspoon sweet paprika
1 tablespoon basil, chopped	A pinch of salt and black pepper
½ teaspoon rosemary, dried	1 tablespoon parsley, chopped

Directions:
Grease the Crock Pot with the oil and mix the lamb with the tomatoes, basil and the other ingredients inside.   Toss, put the lid on, cook on High for 4 hours, divide the mix between plates and serve.
Nutrition Info:calories 276, fat 14, fiber 3, carbs 7, protein 20

Barbecue Crockpot Meatloaf

Servings: 6   Cooking Time: 10 Hours
Ingredients:

1-pound ground beef	2 eggs, beaten
1 cup cheddar cheese	2 tablespoon liquid smoke
Salt and pepper to taste	

Directions:
Place all ingredients in a mixing bowl.   Scoop the mixture into greased ramekins.   Place the ramekins inside the crockpot.   Pour water into the crockpot such that 1/8 of the ramekins are soaked.   Close the lid and cook on low for 10 hours or on high for 7 hours.
Nutrition Info: Calories per serving: 330; Carbohydrates:2 g; Protein:21 g; Fat:17 g; Sugar: 0g; Sodium: 668mg; Fiber: 0.7g

Lamb And Orange Sauce

Servings: 4   Cooking Time: 4 Hours
Ingredients:

2 lamb shanks	1 garlic head, peeled
Salt and black pepper to the taste	Zest of ½ orange
4 tablespoons olive oil	Juice of ½ orange
	½ teaspoon oregano, dried

Directions:
In your Crock Pot, mix lamb with salt, pepper and garlic, cover and cook on High for 4 hours.   In a bowl, mix orange juice with orange zest, salt, pepper, olive oil and oregano and whisk very well. Shred lamb meat, discard bone, divide meat between plates.   Drizzle the orange sauce all over and serve.
Nutrition Info:calories 260, fat 7, fiber 3, carbs 15, protein 12

Pickled Pulled Beef

Servings: 4   Cooking Time: 5 Hours
Ingredients:

1 cup cucumber pickles, chopped	1 teaspoon salt
10 oz beef sirloin	2 cups of water
1 teaspoon ground black pepper	2 tablespoons mayonnaise

Directions:
Pour water in the Crock Pot.   Add beef sirloin, ground black pepper, and salt.   Close the lid and cook the beef on high for 5 hours.   Then drain water and chop the beef.   Put the beef in the big bowl.   Add chopped cucumber pickles and mayonnaise.   Mix the beef well.
Nutrition Info: Per Serving: 162 calories, 21.6g protein, 2.1g carbohydrates, 6.9g fat, 0.1g fiber, 65mg cholesterol, 719mg sodium, 294mg potassium.

Country Style Pie

Servings: 8   Cooking Time: 4 Hours
Ingredients:
- 1 cup cherry tomatoes, halved
- 1 teaspoon dried basil
- 1 zucchini, grated
- ½ cup ground pork
- ½ cup tomato sauce
- 1 tablespoon sunflower oil
- 6 oz puff pastry

Directions:
Brush the Crock Pot bottom with sunflower oil. Then put the puff pastry inside and flatten it in the shape of the pie crust.   In the mixing bowl mix dried basil with ground pork, tomato sauce, and zucchini.   Put the meat mixture over the puff pastry.   Then top the meat with halved cherry tomatoes.   Close the lid and cook the pie on High for 4 hours.
Nutrition Info: Per Serving: 202 calories, 7.3g protein, 12.1g carbohydrates, 14g fat, 1.1g fiber, 18mg cholesterol, 151mg sodium, 252mg potassium

Worcestershire Pork Chops

Servings: 4   Cooking Time: 7 Hours And 12 Minutes
Ingredients:
- 4 medium pork chops
- 1 teaspoon Dijon mustard
- 1 tablespoon Worcestershire sauce
- 1 teaspoon lemon juice
- 1 tablespoon water
- Salt and black pepper to the taste
- 1 teaspoon lemon pepper
- 1 tablespoon olive
- 1 tablespoon chives, chopped

Directions:
In a bowl, mix water with Worcestershire sauce, mustard and lemon juice and whisk well.   Heat up a pan with the oil over medium heat, add pork chops, season with salt, pepper and lemon pepper, cook them for 6 minutes, flip and cook for 6 more minutes and transfer to your Crock Pot.   Add Worcestershire sauce mix, toss, cover and cook on Low for 7 hours.   Divide pork chops on plates, sprinkle chives on top and serve.
Nutrition Info:calories 132, fat 5, fiber 1, carbs 12, protein 18

Wine Dipped Lamb Leg

Servings: 7   Cooking Time: 11 Hr.
Ingredients:
- 2 lbs. lamb leg
- 2 cups dry red wine
- 1 cup of water
- 1 tsp anise
- 1 tsp black peas
- 1 tbsp fresh rosemary
- 1 tbsp cumin seeds
- 1 carrot
- 1 white onion
- ½ tsp ground cinnamon
- 1 tbsp fresh ginger, grated
- 1 tsp olive oil

Directions:
Brush the insert of your Crock Pot with olive oil. Place the lamb leg and add rosemary, cumin seeds, cinnamon, ginger.   Put the cooker's lid on and set the cooking time to hours on High settings.   Add water, red wine, anise, black peas, white onion, and carrot.   Put the cooker's lid on and set the cooking time to 8 hours on Low settings.   Serve warm.
Nutrition Info: Per Serving: Calories: 208, Total Fat: 7.8g, Fiber: 1g, Total Carbs: 3.41g, Protein: 27g

Oregano Pork Chops

Servings: 4   Cooking Time: 8 Hours
Ingredients:
- 4 pork chops
- 1 tablespoon oregano, chopped
- 2 garlic cloves, minced
- 1 tablespoon olive oil
- 15 ounces canned tomatoes, chopped
- 1 tablespoon tomato paste
- Salt and black pepper to the taste
- ¼ cup tomato juice

Directions:
In your Crock Pot, mix pork with oregano, garlic, oil, tomatoes, tomato paste, salt, pepper and tomato juice, cover and cook on Low for 8 hours. Divide everything between plates and serve.
Nutrition Info:calories 210, fat 10, fiber 2, carbs 15, protein 25

Balsamic Beef

Servings: 4   Cooking Time: 9 Hours
Ingredients:
- 1 pound beef stew meat, cubed
- 1 teaspoon cayenne pepper
- 4 tablespoons balsamic vinegar
- ½ cup of water
- 2 tablespoons butter

Directions:
Toss the butter in the skillet and melt it.   Then add meat and roast it for minutes per side on medium heat.   Transfer the meat with butter in the Crock Pot.   Add balsamic vinegar, cayenne pepper, and water.   Close the lid and cook the meal on Low for 9 hours.
Nutrition Info: Per Serving: 266 calories, 34.5g protein, 0.4g carbohydrates, 12.9g fat, 0.1g fiber, 117mg cholesterol, 117mg sodium, 479mg potassium.

Cinnamon Lamb

Servings: 2   Cooking Time: 6 Hours
Ingredients:
- 1 pound lamb chops
- 1 teaspoon cinnamon powder
- 1 red onion, chopped
- 1 tablespoon avocado oil
- 1 tablespoon oregano, chopped
- ½ cup beef stock
- 1 tablespoon chives, chopped

Directions:
In your Crock Pot, mix the lamb chops with the cinnamon and the other ingredients, toss, put the lid on and cook on Low for 6 hours.   Divide the chops between plates and serve with a side salad.
Nutrition Info:calories 253, fat 14, fiber 2, carbs 6, protein 18

Crockpot Beef Picadillo

Servings: 8   Cooking Time: 10 Hours

Ingredients:

2 pounds ground beef	1 red onions, chopped
1 ½ tablespoons chili powder	2 Anaheim peppers, seeded and chopped
2 tablespoon dried oregano	20 green olives, pitted and chopped
1 teaspoon cinnamon powder	8 cloves of garlic, minced
1 cup tomatoes, chopped	Salt and pepper to taste

Directions:

Place all ingredients in the CrockPot.   Give a good stir.   Close the lid and cook on high for 8 hours or on low for 10 hours.

Nutrition Info: Calories per serving: 317; Carbohydrates: 4.5g; Protein: 29.6g; Fat: 19.8g; Sugar: 0g; Sodium: 862mg; Fiber: 2.7g

Flavored Pork Roast

Servings: 6   Cooking Time: 4 Hours

Ingredients:

1 pound sweet potatoes, chopped	1 yellow onion, chopped
3 and ½ pounds pork roast	Grated zest and juice of 1 lemon
8 medium carrots, chopped	4 garlic cloves, minced
Salt and black pepper to the taste	Black pepper to the taste
15 ounces canned tomatoes, chopped	½ cup kalamata olives, pitted
3 bay leaves	

Directions:

Put potatoes in your Crock Pot, add carrots, tomatoes, onions, lemon juice and zest, pork, bay leaves, salt, black pepper and garlic, stir, cover and cook on High for 4 hours.   Transfer meat to a cutting board, slice it and divide between plates. Discard bay leaves, transfer veggies to a bowl, mash them, mix with olives, add next to the meat and serve right away!

Nutrition Info: calories 250, fat 4, fiber 3, carbs 6, protein 13

Lamb Carrot Medley

Servings: 4   Cooking Time: 7 Hrs.

Ingredients:

4 lamb shanks	2 tbsp tomato paste
2 tbsp olive oil	1 tsp oregano, dried
1 yellow onion, finely chopped	1 tomato, roughly chopped
3 carrots, roughly chopped	4 oz. chicken stock
2 garlic cloves, minced	Salt and black pepper to the taste

Directions:

Toss the lamb with carrots and all other ingredients in the insert of the Crock Pot.   Put the cooker's lid on and set the cooking time to 7 hours on Low settings.   Serve warm.

Nutrition Info: Per Serving: Calories: 400, Total Fat: 13g, Fiber: 4g, Total Carbs: 17g, Protein: 24g

Dill Beef Roast

Servings: 8   Cooking Time: 8 Hrs.

Ingredients:

2 and ½ lbs. beef chuck roast	½ cup dry red wine
2 cups carrots, chopped	1/3 cup German mustard
1 tbsp olive oil	A pinch of salt and black pepper
2 cup yellow onion, chopped	¼ tsp cloves, ground
1 cup celery, chopped	2 tbsp flour
¾ cup dill pickle, chopped	2 bay leaves
	2 tbsp beef stock

Directions:

Add beef, carrots, and all other ingredients to the insert of your Crock Pot.   Put the cooker's lid on and set the cooking time to 8 hours on Low settings.   Slice the cooked beef and serve it with the celery sauce.   Serve warm.

Nutrition Info: Per Serving: Calories: 256, Total Fat: 7g, Fiber: 2g, Total Carbs: 10g, Protein: 31g

Egg Salad With Ground Pork

Servings: 2   Cooking Time: 4 Hours

Ingredients:

2 eggs, hard-boiled, peeled, chopped	1 teaspoon salt
¼ cup ground pork	¼ cup plain yogurt
1 teaspoon ground turmeric	1 tablespoon coconut oil
	2 tomatoes, chopped

Directions:

Put the coconut oil in the Crock Pot.   Add ground pork, ground turmeric, salt, and yogurt.   Close the lid and cook the meat on High for 4 hours. After this, transfer the ground pork and all remaining liquid from the Crock Pot in the salad bowl.   Add all remaining ingredients from the list above and mix the salad.

Nutrition Info: Per Serving: 198 calories, 11g protein, 8g carbohydrates, 13.9g fat, 1.7g fiber, 175mg cholesterol, 1262mg sodium, 450mg potassium

Peppercorn Beef Steak

Servings: 4   Cooking Time: 8 Hours

Ingredients:

4 beef steaks	1 tablespoon butter
1 teaspoon salt	1 cup of water
1 teaspoon peppercorns	1 teaspoon dried rosemary

Directions:

Rub the beef steaks with salt and dried rosemary. Then rub the meat with butter and transfer in the Crock Pot.   Add water and peppercorns.   Close the lid and cook the beef steaks on Low for 8 hours.

Nutrition Info: Per Serving: 186 calories, 25.9g protein, 0.5g carbohydrates, 8.3g fat, 0.3g fiber, 84mg cholesterol, 660mg sodium, 354mg potassium.

Lettuce And Pork Wraps

Servings: 2   Cooking Time: 3.5 Hours
Ingredients:

2 lettuce leaves	3 tablespoons water
4 oz ground pork	1 teaspoon white
1 teaspoon ketchup	pepper
1 tablespoon butter	

Directions:
Mix ground pork with water, butter, and white pepper.   Put the meat mixture in the Crock Pot. Close the lid and cook it on High for 5 hours. After this, mix ground pork with ketchup.   Fill the lettuce leaves with ground pork.
Nutrition Info: Per Serving: 138 calories, 15.1g protein, 1.5g carbohydrates, 7.8g fat, 0.3g fiber, 57mg cholesterol, 10mg sodium, 270mg potassium

Naked Beef Enchilada In A Crockpot

Servings: 4   Cooking Time: 6 Hours
Ingredients:

1-pound ground beef	2 cups Mexican
2 tablespoons	cheese blend, grated
enchilada spice mix	¼ cup cilantro,
1 cup cauliflower	chopped
florets	

Directions:
In a skillet, sauté the ground beef over medium flame for 3 minutes.   Transfer to the crockpot and add the enchilada spice mix and cauliflower. Stir to combine.   Add the Mexican cheese blend on top.   Cook on low for 6 hours or on high for 4 hours.   Sprinkle with cilantro on top.
Nutrition Info: Calories per serving: 481; Carbohydrates: 1g; Protein: 35.1g; Fat: 29.4g; Sugar: 0g; Sodium: 536mg; Fiber:0 g

Chili Beef Sausages

Servings: 5   Cooking Time: 4 Hours
Ingredients:

1-pound beef	¼ cup of water
sausages	1 teaspoon chili
1 tablespoon olive oil	powder

Directions:
Pour olive oil in the Crock Pot.   Then sprinkle the beef sausages with chili powder and put in the Crock Pot.   Add water and close the lid.   Cook the beef sausages on high for hours.
Nutrition Info: Per Serving: 385 calories, 12.6g protein, 2.7g carbohydrates, 35.8g fat, 0.2g fiber, 64mg cholesterol, 736mg sodium, 182mg potassium.

Chili Beef Ribs

Servings: 4   Cooking Time: 5 Hours
Ingredients:

10 oz beef ribs,	1 teaspoon hot sauce
chopped	1 tablespoon sesame
1 teaspoon chili	
powder	

	oil
	½ cup of water

Directions:
Mix the beef ribs with chili powder.   Then heat the sesame oil in the skillet until hot.   Add beef ribs and roast them for 2-minutes per side or until they are light brown.   After this, transfer the beef ribs in the Crock Pot.   Add water and hot sauce. Close the lid and cook them on High for 5 hours.
Nutrition Info: Per Serving: 164 calories, 21.6g protein, 0.4g carbohydrates, 7.9g fat, 0.2g fiber, 63mg cholesterol, 86mg sodium, 300mg potassium.

Seasoned Beef

Servings: 6   Cooking Time: 8 Hours
Ingredients:

4 pounds beef roast	1 tablespoon onion
2 cups beef stock	powder
2 sweet potatoes,	1 tablespoon garlic
cubed	powder
6 carrots, sliced	1 tablespoon sweet
7 celery stalks,	paprika
chopped	Salt and black pepper
1 yellow onion,	to the taste
chopped	

Directions:
In your Crock Pot, beef with stock, sweet potatoes, carrots, celery, onion, onion powder, garlic powder, paprika, salt and pepper, stir, cover, cook on Low for 8 hours, slice roast, divide between plates, drizzle sauce from the Crock Pot all and serve with the veggies on the side.
Nutrition Info:calories 372, fat 6, fiber 12, carbs 19, protein 11

Scalloped Potato Casserole

Servings: 4   Cooking Time: 8 Hours
Ingredients:

2 pork chops, sliced	2 tablespoons
3 potatoes, sliced	breadcrumbs
1 egg, beaten	1 oz Parmesan, grated
1 tablespoon butter,	½ cup of coconut
softened	milk

Directions:
Grease the Crock Pot bottom with butter.   Then put the pork chops inside.   Add sliced potatoes over the meat.   Then sprinkle the potatoes with egg and breadcrumbs.   Add parmesan and coconut milk.   Close the lid and cook the casserole on Low for 8 hours.
Nutrition Info: Per Serving: 385 calories, 16.5g protein, 29.5g carbohydrates, 22.9g fat, 4.6g fiber, 88mg cholesterol, 169mg sodium, 889mg potassium

Fall Pork

Servings: 4   Cooking Time: 10 Hours
Ingredients:

9 oz pork tenderloin, chopped	1 cup tomatoes, chopped
½ cup carrot, chopped	1 teaspoon Italian seasonings
½ cup pumpkin, chopped	1 teaspoon salt
2 cups of water	

Directions:
Put all ingredients in the Crock Pot.   Close the lid and cook the meal on Low for 10 hours. Carefully mix the cooked meal before serving.
Nutrition Info: Per Serving: 119 calories, 17.5g protein, 5.7g carbohydrates, 2.8g fat, 1.8g fiber, 47mg cholesterol, 635mg sodium, 484mg potassium

Barbacoa Beef

Servings: 4   Cooking Time: 5 Hours
Ingredients:

1-pound beef chuck roast	½ teaspoon salt
1 teaspoon ground black pepper	¼ lime,
1 teaspoon ground cumin	½ teaspoon ground clove
	2 cups of water

Directions:
Put the beef in the Crock Pot.   Add ground black pepper, salt, ground cumin, ground clove, and water.   Close the lid and cook the meat on High for 5 hours.   Then shred the beef.   Squeeze the line over the meat and carefully mix.
Nutrition Info: Per Serving: 417 calories, 29.9g protein, 1.2g carbohydrates, 31.8g fat, 0.4g fiber, 117mg cholesterol, 369mg sodium, 283mg potassium.

Super-fast Golubkis

Servings: 4   Cooking Time: 8 Hours
Ingredients:

7 oz ground beef	½ cup basmati rice
1 teaspoon garam masala	1 cup tomatoes, chopped
2 cups of water	1 teaspoon tomato paste
2 cups white cabbage, shredded	

Directions:
In the mixing bowl, mix ground beef, garam masala, basmati rice, tomato paste, and tomatoes. Then put ½ part of ground beef mixture in the Crock Pot.   Top it with shredded white cabbage. Then add remaining ground beef mixture and top with remaining shredded cabbage.   Add water and close the lid.   Cook the meal on Low for 8 hours.
Nutrition Info: Per Serving: 195 calories, 17.6g protein, 22.5g carbohydrates, 3.4g fat, 1.8g fiber, 44mg cholesterol, 48mg sodium, 407mg potassium.

Spaghetti Meatballs(1)

Servings: 4   Cooking Time: 4 Hours
Ingredients:

1-pound ground beef	1 teaspoon dried dill
1 teaspoon minced garlic	½ cup marinara sauce
1 teaspoon ricotta cheese	1 tablespoon avocado oil

Directions:
Heat the avocado oil in the skillet well.   Then mix the ground beef with minced garlic, dried dill, and ricotta cheese.   Make the small meatballs and put them in the hot oil.   Roast the meatballs on high heat for 3 minutes per side.   Transfer the meatballs in the Crock Pot and add marinara sauce. Close the lid and cook the meatballs on High for 4 hours.
Nutrition Info: Per Serving: 246 calories, 35.2g protein, 4.9g carbohydrates, 8.5g fat, 1g fiber, 102mg cholesterol, 205mg sodium, 579mg potassium.

Garlic Pork Stew

Servings: 4   Cooking Time: 10 Hours
Ingredients:

1 tablespoon coconut oil	1 onion, diced
1-pound pork shoulder, cut into cubes	2 cups homemade chicken broth
8 cloves of garlic, minced	2 tablespoons mustard
	Salt and pepper to taste

Directions:
Place all ingredients in the CrockPot.   Give a good stir.   Close the lid and cook on high for 8 hours or on low for 10 hours.
Nutrition Info: Calories per serving: 369; Carbohydrates: 4.6g; Protein: 30.4g; Fat: 24.9g; Sugar: 0g; Sodium: 731mg; Fiber: 2.1g

Rich Lamb Shanks

Servings: 4   Cooking Time: 7 Hours
Ingredients:

2 tablespoons olive oil	4 lamb shanks
1 yellow onion, finely chopped	1 teaspoon oregano, dried
3 carrots, roughly chopped	1 tomato, roughly chopped
2 garlic cloves, minced	4 ounces chicken stock
2 tablespoons tomato paste	Salt and black pepper to the taste

Directions:
In your Crock Pot, mix lamb with oil, onion, garlic, carrots, tomato paste, tomato, oregano, stock, salt and pepper, stir, cover and cook on Low for 7 hours.   Divide into bowls and serve hot.
Nutrition Info:calories 400, fat 13, fiber 4, carbs 17, protein 24

Meat And Mushrooms Saute

Servings: 4   Cooking Time: 5 Hours
Ingredients:

8 oz pork sirloin, sliced	1 cup cream
1 cup white mushrooms, chopped	1 teaspoon ground black pepper
1 onion, sliced	1 teaspoon salt

Directions:
Put all ingredients in the Crock Pot and carefully mix with the help of the spatula.   Then close the lid and cook the saute on High for 5 hours.
Nutrition Info: Per Serving: 156 calories, 13g protein, 5.4g carbohydrates, 9g fat, 0.9g fiber, 47mg cholesterol, 634mg sodium, 125mg potassium

Zesty Pesto Pork

Servings: 6   Cooking Time: 11 Hr.
Ingredients:

5 tbsp lime zest	1 tsp chili flakes
2 lbs. pork shoulder	1 tsp ground black pepper
3 garlic cloves, sliced	1 tbsp salt
2 tbsp butter	3 tsp pesto
1 tsp paprika	

Directions:
Whisk lime zest, with paprika, sliced garlic, butter, chili flakes, pesto, salt, and black pepper in a small bowl.   Rub the pork shoulder with the lime zest mixture and wrap it with aluminum foil.   Place the pork should in the insert of the Crock Pot.   Put the cooker's lid on and set the cooking time to 11 hours on Low settings.   Remove the pork shoulder from the foil.   Slice and serve warm.
Nutrition Info: Per Serving: Calories: 153, Total Fat: 6.1g, Fiber: 3g, Total Carbs: 22.42g, Protein: 4g

Herbed Pork Tenderloin

Servings: 6   Cooking Time: 12 Hours
Ingredients:

2 pork tenderloins, skin removed	2 jalapeno peppers, chopped
½ cup extra virgin olive oil	2 tablespoons ginger, grated
½ cup apple cider vinegar	1 teaspoon salt
½ cup cilantro, chopped	½ teaspoon ground black pepper
3 green onions, chopped	½ teaspoon all spice
	1/8 teaspoon ground cloves

Directions:
Mix all ingredients in a bowl and allow meat to marinate in the fridge for at least 2 hours.   Line aluminum foil at the base of the CrockPot.   Place the meat.   Close the lid and cook on high for 10 hours or on low for 12 hours.
Nutrition Info: Calories per serving: 253; Carbohydrates: 5.5g; Protein: 29.8g; Fat: 13.6g; Sugar: 0.3g; Sodium: 739mg; Fiber:2.8 g

Braised Beef Strips

Servings: 4   Cooking Time: 5 Hours
Ingredients:

½ cup mushroom, sliced	1 teaspoon salt
1 onion, sliced	1 teaspoon white pepper
1 cup of water	10 oz beef loin, cut into strips
1 tablespoon coconut oil	

Directions:
Melt the coconut oil in the skillet.   Add mushrooms and roast them for 5 minutes on medium heat.   Then transfer the mushrooms in the Crock Pot.   Add all remaining ingredients and close the lid.   Cook the meal on High for hours
Nutrition Info: Per Serving: 173 calories, 19.6g protein, 3.2g carbohydrates, 9.4g fat, 0.8g fiber, 50mg cholesterol, 624mg sodium, 316mg potassium.

Pork And Lentils Mash

Servings: 4   Cooking Time: 4 Hours
Ingredients:

8 oz pork mince	2.5 cups water
½ cup red lentils	1 teaspoon salt
1 teaspoon chili powder	1 onion, diced
	1 teaspoon olive oil

Directions:
Pour olive oil in the skillet.   Add onion and roast the mixture for 4-5 minutes or until the onion is light brown.   Transfer it in the Crock Pot.   Add red lentils, pork mince, and all remaining ingredients.   Carefully mix the mixture and cook it on High for 4 hours.   Then stir the meal well and transfer it in the serving bowls.
Nutrition Info: Per Serving: 263 calories, 6.6g protein, 52.5g carbohydrates, 3.8g fat, 8.7g fiber, 0mg cholesterol, 595mg sodium, 283mg potassium

Horseradish Pork Chops

Servings: 4   Cooking Time: 5 Hours
Ingredients:

4 pork chops	1 onion, sliced
5 tablespoons horseradish	1 tablespoon avocado oil
½ cup of water	

Directions:
Mix avocado oil with horseradish and rub the pork chops/   Put the pork chops and all remaining horseradish mixture in the Crock Pot.   Add onion and water.   Cook the pork chops on high for 5 hours.
Nutrition Info: Per Serving: 281 calories, 18.5g protein, 4.9g carbohydrates, 20.5g fat, 1.4g fiber, 69mg cholesterol, 117mg sodium, 373mg potassium

Indian Harissa Pork

Servings: 8   Cooking Time: 5 Hrs.

Ingredients:

21 oz pork steak, tenderized	1 tsp ground black pepper
2 tbsp curry	1 tsp salt
1 tsp harissa	1 tsp sugar
1 tbsp garam masala	1 cup cashew, crushed
1 tsp chili flakes	
½ cup cream	1 tsp ground nutmeg

Directions:
Season the pork steaks with harissa, curry, chili flakes, and garam masala.   Place the pork steak in the insert of the Crock Pot.   Add cream, salt, sugar, nutmeg, and black pepper to the pork.   Put the cooker's lid on and set the cooking time to 5 hours on High settings.   Serve warm.
Nutrition Info: Per Serving: Calories: 434, Total Fat: 33.4g, Fiber: 2g, Total Carbs: 12.27g, Protein: 23g

Pork Chops And Pineapple Mix

Servings: 4   Cooking Time: 6 Hours

Ingredients:

2 pounds pork chops	¼ cup ketchup
1/3 cup sugar	5 tablespoons soy sauce
15 ounces pineapple, cubed	
3 tablespoons apple cider vinegar	2 teaspoons garlic, minced
	3 tablespoons flour

Directions:
In a bowl, mix ketchup with sugar, vinegar, soy sauce and tapioca, whisk well, add pork chops, toss well and transfer everything to your Crock Pot Add pineapple and garlic, toss again, cover, cook on Low for 6 hours, divide everything between plates and serve.
Nutrition Info:calories 345, fat 5, fiber 6, carbs 13, protein 14

Thyme Pork Belly

Servings: 6   Cooking Time: 10 Hours

Ingredients:

10 oz pork belly	1 teaspoon salt
1 teaspoon ground thyme	1 teaspoon garlic powder
1 teaspoon ground black pepper	½ cup of water

Directions:
In the shallow bowl mix salt, ground thyme, ground black pepper, and garlic powder.   Then rub the pork belly with the spice mixture and place it in the Crock Pot.   Add water and close the lid.   Cook the pork belly on Low for 10 hours.   Then slice the cooked pork belly into servings.
Nutrition Info: Per Serving: 221 calories, 22g protein, 0.7g carbohydrates, 12.7g fat, 0.2g fiber, 55mg cholesterol, 1152mg sodium, 11mg potassium

Beef Stuffing

Servings: 6   Cooking Time: 5 Hours

Ingredients:

½ teaspoon cumin seeds	12 oz ground beef
1 teaspoon garam masala	2 oz scallions, chopped
1 teaspoon ginger paste	1 cup of water
	1 tablespoon butter
	1 teaspoon salt

Directions:
Put all ingredients in the Crock Pot and carefully mix the mixture.   Close the lid and cook the beef stuffing on High for 5 hours.
Nutrition Info: Per Serving: 152 calories, 21g protein, 1.2g carbohydrates, 6.6g fat, 0.4g fiber, 67mg cholesterol, 531mg sodium, 315mg potassium.

Pan "grilled" Flank Steak

Servings: 4   Cooking Time: 10 Hours

Ingredients:

1 ½ pounds flank steak, fat trimmed	1 tablespoon butter, melted
Salt and pepper to taste	1 tablespoon parsley, chopped
A pinch of rosemary	

Directions:
Season the flank steak with salt and pepper to taste. Rub with a pinch of rosemary.   Pour the butter in the crockpot and add the slices of flank steak. Close the lid and cook on low for 10 hours or on high for 8 hours.   Garnish with parsley before serving.
Nutrition Info: Calories per serving: 397; Carbohydrates: 1g; Protein:26.3 g; Fat: 20.7g; Sugar: 0g; Sodium:644mg; Fiber: 0.3g

Pork Chops And Spinach

Servings: 2   Cooking Time: 4 Hours

Ingredients:

1 pound pork chops	¼ cup tomato passata
1 cup baby spinach	
½ cup beef stock	4 scallions, chopped
½ teaspoon sweet paprika	2 teaspoons olive oil
½ teaspoon coriander, ground	A pinch of salt and black pepper
	1 tablespoon chives, chopped

Directions:
In your Crock Pot, mix the pork chops with the stock, passata and the other ingredients except the spinach, toss, put the lid on and cook on High for 3 hours and 30 minutes.   Add the spinach, cook on High for 30 minutes more, divide the mix between plates and serve.
Nutrition Info:calories 274, fat 14, fiber 2, carbs 6, protein 16

Mustard Ribs

Servings: 2   Cooking Time: 8 Hours
Ingredients:

2 beef short ribs, cut into individual ribs	1 tablespoon balsamic vinegar
Salt and black pepper to the taste	1 tablespoon mustard
½ cup ketchup	1 tablespoon chives, chopped

Directions:
In your Crock Pot, combine the ribs with the ketchup, salt, pepper and the other ingredients, toss, put the lid on and cook on Low for 8 hours. Divide between plates and serve with a side salad.
Nutrition Info:calories 284, fat 7, 4, carbs 18, protein 20

Pork And Zucchini Bowl

Servings: 4   Cooking Time: 5 Hours
Ingredients:

12 oz pork stew meat, cubed	1 teaspoon dried dill
1 cup zucchini, chopped	1 teaspoon salt
1 teaspoon white pepper	½ cup sour cream
	1 cup of water
	1 chili pepper, chopped

Directions:
Put meat in the Crock Pot.   Add white pepper, dried dill, salt, sour cream, water, and chili pepper. Close the lid and cook the meal on High for 4 hours.   Then add zucchini and cook the meal on High for 1 hour more.
Nutrition Info: Per Serving: 249 calories, 26.3g protein, 2.8g carbohydrates, 14.3g fat, 0.5g fiber, 86mg cholesterol, 652mg sodium, 452mg potassium

Maple Rosemary Lamb

Servings: 4   Cooking Time: 9 Hrs.
Ingredients:

3 tbsp mustard	1 tsp salt
5 tbsp olive oil	1 tsp paprika
3 tbsp fresh rosemary	4 tbsp maple syrup
1 tsp ground coriander	1 lb. lamb fillet
1 tsp dried mint	2 tbsp water

Directions:
Whisk olive oil with mustard, rosemary, mint, salt, paprika, and coriander in a small bowl.   Rub the lamb fillet with the mustard mixture then transfer to the insert of Crock Pot.   Add maple syrup and water to the lamb fillet.   Put the cooker's lid on and set the cooking time to 9 hours on Low settings.   Slice the cooked lamb and serve warm with the sauce.
Nutrition Info: Per Serving: Calories: 502, Total Fat: 36.5g, Fiber: 1g, Total Carbs: 14.73g, Protein: 28g

Chili Beef Strips

Servings: 4   Cooking Time: 6 Hours
Ingredients:

1-pound beef loin, cut into strips	2 tablespoons coconut oil
1 chili pepper, chopped	1 teaspoon chili powder
1 teaspoon salt	

Directions:
Sprinkle the beef strips with salt and chili powder. Then put the chili pepper in the Crock Pot.   Add coconut oil and beef strips.   Close the lid and cook the meal on Low for 6 hours.
Nutrition Info: Per Serving: 267 calories, 30.4g protein, 0.5g carbohydrates, 16.4g fat, 0.3g fiber, 81mg cholesterol, 650mg sodium, 401mg potassium.

Beef Mac&cheese

Servings: 4   Cooking Time: 4.5 Hours
Ingredients:

½ cup macaroni, cooked	1 cup Mozzarella, shredded
10 oz ground beef	½ cup of water
½ cup marinara sauce	

Directions:
Mix the ground beef with marinara sauce and water and transfer in the Crock Pot.   Cook it on High for 4 hours.   After this, add macaroni and Mozzarella.   Carefully mix the meal and cook it for 30 minutes more on high.
Nutrition Info: Per Serving: 218 calories, 25.4g protein, 12.4g carbohydrates, 1.2g fat, 68g fiber, 63mg cholesterol, 219mg sodium, 408mg potassium.

Vegetable & Vegetarian Recipes

Lentils Fritters

Servings: 6   Cooking Time: 1.5 Hours
Ingredients:

1 cup red lentils, cooked
1 teaspoon fresh cilantro, chopped
1 teaspoon scallions, chopped

1 tablespoon flour
½ carrot, grated
1 teaspoon flax meal
1 tablespoon coconut oil
¼ cup of water

Directions:
Pour water in the Crock Pot.   Add coconut oil. After this, in the mixing bowl mix all remaining ingredients. Make the small fritters and freeze them for 15-20 minutes in the freezer.   Put the fritters in the Crock Pot and close the lid.   Cook them on High for 1.hours.
Nutrition Info: Per Serving: 141 calories, 8.5g protein, 20.9g carbohydrates, 2.8g fat, 10g fiber, 0mg cholesterol, 6mg sodium, 328mg potassium.

Carrot Strips

Servings: 2   Cooking Time: 1 Hour
Ingredients:

2 tablespoons sunflower oil
1 teaspoon dried thyme

2 carrots, peeled
½ teaspoon salt
½ cup of water

Directions:
Cut the carrots into the strips.   Then heat the sunflower oil in the skillet until hot.   Put the carrot strips in the hot oil and roast for 2-minutes per side.   Pour water in the Crock Pot.   Add salt and dried thyme.   Then add roasted carrot and cook the meal on High for 1 hour.
Nutrition Info: Per Serving: 150 calories, 0.6g protein, 6.3g carbohydrates, 14g fat, 1.7g fiber, 0mg cholesterol, 625mg sodium, 200mg potassium.

Okra Curry

Servings: 4   Cooking Time: 2.5 Hours
Ingredients:

1 cup potatoes, chopped
1 cup okra, chopped
1 cup tomatoes, chopped

1 teaspoon curry powder
1 teaspoon dried dill
1 cup coconut cream
1 cup of water

Directions:
Pour water in the Crock Pot.   Add coconut cream, potatoes, tomatoes, curry powder, and dried dill. Cook the ingredients on High for 2 hours.   Then add okra and carefully mix the meal.   Cook it for 30 minutes on High.
Nutrition Info: Per Serving: 184 calories, 3g protein, 13.3g carbohydrates, 14.6g fat, 3.8g fiber, 0mg cholesterol, 18mg sodium, 508mg potassium.

Tofu Tikka Masala

Servings: 4   Cooking Time: 2 Hours
Ingredients:

1-pound tofu, cubed
1 teaspoon ground cumin
1 teaspoon garam masala
1 teaspoon minced garlic

½ cup coconut cream
1 teaspoon minced ginger
1 tablespoon lemon juice
1 tablespoon avocado oil

Directions:
In the mixing bowl mix avocado oil, lemon juice, minced ginger, garlic, coconut cream, garam masala, and ground cumin.   Then add tofu and carefully mix the mixture.   Leave it for 10 minutes and then transfer in the Crock Pot. Close the lid and cook the meal on Low for 2 hours.
Nutrition Info: Per Serving: 159 calories, 10.2g protein, 4.6g carbohydrates, 12.5g fat, 2g fiber, 0mg cholesterol, 21mg sodium, 281mg potassium.

Sautéed Greens

Servings: 4   Cooking Time: 1 Hour
Ingredients:

1 cup spinach, chopped
2 cups collard greens, chopped

1 cup Swiss chard, chopped
2 cups of water
½ cup half and half

Directions:
Put spinach, collard greens, and Swiss chard in the Crock Pot.   Add water and close the lid.   Cook the greens on High for 1 hour.   Then drain water and transfer the greens in the bowl.   Bring the half and half to boil and pour over greens. Carefully mix the greens.
Nutrition Info: Per Serving: 49 calories, 1.8g protein, 3.2g carbohydrates, 3.7g fat, 1.1g fiber, 11mg cholesterol, 45mg sodium, 117mg potassium.

Buffalo Cremini Mushrooms

Servings: 4   Cooking Time: 6 Hours
Ingredients:

3 cups cremini mushrooms, trimmed	½ cup of water
2 oz buffalo sauce	2 tablespoons coconut oil

Directions:
Pour water in the Crock Pot.   Melt the coconut oil in the skillet.   Add mushrooms and roast them for 4 minutes per side. Transfer the roasted mushrooms in the Crock Pot.   Cook them on Low for hours.   Then add buffalo sauce and carefully mix.   Cook the mushrooms for 2 hours on low.
Nutrition Info: Per Serving: 79 calories, 1.4g protein, 3.2g carbohydrates, 6.9g fat, 0.8g fiber, 0mg cholesterol, 458mg sodium, 242mg potassium.

Paprika Baby Carrot

Servings: 2   Cooking Time: 2.5 Hours
Ingredients:

1 tablespoon ground paprika	2 cups baby carrot
1 teaspoon cumin seeds	1 cup of water
	1 teaspoon vegan butter

Directions:
Pour water in the Crock Pot.   Add baby carrot, cumin seeds, and ground paprika.   Close the lid and cook the carrot on High for 2.5 hours.   Then drain water, add butter, and shake the vegetables.
Nutrition Info: Per Serving: 60 calories, 1.6g protein, 8.6g carbohydrates, 2.7g fat, 4.2g fiber, 5mg cholesterol, 64mg sodium, 220mg potassium.

Fragrant Appetizer Peppers

Servings: 2   Cooking Time: 1.5 Hours
Ingredients:

4 sweet peppers, seeded	1 red onion, sliced
¼ cup apple cider vinegar	½ teaspoon sugar
1 teaspoon peppercorns	¼ cup of water
	1 tablespoon olive oil

Directions:
Slice the sweet peppers roughly and put in the Crock Pot.   Add all remaining ingredients and close the lid.   Cook the peppers on high for 1.5 hours.   Then cool the peppers well and store them in the fridge for up to 6 days.
Nutrition Info: Per Serving: 171 calories, 3.1g protein, 25.1g carbohydrates, 7.7g fat, 4.7g fiber, 0mg cholesterol, 11mg sodium, 564mg potassium.

Curry Couscous

Servings: 4   Cooking Time: 20 Minutes
Ingredients:

1 cup of water	½ cup coconut cream
1 cup couscous	1 teaspoon salt

Directions:
Put all ingredients in the Crock Pot and close the lid.   Cook the couscous on High for   minutes.
Nutrition Info: Per Serving: 182 calories, 5.8g protein, 34.4g carbohydrates, 2g fat, 2.2g fiber, 6mg cholesterol, 597mg sodium, 84mg potassium.

Spaghetti Cheese Casserole

Servings: 8   Cooking Time: 7 Hrs
Ingredients:

1 lb. cottage cheese	3 tbsp white sugar
7 oz. spaghetti, cooked	1 tsp vanilla extract
5 eggs	1 tsp marjoram
1 cup heavy cream	1 tsp lemon zest
5 tbsp semolina	1 tsp butter

Directions:
Start by blending cottage cheese in a blender jug for minute.   Add eggs to the cottage cheese and blend again for 3 minutes.   Stir in semolina, cream, sugar, marjoram, vanilla extract, butter and lemon zest.   Blend again for 1 minute and keep the cheese-cream mixture aside.   Spread the chopped spaghetti layer in the Crock Pot.   Top the spaghetti with 3 tbsp with the cheese-cream mixture.   Add another layer of spaghetti over the mixture.   Continue adding alternate layers in this manner until all ingredients are used.   Put the cooker's lid on and set the cooking time to 7 hours on Low settings.   Slice and serve.
Nutrition Info: Per Serving: Calories 242, Total Fat 13.8g, Fiber 1g, Total Carbs 17.44g, Protein 12g

Paprika Okra

Servings: 4   Cooking Time: 40 Minutes
Ingredients:

4 cups okra, sliced	2 tablespoons coconut oil
1 tablespoon smoked paprika	1 cup organic almond milk
1 teaspoon salt	

Directions:
Pour almond milk in the Crock Pot.   Add coconut oil, salt, and smoked paprika.   Then add sliced okra and gently mix the ingredients.   Cook the okra on High for   minutes. Then cooked okra should be tender but not soft.
Nutrition Info: Per Serving: 119 calories, 2.4g protein, 10.4g carbohydrates, 7.8g fat, 3.9g fiber, 0mg cholesterol, 624mg sodium, 340mg potassium.

Mediterranean Veggies

Servings: 8   Cooking Time: 7 Hrs
Ingredients:

1 zucchini, peeled and diced	2 tbsp olive oil
2 eggplants, peeled and diced	1 tsp ground black pepper
2 red onion, diced	1 tsp paprika
4 potatoes, peeled and diced	1 tsp salt
4 oz. asparagus, chopped	1 tbsp Mediterranean seasoning
	1 tsp minced garlic

Directions:
Mix Mediterranean seasoning with olive oil, paprika, salt, garlic, and black pepper in a large bowl.   Toss in all the veggies to this mixture and mix well.   Spread all the seasoned veggies in the Crock Pot.   Put the cooker's lid on and set the cooking time to 7 hours on Low settings.   Serve warm.
Nutrition Info: Per Serving: Calories 227, Total Fat 3.9g, Fiber 9g, Total Carbs 44.88g, Protein 6g

Avocado Saute

Servings: 4   Cooking Time: 6.5 Hours
Ingredients:

1 cup chickpeas	½ cup fresh parsley, chopped
4 cups of water	
½ cup tomato juice	½ cup coconut cream
1 tablespoon tomato paste	1 avocado, peeled, pitted, chopped

Directions:
Pour water in the Crock Pot. Add chickpeas and tomato juice. Cook the ingredients on low for 6 hours.   Then add tomato paste, fresh parsley, and coconut cream. Cook the meal on High for 30 minutes.   Transfer the cooked meal in the bowls and top with avocado.
Nutrition Info: Per Serving: 365 calories, 11.9g protein, 38.8g carbohydrates, 20.1g fat, 13.3g fiber, 0mg cholesterol, 116mg sodium, 914mg potassium.

Chili Okra

Servings: 6   Cooking Time: 7 Hours
Ingredients:

6 cups okra, chopped	½ teaspoon cayenne pepper
1 cup tomato juice	
1 teaspoon salt	1 tablespoon olive oil
½ teaspoon chili powder	1 cup vegetable stock

Directions:
Put all ingredients from the list above in the Crock Pot.   Mix them gently and cook on Low for 7 hours.
Nutrition Info: Per Serving: 69 calories, 2.4g protein, 9.5g carbohydrates, 2.6g fat, 3.6g fiber, 0mg cholesterol, 514mg sodium, 399mg potassium.

Pumpkin Hummus

Servings: 6   Cooking Time: 4 Hours
Ingredients:

1 cup chickpeas, canned	1 teaspoon harissa
	2 cups of water
1 tablespoon tahini paste	2 tablespoons olive oil
1 cup pumpkin, chopped	1 tablespoon lemon juice

Directions:
Pour water in the Crock Pot.   Add pumpkin and cook it for 4 hours on High or until the pumpkin is soft.   After this, drain water and transfer the pumpkin in the food processor.   Add all remaining ingredients and blend the mixture until smooth.   Add water from pumpkin if the cooked hummus is very thick.
Nutrition Info: Per Serving: 193 calories, 7.4g protein, 24.4g carbohydrates, 8.3g fat, 7.2g fiber, 0mg cholesterol, 26mg sodium, 390mg potassium.

Mushroom Saute

Servings: 4   Cooking Time: 2.5 Hours
Ingredients:

2 cups cremini mushrooms, sliced	1 teaspoon ground black pepper
1 white onion, sliced	¼ cup vegan Cheddar cheese, shredded
½ cup fresh dill, chopped	
1 cup coconut cream	1 tablespoon coconut oil

Directions:
Toss the coconut oil in the skillet and melt it. Add mushrooms and onion.   Roast the vegetables on medium heat for 5 minutes.   Then transfer them in the Crock Pot.   Add all remaining ingredients and carefully mix.   Cook the mushroom saute on High for 2.5 hours.
Nutrition Info: Per Serving: 134 calories, 4.7g protein, 9.7g carbohydrates, 9.4g fat, 1.8g fiber, 19mg cholesterol, 79mg sodium, 436mg potassium.

Coconut Milk Lentils Bowl

Servings: 5   Cooking Time: 9 Hours
Ingredients:

2 cups brown lentils	1 teaspoon ground nutmeg
3 cups of coconut milk	1 teaspoon salt
3 cups of water	

Directions:
Mix the brown lentils with salt and ground nutmeg and put in the Crock Pot.   Add coconut milk and water.   Close the lid and cook the lentils on Low for 9 hours.
Nutrition Info: Per Serving: 364 calories, 5.3g protein, 12.1g carbohydrates, 34.7g fat, 4.9g fiber, 0mg cholesterol, 491mg sodium, 382mg potassium.

Tri-bean Chili

Servings: 6　　Cooking Time: 8 Hrs
Ingredients:
- 15 oz. canned kidney beans, drained
- 30 oz. canned chili beans in sauce
- 15 oz. canned black beans, drained
- 2 green bell peppers, chopped
- 30 oz. canned tomatoes, crushed
- 2 tbsp chili powder
- 2 yellow onions, chopped
- 2 garlic cloves, minced
- 1 tsp oregano, dried
- 1 tbsp cumin, ground
- Salt and black pepper to the taste

Directions:
Add kidney beans, black beans, chili beans, and all the spices and veggies to the Crock Pot.　　Put the cooker's lid on and set the cooking time to 8 hours on Low settings.　　Serve warm.
Nutrition Info: Per Serving: Calories 314, Total Fat 6g, Fiber 5g, Total Carbs 14g, Protein 4g

Soft Sweet Potato Halves

Servings: 4　　Cooking Time: 5 Hours
Ingredients:
- 4 sweet potatoes, halved
- 4 teaspoons coconut oil
- 1 teaspoon salt
- 1 teaspoon dried thyme
- ½ teaspoon dried oregano
- ¼ cup of water

Directions:
Pour water in the Crock Pot.　　Then rub the sweet potato halves with dried thyme, oregano, and salt. Put the sweet potato halves in the Crock Pot. Top every sweet potato halves with coconut oil and close the lid.　　Cook the sweet potato halves for hours on Low.
Nutrition Info: Per Serving: 42 calories, 0.1g protein, 0.6g carbohydrates, 4.6g fat, 0.2g fiber, 0mg cholesterol, 582mg sodium, 14mg potassium.

Curry Paneer

Servings: 2　　Cooking Time: 2 Hours
Ingredients:
- 6 oz paneer, cubed
- 1 teaspoon garam masala
- 1 chili pepper, chopped
- ½ cup coconut cream
- 1 teaspoon olive oil
- ½ onion, diced
- 1 teaspoon garlic paste

Directions:
In the mixing bowl mix diced onion, garlic paste, olive oil, chili pepper, coconut cream, and garam masala.　　Then mix the mixture with cubed paneer and put in the Crock Pot.　　Cook it on Low for 2 hours.
Nutrition Info: Per Serving: 309 calories, 7.1g protein, 22.5g carbohydrates, 22.4g fat, 3.5g fiber, 2mg cholesterol, 415mg sodium, 208mg potassium.

Yam Fritters

Servings: 1　　Cooking Time: 4 Hours

Ingredients:
- 1 yam, grated, boiled
- 1 teaspoon dried parsley
- ¼ teaspoon chili powder
- ¼ teaspoon salt
- 1 egg, beaten
- 1 teaspoon flour
- 5 tablespoons coconut cream
- Cooking spray

Directions:
In the mixing bowl mix grated yams, dried parsley, chili powder, salt, egg, and flour.　　Make the fritters from the yam mixture.　　After this, spray the Crock Pot bottom with cooking spray.　　Put the fritters inside in one layer.　　Add coconut cream and cook the meal on Low for 4 hours.
Nutrition Info: Per Serving: 115 calories, 6.4g protein, 4.9g carbohydrates, 7.9g fat, 0.4g fiber, 175mg cholesterol, 670mg sodium, 110mg potassium.

Rice Stuffed Apple Cups

Servings: 4　　Cooking Time: 6 Hrs
Ingredients:
- 4 red apples
- 1 cup white rice
- 3 tbsp raisins
- 1 onion, diced
- 7 tbsp water
- 1 tsp salt
- 1 tsp curry powder
- 4 tsp sour cream

Directions:
Remove the seeds and half of the flesh from the center of the apples to make apple cups.　　Toss onion with white rice, curry powder, salt, and raisin in a separate bowl.　　Divide this rice-raisins mixture into the apple cups.　　Pour water into the Crock Pot and place the stuffed cups in it.　　Top the apples with sour cream.　　Put the cooker's lid on and set the cooking time to hours on Low settings.　　Serve.
Nutrition Info: Per Serving: Calories 317, Total Fat 1.3g, Fiber 7g, Total Carbs 71.09g, Protein 4g

Baked Onions

Servings: 4　　Cooking Time: 2 Hours
Ingredients:
- 4 onions, peeled
- 1 tablespoon coconut oil
- 1 teaspoon salt
- 1 teaspoon brown sugar
- 1 cup coconut cream

Directions:
Put coconut oil in the Crock Pot.　　Then make the small cuts in the onions with the help of the knife and put in the Crock Pot in one layer.　　Sprinkle the vegetables with salt, and brown sugar.　　Add coconut cream and close the lid.　　Cook the onions on High for 2 hours.
Nutrition Info: Per Serving: 214 calories, 2.6g protein, 14.3g carbohydrates, 17.8g fat, 3.7g fiber, 0mg cholesterol, 595mg sodium, 320mg potassium.

Zucchini Spinach Lasagne

Servings: 7   Cooking Time: 5 Hrs

Ingredients:

1 lb. green zucchini, sliced	1 tbsp minced garlic
7 tbsp tomato sauce	1 onion, chopped
½ cup fresh parsley, chopped	4 tbsp ricotta cheese
1 tbsp fresh dill, chopped	5 oz. mozzarella, shredded
7 oz. Parmesan, shredded	2 eggs
	½ cup baby spinach
	1 tsp olive oil

Directions:

Grease the base of your Crock Pot with olive oil. Spread 3 zucchini slices at the bottom of the cooker.   Whisk tomato sauce with garlic, onion, dill, ricotta cheese, parsley, and spinach.   Stir in shredded parmesan, mozzarella, and eggs, then mix well.   Add a layer of this tomato-cheese mixture over the zucchini layer.   Again, place the zucchini slices over this tomato mixture layer.   Continue adding alternating layers of zucchini and tomato sauce   Put the cooker's lid on and set the cooking time to 5 hours on High settings.   Slice and serve warm.

Nutrition Info: Per Serving: Calories 233, Total Fat 6.4, Fiber 3g, Total Carbs 20.74g, Protein 23g

Wild Rice Peppers

Servings: 5   Cooking Time: 7.5 Hrs

Ingredients:

1 tomato, chopped	1 tsp turmeric
1 cup wild rice, cooked	1 tsp curry powder
4 oz. ground chicken	1 cup chicken stock
2 oz. mushroom, sliced	2 tsp tomato paste
½ onion, sliced	1 oz. black olives
1 tsp salt	5 red sweet pepper, cut the top off and seeds removed

Directions:

Toss rice with salt, turmeric, olives, tomato, onion, chicken, mushrooms, curry powder in a bowl. Pour tomato paste and chicken stock into the Crock Pot.   Stuff the sweet peppers with chicken mixture.   Place the stuffed peppers in the cooker. Put the cooker's lid on and set the cooking time to 7 hours 30 minutes on Low settings.   Serve warm with tomato gravy.

Nutrition Info: Per Serving: Calories 232, Total Fat 3.7g, Fiber 5g, Total Carbs 41.11g, Protein 12g

Vegetarian Keto Burgers

Servings: 4   Cooking Time: 4 Hours

Ingredients:

2 Portobello mushrooms, chopped	1 clove of garlic, minced
2 tablespoons basil, chopped	½ cup boiled cauliflower, mashed
1 egg, beaten	

Directions:

Line the bottom of the crockpot with foil.   In a food processor, combine all ingredients.   Make 4 burger patties using your hands and place gently in the crockpot.   Close the lid and cook on low for hours or on high for 3 hours.

Nutrition Info: Calories per serving: 134; Carbohydrates: 18g; Protein: 10g; Fat: 3.1g; Sugar:0.9g; Sodium:235mg; Fiber: 5g

Broccoli And Cheese Casserole

Servings: 4   Cooking Time: 4 Hours

Ingredients:

¾ cup almond flour	Salt and pepper to taste
1 head of broccoli, cut into florets	½ cup mozzarella cheese
2 large eggs, beaten	

Directions:

Place the almond flour and broccoli in the crockpot. Stir in the eggs and season with salt and pepper to taste.   Sprinkle with mozzarella cheese.   Close the lid and cook on low for hours or on high for 2 hours.

Nutrition Info: Calories per serving: 78; Carbohydrates: 4g; Protein: 8.2g; Fat:5.8 g; Sugar: 0g; Sodium: 231mg; Fiber:2.3 g

Vegan Pepper Bowl

Servings: 4   Cooking Time: 3.5 Hours

Ingredients:

2 cups bell pepper, sliced	4 tablespoons water
1 tablespoon olive oil	5 oz tofu, chopped
1 tablespoon apple cider vinegar	½ cup of coconut milk
	1 teaspoon curry powder

Directions:

Put the sliced bell peppers in the Crock Pot. Sprinkle them with olive oil, apple cider vinegar, and water.   Close the lid and cook the vegetables on low for hours.   Meanwhile, mix curry powder with coconut milk. Put the tofu in the curry mixture and leave for 15 minutes.   Add the tofu and all remaining curry mixture in the Crock Pot. Gently mix it and cook for 30 minutes on low.

Nutrition Info: Per Serving: 145 calories, 4.3g protein, 7.1g carbohydrates, 12.4g fat, 2g fiber, 0mg cholesterol, 11mg sodium, 254mg potassium.

Rice Stuffed Eggplants

Servings: 4   Cooking Time: 8 Hrs

Ingredients:

4 medium eggplants	1 tsp paprika
1 cup rice, half-cooked	½ cup fresh cilantro
½ cup chicken stock	3 tbsp tomato sauce
1 tsp salt	1 tsp olive oil

Directions:

Slice the eggplants in half and scoop 2/3 of the flesh from the center to make boats.   Mix rice with tomato sauce, paprika, salt, and cilantro in a bowl.   Now divide this rice mixture into the eggplant boats.   Pour stock and oil into the Crock Pot and place the eggplants in it.   Put the cooker's lid on and set the cooking time to 8 hours on Low settings.   Serve warm.

Nutrition Info: Per Serving: Calories 277, Total Fat 9.1g, Fiber 24g, Total Carbs 51.92g, Protein 11g

Pinto Beans With Rice

Servings: 6   Cooking Time: 3 Hrs

Ingredients:

1 lb. pinto beans, dried	½ tsp cumin, ground
1/3 cup hot sauce	1 tbsp chili powder
Salt and black pepper to the taste	3 bay leaves
	½ tsp oregano, dried
1 tbsp garlic, minced	1 cup white rice, cooked
1 tsp garlic powder	

Directions:

Add pinto beans along with the rest of the ingredients to your Crock Pot.   Put the cooker's lid on and set the cooking time to 3 hours on High settings.   Serve warm on top of rice.

Nutrition Info: Per Serving: Calories 381, Total Fat 7g, Fiber 12g, Total Carbs 35g, Protein 10g

Masala Eggplants

Servings: 2   Cooking Time: 2 Hours

Ingredients:

½ cup coconut cream	½ cup of water
1 teaspoon garam masala	2 eggplants, chopped
	1 teaspoon salt

Directions:

Sprinkle the eggplants with salt and leave for minutes.   Then drain eggplant juice and transfer the vegetables in the Crock Pot.   Add garam masala, water, and coconut cream.   Cook the meal on High for 2 hours.

Nutrition Info: Per Serving: 275 calories, 6.8g protein, 35.5g carbohydrates, 15.3g fat, 20.7g fiber, 0mg cholesterol, 1186mg sodium, 1414mg potassium.

Cashew And Tofu Casserole

Servings: 4   Cooking Time: 3.5 Hours

Ingredients:

1 oz cashews, crushed	¼ cup of soy sauce
6 oz firm tofu, chopped	¼ cup maple syrup
1 cup broccoli, chopped	1 tablespoon cornstarch
1 red onion, sliced	½ cup of water
1 tablespoon avocado oil	1 teaspoon garlic powder

Directions:

Pour the avocado oil in the Crock Pot.   Then sprinkle the broccoli with garlic powder and put it in the Crock Pot.   Add cornstarch.   After this, add maple syrup, soy sauce, onion, and tofu.   Add cashews and water.   Close the lid and cook the casserole on Low for 3.5 hours.

Nutrition Info: Per Serving: 164 calories, 6.7g protein, 24g carbohydrates, 5.7g fat, 2.1g fiber, 0mg cholesterol, 917mg sodium, 309mg potassium.

Creamy White Mushrooms

Servings: 4   Cooking Time: 8 Hours

Ingredients:

1-pound white mushrooms, chopped	1 teaspoon ground black pepper
1 cup cream	1 tablespoon dried parsley
1 teaspoon chili flakes	

Directions:

Put all ingredients in the Crock Pot.   Cook the mushrooms on low for 8 hours.   When the mushrooms are cooked, transfer them in the serving bowls and cool for 10-15 minutes.

Nutrition Info: Per Serving: 65 calories, 4.1g protein, 6g carbohydrates, 3.7g fat, 1.3g fiber, 11mg cholesterol, 27mg sodium, 396mg potassium.

Tofu And Cauliflower Bowl

Servings: 3   Cooking Time: 2.15 Hours

Ingredients:

5 oz firm tofu, chopped	¼ cup of coconut milk
1 teaspoon curry paste	1 tablespoon sunflower oil
1 teaspoon dried basil	2 cups cauliflower, chopped
	1 cup of water

Directions:

Put cauliflower in the Crock Pot.   Add water and cook it on High for hours.   Meanwhile, mix curry paste with coconut milk, dried basil, and sunflower oil.   Then add tofu and carefully mix the mixture.   Leave it for 30 minutes.   When the cauliflower is cooked, drain water.   Add tofu mixture and shake the meal well. Cook it on High for 15 minutes.

Nutrition Info: Per Serving: 148 calories, 5.7g protein, 5.9g carbohydrates, 12.5g fat, 2.5g fiber, 0mg cholesterol, 31mg sodium, 326mg potassium.

Mung Beans Salad

Servings: 4   Cooking Time: 3 Hours

Ingredients:

½ avocado, chopped
1 cup cherry tomatoes, halved
½ cup corn kernels, cooked
1 cup mung beans

3 cups of water
1 tablespoon lemon juice
1 tablespoon avocado oil

Directions:
Put mung beans in the Crock Pot.   Add water and cook them on High for 3 hours.   Then drain water and transfer the mung beans in the salad bowl.   Add avocado, cherry tomatoes, corn kernels, and shake well.   Then sprinkle the salad with avocado oil and lemon juice.

Nutrition Info: Per Serving: 287 calories, 13.9g protein, 40g carbohydrates, 9.4g fat, 11.2g fiber, 0mg cholesterol, 20mg sodium, 932mg potassium.

Lazy Minestrone Soup

Servings: 4   Cooking Time: 3 Hours

Ingredients:

1 cup zucchini, sliced
1 package diced vegetables of your choice

2 cups chicken broth
2 tablespoons basil, chopped
½ cup diced celery

Directions:
Place all ingredients in the crockpot.   Season with salt and pepper to taste.   Close the lid and cook on low for hours or on high for 1 hour.

Nutrition Info: Calories per serving: 259; Carbohydrates: 13.5g; Protein:30.3 g; Fat: 8.3g; Sugar: 0.4g; Sodium: 643mg; Fiber: 4.2g

Garlic Butter

Servings: 8   Cooking Time: 20 Minutes

Ingredients:

1 cup vegan butter
1 tablespoon garlic powder

¼ cup fresh dill, chopped

Directions:
Put all ingredients in the Crock Pot and cook on High for 20 minutes.   Then pour the liquid in the ice cubes molds and refrigerate for 30 minutes or until butter is solid.

Nutrition Info: Per Serving: 211 calories, 0.7g protein, 1.6g carbohydrates, 23.1g fat, 0.3g fiber, 61mg cholesterol, 167mg sodium, 68mg potassium.

Sugar Yams

Servings: 4   Cooking Time: 2 Hours

Ingredients:

4 yams, peeled
1 cup of water
1 tablespoon sugar

2 tablespoons vegan butter

Directions:
Cut the yams into halves and put them in the Crock Pot.   Add water and cook for hours on high. Then melt the butter in the skillet.   Add sugar and heat it until sugar is melted.   Then drain water from the yams.   Put the yams in the sugar butter and roast for 2 minutes per side.

Nutrition Info: Per Serving: 63 calories, 0.1g protein, 3.3g carbohydrates, 5.8g fat, 0g fiber, 15mg cholesterol, 43mg sodium, 9mg potassium.

Teriyaki Kale

Servings: 6   Cooking Time: 30 Minutes

Ingredients:

5 cups kale, roughly chopped
1/2 cup teriyaki sauce
1 teaspoon sesame seeds

1 cup of water
1 teaspoon garlic powder
2 tablespoons coconut oil

Directions:
Melt the coconut oil and mix it with garlic powder, water, sesame seeds, and teriyaki sauce.   Pour the liquid in the Crock Pot.   Add kale and close the lid.   Cook the kale on High for 30 minutes. Serve the kale with a small amount of teriyaki liquid.

Nutrition Info: Per Serving: 92 calories, 3.3g protein, 10g carbohydrates, 4.8g fat, 1g fiber, 0mg cholesterol, 945mg sodium, 336mg potassium.

Potato Salad

Servings: 2   Cooking Time: 3 Hours

Ingredients:

1 cup potato, chopped
1 cup of water
1 teaspoon salt
2 oz celery stalk, chopped

2 oz fresh parsley, chopped
¼ onion, diced
1 tablespoon mayonnaise

Directions:
Put the potatoes in the Crock Pot.   Add water and salt.   Cook the potatoes on High for hours. Then drain water and transfer the potatoes in the salad bowl.   Add all remaining ingredients and carefully mix the salad.

Nutrition Info: Per Serving: 129 calories, 5.5g protein, 12.4g carbohydrates, 6.7g fat, 2.5g fiber, 12mg cholesterol, 1479mg sodium, 465mg potassium.

Creamy Puree

Servings: 4   Cooking Time: 4 Hours

Ingredients:

2 cups potatoes, chopped
1 tablespoon vegan butter

3 cups of water
¼ cup cream
1 teaspoon salt

Directions:
Pour water in the Crock Pot.   Add potatoes and salt.   Cook the vegetables on high for 4 hours. Then drain water, add butter, and cream.   Mash the potatoes until smooth.

Nutrition Info: Per Serving: 87 calories, 1.4g protein, 12.3g carbohydrates, 3.8g fat, 1.8g fiber, 10mg cholesterol, 617mg sodium, 314mg potassium

Parsnip Balls

Servings: 4   Cooking Time: 3 Hours

Ingredients:

8 oz parsnip, peeled, grated
1 tablespoon coconut cream
1 tablespoon coconut oil
1/3 cup coconut flour
1 carrot, boiled, peeled, mashed
1 teaspoon salt
1 teaspoon chili powder

Directions:

In the mixing bowl mix grated parsnip, coconut cream, coconut flour, mashed carrot, salt, and chili powder.   With the help of the scooper make the small balls and freeze them for 10-15 minutes. Then put coconut oil in the Crock Pot.   Add frozen parsnip balls and cook them on Low for 3 hours.

Nutrition Info: Per Serving: 129 calories, 2.3g protein, 18.9g carbohydrates, 5.6g fat, 7.5g fiber, 0mg cholesterol, 605mg sodium, 284mg potassium.

Corn Pudding

Servings: 4   Cooking Time: 5 Hours

Ingredients:

3 cups corn kernels
3 tablespoons muffin mix
2 cups heavy cream
1 oz Parmesan, grated

Directions:

Mix heavy cream with muffin mix and pour the liquid in the Crock Pot.   Add corn kernels and Parmesan. Stir the mixture well.   Close the lid and cook the pudding on Low for 5 hours.

Nutrition Info: Per Serving: 371 calories, 21.8g protein, 31.4g carbohydrates, 26.3g fat, 3.2g fiber, 87mg cholesterol, 180mg sodium, 378mg potassium.

Rainbow Bake

Servings: 4   Cooking Time: 6 Hours

Ingredients:

1 zucchini, sliced
1 tomato, sliced
1 eggplant, sliced
1 red onion, sliced
1 tablespoon coconut oil
1 teaspoon salt
1 teaspoon dried parsley
1 teaspoon chili powder
1 cup of water

Directions:

Carefully grease the Crock Pot bowl with coconut oil.   Then put zucchini, tomato, eggplant, and onion in the Crock Pot one-by-one.   Sprinkle the vegetables with salt, dried parsley, and chili powder.   Add water and close the lid.   Cook the meal on Low for 6 hours.

Nutrition Info: Per Serving: 82 calories, 2.2g protein, 11.9g carbohydrates, 3.9g fat, 5.6g fiber, 0mg cholesterol, 597mg sodium, 482mg potassium.

Marjoram Carrot Soup

Servings: 9   Cooking Time: 12 Hrs

Ingredients:

1 lb. carrot
1 tsp ground cardamom
¼ tsp nutmeg
1 tsp salt
3 tbsp fresh parsley
1 tsp honey
1 tsp marjoram
5 cups chicken stock
½ cup yellow onion, chopped
1 tsp butter

Directions:

Add butter and all the veggies to a suitable pan. Sauté these vegetables on low heat for 5 minutes then transfer to the Crock Pot.   Stir in cardamom, salt, chicken stock, marjoram, and nutmeg.   Put the cooker's lid on and set the cooking time to 12 hours on Low settings.   Puree the cooked veggie mixture using an immersion blender until smooth.   Garnish with honey and parsley.   Devour.

Nutrition Info: Per Serving: Calories 80, Total Fat 2.7g, Fiber 2g, Total Carbs 10.19g, Protein 4g

Cheddar Mushrooms

Servings: 4   Cooking Time: 6 Hours

Ingredients:

4 cups cremini mushrooms, sliced
1 teaspoon dried oregano
1 teaspoon ground black pepper
½ teaspoon salt
1 cup Cheddar cheese, shredded
1 cup heavy cream
1 cup of water

Directions:

Pour water and heavy cream in the Crock Pot. Add salt, ground black pepper, and dried oregano. Then add sliced mushrooms, and Cheddar cheese. Cook the meal on Low for 6 hours.   When the mushrooms are cooked, gently stir them and transfer in the serving plates.

Nutrition Info: Per Serving: 239 calories, 9.6g protein, 4.8g carbohydrates, 20.6g fat, 0.7g fiber, 71mg cholesterol, 484mg sodium, 386mg potassium.

Sweet Onions

Servings: 4   Cooking Time: 4 Hours

Ingredients:

2 cups white onion, sliced
½ cup vegan butter
1 teaspoon ground black pepper
¼ cup of water
1 tablespoon maple syrup
1 teaspoon lemon juice

Directions:

Put all ingredients in the Crock Pot.   Close the lid and cook the onions on low for 4 hours.

Nutrition Info: Per Serving: 241 calories, 0.9g protein, 9.1g carbohydrates, 23.1g fat, 1.4g fiber, 61mg cholesterol, 167mg sodium, 109mg potassium.

Light Chana Masala

Servings: 4   Cooking Time: 8 Hours
Ingredients:

1 teaspoon ginger, peeled, minced
1 teaspoon minced garlic
¼ cup fresh cilantro, chopped
1 jalapeno, chopped
1 cup tomatoes, pureed
1 cup chickpeas
4 cups of water

Directions:
Put all ingredients in the Crock Pot and close the lid.   Cook the meal on Low for 8 hours.
Nutrition Info: Per Serving: 194 calories, 10.2g protein, 32.9g carbohydrates, 3.2g fat, 9.4g fiber, 0mg cholesterol, 22mg sodium, 568mg potassium.

Crockpot Mediterranean Eggplant Salad

Servings: 2   Cooking Time: 4 Hours
Ingredients:

1 red onion, sliced
2 bell peppers, sliced
3 extra virgin olive oil
1 eggplant, quartered
1 cup tomatoes, crushed
1 tablespoon smoked paprika
2 teaspoons cumin
Juice from 1 lemon, freshly squeezed
Salt and pepper to taste

Directions:
Place all ingredients in the CrockPot.   Give a good stir.   Close the lid and cook on high for hours or on low for 4 hours.
Nutrition Info: Calories per serving: 312; Carbohydrates: 30.2g; Protein: 5.6g; Fat: 22g; Sugar: 0.4g; Sodium: 519mg; Fiber: 27.1g

Herbed Mushrooms

Servings: 4   Cooking Time: 4.5 Hours
Ingredients:

1-pound cremini mushrooms
1 teaspoon cumin seeds
1 teaspoon coriander seeds
2 cups of water
1 teaspoon fennel seeds
3 tablespoons sesame oil
1 teaspoon salt
3 tablespoons lime juice

Directions:
Pour water in the Crock Pot. Add mushrooms. Close the lid and cook them on High for 4.5 hours. Then drain water and transfer mushrooms in the big bowl.   Sprinkle them with cumin seeds, coriander seeds, fennel seeds, sesame oil, salt, and lime juice.   Carefully mix the mushrooms and leave them to marinate for 30 minutes.
Nutrition Info: Per Serving: 125 calories, 3g protein, 5.4g carbohydrates, 10.5g fat, 1g fiber, 0mg cholesterol, 594mg sodium, 531mg potassium.

Garam Masala Potato Bake

Servings: 2   Cooking Time: 6 Hours
Ingredients:

1 cup potatoes, chopped
1 teaspoon garam
3 eggs, beaten
1 tablespoon vegan butter
masala
½ cup vegan mozzarella, shredded
2 tablespoons coconut cream

Directions:
Mix potatoes with garam masala.   Then put them in the Crock Pot.   Add vegan butter and mozzarella.   After this, mix coconut cream with eggs and pour the liquid over the mozzarella. Close the lid and cook the meal on Low for 6 hours.
Nutrition Info: Per Serving: 199 calories, 12.1g protein, 16.8g carbohydrates, 9.4g fat, 1.9g fiber, 252mg cholesterol, 156mg sodium, 398mg potassium.

Apples Sauté

Servings: 4   Cooking Time: 2 Hours
Ingredients:

4 cups apples, chopped
1 cup of water
1 teaspoon ground cinnamon
1 teaspoon sugar

Directions:
Put all ingredients in the Crock Pot.   Cook the apple sauté for hours on High.   When the meal is cooked, let it cool until warm.
Nutrition Info: Per Serving: 121 calories, 0.6g protein, 32.3g carbohydrates, 0.4g fat, 5.7g fiber, 0mg cholesterol, 4mg sodium, 242mg potassium.

Braised Root Vegetables

Servings: 4   Cooking Time: 8 Hours
Ingredients:

1 cup beets, chopped
1 cup carrot, chopped
2 cups vegetable stock
1 teaspoon raisins
1 teaspoon salt
1 teaspoon onion powder

Directions:
Put all ingredients in the Crock Pot.   Close the lid and cook them on Low for 8 hours.
Nutrition Info: Per Serving: 39 calories, 1g protein, 9g carbohydrates, 1.1g fat, 1.6g fiber, 0mg cholesterol, 993mg sodium, 229mg potassium.

Couscous Halloumi Salad

Servings: 5   Cooking Time: 4 Hrs
Ingredients:

1 cup couscous
1 green sweet pepper, chopped
2 garlic cloves
1 cup beef broth
1 tsp chives
½ cup cherry tomatoes halved
1 zucchini, diced
7 oz. halloumi cheese, chop
1 tsp olive oil
1 tsp paprika
¼ tsp ground cardamom
1 tsp salt

Directions:
Add couscous, cardamom, salt, and paprika to the Crock Pot.   Stir in garlic, zucchini, and beef broth to the couscous.   Put the cooker's lid on and set the cooking time to 4 hours on High settings. Stir in the remaining ingredients and toss it gently. Serve.
Nutrition Info: Per Serving: Calories 170, Total Fat 9.6g, Fiber 1g, Total Carbs 12.59g, Protein 9g

Shredded Cabbage Saute

Servings: 4   Cooking Time: 6 Hours
Ingredients:

3 cups white cabbage, shredded	1 teaspoon dried oregano
1 cup tomato juice	3 tablespoons olive oil
1 teaspoon salt	1 cup of water
1 teaspoon sugar	

Directions:
Put all ingredients in the Crock Pot.   Carefully mix all ingredients with the help of the spoon and close the lid.   Cook the cabbage saute for 6 hours on Low.
Nutrition Info: Per Serving: 118 calories, 1.2g protein, 6.9g carbohydrates, 10.6g fat, 1.7g fiber, 0mg cholesterol, 756mg sodium, 235mg potassium

Eggplant Parmesan Casserole

Servings: 3   Cooking Time: 3 Hours
Ingredients:

1 medium eggplant, sliced	1 large egg
Salt and pepper to taste	1 cup almond flour
	1 cup parmesan cheese

Directions:
Place the eggplant slices in the crockpot.   Pour in the eggs and season with salt and pepper.   Stir in the almond flour and sprinkle with parmesan cheese.   Stir to combine everything.   Close the lid and cook on low for 3 hours or on high for 2 hours.
Nutrition Info: Calories per serving: 212; Carbohydrates: 17g; Protein: 15g; Fat:12.1 g; Sugar: 1.2g; Sodium: 231mg; Fiber:8.1 g

Spicy Okra

Servings: 2   Cooking Time: 1.5 Hours
Ingredients:

2 cups okra, sliced	1 teaspoon chili flakes
½ cup vegetable stock	1 teaspoon dried oregano
1 teaspoon chili powder	1 tablespoon butter
½ teaspoon ground turmeric	

Directions:
Put okra in the Crock Pot.   Add vegetable stock, chili powder, ground turmeric, chili flakes, and dried oregano.   Cook the okra on High for 1.5 hours.   Then add butter and stir the cooked okra well.
Nutrition Info: Per Serving: 102 calories, 2.5g protein, 9.2g carbohydrates, 6.4g fat, 4.1g fiber, 15mg cholesterol, 252mg sodium, 358mg potassium.

Cardamom Pumpkin Wedges

Servings: 4   Cooking Time: 6 Hours
Ingredients:

2-pound pumpkin, peeled	2 tablespoons lemon juice
1 teaspoon ground cardamom	1 teaspoon lemon zest, grated
2 tablespoons sugar	1 cup of water

Directions:
Cut the pumpkin into wedges and place them in the Crock Pot.   Add water.   Then sprinkle the pumpkin with ground cardamom, lemon juice, lemon zest, and sugar.   Close the lid and cook the pumpkin on Low for 6 hours.   Serve the pumpkin wedges with sweet liquid from the Crock Pot.
Nutrition Info: Per Serving: 103 calories, 2.6g protein, 25g carbohydrates, 0.7g fat, 6.8g fiber, 0mg cholesterol, 15mg sodium, 484mg potassium.

Potato Balls

Servings: 6   Cooking Time: 1.5 Hours
Ingredients:

2 cups mashed potato	1 teaspoon dried dill
1 tablespoon coconut cream	2 oz scallions, diced
3 tablespoons breadcrumbs	1 egg, beaten
	2 tablespoons flour
	½ cup of coconut milk

Directions:
In the mixing bowl mix mashed potato with coconut cream, breadcrumbs, dried dill, scallions, egg, and flour.   Make the potato balls and put them in the Crock Pot.   Add coconut milk and cook the meal on High for 1.5 hours.
Nutrition Info: Per Serving: 132 calories, 3.4g protein, 17.5g carbohydrates, 5.5g fat, 1.6g fiber, 28mg cholesterol, 273mg sodium, 287mg potassium.

Cream Zucchini Pasta

Servings: 2   Cooking Time: 2 Hours
Ingredients:

2 large zucchinis, trimmed	1 cup coconut cream
1 teaspoon white pepper	2 oz vegan Parmesan, grated

Directions:
Make the strips from zucchini with the help of a spiralizer and put in the Crock Pot.   Add white pepper and coconut cream.   Then top the zucchini with grated vegan Parmesan and close the lid.   Cook the meal on low for 2 hours.
Nutrition Info: Per Serving: 223 calories, 14.1g protein, 16.3g carbohydrates, 13.4g fat, 3.8g fiber, 43mg cholesterol, 335mg sodium, 904mg potassium.

Corn Fritters

Servings: 4   Cooking Time: 3 Hours
Ingredients:

1 cup mashed potato	1 teaspoon ground turmeric
1/3 cup corn kernels, cooked	½ teaspoon chili powder
1 egg, beaten	2 tablespoons coconut oil
2 tablespoons flour	
1 teaspoon salt	

Directions:
Put the coconut oil in the Crock Pot and melt it on low for minutes.   Meanwhile, mix mashed potato with corn kernels, egg, flour, salt, ground turmeric, and chili powder.   Make the medium size fritters and put them in the Crock Pot.   Cook them on Low for 3 hours.
Nutrition Info: Per Serving: 162 calories, 3.3g protein, 14.9g carbohydrates, 10.4g fat, 1.5g fiber, 41mg cholesterol, 777mg sodium, 246mg potassium.

Carrot And Lentils Sauté

Servings: 4   Cooking Time: 5 Hours

Ingredients:

1 cup red lentils	1 teaspoon cayenne
1 cup carrot, diced	pepper
1 cup fresh parsley,	1 teaspoon salt
chopped	1 tablespoon tomato
4 cups vegetable	paste
stock	

Directions:
Put all ingredients in the Crock Pot and gently stir. Close the lid and cook the meal on low for 5 hours.
Nutrition Info: Per Serving: 201 calories, 13.3g protein, 35.5g carbohydrates, 2.7g fat, 16.1g fiber, 0mg cholesterol, 1336mg sodium, 679mg potassium.

Tender Stuffing

Servings: 4   Cooking Time: 4 Hours

Ingredients:

8 oz celery stalks,	2 tablespoons
chopped	coconut oil
¼ cup breadcrumbs	½ cup tomatoes,
1 white onion, diced	chopped
1 teaspoon dried sage	1 cup of coconut milk

Directions:
Put all ingredients in the Crock Pot and gently mix. Then close the lid and cook the stuffing on Low for 4 hours.
Nutrition Info: Per Serving: 248 calories, 3.2g protein, 13.4g carbohydrates, 21.7g fat, 3.5g fiber, 0mg cholesterol, 106mg sodium, 414mg potassium.

Tofu Curry

Servings: 4   Cooking Time: 3 Hours

Ingredients:

1 cup chickpeas,	½ cup of coconut
cooked	milk
8 oz firm tofu,	1 teaspoon ground
chopped	coriander
1 teaspoon curry	1 cup vegetable stock
powder	1 red onion, diced

Directions:
In the mixing bowl mix curry powder, coconut milk, ground coriander, and red onion.   Mix the curry mixture with tofu.   Then pour the vegetable stock in the Crock Pot.   Add chickpeas, tofu, and all remaining curry mixture.   Close the lid and cook the meal on Low for 3 hours. Don't stir the cooked meal.
Nutrition Info: Per Serving: 306 calories, 15.3g protein, 36.3g carbohydrates, 13.1g fat, 10.6g fiber, 0mg cholesterol, 205mg sodium, 649mg potassium.

Beans Bake

Servings: 4   Cooking Time: 5 Hours

Ingredients:

1-pound green beans	1 teaspoon salt
1 tablespoon olive oil	2 tablespoons
½ teaspoon ground	breadcrumbs
black pepper	4 eggs, beaten

Directions:
Chop the green beans roughly and sprinkle them with salt and ground black pepper.   Then put them in the Crock Pot.   Sprinkle the vegetables with breadcrumbs and eggs.   Close the lid and cook the beans bake on Low for 5 hours.
Nutrition Info: Per Serving: 142 calories, 8.1g protein, 11g carbohydrates, 8.2g fat, 4.1g fiber, 164mg cholesterol, 675mg sodium, 306mg potassium.

Swedish Style Beets

Servings: 4   Cooking Time: 8 Hours

Ingredients:

¼ cup apple cider	1-pound beets
vinegar	1 teaspoon salt
1 tablespoon olive oil	½ teaspoon sugar
	3 cups of water

Directions:
Put beets in the Crock Pot.   Add water and cook the vegetables for 8 hours on Low.   Then drain water and peel the beets.   Chop the beets roughly and put in the big bowl.   Add all remaining ingredients and leave the beets for 2-3 hours to marinate.
Nutrition Info: Per Serving: 85 calories, 1.9g protein, 11.9g carbohydrates, 3.7g fat, 2.3g fiber, 0mg cholesterol, 675mg sodium, 359mg potassium.

Chili Dip

Servings: 5   Cooking Time: 5 Hours

Ingredients:

5 oz chilies, canned,	1 tomato, chopped
chopped	½ cup milk
3 oz Mozzarella,	1 teaspoon cornflour
shredded	

Directions:
Mix milk with cornflour and whisk until smooth. Pour the liquid in the Crock Pot.   Then add chilies, Mozzarella, and tomato.   Close the lid and cook the dip on low for 5 hours.
Nutrition Info: Per Serving: 156 calories, 8.7g protein, 22.5g carbohydrates, 5.2g fat, 8.3g fiber, 11mg cholesterol, 140mg sodium, 575mg potassium.

Thyme Fennel Bulb

Servings: 4   Cooking Time: 3 Hours
Ingredients:
  16 oz fennel bulb
  1 tablespoon thyme
  1 cup of water
  1 teaspoon salt
  1 teaspoon peppercorns
Directions:
Chop the fennel bulb roughly and put it in the Crock Pot.   Add thyme, water, salt, and peppercorns.   Cook the fennel on High for hours. Then drain water, remove peppercorns, and transfer the fennel in the serving plates.
Nutrition Info: Per Serving: 38 calories, 1.5g protein, 9g carbohydrates, 0.3g fat, 3.9g fiber, 0mg cholesterol, 643mg sodium, 482mg potassium.

Marinated Poached Aubergines

Servings: 6   Cooking Time: 4 Hours
Ingredients:
  ½ cup apple cider vinegar
  1-pound eggplants, chopped
  1 cup of water
  ¼ cup avocado oil
  3 garlic cloves, diced
  1 teaspoon salt
  1 teaspoon sugar
Directions:
Put all ingredients in the Crock Pot.   Cook the meal on Low for 4 hours.   Cool the cooked aubergines well.
Nutrition Info: Per Serving: 40 calories, 1g protein, 6.3g carbohydrates, 1.3g fat, 3.1g fiber, 0mg cholesterol, 392mg sodium, 224mg potassium.

Crockpot Eggplant Lasagna

Servings: 4   Cooking Time: 4 Hours
Ingredients:
  1 cup beefsteak tomatoes
  ½ cup basil leaves
  ½ teaspoon thyme leaves
  1 onion, diced
  1 red bell pepper diced
  Salt and pepper to taste
  1 cup chopped walnuts
  2 large eggs, beaten
  1 cup heavy cream
  2 tablespoons olive oil
  1 eggplant, sliced using a mandolin
  1 cup mozzarella cheese
Directions:
In a blender or food processor, combine the tomatoes, basil leaves, thyme leaves, onion, and red bell pepper. Season with salt and pepper then pulse until smooth.   Place in a bowl and add the chopped walnuts.   In another bowl, combine the eggs and heavy cream. Set aside.   Grease the bottom of the CrockPot with olive oil.   Arrange the eggplant slices first and pour in a generous amount of the tomato sauce mixture.   Pour the egg mixture and cheese on top.   Repeat the layering until all ingredients are used up.   Close the lid and cook on high for 3 hours or on low for 4 hours.
Nutrition Info: Calories per serving: 373; Carbohydrates: 19g; Protein: 23g; Fat: 14g; Sugar: 1.2g; Sodium: 963mg; Fiber: 13.8g!Follow

White Beans Luncheon

Servings: 10   Cooking Time: 4 Hrs
Ingredients:
  2 lbs. white beans
  3 celery stalks, chopped
  2 carrots, chopped
  1 bay leaf
  1 yellow onion, chopped
  3 garlic cloves, minced
  1 tsp rosemary, dried
  1 tsp oregano, dried
  1 tsp thyme, dried
  10 cups water
  Salt and black pepper to the taste
  28 oz. canned tomatoes, chopped
  6 cups chard, chopped
Directions:
Add beans, carrots, and all other ingredients to a Crock Pot.   Put the cooker's lid on and set the cooking time to 4 hours on High settings.   Serve warm.
Nutrition Info: Per Serving: Calories 341, Total Fat 8, Fiber 12, Total Carbs 20, Protein 6

Quinoa Avocado Salad(2)

Servings: 6   Cooking Time: 7 Hrs
Ingredients:
  ½ lemon, juiced
  1 avocado, pitted, peeled and diced
  1 red onion, diced
  1 cup white quinoa
  1 cup of water
  1 tsp canola oil
  ½ cup fresh dill
  1 cup green peas, frozen
  1 tsp garlic powder
Directions:
Add quinoa, green peas and water to the Crock Pot. Put the cooker's lid on and set the cooking time to 7 hours on Low settings.   Transfer the cooked quinoa and peas to a salad bowl.   Stir in the remaining ingredients for the salad and toss well. Serve fresh.
Nutrition Info: Per Serving: Calories 195, Total Fat 7.7g, Fiber 6g, Total Carbs 26.77g, Protein 6g

Chorizo Cashew Salad

Servings: 6   Cooking Time: 4 Hours 30 Minutes
Ingredients:
  8 oz. chorizo, chopped
  1 tsp olive oil
  1 tsp cayenne pepper
  1 tsp chili flakes
  1 tsp ground black pepper
  1 tsp onion powder
  2 garlic cloves
  3 tomatoes, chopped
  1 cup lettuce, torn
  1 cup fresh dill
  1 tsp oregano
  3 tbsp crushed cashews
Directions:
Add chorizo sausage to the Crock Pot.   Put the cooker's lid on and set the cooking time to 4 hours on High settings.   Mix chili flakes, cayenne pepper, black pepper, and onion powder in a bowl. Now add tomatoes to the Crock Pot and cover again.   Crock Pot for another 30 minutes on High setting.   Stir in oregano and dill then mix well. Add sliced garlic and torn lettuce to the mixture. Garnish with cashews.   Serve.
Nutrition Info: Per Serving: Calories 249, Total Fat 19.8g, Fiber 2g, Total Carbs 7.69g, Protein 11g

Sesame Asparagus

Servings: 4   Cooking Time: 3 Hours

Ingredients:

1-pound asparagus
½ cup of soy sauce
1 teaspoon sesame seeds
½ cup vegetable stock
1 tablespoon vegan butter

Directions:

Trim the asparagus and put it in the Crock Pot. Add soy sauce and vegetable stock.   Then add sesame seeds and butter.   Close the lid and cook the meal on High for 3 hours.

Nutrition Info: Per Serving: 71 calories, 4.7g protein, 7.1g carbohydrates, 3.5g fat, 2.7g fiber, 8mg cholesterol, 1915mg sodium, 304mg potassium.

Fragrant Jackfruit

Servings: 4   Cooking Time: 2 Hours

Ingredients:

1-pound jackfruit, canned, chopped
1 teaspoon tomato paste
1 onion, diced
1 teaspoon taco seasoning
½ cup coconut cream
1 teaspoon chili powder

Directions:

In the mixing bowl mix taco seasoning, chili powder, tomato paste, and coconut cream.   Put the jackfruit and diced onion in the Crock Pot. Pour the tomato mixture over the vegetables and gently mix them.   Close the lid and cook the meal on High for 2 hours.

Nutrition Info: Per Serving: 145 calories, 2.4g protein, 32.4g carbohydrates, 2.2g fat, 2.7g fiber, 6mg cholesterol, 127mg sodium, 421mg potassium.

Tarragon Pumpkin Bowl

Servings: 2   Cooking Time: 4 Hours

Ingredients:

2 cups pumpkin, chopped
1 teaspoon dried tarragon
1 tablespoon coconut oil
1 cup of water
1 teaspoon salt

Directions:

Put all ingredients in the Crock Pot. Gently mix them.   Close the lid and cook pumpkin on High for 4 hours.

Nutrition Info: Per Serving: 143 calories, 2.8g protein, 20g carbohydrates, 7.5g fat, 7.1g fiber, 0mg cholesterol, 1179mg sodium, 515mg potassium.

Zucchini Latkes

Servings: 4   Cooking Time: 40 Minutes

Ingredients:

2 large zucchinis, grated
1 onion, minced
1 egg, beaten
1 teaspoon ground black pepper
2 tablespoons flour
1 oz vegan parmesan, grated
1 tablespoon olive oil
½ cup of water

Directions:

In the mixing bowl mix grated zucchini, minced onion, egg, flour, ground black pepper, and vegan parmesan.   After this, heat the olive oil in the skillet well.   Make the small latkes from the zucchini mixture and transfer in the hot oil. Roast the zucchini latkes for 2 minutes per side on high heat.   Then transfer the latkes in the Crock Pot.   Add water and close the lid.   Cook the meal on High for 40 minutes.

Nutrition Info: Per Serving: 121 calories, 6.4g protein, 11.6g carbohydrates, 6.5g fat, 2.6g fiber, 46mg cholesterol, 100mg sodium, 489mg potassium.

Braised Sesame Spinach

Servings: 4   Cooking Time: 35 Minutes

Ingredients:

1 tablespoon sesame seeds
2 tablespoons sesame oil
¼ cup of soy sauce
4 cups spinach, chopped
1 cup of water

Directions:

Pour water in the Crock Pot.   Add spinach and cook it on High for 35 minutes.   After this, drain water and transfer the spinach in the big bowl. Add soy sauce, sesame oil, and sesame seeds. Carefully mix the spinach and transfer in the serving plates/bowls.

Nutrition Info: Per Serving: 88 calories, 2.3g protein, 2.8g carbohydrates, 8.1g fat, 1.1g fiber, 2.8mg cholesterol, 924mg sodium, 213mg potassium.

Hot Tofu

Servings: 4   Cooking Time: 4 Hours

Ingredients:

1-pound firm tofu, cubed
½ cup vegetable stock
1 tablespoon hot sauce
1 teaspoon miso paste

Directions:

Mix vegetables tock with miso paste and pour in the Crock Pot.   Add hot sauce and tofu.   Close the lid and cook the meal on Low for 4 hours. Then transfer the tofu and liquid in the serving bowls.

Nutrition Info: Per Serving: 83 calories, 9.5g protein, 2.5g carbohydrates, 4.8g fat, 1.2g fiber, 0mg cholesterol, 168mg sodium, 176mg potassium.

Cauliflower Rice

Servings: 6   Cooking Time: 2 Hours

Ingredients:

4 cups cauliflower, shredded
1 cup vegetable stock
1 cup of water
1 tablespoon cream cheese
1 teaspoon dried oregano

Directions:

Put all ingredients in the Crock Pot.   Close the lid and cook the cauliflower rice on High for hours.

Nutrition Info: Per Serving: 25 calories, 0.8g protein, 3.9g carbohydrates, 0.8g fat, 1.8g fiber, 2mg cholesterol, 153mg sodium, 211mg potassium

Dessert Recipes

Banana Almond Foster

Servings: 4   Cooking Time: 4 Hrs.
Ingredients:

1 lb. banana, peeled and chopped	1 tsp ground cinnamon
3 oz butter	3 tbsp coconut flakes
1 cup white sugar	½ tsp vanilla extract
2 tsp rum	4 tbsp almond, crushed

Directions:
Add bananas, white sugar, rum, coconut flakes, ground cinnamon, crushed almonds, and vanilla extract to the insert of Crock Pot.   Put the cooker's lid on and set the cooking time to 4 hours on Low settings.   Serve with whipped cream.
Nutrition Info: Per Serving: Calories: 689, Total Fat: 30.7g, Fiber: 13g, Total Carbs: 109.32g, Protein: 6g

Pear And Apple Butter

Servings: 6   Cooking Time: 6 1/2 Hours
Ingredients:

6 large red apples, peeled, cored and sliced	1 cup white sugar
	1 cup light brown sugar
4 ripe pears, peeled, cored and sliced	1 cinnamon stick
1 1/2 cups fresh apple juice	4 cardamom pods, crushed

Directions:
Combine all the ingredients in your Crock Pot. Cover the pot and cook on low settings for 6 hours. When done, pour the mixture into glass jars and seal them with a lid.   Allow to cool before serving.

Sweet Potato Chocolate Cake

Servings: 8   Cooking Time: 4 1/4 Hours
Ingredients:

1 cup all-purpose flour	1/2 teaspoon salt
1/2 cup cocoa powder	2 eggs
1 teaspoon baking soda	1 cup buttermilk
1 teaspoon cinnamon powder	1/2 cup canola oil
	1cup sweet potato puree

Directions:
Mix the dry ingredients in a bowl then add the wet ingredients and mix with a whisk just until combined.   Pour the batter in your greased Crock Pot and bake for 4 hours on low settings.   Allow the cake to cool in the pot before slicing and serving.

Cracked Chocolate Cookies

Servings: 3   Cooking Time: 2 Hours
Ingredients:

¼ cup of cocoa powder	½ teaspoon baking powder
4 tablespoons flour	3 tablespoons of sugar powder
1 tablespoon sugar	
2 tablespoons butter	

Directions:
Mix cocoa powder with flour and sugar.   Add baking powder and butter. Knead the soft dough. Make the medium-size balls from the dough and coat them in the sugar powder.   Put the coated cocoa balls in the Crock Pot and close the lid. Cook the cookies on high for 2 hours.
Nutrition Info: Per Serving: 169 calories, 2.5g protein, 24.3g carbohydrates, 8.7g fat, 2.4g fiber, 20mg cholesterol, 57mg sodium, 277mg potassium.

Spiced Applesauce Cake

Servings: 10   Cooking Time: 4 1/2 Hours
Ingredients:

2 cups all-purpose flour	1/4 teaspoon ground whole cloves
1 teaspoon baking soda	1/2 cup butter, softened
1/2 teaspoon baking powder	1/2 cup white sugar
1 teaspoon cinnamon powder	1/4 cup light brown sugar
1/2 teaspoon ground ginger	2 eggs
	1 cup applesauce

Directions:
Mix the dry ingredients in a bowl.   Mix the butter, sugar and eggs in a bowl until creamy. Fold in the dry ingredients, alternating them with the applesauce.   Mix just until combined then transfer the batter in your Crock Pot.   Cover the pot and bake on low settings for 4 hours.   Allow the cake to cool in the pot before slicing and serving.

Orange Ginger Cheesecake

Servings: 8   Cooking Time: 7 1/2 Hours

Ingredients:

Crust:	4 eggs
6 oz. graham crackers, crushed	1 tablespoon cornstarch
1/2 cup butter, melted	1 teaspoon grated ginger
1 tablespoon grated orange zest	1 teaspoon grated orange zest
Filling:	1/2 cup white sugar
20 oz. cream cheese	1 pinch salt
1 cup sour cream	

Directions:

For the crust, mix the two ingredients together in a bowl then transfer in your crock pot and press the mixture well on the bottom of the pot.   For the filling, mix all the ingredients in a bowl then pour the mix over the crust.   Cover the pot and cook on low settings for 7 hours.   Allow the cheesecake to cool before slicing and serving.

Cherry Jam

Servings: 4   Cooking Time: 3 Hours

Ingredients:

2 cups cherries, pitted	1 tablespoon agar
1/2 cup of sugar	3 tablespoons water

Directions:

Mix sugar with cherries and put in the Crock Pot. Then mix water and agar and pour the liquid in the Crock Pot too.   Stir well and close the lid.   Cook the jam on high for 3 hours.   Then transfer the jam in the glass cans and store it in the fridge for up to 2 months.

Nutrition Info: Per Serving: 139 calories, 0.5g protein, 36.1g carbohydrates, 0g fat, 1.5g fiber, 0mg cholesterol, 0mg sodium, 3mg potassium.

Pavlova

Servings: 6   Cooking Time: 3 Hours

Ingredients:

5 egg whites	1 teaspoon vanilla extract
1 cup of sugar powder	
1 teaspoon lemon juice	1/2 cup whipped cream

Directions:

Mix egg whites with sugar powder, lemon juice, and vanilla extract and whisk until you get firm peaks.   Then line the Crock Pot with baking paper and put the egg white mixture inside. Flatten it and cook for hours on low.   When the egg white mixture is cooked, transfer it in the serving plate and top with whipped cream.

Nutrition Info: Per Serving: 124 calories, 3.2g protein, 20.5g carbohydrates, 3.2g fat, 0g fiber, 11mg cholesterol, 32mg sodium, 57mg potassium.

Rocky Road Chocolate Cake

Servings: 10   Cooking Time: 4 1/2 Hours

Ingredients:

1 1/2 cups all-purpose flour	1 teaspoon vanilla extract
1/2 cup cocoa powder	2 eggs
1 teaspoon baking soda	1/2 cup mini marshmallows
1/2 teaspoon salt	1/2 cup pecans, chopped
1/2 cup canola oil	
1 cup buttermilk	1/2 cup white chocolate chips
1/2 cup whole milk	

Directions:

Mix the flour, cocoa powder, baking soda, salt, canola oil, buttermilk, milk, vanilla and eggs in a bowl. Give it a quick mix then pour the batter in your Crock Pot.   Top the batter with mini marshmallows, pecans and chocolate chips. Cover the pot and cook on low settings for 4 hours. Allow the cake to cool completely before serving.

Mixed-berry Marmalade

Servings: 12   Cooking Time: 3 Hrs.

Ingredients:

1 lb. cranberries	2 lbs. sugar
1 lb. strawberries	Zest of 1 lemon
1/2 lb. blueberries	2 tbsp water
3.5 oz. black currant	

Directions:

Toss all the berries with sugar, water, and lemon zest in the insert of Crock Pot.   Put the cooker's lid on and set the cooking time to 3 hours on High settings.   Divide the marmalade mixture into the jars and allow it to cool.   Serve.

Nutrition Info: Per Serving: Calories: 100, Total Fat: 4g, Fiber: 3g, Total Carbs: 12g, Protein: 3g

Golden Syrup Pudding

Servings: 8   Cooking Time: 4 1/4 Hours

Ingredients:

1/2 cup golden syrup	1 1/2 cups all-purpose flour
1/2 cup butter, softened	1/4 teaspoon salt
1/4 cup light brown sugar	1/2 teaspoon baking soda
2 eggs	3/4 cup whole milk

Directions:

Mix the dry ingredients in a bowl and the wet ingredients in another bowl. Combine the dry and wet ingredients in a bowl and give it a quick mix. Spoon the batter in your Crock Pot and bake on low settings for 4 hours.   Allow the pudding cool before serving.

Almond Rice Pudding

Servings: 2   Cooking Time: 1 Hour
Ingredients:

2 tablespoons almonds, chopped
1 cup white rice
2 cups almond milk
1 tablespoons maple syrup
1 tablespoon sugar
¼ teaspoon cinnamon powder
¼ teaspoon ginger, grated

Directions:
In your Crock Pot, mix the milk with the rice, sugar and the other ingredients, toss, put the lid on and cook on High for hour.   Divide the pudding into bowls and serve cold
Nutrition Info:calories 205, fat 2, fiber 7, carbs 11, protein 4

Lemon Berry Cake

Servings: 10   Cooking Time: 4 1/2 Hours
Ingredients:

1 cup butter, softened
1 cup white sugar
1 teaspoon vanilla extract
2 teaspoons lemon zest
4 eggs
1 cup all-purpose flour
1 teaspoon baking powder
1/4 teaspoon salt
1 cup fresh mixed berries

Directions:
Mix the butter, sugar and vanilla in a bowl until creamy.   Add the eggs, one by one, as well as the lemon zest and mix for 1 minute on high speed. Fold in the flour, baking powder and salt then spoon the batter in your Crock Pot.   Cover the pot and cook for hours on low settings.   Allow the cake to cool before serving.

Sponge Cake

Servings: 6   Cooking Time: 7 Hours
Ingredients:

2 egg yolks
4 egg whites
1 cup of sugar
½ cup flour
1 teaspoon vanilla extract
Cooking spray

Directions:
Spray the Crock Pot with cooking spray from inside.   Then whisk the egg whites until you get soft peaks.   After this, mix egg yolks with sugar and blend until smooth.   Add flour and vanilla extract.   Then add egg whites and carefully mix the mixture until homogenous.   Pour it in the Crock Pot and close the lid.   Cook the sponge cake on Low for hours.
Nutrition Info: Per Serving: 194 calories, 4.4g protein, 41.7g carbohydrates, 1.6g fat, 0.3g fiber, 70mg cholesterol, 25mg sodium, 54mg potassium.

Dates And Rice Pudding

Servings: 2   Cooking Time: 3 Hours
Ingredients:

1 cup dates, chopped
½ cup white rice
2 tablespoons brown sugar
1 cup almond milk
1 teaspoon almond extract

Directions:
In your Crock Pot, mix the rice with the milk and the other ingredients, whisk, put the lid on and cook on Low for 3 hours.   Divide the pudding into bowls and serve.
Nutrition Info:calories 152, fat 5, fiber 2, carb 6, protein 3

Orange Bowls

Servings: 2   Cooking Time: 3 Hours
Ingredients:

½ pound oranges, peeled and cut into segments
½ tablespoon almonds, chopped
1 cup heavy cream
1 tablespoon chia seeds
1 tablespoon sugar

Directions:
In your Crock Pot, mix the oranges with the cream and the other ingredients, toss, put the lid on and cook on Low for 3 hours.   Divide into bowls and serve.
Nutrition Info:calories 170, fat 0, fiber 2, carbs 7, protein 4

Saucy Peach And Apple Dessert

Servings: 4   Cooking Time: 4 1/4 Hours
Ingredients:

2 Granny Smith apples, peeled, cored and sliced
2 ripe peaches, pitted and sliced
1 cup fresh orange juice
1 cinnamon stick
1 teaspoon orange zest
3 tablespoons honey
1 teaspoon cornstarch
Ice cream or whipped cream for serving

Directions:
Combine all the ingredients in your Crock Pot. Cover the pot and cook for 4 hours on low settings. Allow the dessert to cool in the pot before serving. Ice cream or whipped cream can be a great match for this dessert.

Cauliflower Pudding

Servings: 6   Cooking Time: 2 Hours
Ingredients:

1 tablespoon butter, melted
7 ounces cauliflower rice
4 ounces water
16 ounces milk
3 ounces sugar
1 egg
1 teaspoon cinnamon powder
1 teaspoon vanilla extract

Directions:
In your Crock Pot, mix butter with cauliflower rice, water, milk, sugar, egg, cinnamon and vanilla extract, stir, cover and cook on High for 2 hours. Divide pudding into bowls and serve cold.
Nutrition Info:calories 202, fat 2, fiber 6, carbs 18, protein 4

Melon Pudding

Servings: 3   Cooking Time: 3 Hours

Ingredients:

1 cup melon, chopped
2 tablespoons cornstarch
¼ cup of coconut milk
1 teaspoon vanilla extract

Directions:

Blend the melon until smooth and mix with coconut milk, cornstarch, and vanilla extract. Transfer the mixture in the Crock Pot and cook the pudding on low for 3 hours.

Nutrition Info: Per Serving: 88 calories, 0.9g protein, 10.4g carbohydrates, 4.9g fat, 1g fiber, 0mg cholesterol, 12mg sodium, 194mg potassium.

Crock Pot Fudge

Servings: 12   Cooking Time: 1 1/4 Hours

Ingredients:

2 1/2 cups dark chocolate chips
1/2 cup heavy cream
1/2 cup honey
1 teaspoon vanilla extract
1/2 cup chopped walnuts

Directions:

Combine the dark chocolate chips, cream, honey and vanilla in your Crock Pot.   Cover the pot and cook for 1 hour on high settings.   When done, stir in the walnuts and allow to cool completely and to set.   Cut into small squares and serve.

Thick Pear Puree

Servings: 6   Cooking Time: 2.5 Hours

Ingredients:

3 cups pears, chopped
3 tablespoons lemon juice
1 teaspoon vanilla extract
1 tablespoon sugar
1 tablespoon corn starch
¼ cup of water

Directions:

Mix pears with lemon juice, sugar, vanilla extract, and water, and transfer in the Crock Pot.   Close the lid and cook the mixture on High for hours. Then blend it with the help of the immersion blender.   Add cornflour and stir until smooth. Close the lid and cook the puree on High for 30 minutes.   Transfer the cooked dessert in the ramekins and cool to room temperature.

Nutrition Info: Per Serving: 64 calories, 0.4g protein, 16g carbohydrates, 0.2g fat, 2.5g fiber, 0mg cholesterol, 3mg sodium, 104mg potassium.

Coconut Soufflé

Servings: 4   Cooking Time: 6 Hours

Ingredients:

4 egg yolks
1 cup of sugar
2 cups of coconut milk
1 tablespoon cornstarch
1 tablespoon butter, softened

Directions:

Mix coconut milk with cornstarch and pour in the ramekins.   Add sugar and butter in every ramekin and cover with foil.   Pierce the foil and transfer the ramekins in the Crock Pot.   Cook the soufflé on low for 6 hours.

Nutrition Info: Per Serving: 550 calories, 5.5g protein, 59.1g carbohydrates, 36g fat, 2.7g fiber, 217mg cholesterol, 47mg sodium, 335mg potassium.

Coffee Cinnamon Roll

Servings: 4   Cooking Time: 4 Hrs.

Ingredients:

3 tbsp butter
3 tbsp ground cinnamon
1 tbsp instant coffee powder
1 tsp vanilla extract
3 tbsp sugar, brown
½ tsp yeast
¼ cup whey
½ cup flour
¼ tsp salt
1 tsp white sugar
1 egg yolk
½ tsp canola oil

Directions:

Whisk yeast with sugar and whey in a bowl.   Stir in flour, salt, vanilla, and enough water to make a smooth dough.   Roll this dough into ¼ inch thick sheet.   Mix cinnamon with coffee powder, brown sugar, and butter in a small bowl.   Spread this cinnamon-butter mixture over the dough sheet. Start rolling the dough from one to make a cinnamon roll.   Grease the insert of your Crock Pot with canola oil and place the cinnamon roll it. Brush the top of this roll with whisked egg yolk. Put the cooker's lid on and set the cooking time to 4 hours on High settings.   Slice the roll and serve.

Nutrition Info: Per Serving: Calories: 203, Total Fat: 10.8g, Fiber: 4g, Total Carbs: 24.52g, Protein: 3g

Vanilla And Cocoa Pudding

Servings: 2   Cooking Time: 7 Hours

Ingredients:

1 cup of coconut milk
1 tablespoon cornflour
1 teaspoon vanilla extract
1 tablespoon brown sugar
1 tablespoon butter
2 tablespoons cocoa powder

Directions:

Mix coconut milk with cocoa powder, brown sugar, vanilla extract, and cornflour.   Whisk the mixture until smooth and transfer in the Crock Pot.   Add butter and close the lid.   Cook the pudding on Low for 7 hours.   Then transfer it in the serving bowls and cool to the room temperature.

Nutrition Info: Per Serving: 375 calories, 4.1g protein, 17.1g carbohydrates, 35.2g fat, 4.5g fiber, 15mg cholesterol, 62mg sodium, 473mg potassium.

Stewed Grapefruit

Servings: 6   Cooking Time: 2 Hours

Ingredients:
- 1 cup water
- 1 cup maple syrup
- 64 ounces red grapefruit juice
- ½ cup mint, chopped
- 2 grapefruits, peeled and chopped

Directions:
In your Crock Pot, mix grapefruit with water, maple syrup, mint and grapefruit juice, stir, cover and cook on High for 2 hours.   Divide into bowls and serve cold.

Nutrition Info: calories 170, fat 1, fiber, 2, carbs 5, protein 1

Peppermint Chocolate Clusters

Servings: 20   Cooking Time: 4 1/4 Hours

Ingredients:
- 2 cups pretzels, chopped
- 1 1/2 cups dark chocolate chips
- 1 cup pecans, chopped
- 1/2 cup milk chocolate chips
- 1 teaspoon peppermint extract

Directions:
Combine all the ingredients in your Crock Pot. Cover the pot and cook on low settings for 4 hours. When done, drop small clusters of mixture on a baking tray lined with baking paper.   Allow to cool and set before serving.

Wine Dipped Pears

Servings: 6   Cooking Time: 1 Hr. 30 Minutes

Ingredients:
- 6 green pears
- 1 vanilla pod
- 1 clove
- A pinch of cinnamon
- 7 oz. sugar
- 1 glass red wine

Directions:
Add pears, cinnamon, vanilla, wine, cloves, and sugar to the insert of Crock Pot.   Put the cooker's lid on and set the cooking time to 1.5 hours on High settings.   Serve the pears with wine sauce.

Nutrition Info: Per Serving: Calories: 162, Total Fat: 4g, Fiber: 3g, Total Carbs: 6g, Protein: 3g

Butternut Squash Sweet Mix

Servings: 8   Cooking Time: 3 Hours

Ingredients:
- 2 pounds butternut squash, steamed, peeled and mashed
- 2 eggs
- 1 cup milk
- ¾ cup maple syrup
- 1 teaspoon cinnamon powder
- ½ teaspoon ginger powder
- ¼ teaspoon cloves, ground
- 1 tablespoon cornstarch
- Whipped cream for serving

Directions:
In a bowl, mix squash with maple syrup, milk, eggs, cinnamon, cornstarch, ginger, cloves and cloves and stir very well.   Pour this into your Crock Pot, cover, cook on Low for hours, divide into cups and serve with whipped cream on top.

Nutrition Info: calories 152, fat 3, fiber 4, carbs 16, protein 4

Apple Cinnamon Brioche Pudding

Servings: 8   Cooking Time: 6 1/2 Hours

Ingredients:
- 16 oz. brioche bread, cubed
- 4 Granny Smith apples, peeled and cubed
- 1 teaspoon cinnamon powder
- 1/2 teaspoon ground ginger
- 2 tablespoons white sugar
- 1 cup evaporated milk
- 1 cup sweetened condensed milk
- 1 cup whole milk
- 4 eggs
- 1 teaspoon vanilla extract

Directions:
Mix the brioche bread, apples, cinnamon, ginger and sugar in your crock pot.   Combine the three types of milk in a bowl. Add the eggs and vanilla and mix well.   Pour this mix over the bread then cover the pot and cook for 6 hours on low settings. The pudding is best served slightly warm.

Pears And Apples Bowls

Servings: 2   Cooking Time: 2 Hours

Ingredients:
- 1 teaspoon vanilla extract
- 2 pears, cored and cut into wedges
- 2 apples, cored and cut into wedges
- 1 tablespoon walnuts, chopped
- 2 tablespoons brown sugar
- ½ cup coconut cream

Directions:
In your Crock Pot, mix the pears with the apples, nuts and the other ingredients, toss, put the lid on and cook on Low for 2 hours.   Divide the mix into bowls and serve cold.

Nutrition Info: calories 120, fat 2, fiber 2, carbs 4, protein 3

Raspberry Nutmeg Cake

Servings: 8   Cooking Time: 7 Hrs.

Ingredients:
- 4 eggs
- 1 cup sugar
- 1 cup flour
- 1 tsp vanilla extract
- 1 cup raspberry
- 1/3 cup sugar, brown
- 1 tbsp butter
- ¼ tsp nutmeg
- 1 tbsp cornstarch

Directions:
Separate the egg yolks from egg whites and keep them in a separate bowl.   Beat egg yolks with sugar, vanilla extract, cornstarch and nutmeg in a mixer.   Now beat the egg whites in an electric mixer until it forms peaks.   Add this egg white foam to the egg yolk mixture.   Mix gently, then add brown sugar and raspberry and blend again. Grease the insert of your Crock Pot with butter. Spread the raspberry batter in the cooker.   Put the cooker's lid on and set the cooking time to 7 hours on Low settings.   Slice and serve when chilled.

Nutrition Info: Per Serving: Calories: 234, Total Fat: 6.5g, Fiber: 6g, Total Carbs: 37.51g, Protein: 6g

Vanilla Bean Caramel Custard

Servings: 6   Cooking Time: 6 1/4 Hours
Ingredients:

1 cup white sugar for melting	4 eggs
4 cups whole milk	1 tablespoon vanilla bean paste
1 cup heavy cream	2 tablespoons white sugar
2 egg yolks	

Directions:
Caramelize cup of sugar in a thick saucepan until it has an amber color. Pour the caramel in your Crock Pot and swirl to coat the bottom and sides as much as possible.   Mix the milk, cream, egg yolks, eggs, vanilla bean paste and sugar in a bowl. Pour this mixture over the caramel.   Cover the pot and cook on low settings for 6 hours.   Serve the custard chilled.

Marshmallow Hot Drink

Servings: 3   Cooking Time: 5 Hours
Ingredients:

½ cup of chocolate chips	1 teaspoon butter
4 oz marshmallows	2 cups of milk

Directions:
Put all ingredients in the Crock Pot and close the lid.   Cook the drink on Low for 5 hours. Stir it every hours.
Nutrition Info: Per Serving: 364 calories, 7.8g protein, 54.g carbohydrates, 13g fat, 1g fiber, 23mg cholesterol, 138mg sodium, 200mg potassium.

Cinnamon Butter

Servings: 6   Cooking Time: 6 Hours
Ingredients:

2 cups apples, chopped	1 teaspoon ground cinnamon
½ cup butter	2 tablespoons sugar

Directions:
Mix sugar with apples and put in the Crock Pot. Leave the apples for 5-10 minutes or until they start to give the juice. Add ground cinnamon.   Then add butter and close the lid.   Cook the cinnamon butter on Low for 6 hours.   Then blend it with the help of the blender and transfer in the ramekins. Cool it.
Nutrition Info: Per Serving: 190 calories, 0.4g protein, 14.6g carbohydrates, 15.5g fat, 2g fiber, 41mg cholesterol, 110mg sodium, 86mg potassium.

Avocado Jelly

Servings: 2   Cooking Time: 1.5 Hours
Ingredients:

1 avocado, pitted, chopped	1 tablespoon gelatin
1 cup of orange juice	3 tablespoons brown sugar

Directions:
Pour orange juice in the Crock Pot.   Add brown sugar and cook the liquid on High for 1.5 hours. Then add gelatin and stir the mixture until smooth. After this, blend the avocado until smooth, add orange juice liquid and mix until homogenous. Pour it in the cups and refrigerate until solid.

Nutrition Info: Per Serving: 324 calories, 5.8g protein, 34.8g carbohydrates, 19.9g fat, 7g fiber, 0mg cholesterol, 18mg sodium, 754mg potassium.

Vanilla Cheesecake

Servings: 8   Cooking Time: 3 Hrs.
Ingredients:

2 cups cream cheese	½ cup butter, melted
½ cup sour cream	1 cup of sugar
5 eggs	1 tsp vanilla extract
8 oz graham cookies	1 tsp lemon zest

Directions:
Whisk cream cheese, sour cream, sugar, lemon zest, and vanilla extract in a mixing bowl.   Add eggs to the mixture while beating it with a hand mixer.   Mix melted butter and crushed graham cookies in a blender.   Spread this mixture in a pan lined with a parchment sheet.   Fill this crust with the cream cheese mixture.   Add 1 cup water into the insert of Crock Pot and place steel rack inside.   Place the baking pan with the prepared cheesecake batter in the Crock Pot.   Put the cooker's lid on and set the cooking time to 3 hours on Low settings.   Slice and serve when chilled.
Nutrition Info: Per Serving: Calories: 551, Total Fat: 39.2g, Fiber: 1g, Total Carbs: 38.36g, Protein: 12g

Cantaloupe Cream

Servings: 2   Cooking Time: 1 Hour
Ingredients:

2 cups cantaloupe, peeled and cubed	1 tablespoon butter
2 tablespoons sugar	1 tablespoon lemon zest, grated
1 cup coconut cream	Juice of ½ lemon

Directions:
In your Crock Pot, mix the cantaloupe with the sugar, cream and the other ingredients, toss, put the lid on and cook on High for hour.   Blend using an immersion blender, divide into bowls and serve cold.
Nutrition Info:calories 100, fat 2, fiber 3, carbs 6, protein 1

Crème Brule

Servings: 4   Cooking Time: 8 Hours
Ingredients:

6 egg yolks	½ cup of sugar
1 ½ cup heavy cream	1 teaspoon flour

Directions:
Blend the egg yolks with sugar until you get a smooth lemon color mixture.   Add heavy cream and flour. Mix the liquid until smooth.   Pour the liquid in the ramekins and place in the Crock Pot. Cover the ramekins with foil and close the lid of the Crock Pot.   Cook the dessert on Low for 8 hours.
Nutrition Info: Per Serving: 332 calories, 5g protein, 27.7g carbohydrates, 23.4g fat, 0g fiber, 376mg cholesterol, 29mg sodium, 62mg potassium.

Buttery Chocolate Cake

Servings: 10   Cooking Time: 4 1/4 Hours

Ingredients:

3/4 cup butter, softened	1/2 cup sour cream
3/4 cup light brown sugar	1 1/4 cups all-purpose flour
4 eggs	1/4 cup cocoa powder
1 cup dark chocolate, melted and chilled	1 1/2 teaspoons baking powder
	1/4 teaspoon salt

Directions:

Mix the butter and sugar in a bowl until creamy. Add the eggs, one by one, then stir in the melted chocolate and sour cream.   Fold in the flour, cocoa powder, baking powder and salt.   Spoon the batter in your Crock Pot and cook on low settings for 4 hours.   Allow the cake to cool in the pot before serving.

Banana Muffins

Servings: 2   Cooking Time: 2.5 Hours

Ingredients:

2 eggs, beaten	4 tablespoons flour
2 bananas, chopped	1/2 teaspoon baking powder
1/2 teaspoon vanilla extract	

Directions:

Mash the chopped bananas and mix them with eggs.   Then add vanilla extract and baking powder.   Add flour and stir the mixture until smooth.   Pour the banana mixture in the muffin molds (fill 1/2 part of every muffin mold) and transfer in the Crock Pot.   Cook the muffins on High for 2.hours.

Nutrition Info: Per Serving: 229 calories, 84g protein, 39.9g carbohydrates, 4.9g fat, 3.5g fiber, 164mg cholesterol, 64mg sodium, 626mg potassium.

Amaretto Pear Butter

Servings: 6   Cooking Time: 6 1/2 Hours

Ingredients:

1 1/2 cups white sugar	4 pounds ripe pears, peeled, cored and sliced
1/4 cup dark brown sugar	1/2 teaspoon cinnamon powder
1/4 cup Amaretto liqueur	

Directions:

Combine all the ingredients in your Crock Pot. Cover the pot and cook on low settings for 6 hours. When done, pour the batter in your glass jars and seal with a lid while still hot.   Allow to cool before serving.

Maple Pears

Servings: 4   Cooking Time: 4 Hours

Ingredients:

4 pears, peeled and tops cut off and cored	2 cups orange juice
5 cardamom pods	1/4 cup maple syrup
	1 cinnamon stick
	1-inch ginger, grated

Directions:

Put the pears in your Crock Pot, add cardamom, orange juice, maple syrup, cinnamon and ginger, cover and cook on Low for 4 hours.   Divide pears between plates and serve them with the sauce on top.

Nutrition Info:calories 200, fat 4, fiber 2, carbs 3, protein 4

Cardamom Plums

Servings: 6   Cooking Time: 5 Hours

Ingredients:

4 cups plums, pitted, halved	1/4 cup of sugar
1 teaspoon ground cardamom	1 teaspoon lemon juice
	1 cup of water

Directions:

Put plums in the Crock Pot and sprinkle them with ground cardamom, sugar, and lemon juice.   Add water and close the lid.   Cook the plums on Low for 5 hours.   Carefully stir the cooked dessert and transfer in the serving ramekins.

Nutrition Info: Per Serving: 52 calories, 0.4g protein, 13.9g carbohydrates, 0.2g fat, 0.7g fiber, 0mg cholesterol, 1mg sodium, 74mg potassium.

Glazed Carrot With Whipped Cream

Servings: 6   Cooking Time: 2.5 Hours

Ingredients:

1 cup whipped cream	1 tablespoon lemon juice
3 cups baby carrot	1 teaspoon lime zest, grated
4 tablespoons maple syrup	1/2 cup of water
1 teaspoon ground cinnamon	

Directions:

Mix carrot with ground cinnamon, lemon juice, lime zest, and water.   Add maple syrup and transfer the mixture in the Crock Pot.   Cook the carrots on High for 2.5 hours.   Then cool the carrots and transfer them in the bowls.   Top the dessert with whipped cream.

Nutrition Info: Per Serving: 120 calories, 0.9g protein, 5.8g carbohydrates, 6.3g fat, 2.3g fiber, 22mg cholesterol, 64mg sodium, 220mg potassium.

Orange Muffins

Servings: 4   Cooking Time: 3 Hours
Ingredients:

1 egg, beaten
1 teaspoon orange zest, grated
1 tablespoon butter, melted
½ cup of orange juice
1 cup flour
1 teaspoon baking powder

Directions:
Mix egg with orange juice and butter.   Then add baking powder and flour. Stir it until you get the smooth butter.   Add orange zest and stir the batter with the help of the spoon.   Transfer the batter in the muffin molds, filling ½ part of every mold.   Then place them in the Crock Pot and close the lid.   Cook the muffins on high for 3 hours.
Nutrition Info: Per Serving: 171 calories, 4.9g protein, 27.9g carbohydrates, 4.4g fat, 1g fiber, 49mg cholesterol, 38mg sodium, 238mg potassium.

S'mores Baked Sweet Potatoes

Servings: 8   Cooking Time: 3 1/2 Hours
Ingredients:

1 teaspoon cinnamon powder
2 tablespoons brown sugar
1 1/2 cups crushed graham crackers
1/4 cup butter, melted
2 large sweet potatoes, peeled and diced
1 1/2 cups dark chocolate chips
2 cups mini marshmallows

Directions:
Mix the crackers and butter in a bowl. Transfer this mixture in your Crock Pot and press it well on the bottom of the pot.   Mix the sweet potatoes with the cinnamon and brown sugar then transfer this mix over the crackers crust.   Top the potatoes with chocolate chips, followed by marshmallows. Cook on low settings for 3 hours.   Allow the dessert to cool down slightly before serving.

S'mores Cake

Servings: 6   Cooking Time: 2 Hours
Ingredients:

1 cup chocolate cake mix
1/4 cup pudding mix
3 eggs, beaten
3 tablespoons butter, melted
1/4 cup plain yogurt
3 oz marshmallows
3 oz graham crackers, crushed
Cooking spray

Directions:
Mix chocolate cake mix with pudding mix.   Add eggs, plain yogurt, and butter. Stir it until homogenous.   After this, add graham crackers and carefully mix them again.   Spray the Crock Pot bottom with cooking spray and put the chocolate mixture inside.   Cook it on high for 2 hours.   Then add marshmallows and broil the mixture.
Nutrition Info: Per Serving: 390 calories, 7.1g protein, 56.7g carbohydrates, 16.4g fat, 1.5g fiber, 98mg cholesterol, 579mg sodium, 219mg potassium.

Raisin Cookies

Servings: 2   Cooking Time: 2 Hours And 30 Minutes
Ingredients:

1 tablespoon coconut oil, melted
2 eggs, whisked
1/4 cup brown sugar
1/2 cup raisins
1/4 cup almond milk
1/4 teaspoon vanilla extract
1/4 teaspoon baking powder
1 cup almond flour

Directions:
In a bowl, mix the eggs with the raisins, almond milk and the other ingredients and whisk well. Line your Crock Pot with parchment paper, spread the cookie mix on the bottom of the pot, put the lid on, cook on Low for hours and 30 minutes, leave aside to cool down, cut with a cookie cutter and serve.
Nutrition Info:calories 220, fat 2, fiber 1, carbs 6, protein 6

Maple Plums And Mango

Servings: 2   Cooking Time: 1 Hour
Ingredients:

2 teaspoons orange zest
1 tablespoon orange juice
1 cup plums, pitted and halved
1 cup mango, peeled and cubed
1 tablespoon maple syrup
3 tablespoons sugar

Directions:
In your Crock Pot, mix the plums with the mango and the other ingredients, toss, put the lid on and cook on High for hour.   Divide into bowls and serve cold
Nutrition Info:calories 123, fat 1, fiber 2, carbs 20, protein 3

Brownie Bars

Servings: 8   Cooking Time: 5 Hours
Ingredients:

1/2 cup of cocoa powder
1/2 cup flour
1 teaspoon baking powder
1/4 cup butter, melted
1 teaspoon vanilla extract
3 eggs, beaten
1/4 cup of sugar
2 oz chocolate chips

Directions:
Mix all ingredients in the bowl and stir until smooth.   Line the Crock Pot with baking paper and transfer the mixture inside.   Close the lid and cook the brownie on low for 5 hours.   When the brownie is cooked, let it cool little.   Cut the dessert into bars.
Nutrition Info: Per Serving: 178 calories, 4.5g protein, 19.9g carbohydrates, 10.3g fat, 2.1g fiber, 78mg cholesterol, 71mg sodium, 258mg potassium.

Flax Seeds Bars

Servings: 8   Cooking Time: 4 Hours
Ingredients:

1 cup flax seeds	3 oz nuts, chopped
1 cup of chocolate chips	1 tablespoon coconut oil
¼ cup cream	

Directions:
Line the Crock Pot bottom with baking paper. Then put all ingredients inside and close the lid. Cook the mixture on low for 4 hours.   Then open the lid and make the mixture homogenous. Transfer it in the silicone mold and flatten well. Refrigerate it until solid and crush into bars.
Nutrition Info: Per Serving: 269 calories, 6.1g protein, 19.4g carbohydrates, 18.2g fat, 5.5g fiber, 6mg cholesterol, 94mg sodium, 258mg potassium.

Browned Butter Pumpkin Cheesecake

Servings: 8   Cooking Time: 6 1/2 Hours
Ingredients:

Crust:	4 eggs
1 1/4 cups crushed graham crackers	1 pinch salt
1/2 cup butter	1 teaspoon cinnamon powder
Filling:	1 teaspoon ground ginger
1 cup pumpkin puree	
24 oz. cream cheese	1/2 teaspoon cardamom powder
1/2 cup light brown sugar	1/4 cup butter

Directions:
To make the curst, start by browning the butter. Place the butter in a saucepan and cook for a few minutes until it starts to look golden. Allow to cool slightly.   Mix the browned butter with crushed crackers then transfer the mixture in your crock pot and press it well on the bottom of the pot.   For the filling, brown 1/4 cup butter as described above then stir in the pumpkin puree, cream cheese, eggs, sugar, salt, cinnamon, ginger and cardamom. Pour the mixture over the curst and cook on low settings for 6 hours.   Allow the cheesecake to cool down before slicing and serving.

Peach Bread Pudding

Servings: 6   Cooking Time: 6 Hours
Ingredients:

5 oz white bread, chopped	1 cup heavy cream
2 eggs, beaten	1 teaspoon flour
½ cup peaches, chopped	1 teaspoon coconut oil
	2 tablespoons sugar

Directions:
Grease the Crock Pot bottom with coconut oil. Then add white bread.   Mix heavy cream with eggs, flour, sugar, and pour over the bread.   Then add peaches and close the lid.   Cook the pudding on Low for 6 hours.
Nutrition Info: Per Serving: 181 calories, 4.2g protein, 18.1g carbohydrates, 10.4g fat, 0.8g fiber, 82mg cholesterol, 189mg sodium, 82mg potassium.

Rice Pudding

Servings: 6   Cooking Time: 2 Hours

Ingredients:

1 tablespoon butter	3 ounces sugar
7 ounces long grain rice	1 egg
4 ounces water	1 tablespoon cream
16 ounces milk	1 teaspoon vanilla extract

Directions:
In your Crock Pot, mix butter with rice, water, milk, sugar, egg, cream and vanilla, stir, cover and cook on High for 2 hours.   Stir pudding one more time, divide into bowls and serve.
Nutrition Info:calories 152, fat 4, fiber 4, carbs 6, protein 4

Apple Sour Cream Crostata

Servings: 8   Cooking Time: 6 1/2 Hours
Ingredients:

2 pounds Granny Smith apples, peeled, cored and sliced	1 1/2 cups all-purpose flour
1 tablespoon cornstarch	1/2 cup butter, chilled and cubed
1 teaspoon cinnamon powder	1 pinch salt
1/4 cup light brown sugar	2 tablespoons white sugar
	1/2 cup sour cream

Directions:
Mix the butter, flour, salt and white sugar in a bowl. Rub the mix well with your fingertips until grainy then stir in the sour cream and knead for a few times.   Roll the dough on a floured working surface to match the size of your crock pot. Transfer the dough in your Crock Pot.   For the topping, mix the apples, cornstarch, cinnamon and light brown sugar in a bowl. Place the mix over the dough.   Cover the pot and cook on low settings for 6 hours.   Serve the crostata chilled.

Soft Sable Cookies

Servings: 2   Cooking Time: 2 Hours
Ingredients:

1 teaspoon sesame seeds	1 egg yolk, whisked
2 tablespoons butter, softened	2 teaspoons brown sugar
½ teaspoon baking powder	1/3 cup flour
	½ teaspoon olive oil

Directions:
Mix butter with baking powder, brown sugar, and flour.   Knead a soft dough and cut into pieces. Then roll the balls from the dough and press them gently.   Brush every ball with the help of the egg yolk and sprinkle with sesame seeds.   Brush the Crock Pot bowl with olive oil and put the cookies inside.   Cook them on High for 2 hours. Then cool the cookies well.
Nutrition Info: Per Serving: 236 calories, 3.9g protein, 20.1g carbohydrates, 15.9g fat, 0.8g fiber, 135mg cholesterol, 88mg sodium, 172mg potassium.

Monkey Bread

Servings: 8   Cooking Time: 5 1/4 Hours

Ingredients:

3 cups all-purpose flour	1 teaspoon active dry yeast
4 eggs	3/4 cup butter, melted
1/4 cup white sugar	1 cup white sugar
1 teaspoon vanilla extract	1 1/2 teaspoons cinnamon powder
1 1/4 cups warm milk	

Directions:

Mix the flour, salt, eggs, 4 cup white sugar, warm milk, vanilla and active dry yeast in the bowl of your mixer and knead for 10 minutes. Allow the dough to rise for 1 hour.   Transfer the dough on a floured working surface and cut it into -30 small pieces of dough. Roll each piece of dough into a ball.   Mix the sugar with cinnamon powder. To finish the bread, dip each ball of dough into melted butter then roll through the cinnamon sugar.   Grease your crock pot and place the dough balls in the pot.   Cook on low settings for 4 hours.   Allow to cool before serving.

Hazelnut Crumble Cheesecake

Servings: 8   Cooking Time: 6 1/2 Hours

Ingredients:

Crust and topping:	Filling:
3/4 cup butter, chilled and cubed	20 oz. cream cheese
1 1/4 cups all-purpose flour	1/2 cup sour cream
	1/2 cup white sugar
1 cup ground hazelnuts	1 teaspoon vanilla extract
1/4 cup buttermilk	2 tablespoons Grand Marnier
1 pinch salt	1 tablespoon cornstarch
2 tablespoons light brown sugar	2 eggs

Directions:

For the crust and topping, combine all the ingredients in a food processor and pulse until a dough comes together. Cut the dough in half. Wrap one half in plastic wrap and place in the fridge. The remaining dough, roll it into a thin sheet and place it in your Crock Pot, trimming the edges if needed. For the filling, mix all the ingredients in a large bowl. Pour this mixture over the crust.   For the topping, remove the dough from the fridge then grate it on a large grater over the cheesecake filling. Cover the pot and bake for 6 hours on low settings. Allow to cool completely before slicing and serving.

Apricot Marmalade

Servings: 2   Cooking Time: 3 Hours

Ingredients:

1 cup apricots, chopped	2 tablespoons lemon juice
½ cup water	1 teaspoon fruit pectin
1 teaspoon vanilla extract	2 cups sugar

Directions:

In your Crock Pot, mix the apricots with the water, vanilla and the other ingredients, whisk, put the lid on and cook on High for 3 hours.   Stir the marmalade, divide into bowls and serve cold.

Nutrition Info: calories 100, fat 1, fiber 2, carbs 20, protein 1

Bread And Quinoa Pudding

Servings: 2   Cooking Time: 3 Hours

Ingredients:

1 cup quinoa	1 teaspoon cinnamon powder
1 cup bread, cubed	
2 cups almond milk	1 teaspoon nutmeg, ground
2 tablespoons honey	

Directions:

In your Crock Pot, mix the quinoa with the milk and the other ingredients, whisk, put the lid on and cook on Low for 3 hours.   Divide the pudding into bowls and serve.

Nutrition Info: calories 981, fat 63.4, fiber 11.9, carbs 94.6, protein 19

Cottage Cheese Dip

Servings: 4   Cooking Time: 4 Hours

Ingredients:

4 bananas, mashed	1 egg, beaten
1 cup cottage cheese	¼ cup milk
1 tablespoon butter	

Directions:

Put the bananas in the blender.   Add cottage cheese, butter, egg, and milk.   Blend the mixture until smooth and pour it in the Crock Pot.   Close the lid and cook it on Low for hours.

Nutrition Info: Per Serving: 205 calories, 11g protein, 29.8g carbohydrates, 5.8g fat, 3.1g fiber, 54mg cholesterol, 274mg sodium, 501mg potassium.

Cardamom Lemon Pie

Servings: 6   Cooking Time: 7 Hrs.

Ingredients:

3 lemons, sliced	1 tsp baking powder
1 tsp ground cardamom	1 tbsp lemon juice
5 eggs, whisked	1 cup of sugar
1 cup whey	1 tsp lime zest
½ cup cottage cheese	2 tsp ground ginger
2 cups flour	

Directions:

Start by mixing whey, lemon juice, baking powder, cottage cheese, sugar, ground cardamom, lime zest, and ground ginger in a mixer.   Stir in flour and whisk until it forms a smooth whey batter.   Fold in the sliced lemons and mix gently.   Layer the base of the insert of Crock Pot with a parchment sheet.   Spread the lemon-whey batter in the insert of Crock Pot.   Put the cooker's lid on and set the cooking time to 7 hours on Low settings. Slice and serve chilled.

Nutrition Info: Per Serving: Calories: 363, Total Fat: 9.5g, Fiber: 1g, Total Carbs: 54.92g, Protein: 14g

Amaranth Bars

Servings: 7   Cooking Time: 1 Hour
Ingredients:
  ½ cup amaranth   3 oz milk chocolate,
  4 oz peanuts,   chopped
  chopped
  ¼ cup of coconut oil
Directions:
Put all ingredients in the Crock Pot and cook on
High for hour.   Then transfer the melted
amaranth mixture in the silicone mold, flatten it,
and refrigerate until solid.   Cut the dessert into
bars.
Nutrition Info: Per Serving: 276 calories, 7.1g
protein, 19.1g carbohydrates, 20.3g fat, 3.1g fiber,
3mg cholesterol, 15mg sodium, 210mg potassium.

Summer Fruits Compote

Servings: 6   Cooking Time: 3 Hours
Ingredients:
  1 cup apricots, pitted,   1 cup strawberries
  chopped   ¼ cup blackberries
  ½ cup cherries,
  pitted   ½ cup of sugar
                              8 cups of water
Directions:
Put all ingredients in the Crock Pot.   Cook
compote on High for 3 hours.   Cool it and serve
with ice cubes.
Nutrition Info: Per Serving: 93 calories, 0.7g
protein, 23.9g carbohydrates, 0.3g fat, 1.4g fiber,
0mg cholesterol, 11mg sodium, 117mg potassium.

Citron Vanilla Bars

Servings: 10   Cooking Time: 4 Hrs.
Ingredients:
  6 tbsp sugar   1 tbsp lemon zest
  9 tbsp butter   ¼ tsp olive oil
  1 ½ cup flour
  7 oz lemon curd   1 large egg, beaten
                            1 tsp vanilla extract
Directions:
Mix softened butter with lemon zest, egg, sugar,
and flour in a bowl.   Stir in vanilla extract, then
mix well until it forms a smooth dough.   Spread
this dough into a sheet then place this dough in the
insert of Crock Pot.   Add lemon curd over the
dough evenly.   Put the cooker's lid on and set the
cooking time to 4 hours on High settings.   Slice
and serve.
Nutrition Info: Per Serving: Calories: 191, Total
Fat: 11.2g, Fiber: 1g, Total Carbs: 20.69g, Protein:
2g

Cheese Cake

Servings: 8   Cooking Time: 8 Hours
Ingredients:
  6 oz cookies, crushed   2 cups cream cheese
  2 tablespoon butter,   3 eggs, beaten
  softened
  1 teaspoon vanilla   ¼ cup of sugar
  extract   1 cup of water
Directions:

Mix cookies with butter and transfer the mixture in
the cheesecake mold.   Flatten the cookies
mixture in the shape of the pie crust.   Then blend
sugar with eggs, vanilla extract, and cream cheese.
Pour the cream cheese mixture over the pie crust.
Then pour water in the Crock Pot and insert the
mold with cheesecake inside.   Close the lid and
cook the dessert on Low for 8 hours.
Nutrition Info: Per Serving: 357 calories, 7.4g
protein, 25.8g carbohydrates, 25.3g fat, 0.3g fiber,
133mg cholesterol, 273mg sodium, 101mg
potassium.

Coconut And Macadamia Cream

Servings: 4   Cooking Time: 1 Hour And 30
Minutes
Ingredients:
  4 tablespoons   2 tablespoons sugar
  vegetable oil   1 cup heavy cream
  3 tablespoons   5 tablespoons
  macadamia nuts,   coconut powder
  chopped
Directions:
Put the oil in your Crock Pot, add nuts, sugar,
coconut powder and cream, stir, cover, cook on
Low for hour and 30 minutes.   Stir well, divide
into bowls and serve.
Nutrition Info:calories 154, fat 1, fiber 0, carbs 7,
protein 2

Milk Fondue

Servings: 3   Cooking Time: 4 Hours
Ingredients:
  5 oz milk chocolate,   1 teaspoon vanilla
  chopped   extract
  1 tablespoon butter   ¼ cup milk
Directions:
Put the chocolate in the Crock Pot in one layer.
Then top it with butter, vanilla extract, and milk.
Close the lid and cook the dessert on Low for 4
hours.   Gently stir the cooked fondue and
transfer in the ramekins.
Nutrition Info: Per Serving: 301 calories, 4.3g
protein, 29.3g carbohydrates, 18.3g fat, 1.6g fiber,
23mg cholesterol, 74mg sodium, 191mg potassium.

Green Tea Pudding

Servings: 2   Cooking Time: 1 Hour
Ingredients:
  1 and ½ cup avocado,   ½ cup coconut milk
  pitted and peeled
  2 tablespoons green   2 teaspoons lime zest,
  tea powder   grated
                            1 tablespoon sugar
Directions:
In your Crock Pot, mix coconut milk with avocado,
tea powder, lime zest and sugar, stir, cover and
cook on Low for hour.   Divide into cups and
serve cold.
Nutrition Info:calories 107, fat 5, fiber 3, carbs 6,
protein 8

Sweet Strawberry Mix

Servings: 10   Cooking Time: 3 Hours
Ingredients:

2 tablespoons lemon juice	1 teaspoon cinnamon powder
2 pounds strawberries	1 teaspoon vanilla extract
4 cups sugar	

Directions:
In your Crock Pot, mix strawberries with sugar, lemon juice, cinnamon and vanilla, cover, cook on Low for 3 hours, divide into bowls and serve cold.
Nutrition Info:calories 100, fat 1, fiber 1, carbs 6, protein 2

Fresh Cream Mix

Servings: 6   Cooking Time: 1 Hour
Ingredients:

2 cups fresh cream	Zest of 1 orange, grated
1 teaspoon cinnamon powder	A pinch of nutmeg for serving
6 egg yolks	4 tablespoons sugar
5 tablespoons white sugar	2 cups water

Directions:
In a bowl, mix cream, cinnamon and orange zest and stir.   In another bowl, mix the egg yolks with white sugar and whisk well.   Add this over the cream, stir, strain and divide into ramekins.   Put ramekins in your Crock Pot, add 2 cups water to the Crock Pot, cover, cook on Low for 1 hour, leave cream aside to cool down and serve.
Nutrition Info:calories 200, fat 4, fiber 5, carbs 15, protein 5

Banana Cake

Servings: 6   Cooking Time: 2 Hours
Ingredients:

¾ cup sugar	3 bananas, mashed
1/3 cup butter, soft	1 and ½ cups flour
1 teaspoon vanilla	
1 egg	½ teaspoons baking soda
1 teaspoon baking powder	1/3 cup milk
	Cooking spray

Directions:
In a bowl, mix butter with sugar, vanilla extract, eggs, bananas, baking powder, flour, baking soda and milk and whisk.   Grease your Crock Pot with the cooking spray, add the batter, spread, cover and cook on High for hours.   Leave the cake to cool down, slice and serve.
Nutrition Info:calories 300, fat 4, fiber 4, carbs 27, protein 4

Tomato Jam

Servings: 2   Cooking Time: 3 Hours
Ingredients:

½ pound tomatoes, chopped	2 tablespoons red wine vinegar
1 green apple, grated	4 tablespoons sugar

Directions:
In your Crock Pot, mix the tomatoes with the apple and the other ingredients, whisk, put the lid on and cook on Low for 3 hours.   Whisk the jam well, blend a bit using an immersion blender, divide into bowls and serve cold.
Nutrition Info:calories 70, fat 1, fiber 1, carbs 18, protein 1

Rhubarb Stew

Servings: 2   Cooking Time: 2 Hours
Ingredients:

½ pound rhubarb, roughly sliced	½ teaspoon lemon extract
2 tablespoons sugar	1 tablespoon lemon juice
½ teaspoon vanilla extract	¼ cup water

Directions:
In your Crock Pot, mix the rhubarb with the sugar, vanilla and the other ingredients, toss, put the lid on and cook on Low for 2 hours.   Divide the mix into bowls and serve cold.
Nutrition Info:calories 60, fat 1, fiber 0, carbs 10, protein 1

Mango Muffins

Servings: 2   Cooking Time: 3 Hours
Ingredients:

3 tablespoons mango puree	1 teaspoon vanilla extract
1 tablespoon butter, softened	¼ teaspoon baking powder
3 tablespoons flour	

Directions:
Mix mango puree with butter, vanilla extract, flour, and baking powder.   Stir the mixture until you get a smooth batter.   Then fill the muffin molds with batter (fill ½ part of every muffin mold) and transfer them in the Crock Pot.   Close the lid and cook the muffins on High for 3 hours.
Nutrition Info: Per Serving: 110 calories, 1.4g protein, 11.8g carbohydrates, 5.9g fat, 0.6g fiber, 15mg cholesterol, 42mg sodium, 107mg potassium.

Cardamom Carrot Cake

Servings: 8   Cooking Time: 4 1/2 Hours

Ingredients:

Cake:	1/2 cup canola oil
4 eggs	1 1/2 cups all-purpose
1 cup white sugar	flour
1 teaspoon vanilla	1 teaspoon baking
extract	powder
1 cup crushed	1/2 teaspoon baking
pineapple	soda
1 1/2 cups grated	1/2 teaspoon salt
carrot	Frosting:
1 1/2 teaspoons	1 cup mascarpone
ground cardamom	cream
1/2 teaspoon ground	1/4 cup powdered
ginger	sugar
1 teaspoon cinnamon	1/2 cup heavy cream,
powder	whipped

Directions:

Mix the eggs, sugar and vanilla in a bowl for 5-7 minutes until pale and fluffy.   Add the oil and mix well then stir in the pineapple, carrot, cardamom, finger and cinnamon.   In a bowl, sift the flour with baking powder, baking soda and salt then fold this dry mixture into the batter.   Pour the batter in your Crock Pot and bake for hours on low settings.   Allow the cake to cool completely when done.   For the frosting, mix the mascarpone cream with the sugar until fluffy. Fold in the whipped cream/   Top the cake with this frosting before serving.

Coconut Blueberry Crumble

Servings: 6   Cooking Time: 2 1/4 Hours

Banana Bread

Servings: 6   Cooking Time: 3 Hours

Ingredients:

¾ cup sugar	
1/3 cup butter, soft	1 and ½ cups flour
1 teaspoon vanilla	
extract	½ teaspoons baking
1 egg	soda
2 bananas, mashed	1/3 cup milk
1 teaspoon baking	
powder	1 and ½ teaspoons
	cream of tartar
	Cooking spray

Directions:

In a bowl, combine milk with cream of tartar and stir well.   Add sugar, butter, egg, vanilla and bananas and stir everything.   In another bowl, mix flour with salt, baking powder and soda. Combine the 2 mixtures and stir them well. Grease your Crock Pot with cooking spray, add bread batter, cover, cook on High for 3 hours. Leave the bread to cool down, slice and serve it.

Ingredients:

1 pound fresh	1/4 cup white sugar
blueberries	1/2 cup all-purpose
1 tablespoon	flour
cornstarch	1/4 cup butter,
1 lemon, zested and	chilled
juiced	2 tablespoons
1 cup shredded	coconut milk, chilled
coconut	

Directions:

Mix the blueberries, cornstarch, white sugar, lemon zest and lemon juice in your Crock Pot.   For the topping, combine the coconut, flour and butter in a bowl. Mix until sandy then stir in the coconut milk. Spread the mixture over the blueberries and cook on high settings for 2 hours.   Allow the crumble to cool before serving.

Egyptian Rice Pudding

Servings: 6   Cooking Time: 4 1/4 Hours

Ingredients:

1 1/2 cups white rice	4 cups whole milk
1 vanilla pod, cut in	1/4 cup cold water
half lengthwise	1/2 cup sugar
2 tablespoons	1 teaspoon cinnamon
cornstarch	powder

Directions:

Mix the rice, milk, vanilla pod and sugar in your crock pot.   Cook on low settings for 3 hours. Combine the water and cornstarch in a bowl then pour this mixture over the rice pudding.   Cover the pot again and cook on low settings for 1 additional hour.   Serve the pudding warm or chilled, sprinkled with cinnamon powder.

Nutrition Info: calories 300, fat 3, fiber 4, carbs 28, protein 5

Berry Pudding

Servings: 2   Cooking Time: 5 Hours

Ingredients:

¼ cup strawberries,	1 tablespoon corn
chopped	starch
2 tablespoons sugar	1 teaspoon vanilla
2 cups of milk	extract

Directions:

Mix milk with corn starch and pour liquid in the Crock Pot.   Add vanilla extract, sugar, and strawberries.   Close the lid and cook the pudding on low for 5 hours.   Carefully mix the dessert before serving.

Nutrition Info: Per Serving: 196 calories, 8.1g protein, 30.2g carbohydrates, 5.1g fat, 0.4g fiber, 20mg cholesterol, 115mg sodium, 171mg potassium.

21-Day Meal Plan

Day 1
Breakfast: Cauliflower And Eggs Bowls
Lunch: Autumnal Stew
Dinner: Spicy Hot Chicken Thighs

Day 2
Breakfast: Milk Oatmeal
Lunch: Turnip And Beans Casserole
Dinner: Ricotta Veggie Lasagna

Day 3
Breakfast: Asparagus Egg Casserole
Lunch: Button Mushroom Beef Stew
Dinner: Bbq Chicken Thighs

Day 4
Breakfast: Vanilla Maple Oats
Lunch: Madras Lentils
Dinner: Whole Roasted Cauliflower

Day 5
Breakfast: Eggplant Pate
Lunch: Chicken And Cabbage Mix
Dinner: Beef And Veggie Stew

Day 6
Breakfast: Raspberry Oatmeal
Lunch: Pesto Pork Shanks
Dinner: Beef Stroganoff

Day 7
Breakfast: Pork And Eggplant Casserole
Lunch: Apple And Onion Lunch Roast
Dinner: Fennel Infused Pork Ham

Day 8
Breakfast: Baby Spinach Rice Mix
Lunch: Lime Bean Stew
Dinner: Caramelized Onion Beef Pot Roast

Day 9
Breakfast: Baby Carrots In Syrup
Lunch: Red Wine Braised Oxtail
Dinner: Chicken Stew

Day 10
Breakfast: Green Muffins
Lunch: Banana Chicken Curry
Dinner: Navy Bean Stew

Day 11
Breakfast: Scallions And Bacon Omelet

Lunch: White Bean Casoulet
Dinner: Bacon Potato Stew

Day 12
Breakfast: Breakfast Meat Rolls
Lunch: Spiced Pork Belly
Dinner: Rich Chicken Rice Stew

Day 13
Breakfast: Cowboy Breakfast Casserole
Lunch: Jamaican Jerk Chicken
Dinner: Bbq Beef Brisket

Day 14
Breakfast: Maple Banana Oatmea
Lunch: Creamy Chicken And Mushroom Pot Pie
Dinner: Spicy Hot Chicken Thighs

Day 15
Breakfast: Potato Muffins
Lunch: Honey Sesame Glazed Chicken
Dinner: Chicken Drumsticks And Buffalo Sauce

Day 16
Breakfast: Eggs And Sweet Potato Mix
Lunch: Cheesy Chicken Burrito Filling
Dinner: Beef Roast Au Jus

Day 17
Breakfast: Veggie Hash Brown Mix
Lunch: Rich Stout Beef Casserole
Dinner: Beer Braised Beef

Day 18
Breakfast: Butter Oatmeal
Lunch: Red Chile Pulled Pork
Dinner: Mustard Baked Potatoes

Day 19
Breakfast: Veggies Casserole
Lunch: Lemon Roasted Pork Tenderloin
Dinner: Puttanesca Pizza

Day 20
Breakfast: Mixed Egg And Sausage Scramble
Lunch: Rice And Chorizo Bowl
Dinner: Mediterranean Beef Brisket

Day 21
Breakfast: Chicken Burrito Bowl
Lunch: Beef Strips With Egg Noodles
Dinner: Paprika Pork And Chickpeas

Appendix : Recipes Index